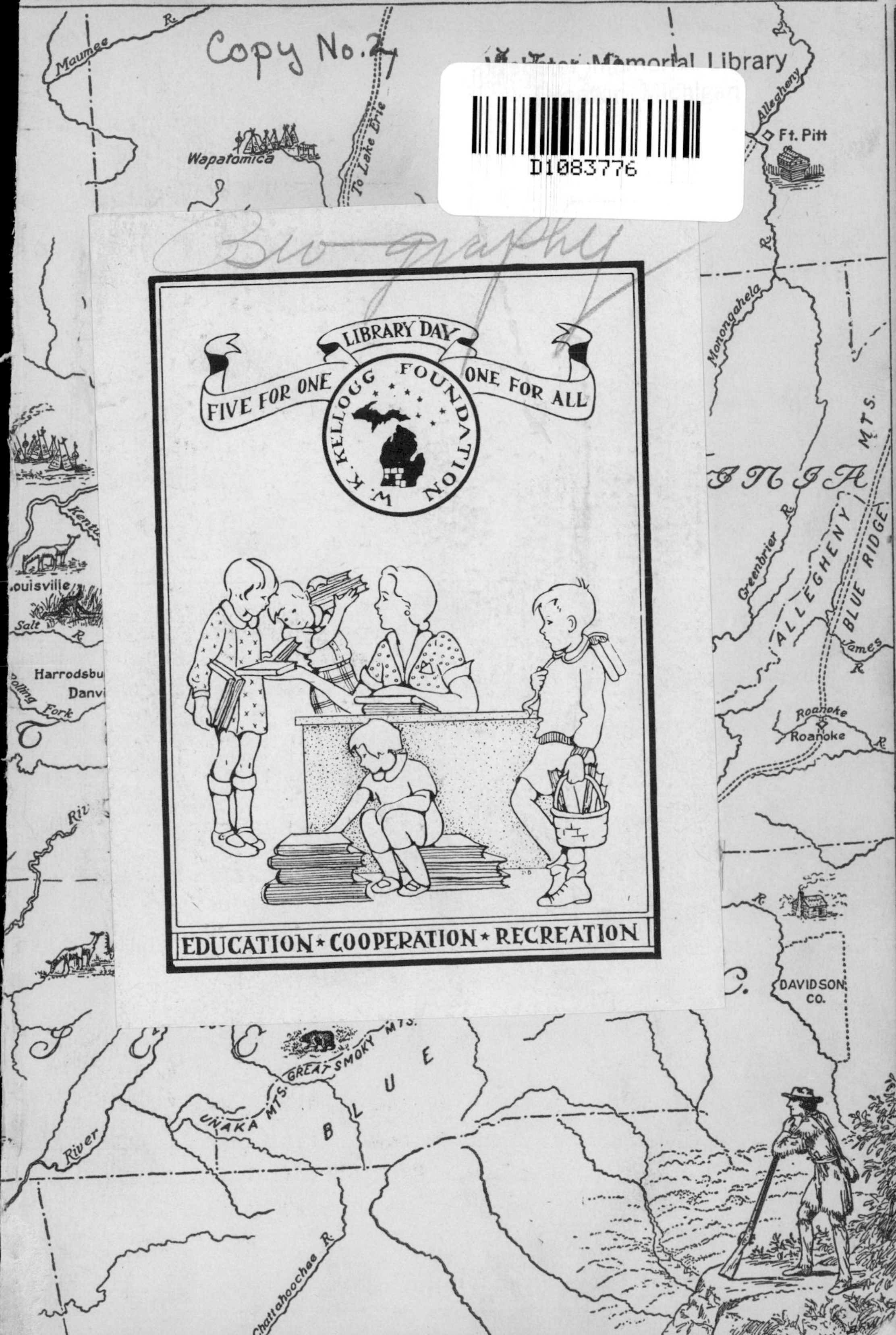
Maumee R.
Wapatomica
To Lake Erie
Allegheny
Ft. Pitt
Monongahela R.
Greenbrier R.
ALLEGHENY MTS.
BLUE RIDGE
James R.
Roanoke
Roanoke R.
Kentu
Louisville
Salt R.
Harrodsbu
Danvi
Rolling Fork
DAVIDSON CO.
GREAT SMOKY MTS.
UNAKA MTS.
B L U E
River
Chattahoochee R.
LIBRARY DAY
FIVE FOR ONE
ONE FOR ALL
W. K. KELLOGG FOUNDATION
EDUCATION ★ COOPERATION ★ RECREATION

TO

ERNEST C. OBERHOLTZER

a modern master of the wilderness

Contents

Illustrations

Introduction

ALTHOUGH Daniel Boone early became an American hero and the subject of innumerable popular sketches of varying merit, he has not hitherto been made the subject of a documented biography based on original sources.

The present study is the result of personal examination of all known original Boone manuscripts, except a few in distant county courthouses or private collections, which have been examined for me and sometimes copied by local investigators. It endeavors to bring together the entire story of Daniel Boone's life without entering into details of merely local interest, such as the exact routes he followed or the exact sites of his camps. Matters of this sort, though of great interest to local historians, who debate them vigorously, are of no special significance to anyone else.

In general, I have ignored mere rumor, except where it is so widespread as to deserve at least passing mention, plainly labeled for what it is. Stories like the one which provides Boone with a Shawnee squaw for his "Indian wife" I have passed over in silence. They are, in the first place, unsupported by anything except folk stories dating from long after Boone's death. They are, in the second place, usually in conflict with the known facts. The Shawnee wife story, for example, is hard to believe not merely in view of Daniel Boone's devotion to his legitimate wife, but also in view of the fact that, except for one captivity of a few months, Boone never lived among the Shawnees. Similarly, the story that Rebecca Boone had a child by one of Daniel's brothers during one of her husband's long absences in the woods, but that Daniel kept the baby and brought it up as his own, conflicts with the known dates of her children's births.

Much of the material appears in print for the first time; fully half of it has never appeared anywhere except in valuable but obscure local historical journals of strictly limited circulation; and the entire story of Boone's life is here first presented with complete documentation.

I should perhaps add a word as to the direct quotations found in the text. In every case but one, these come directly from first-hand original manuscript sources and are there given as direct quotations. In the one exception (page 382) I have shifted indirect to direct quotation without any change except the personal pronouns. This particular change seems justified, since the manuscript authority is otherwise plainly quoting Boone's exact words, and since the minor alteration is plainly indicated in a note. It should be needless to remark that even manuscript accounts of conversations cannot pretend to stenographic accuracy. In every case where the original manuscript still exists, I have checked quotations by it; where it has disappeared, I have used the best copy available.

Both Professor Jonathan Truman Dorris and Dr. Louise Phelps Kellogg have read the entire manuscript to suggest corrections and improvements. In gratefully acknowledging their assistance, I should add that obviously I accept entire responsibility for any errors that may have crept into my account of a life which is highly controversial at every point.

JOHN BAKELESS

New York, N. Y.

DANIEL BOONE

1. The Boones of Pennsylvania

IN peaceful Devon, loveliest of the English counties, a family of English Quakers was growing restless as the eighteenth century began. Queen Anne was on the throne; Marlborough was winning renown and cash for himself, and honor for the British arms; it was a wonderful period in England's history. In London, Dean Swift was being witty and extremely caustic. Mr. Dryden had recently died. Mr. Pope's poetry was beginning to be greatly admired. But none of these worldly vanities meant much to George Boone, a humble Quaker weaver in the village of Cullompton, near Exeter.

Dissenters of every sort had troubles of their own in those days, the Quakers not least. Stories began to spread among the Society of Friends about the new Province of Pennsylvania, founded by one of the few Quakers whom the Lord had blessed with wealth and social position. In the new colony religious toleration, they heard, was complete. The Friends were really in control of the government. Further, there was land.

They were an adventurous breed, the Boones. For the next four generations they were always to be pulling up stakes and moving westward. Once, centuries earlier, they had been Bohuns, Normans. Even then they had been fighters and adventurers, who had moved westward into the newly conquered England. Even then they went to acquire land.

With their adventurous nature went a singular caution.

Any Boone would run any risk; but first, if he could, he must look over the ground, consider, ponder, reconnoiter. George Boone was middle-aged, well into his forties. The fact may have accentuated that native caution. After forty, a man looks before he leaps—that is, if there is time, and an Indian is not too close behind.

The cautious weaver of Cullompton had heard glowing tales of Pennsylvania. But a man cannot believe all he hears. A man must be sure. Sometime before 1713 his son, George Boone the younger, his daughter Sarah, and another son, Squire Boone, took ship to investigate this new land that promised so well. Squire shipped as cabin boy.

As it turned out, the new land pleased them. Squire and Sarah stayed. Their brother is said to have returned to Devon to report to his father—the elder George Boone still was cautious. If he did so, it was a hasty trip, for he was back in Pennsylvania, marrying an American girl, by May, 1713. Not for four years, however, was the rest of the family ready to leave Devon's peaceful meadows for the wild Pennsylvania country with its thin fringe of settlements running along the eastern edge. They sailed August 17, 1717. It was a long voyage, but on October 10 they were in Philadelphia, already a small city.

Though Quakers dominated Pennsylvania, complete religious freedom prevailed. The Mennonites, German pacifists and pietists, had arrived nearly as early as the Quakers. The Amish branch of the sect had settled in Berks County just before the Boones arrived and were soon followed by the German Baptist Brethren, or Dunkers, a similar sect. Each had its special costume. The Quakers wore their sober gray. The Amish, frowning upon the sinful vanity of buttons, wore only invisible hooks-and-eyes. The men bobbed their hair below the ears in "Dutch cut," and after marriage shaved only the upper lip. The Dunkers were equally sober yet equally picturesque.

The country itself was only partly cleared of forest. Even the best fields were still full of stumps. In others the farmers had merely killed the trees by girdling and left them standing, cultivating as best they could the soil between the trunks. The time had not yet come for the rich fields, enormous barns, and fat pure-bred cattle for which southeastern Pennsylvania is famous now. The livestock ran wild. Even in winter it had no shelter. Horses were almost unknown. The farmers plowed with oxen. Cattle were stunted and so poor that a gallon of milk a day was thought a good yield for a cow.

It was in some such country as this that all the Boones settled together at Abingdon, twelve or fourteen miles north of Philadelphia. But they did not stay. There was always a branch of the Boone family that never stayed. The Boones were wanderers born. They had the itching foot. Something called. Something beyond the mountains always whispered. They heard of distant lands and knew that they must go there.

Old George Boone was like that. His sons George and Squire were wanderers both. His grandsons Daniel Boone and Squire Boone the younger wandered all their lives. Daniel's sons moved with their father, west to Kentucky, westward again to Missouri. Daniel's own grandsons moved on toward the Rockies. Other pioneer families have such a history behind them, but it is marked most clearly in the Boones.

The first move was not very distant. Abingdon Meeting granted them a certificate permitting them "to settle in and towards Oley and join themselves to Gwynedd Meeting." They went to North Wales, Gwynedd Township, southwest of the city. They went because they wanted land—the Boones always wanted land. In 1718, young George Boone took out a warrant for four hundred acres in Oley Township, near Reading. The Boones were always careful to provide their sons with land, and his father guaranteed the purchase. It was the first of many deals, which eventually made the younger George Boone an extensive land-owner.

The Boones were Quakers, but they do not seem to have been particularly devout. The younger George Boone did not bother to present a certificate from the Friends in England testifying to his "orderly and good conversation while he lived there," until he wanted to get married. His father, arriving later, took two months before producing at Gwynedd Meeting "a Certificate of his Good Life and Conversation from the Monthly att Callumpton In Great Brittain wch was read and Well recd."

Within two years, Squire Boone and Sarah Morgan, future parents of Daniel Boone, announced to the Meeting "their Intention of Marriage with each Other ye first time." The usual committee was appointed to investigate the prospective bridegroom and particularly to "inspect his Clearness from Other Women." They found no obstacle; but there were other matrimonial prospects in the Boone family about which the godly Friends held other views. Under compulsion, George Boone, Squire's father, "openly Acknowledged in this Meetting his forwardness in giving his Consent to John Webb to keep Company wth his Daughter in order to Marry Contrary to ye Establish'd order amongst us."

John Webb may have been a "worldling," or non-Quaker. More probably, however, the Meeting simply wanted more information about him. The sins of the father were not in this case visited upon the children. After a committee had been named "to Inspect into his Conversation," the Meeting relented. John Webb and Mary Boone were allowed to declare their intentions and to get married on the same day as the other pair.

On July 23, 1720, the marriage of Friend Squire Boone and Friend Sarah Morgan, daughter of Friend John Morgan, was "decently Accomplish'd" by Quaker ceremony. Marriage among the Society of Friends was a serious but very simple affair. There was no clergyman and no ritual. It could hardly be called a ceremony at all. "Ye Said Squire Boone Took ye Said Sarah Morgan by ye Hand Did in A Solemn Manner Openly Declare he Took her To Be his Wife Promising To be Unto Her A Faithfull and Loveing Husband Untill Death Should Seperate Them And Then & There In the Said Assembly the said Sarah Morgan did likewise Declare." Then, after the usual Quaker custom, everyone present signed the marriage lines as a witness. In the early days of English Quakerism, there had been some doubt of the legality of Quaker marriage, and it had become a custom to have as many witnesses as possible at every wedding.

The couple went to live at Gwynedd. Squire Boone had learned his father's trade and settled down to support his wife as a weaver. But a mere trade was not enough. He was a Boone. He wanted land. There was a promising tract of 147 acres in New Britain Township, Bucks County. He bought it on December 3, 1728. Two years later he bought another tract, adjoining his father's farm in Oley Township, now Berks County. Here he seems to have settled and here, presumably, his sixth son was born, November 2, 1734.* They called him Daniel; it was an old Boone name. They called another son Squire—no one knows why. That, too, was a Boone name, not so unusual as it sounds in modern ears, for it turns up in at least one other colonial family.

The early life of Daniel Boone is mainly legend, but there is abundant evidence that it was exactly the kind of life a small boy enjoys. There was game everywhere—deer, bear, wild turkeys. "Flying Hill" took its name from the perpetual flutter of wild turkeys there. Even buffalo appeared in Pennsylvania,

* This is the date by our modern calendar. It is October 22, 1734, Old Style, which Boone himself insisted on using throughout his life.

though by this time they probably did not come so far east as Berks County.

There were Indians, too. The red men were beginning to move westward—where Daniel Boone would find plenty of them later on. But there were still villages of clustered wigwams in the Tulpehocken and Ontelaunee Valleys, beyond the mountains, north of the Boone farms.

The Quaker policy of peace and fair dealing had borne fruit, however. The Society of Friends had treated these Indians fairly and paid honestly for the land, even though King Charles had already awarded it to the Penns by English law. The Indians were friendly.

The peaceful Quakers were startled on one occasion by the arrival of a party of braves brilliantly painted for war. But it was a false alarm. The Indians had heard that their peaceful white brothers were in danger from other Indians and had hurried down to protect them!

On the whole, it was a good thing for the Indians that they were so well disposed. These early Quaker Boones were peaceful enough, but they were also ready to fight when necessary. Indeed, Boone pacifism was always just a little theoretical. When in 1728 Indian friendship had worn rather thin and it was feared that "the Indians will fall down upon us very suddenly," the inhabitants "Generally fled." But George Boone, justice of the peace, wrote stoutly to the governor: "There remains about twenty men with me to guard my mill, where I have about 1000 bushels of wheat and fflour; and we are resolved to defend ourselves to ye last Extremity."

By the time Daniel Boone was born, friendship had been restored, and Indians were among the child's earliest recollections. In 1736, when he was barely out of the cradle, a party of twenty-five Delawares halted one day to visit the farm of his grandfather, George Boone. Indians enlivened even the church services. In 1742, when little Daniel was only eight, Count Zinzendorf, the Moravian missionary, held a synod in one of the Oley barns; and there was preaching to the Delawares by three recently converted warriors which lasted all through the night.

From these friendly aborigines the future Indian fighter was learning the red man's habits, character, and way of life, mastering the kinks and quirks of red psychology, gaining that amazing ability to "think Indian" which in after life enabled him, when trailing Indians, to know exactly what they were going to do next. Many a pioneer document from the desperate and bloody Kentucky years shows Daniel Boone quietly assuring his companions that the Indians would soon do thus-and-so—as invariably they did!

The fascination which the wilderness exercised on Daniel Boone to the end of his life began almost as early as his knowledge of Indians. The excitement of hunting, the odd ways of wild animals, or just the charm of complete solitude never failed to stir him. When, in 1744, Squire Boone, his father, bought twenty-five acres some miles distant from the farm, he used it mainly for grazing and dairying. The early settlers often sent their cattle miles away to graze for a whole season, and this pasture was too far away to bring the cows home at night. Year after year, from about the time Daniel was ten years old, the boy and his mother used to take the cattle out in the grazing season and live there in a cabin, while Squire Boone stayed at home, managing his blacksmith shop and the modest weaving establishment which now required five or six looms.

From the age of ten to sixteen, young Daniel did little but watch the cattle and roam the woods. The cows may sometimes have been neglected; Boone himself in after life attributed his love of the wild to the carefree roving of these early formative years. As a kinsman remarked, he remained "ever unpracticed in the business of farming, but grew up a woodsman & a hunter."

Still too young to be trusted with a rifle, he whittled a sapling into a kind of javelin, sharpening its tough roots to a point, and managed to kill game without firearms. When he was twelve or thirteen, his father at last gave him a rifle, and Daniel Boone began that perpetual ranging of the forests, plains, and mountains that was to continue for more than seventy years. In the forests, and on the mountains around the half-settled farm land of Berks County, he acquired the iron steadiness of the rifleman's hands and learned to squint an infallibly keen blue eye along the long barrel to the "bead" above the muzzle.

As to his education, there is dispute. Scores of Boone manuscripts—letters, accounts, bonds, militia orders, survey books—show that whatever Daniel Boone's schooling may have been, his book-learning never amounted to very much. His handwriting was a scrawl. His spelling always had a wild, free, original flavor, like his life. In its way it was magnificent. It served its purpose well enough. But it was never gained by prolonged study.

"In Oley sind die Schulen sehr entfernt," observed an old Lutheran preacher in 1748, when Daniel was fourteen. Even these "very isolated" schools were Lutheran church schools to which Quakers would hesitate to send their children.

Such as it was, Daniel Boone got most of his education at home. In his father's blacksmith shop the boy acquired a practical knowledge of metal work under the tuition of his lifelong friend Henry Miller. It was a matter of some importance later, since it enabled him to repair his own rifle, and—as a prisoner—those of the Indians. The Boone family could also provide a good deal of book-learning. The family reputation for literacy has suffered unjustly from the fact that its most famous member spelled after a wild fashion of his own devising. Actually, Daniel Boone was the only bad speller among George Boone's forty-five surviving grandchildren. And even he was no worse than frontier heroes like Simon Kenton, George Rogers Clark, Benjamin Logan, and many another.

As for Daniel's forebears, they were remarkably well educated for their place and time. Old George Boone III is said to have mastered "the several branches of English learning"; John Boone, Daniel's uncle or great-uncle, became a teacher; James Boone, Jr., another relative, became a mathematician of local repute. According to Nathan Boone, young Daniel was taught by Sarah Day Boone, wife of his brother Samuel, and later taught himself to write a little better. According to another legend, Uncle John Boone took a hand, and when he despaired of Daniel's impressionistic orthography, was met by Squire Boone's rejoinder: "Let the girls do the spelling and Dan will do the shooting"—which, as matters turned out, was what happened.

According to another tale, young Daniel attended one of the wretched little country schools of the period. It was, says the legend, taught by a dissipated Irishman, who kept a bottle of whiskey hidden in a thicket near the schoolhouse, which he visited for frequent potations to brighten his pedagogical labors. Daniel Boone, chasing a squirrel, found the flask, which the schoolboys filled with an emetic. When the schoolmaster next returned from the thicket, he was in a very bad humor. Daniel, at that unfortunate moment, made a mistake in arithmetic and was promptly flogged. There was a scuffle. The other children "shouted and roared." Daniel, being large for his age, knocked the teacher flat and ran for his life. The teacher, not the pupil, was dismissed, but young Daniel never went back to school.

The story may or may not be true. Daniel himself liked to

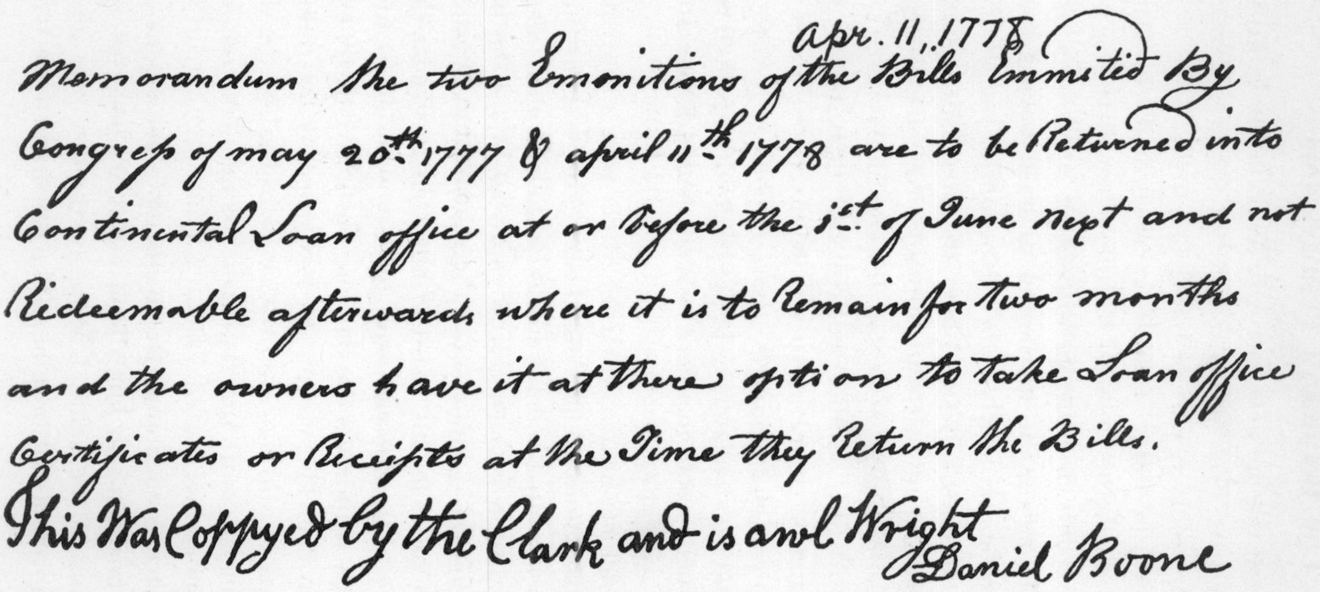
Memorandum the two Emmitions of the Bills Emmitied By Congress of may 20th 1777 & april 11th 1778 are to be Returned into Continental Loan office at or before the 1st of June next and not Reedeemable afterwards where it is to Remain for two months and the owners have it at there option to take Loan office Certificates or Receipts at the Time they Return the Bills.

Apr. 11, 1778

This Was Coppyed by the Clark and is awl Wright
Daniel Boone

DANIEL BOONE MAKES A LEGAL NOTE

The document is an extract from legal records, in a clerk's hand. The annotation is by Boone, who habitually used this spelling. Reproduced by permission from the original in the Durrett Collection, University of Chicago Library.

tell his children that he never went to school a day in his life, but that may have been just a manner of speaking. At least, the schoolhouse story is part of the Boone myth.

Quaker pacifism never appealed very strongly to Daniel Boone. He was a fighter most of his life, when there was need of fighting; records of fisticuffs with other small boys begin early. Nor did he confine his battles to small boys. Frontier humor was crude and hearty rather than subtle; and the ideas of chivalry entertained by small boys are often a little mixed. Hence the two playful girls who emptied a pail of fish entrails upon little Daniel Boone as he lay sleeping under a tree went crying home to their mother with swollen faces and bloody noses. But maternal complaint to Mrs. Squire Boone about her ungallant son's misdeed brought a tart response: "If thee has not brought up thy daughters to better behavior, it is high time they were taught good manners."—Well, Sarah Boone stood by her son.

Young Daniel and his friend Henry Miller were a lively pair. The young blacksmiths knew all about taking wagons apart. Farmers who affronted them were likely to find their wagon wheels depending from tree-tops or tucked away on the barn roof. An incautious neophyte who borrowed a long musket from Daniel's father for his first deer hunt was knocked sprawling at the first shot. The two boys, already experienced hunters, had quietly withdrawn the ball and put in five or six extra charges of powder. The victim was so startled by the tremendous bang that he did not even notice he had killed the deer he was aiming at, until the repentant Daniel went out and hunted up the carcass.

Another illicit excursion ended in disaster when Boone and Miller tried one night to jump Squire Boone's horse over an old cow resting in the fields. Unhappily, the cow rose just as the horse was in mid-air above her. The nag crashed down and broke its neck. Matters looked serious. Quaker lads were not encouraged to go gallivanting about by night. The demise of the horse would be hard enough to explain; the little nocturnal excursion would be still harder. The boys, since no one knew they had the horse out, slipped saddle and bridle back into the barn, leaving the head of the family to speculate in vain how his steed could possibly have perished in so strange a way.

Still another escapade of Daniel Boone's childhood is a good example of the impatience of restraint which marks his later career. Smallpox, scourge of the frontier, developed near the Boone homestead. To protect her children from the disease, Sarah Boone kept them at home. Finding confinement irksome, Daniel and his sister Elizabeth decided that if they once caught the disease and became immune, their mother would let them go where they pleased. Slipping out of bed one night, the two children ran off to a neighbor's house, crawled into bed with a smallpox patient, and then came home undiscovered, cheerfully anticipating the worst. It soon happened.

When the disease developed, their mother got the story by taking her son aside with an admonitory: "Now, Daniel, I want thee to tell thy mother the whole truth."

Daniel confessed, and Sarah Boone was immensely vexed. But one cannot punish a smallpox patient, and the small boy, who with his sister had endangered the entire household, got off with a very mild scolding: "Thee naughty little gorrel, why did thee not tell me before so that I could have had thee better prepared?" All the children escaped with light cases and Daniel was again free to wander. The smallpox had, on the whole, been a great success.

2. To the Yadkin Valley

THERE was a steady trickle of settlers in those years out of Pennsylvania into the rich lands of the Shenandoah Valley and onward into North Carolina. But beyond lay the mountains, running north and south, dark, grim and thickly wooded, tangled with underbrush, blocking the westward traveler. No roads ran that way except the "Warriors' Path," a mere "trace" used only by red hunters or war parties, which wound through the Cumberland Gap and vanished, no white man knew whither.

Toward that forbidden land no settler had ever ventured. A stray half dozen hunters and explorers, taking their lives in their hands, had penetrated the wilderness briefly. Adventurers by water had skirted the Ohio and Mississippi shores of Kentucky. The natural trend of wanderers with families in search of farm land was not at first into that dangerous and unknown country, but southward, along the valley that paralleled the coast and the settlements. Many of Squire Boone's Pennsylvania neighbors undertook the journey.

Squire Boone and his family were beginning to find Berks County an unpleasant place to live in. There was friction with the godly Friends of Exeter Meeting, who had been horrified by the marriages of the Boone children. In 1742, Daniel's sister Sarah was "treated with for marrying out"—that is, "out of Unity with Friends." Sarah Boone was a dreadful example of eighteenth-century flaming youth. To begin with, she had married a "worldling," though as the minutes charitably record, it was "1st offence of this kind." Then there is a further note: "Fr[ien]ds. appointed to speak to her Father, Squire Boone." The Meeting had meantime heard still darker rumors. It was bad enough to marry a worldling. The Friends now began to suspect that she had not married him nearly soon enough. Two Quakeresses were appointed to investigate. It was true. Sarah Boone had been with child before the wedding. The little community buzzed. The distressed father abased himself before the Meeting:

> Squire [Boone] declareth, that he was no ways Countenancing or Consenting to the said Marriage; but, confesseth himself in a Fault in keeping them in his House after he knew of their keeping Company, (but that he was in a great streight in not knowing what to do, seeing he was somewhat Sensible that they had been too Conversant before) and hopeth to be more Careful for the future.

More trouble was in store. In 1747, on the thirty-first day of the tenth month (Quaker dating, since these strict Friends refused to use the heathen names of the months), Squire's son Israel was also "testified against" in Meeting for "marrying out." Again the poor father was called to account for a "disorderly marriage," though there was no breath of scandal beyond the fact that Israel's bride was not a Quakeress. Even legitimate marriage to such a creature, the Quakers thought, was pretty serious. This time Squire Boone appears to have been firmer in dealing with the Meeting. He insisted on his son's right to marry whom he pleased. The Society of Friends did not countenance such goings-on and within a few months Squire Boone was "disowned"—a kind of Quaker excommunication. He was accused of "giving Room to a reflecting Spirit even against his Friends who sought his everlasting Peace and

Welfare." They tried to "bring him to a Sense of his Outgoings" and make him "sensible of his coming to a Godly Sorrow in himself," but it was not much use. Squire remained stubborn.

Thereafter he found himself in an exceedingly uncomfortable position. Hitherto he had been rather prominent in the Meeting. He had been an "overseer," also a trustee of the little burial ground. His daughter's forced marriage was disgrace enough, but now he had been cast out of the Meeting merely because of his son's entirely respectable marriage. Even though his wife and the rest of the family were still in good standing, the Friends could—and they probably did—make things very unpleasant.

Squire Boone stuck it out only a little while; then he sold all that he owned. He wanted to leave Berks County forever, but he does not seem to have been quite sure where he was going, for his wife, still in good standing with the Friends, asked for and duly received letters addressed to Meetings in Virginia, North Carolina, and apparently Maryland as well.

There were other and less painful motives for Squire Boone's departure. The crude agriculture of that period exhausted the land quickly. There was no rotation of crops and little fertilization of the fields. At first it had been easy to move on to better land. But now the good land in Pennsylvania was filling up. Since 1735 Dutch and Quaker settlers had been moving steadily to the "southwest"—as North Carolina was then called.

By 1750 more and more Berks County families were moving down the Cumberland and Shenandoah Valleys. John Lincoln, the great-grandfather of the Emancipator, moved off about this time and settled permanently in Virginia, whence his restless son, Abraham, later took his own son Thomas and set off for Kentucky. It was Thomas Lincoln who became father of the Emancipator. Another Berks County family migrated at nearly the same time—the Hankses, to whom Lincoln's mother was in some way related. The Boones and Lincolns had always been closely associated. The Boones were soon to be even more closely linked with the family of Morgan Bryan, who also started for North Carolina. Squire Boone joined the trend. Perhaps he would have done so anyway; but resentment at being disowned by the Friends, his daughter's disgrace, the turmoil over his son's marriage, must have urged him on.

It was the spring of 1750 when Squire and Sarah Boone set off with their family. They had sold their land April 11, and on the first of May they started. West across Pennsylvania. Probably through the old colonial town of Carlisle—who would have supposed they would found a school for the Indians there, some day? Down the Cumberland Valley, where, later, Lee's army would come sweeping into Pennsylvania. On down the Shenandoah, where Stonewall Jackson's men would march and countermarch in years to come.

It was such interesting country that Squire Boone dallied on the way, perhaps with his friend John Lincoln on Linnville Creek, Rockingham County, Virginia. Here Henry Miller, Daniel Boone's boyhood friend, left the Boones, to settle permanently. When the two friends next met, nearly thirty years later, one was a prosperous business man, the other the most celebrated frontiersman in America.

Not until the late autumn of 1751 or sometime in 1752 did Squire Boone reach the Yadkin Valley in North Carolina; and not until December 29, 1753, did he buy land. He purchased directly from agents of the Earl of Granville, to whom the King had granted an enormous tract. The terms of the sale would worry a modern lawyer. It was not a clear title. King George II retained the right to half of any gold or silver Squire Boone might find. The noble earl himself retained a right to half the rest. The purchaser could have the remaining one quarter. It was all rather futile, for no ore was ever found. But there was a further irksome stipulation. Even though he owned the land, Squire Boone had to pay annual rental, and he was obligated to clear three out of every hundred acres every three years. Clearing forest land was a tremendous task—trees to be cut down, stumps to be dug out, underbrush to be chopped away, stones to be moved, and the earth itself a hopeless tangle of matted roots. An acre a year meant back-breaking work.

Squire Boone had chosen a hill overlooking the Yadkin River in what was then Rowan, and is today Davidson County. Here he built a cabin whose ruins—including part of the stone chimney and a stone marked "D. Boone"—survived until about 1900.

It was wilder country than Pennsylvania. There were less than twenty-five thousand people in the entire colony of North Carolina, and the Yadkin was on its extreme western frontier. Game was everywhere—even a few buffalo wandered across the mountain in winter from the mysterious wilderness beyond. In the beginning a hunter could take thirty deer a day without leaving the valley. The market town of Salisbury was near enough to provide a market for deerskins and furs and to supply the few commodities that a frontier farmer could not provide for himself.

It was an exciting time, too. The Indians about the Yadkin Valley were mostly Catawbas who were usually friendly, but beyond them were the powerful Cherokees, one of the most advanced of all the tribes, whose friendship was a very uncertain quantity. Worse still, news began to trickle through the wilderness and into the settlements that the French were encroaching on the King's lands in the Ohio Valley. A young officer of the Virginia militia, named Washington, went up to warn them off, was rebuffed, and nearly murdered. He went back again with troops, won a small skirmish, lost a large one, and was forced to surrender. From somewhere beyond the mountains—no one knew just where until Daniel Boone and his men found out years later—parties of Shawnees came down along the Warriors' Path to attack the Cherokees. White men who had been unfortunate enough to settle near the famous warpath were attacked too, with entire impartiality. The Shawnees wanted scalps. Redskin or paleface, any scalp would do. Some of the raiders in the Yadkin in 1753 bore French arms and ornaments, proof positive, if any were needed, that the French were stirring up the tribes against the British settlements.

So far Daniel Boone had never even seen a hostile Indian. He had his first experience in the Yadkin Valley when he incurred the enmity of a Catawba brave known to the whites as Saucy Jack, who was jealous because of Daniel's superior marksmanship, displayed in many a frontier shooting-match. Saucy Jack threatened to kill his rival, who was absent at the time on a hunting trip in the forests where he could have been easily ambushed. Learning of the danger, the old Quaker father seized a hatchet, remarked: "Well, I'll be first," and set out in search of Saucy Jack, who prudently vanished. Years afterward, as an Indian prisoner, Daniel Boone, shooting at targets with his captors, was careful not to shoot too well and so rouse enmity.

He was shortly to learn the first of many lessons in Indian warfare, for the secret hostility of the French soon led to the open hostilities of the French and Indian War.

Early in 1755, Major-General Edward Braddock of the British Regular Army arrived to command an expedition against the French Fort Duquesne, at what is now Pittsburgh. His force was a mixture of British Regulars and American militia, including two officers who twenty years later were to command

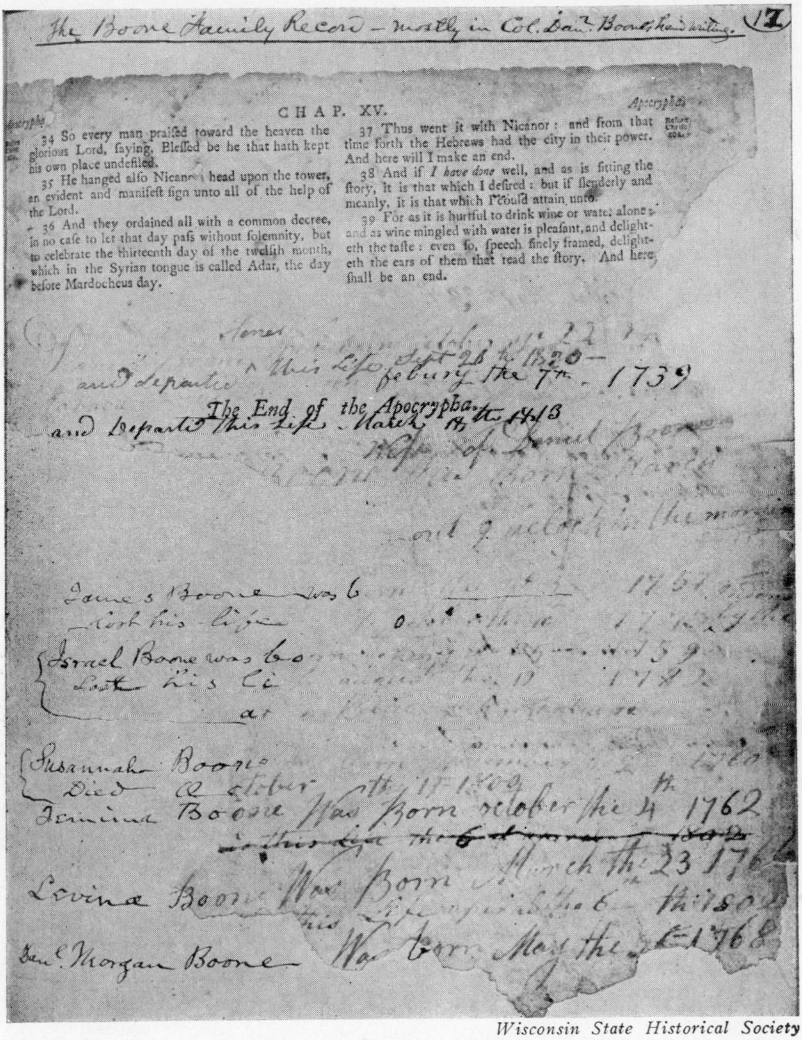
The Boone Family Record — mostly in Col. Danl. Boone's handwriting. 17

CHAP. XV.

34 So every man praised toward the heaven the glorious Lord, saying, Blessed be he that hath kept his own place undefiled.

35 He hanged also Nicanor's head upon the tower, an evident and manifest sign unto all of the help of the Lord.

36 And they ordained all with a common decree, in no case to let that day pass without solemnity, but to celebrate the thirteenth day of the twelfth month, which in the Syrian tongue is called Adar, the day before Mardocheus day.

37 Thus went it with Nicanor: and from that time forth the Hebrews had the city in their power. And here will I make an end.

38 And if *I have done* well, and as is fitting the story, it is that which I desired: but if slenderly and meanly, it is that which I could attain unto.

39 For as it is hurtful to drink wine or water alone; and as wine mingled with water is pleasant, and delighteth the taste: even so, speech finely framed, delighteth the ears of them that read the story. And here shall be an end.

The End of the Apocrypha.

and departed this life Sept 26th 1820

febury the 7th 1739

and Departed this life March 18th 1813

Wife of Daniel Boone

James Boone was born [illegible] 1757

lost his life [illegible] 1773

Israel Boone was born [illegible] 1759

Lost his life [illegible] 1782

Susannah Boone [illegible] 1760

Died October [illegible] 1800

Jemima Boone Was Born october the 4th 1762

Levina Boone Was Born March the 23 176[illegible]

Danl. Morgan Boone Was Born May the [illegible] 1768

Wisconsin State Historical Society

BOONE FAMILY RECORD

Detached leaf of a Boone Bible now in the Draper Collection. Largely in Boone's handwriting, the annotations are by Lyman C. Draper.

opposing armies in the Revolution. Young Colonel Washington had stood on his dignity and resigned when informed that officers with commissions from the King would outrank militia officers with nothing but commissions from the provincial governors. But Colonel Washington was a valuable man. He knew better than any other soldier the country where the campaign was to be fought, and his influence in Virginia was not to be ignored. The wounded dignity of the Washingtons was assuaged by a position on General Braddock's staff. As representative of the commanding general, the colonel could look down his nose at any mere line officer, no matter whose commission he held.

A certain Lieutenant-Colonel Gage commanded the advance guard. Twenty years later, in the spring of 1775, he would be penned up in Boston and bombarded by Braddock's young Virginia aide.

Dr. Benjamin Franklin, postmaster of Pennsylvania, was very helpful to the British general in getting the troops provisioned and started. Like Colonel Washington, Dr. Franklin, too, was later to be in some danger of hanging at his Majesty's hands. The principal commissary of the expedition was that very Dr. Thomas Walker who had been one of the earliest explorers of Kentucky. One of the leading scouts was Christopher Gist, the veteran woodsman who had been Washington's guide, a neighbor of the Boones in the Yadkin Valley.

With them, probably as a wagoner, went John Finley, who only a year or so before had returned from trading with the Indians, and who had accompanied them on a hunting trip in the new and miraculous land beyond the mountains. With the expedition also was young Daniel Boone, not a soldier, just a wagoner in the North Carolina militia commanded by Major Edward Brice Dobbs, son of the Governor of North Carolina.

Major Dobbs was an officer of the British Regular Army.

Since he was in North Carolina when the war broke out, he was given a company and sent into Virginia to aid the general defense of the colonies. Later, he was promoted major and placed in command of the entire force.

Braddock's expedition was in difficulties from the start. The general had spent his last evening in London visiting a young lady of dubious repute for whom he entertained an allegedly platonic affection. In parting, he had observed to her, "Dear Pop, we are sent like sacrifices to the altar." It was an accurate prophecy.

When the general reached the Colonies, the promised preparations were a chaos. Neither the provincial troops nor the supplies that had been promised were ready. Dr. Franklin, however, was able to terrorize his Pennsylvania Dutch farmers into providing the necessary wagons for Braddock's field train. He solved the problem with typical shrewdness. The hussars would come and take the wagons if the farmers did not voluntarily provide them, he let it be known. The Pennsylvania Dutch had certain vivid recollections of what hussars had been like in the Rhine Valley. They hurriedly provided the wagons—for which eventually they got paid.

After endless delays the expedition crawled slowly off through the western Pennsylvania wilderness, its pioneers, ahead, chopping energetically to make a road which would keep the line of supplies permanently open and enable Braddock to advance as far as necessary.

The march seemed endless. The expedition halted early each day to fortify camp for the night, and there was plenty of time for talk by the camp fires. Boone and Finley met. Many a long night, by the embers of a log-fire, the North Carolina farmer boy listened open-eyed to tales of that new land called Kentucky, that hunter's paradise, that wonderful wild area of rich land, good farm land that a young man with a family could have for the taking, land where deer and buffalo, beaver, otter, and game of every kind abounded. Sixty years later Daniel Boone still remembered the thrill of it. He may have heard similar tales from the scout Christopher Gist, who had already seen it, or from his own hunting companion, Nathaniel Gist, the great scout's son. He could have heard tales of Kentucky quite as marvelous from Dr. Thomas Walker, the explorer who had reached Kentucky in 1750, but it is doubtful whether the expedition's commissary even knew the young wagoner existed. General Braddock and all his staff officers had plenty of other things to think about just then.

Major-General Edward Braddock has been greatly maligned. He was an irritating and irritable man, but the conditions he found on his arrival in America more or less justified his exasperation. He was completely self-satisfied and of course wholly ignorant of forest warfare. So were his Regulars. But within his limits he was the very model of an eighteenth-century major-general. Not very bright, but careful, courageous, and conscientious.

Every precaution against surprise that the drill book called for, Braddock took. His tactical dispositions and reconnoissance on the march and in bivouac were models. Even on that fatal day at Turtle Creek, near Pittsburgh, only his advance guard was taken by surprise (which is more or less the function of advance guards). The small force of French and Indians ahead of Gage's troops were outnumbered two to one. They could have been brushed aside or smashed in a twinkling if either the general or his officers had had the least idea of how to fight Indians. As it was, Braddock and his army gave a magnificent display of bulldog courage, and got themselves killed off like flies by a force ridiculously inferior to their own but with the advantage of knowing nothing about a drill book meant for another kind of war in another kind of terrain.

The French, terrified at Braddock's approach, had already been preparing to surrender, when Beaujeu, a subordinate officer, begged his commander to let him at least make an attempt to stop the apparently irresistible advance of the overwhelming British force. Hurrying off to the neighboring Indians, he urged them to join his handful of Frenchmen in an attack. The Indians, also frightened, at first refused. Eventually, about eight hundred joined in forming an ambush across a ravine through which Braddock's army would have to pass.

The rest is familiar history; how Lieutenant-Colonel Gage, the British Regular, ran into the ambushed Indians and stood them off. How Braddock, Washington, and the main body came up—some of the officers, caught lunching, with napkins still under their chins. How Braddock raged up and down the field, after the best European tradition, keeping his troops out in the open where their red coats gave the Indians easy target practice. How the Virginians took cover and fought Indians Indian-style. How Washington, who had been carried for the last day or so in a wagon, riddled with fever, crawled into the saddle, fever or no fever, and rode into fire. How at last the troops could stand no more and bolted. How the wounded Braddock was carried back dying and was buried under the military road his pioneers had built so carefully. How the wagons were driven above his grave to save the dead general's scalp by concealing the spot where he lay. How years later road menders came upon the grave and recognized the body by the insignia of a general officer. How the rumor later spread that Braddock had cut down one of the Virginia riflemen with his sword and had promptly been shot by the slain man's brother.

Major Dobbs' North Carolina troops did not get into this action very heavily, if indeed they were involved at all. According to one account they happened to be marching with the reserve, far to the rear. According to another account, Major Dobbs and his men were absent on reconnoissance. All accounts agree, however, that Boone and the North Carolina wagon train, which of course could not accompany reconnoissance in that wooded country, were somewhere in the rear with the rest of Braddock's field train.

As the troops broke, out in front of them, Daniel Boone and the other wagoners saw the terrorized mob come pouring back with the Indian knives and tomahawks flashing among them. Unable to get their wagons away, Boone and the rest slashed the traces and rode for their lives. A few wagoners were killed, but Boone and Finley escaped. The rout was finally stopped, some wagons were collected, troops reorganized, miles away. The army was so shaken that there was nothing to do but limp homeward, leaving the frontier completely open.

Some of Braddock's British grenadiers, fresh from the old country and knowing nothing of cruel wilderness ways, had surrendered to the Indians. They probably expected the ordinary treatment of prisoners of war when they were brought to the vicinity of Fort Duquesne. Even being stripped and painted black, the usual preparation for the stake, may not at first have undeceived them.

The poor devils soon learned the worst. One after another, while the rest watched in horror, they were dragged to the stake, tortured a while, and then burned to death. In the fort, close at hand, the French commander and his disciplined troops went unconcernedly about their military routine, paying no heed to the long-drawn screams of agony and the fierce yells of the torturers that echoed through the forest hour after tormented hour.

In all that wilderness from which their comrades had fled, there was only one human being to pity them. James Smith, a

British prisoner taken by the French some time before, was in the fort. Safe enough from the Indians himself, since he was in French hands, he stood in despair on the stockade, watching the prisoners brought to the warriors' camp outside, knowing well enough what was to happen. When the torture began he went back to his quarters to avoid seeing it, but no log cabin could shut out the horrible sounds.

News of the English defeat spread swiftly through the forests; but both the Catawbas and Cherokees of North Carolina remained friendly and in 1757 actually sent four hundred warriors to assist the Virginians. The Cherokees even encouraged the building of white men's forts in their country, for defense against the French and the northern Indians.

Daniel Boone was soon back in his father's cabin in the Yadkin Valley, trying to forget the horrors he had seen. His mind was occupied by pleasanter matters. He was thinking of getting married, and prudently brought a little furniture home with him from his travels.

Near Squire Boone's farm lived the family of Joseph Bryan. Mary Boone, Daniel's sister, had married William Bryan, Joseph's brother, and at their wedding young Daniel Boone, off for the wars, first saw his future wife. She was Joseph Bryan's daughter Rebecca, then only fifteen but quite old enough for marriage by the standards of that time and place.

The pair next met in a group of young people, indulging in a little mild flirtation in a cherry orchard. Rebecca was wearing a white cambric apron, priceless finery in the eyes of a frontier girl. Daniel, entranced by the dark comeliness of the strapping young creature at his side, had, none the less, certain doubts. For all their daring, the Boones were a cautious breed. Frontier matrons, with much to try their patience, were sometimes termagants. Rebecca was charming, but what about her disposition? Daniel, as he afterward confessed, slyly proceeded to "try her temper." Out of its sheath came the ever present hunting knife. Young Daniel, in apparent absent-mindedness, began to cut idly at the green turf on which he was lounging beside Rebecca. Slash, slash, a pick and a cut at a blade of grass. The absent-minded young man had cut a great hole in the precious garment. He watched Rebecca.

Rebecca was very nice about it. In fact, she was so nice that there is an alarming possibility she had seen through the whole maneuver from the very beginning. At any rate, the test having proved the lady's good temper and equanimity, on August 14, 1756, wedlock followed.

Of their courtship, only two other incidents are recorded, one of them almost certainly apocryphal. Like other North Carolina hunters, Daniel Boone occasionally brought down his deer by "fire hunting." Moving silently through the woods or floating in a canoe, the hunters flashed torches until they attracted the deer, always curious when a light shows in the woods at night. They fired at the light reflected in the animals' eyes. Daniel Boone, says the tale, caught the gleam of eyes in the woods one night, raised his rifle, and discovered just in time the figure of Rebecca. The girl rushed home to her father's cabin exclaiming that she had been chased by a panther. Not even their children ever believed the story, in spite of its wide currency.

It was the custom for a betrothed lover to bring a deer to his sweetheart's cabin and cut up the venison in her presence, proof of his skill as a hunter and ability to provide for a family. Daniel and the deer duly appeared at the Bryan cabin where Daniel flayed and prepared the carcass before an audience of girls who were not so admiring as they might have been. Daniel was skillful enough, but the young ladies commented flippantly on the amount of grease and blood with which his hunting shirt was besmeared in the process. Not that they were squeamish—Rebecca was handy enough with the rifle to kill an occasional deer herself—but women for some reason always enjoyed teasing Daniel Boone.

The young hunter pretended to notice nothing. But as they all sat down to supper a little later he picked up his bowl of milk, glanced into it, and quietly addressed the bowl: "You, like my hunting shirt, have missed many a good washing." There was a gasp from the girls at the reflection on their housekeeping. Daniel, it was agreed, had evened up the score. Not, one would say, an overwhelmingly funny joke; and yet the backwoods chuckled over it for years.

The marriage of Daniel and Rebecca Boone must have been very much like other frontier weddings. The bride customarily rode to the altar on a pillion behind her father's saddle. After the wedding, the pillion was taken off and strapped on behind her bridegroom's saddle. His wife mounted his horse with him and rode off on her honeymoon.

It was not very private. The entire wedding party gathered in the cabin where the couple were to spend their wedding night. There was a feast, with the rough plenty of the backwoods. The bottle of corn whiskey circulated. The jests were far from mealy-mouthed, for the frontier had no doubt that marriage was indeed "ordained for the procreation of children."

When the evening was partly over, a bevy of young girls, together with the bride, slipped one by one up the ladder that led to the rough loft above the cabin and there put the bride to bed. When they were gone, a group of young men followed, performed a like office for the bridegroom, and left the pair together in such privacy as the loft of a one- or two-room cabin could afford. Late in the night, food was sent up the ladder to the newly married couple and the wedding guests gradually departed.

It was all very rough and crude and primitive; but the marriage of Daniel and Rebecca led to a lifelong devotion, a working partnership such as few sophisticated moderns achieve. Daniel may have strayed from the path of complete fidelity once or twice. There are some very queer—and probably slanderous—tales about Rebecca herself. The frontier was a rough place with a rough relish for rough jokes; it is hard now to tell what the facts are. But whatever the truth may be, there is no doubt that they forgave and forgot whatever there was to forgive and forget, working and struggling together for a long, hard, and rather happy lifetime.

The Boone and Bryan families, thus intimately linked, were never afterwards separated. Both were represented in Boone's disastrous first efforts to settle Kentucky in 1773. Both actually did settle in Kentucky later. Both moved together to the Missouri settlements when Kentucky became crowded. This was not unusual in those days, for, where communities were small and travel was restricted, family relationships meant a great deal. Families tended to intermarry, and then lived and worked together their whole lives long.

What was Rebecca Boone like? Except that she was a rather tall brunette, nobody knows now, because then it was not thought of enough importance to record. Subsequently one of the early biographers was inspired to lyric invention: "Rebecca Bryan, whose brow had now been fanned by the breezes of seventeen summers, was, like Rebecca of old, 'very fair to look upon,' with jet black hair and eyes, complexion rather dark, and something over the common size of her sex; her whole demeanor, expressive of her childlike artlessness, pleasing in her address, and unaffectedly kind in all her deportment. Never was there a more gentle, affectionate, forbearing creature, than this same fair youthful bride of the Yadkin." But that is just the way mid-nineteenth-century biographers went on.

The only way you can know what Rebecca Boone was really like is to know what she did. She married her Daniel in the Yadkin as a girl of seventeen, and she died, still with her Daniel, in Missouri as an old woman of seventy-three. Once she despaired and gave him up for dead. Many a time she had reason to despair. Two mortal years she lived alone on the Yadkin, bringing up the children while Daniel was in the wilderness. She molded bullets and she helped to fight the redskins off. She saw her husband wounded with a tomahawk and her daughter with a bullet. For a good part of her married life she was not quite sure whether her husband was alive or dead. The chances always were the Indians had killed him. The chances, as a matter of fact, were always wrong. But still it was disturbing to a married woman with a family.

Quite an ordinary girl. Quite an ordinary woman. There were a lot like that in the backwoods. It has been, on the whole, a good thing for these United States.

As Daniel Boone himself used to say, all you needed for happiness was "a good gun, a good horse, and a good wife." Now he had them all, and there is no reason for supposing that despite all his arduous labors and cruel disappointments he was ever anything but happy.

The young couple are said to have settled down after their marriage in a cabin in Squire Boone's yard, but not for long. From 1758 to 1760 there was a series of Indian wars of which the North Carolina frontier bore the brunt.

The Cherokees had remained friendly, even after such a blow to English prestige as Braddock's defeat; but there were plenty of white ruffians on the frontier to whom the only good Indian was a dead one. There were several wanton killings of Cherokees by treacherous white men. Cherokee feeling changed abruptly. The proud and powerful tribe, faithful to the red man's notions of revenge, went out on the warpath. In April of 1759 war parties were raiding the Yadkin Valley, where the

Boones and Bryans had their farms. White settlers fled to escape the carnage. Many of the Boones "forted up" in Fort Dobbs, which was besieged by the red warriors; but Squire Boone and his son took their families to safety in the East.

It is said that old Squire Boone retired to Maryland until the Indian wars were over. His son Squire, who had been learning the blacksmith's trade from Samuel Boone in Pennsylvania—rather more thoroughly than his brother Daniel—had moved with Samuel Boone's family to Maryland. This was the old man's natural refuge.

Daniel and Rebecca, however, took a two-horse wagon and went to Culpeper County, Virginia, near Fredericksburg. Here Daniel Boone probably met George Washington, whose acquaintance he claimed in after life. The young husband worked as a wagoner, hauling tobacco to market, hunting a little, shooting at targets, occasionally scouting even here for Indian "sign."

Though the books never say so, Daniel Boone almost certainly accompanied the Virginia troops who marched with General John Forbes in 1758 on his expedition across Pennsylvania with an overwhelming force to retrieve Braddock's defeat and drive the French out of Fort Duquesne once for all. In his old age Boone told a friend that he had killed his first Indian by throwing him off the "Juniata bridge" to the rocks forty feet below while serving as wagon-master with troops campaigning in Pennsylvania. Forbes' expedition is the only one with which Boone could possibly have crossed the Juniata River. Braddock's was never anywhere near it.

However that may be, he was soon back in the Yadkin country, for on October 12, 1759, while the Indian wars still raged, Daniel Boone was buying 640 acres of land from his father in Rowan County. A note added to the original deed explains: "Daniel Boone, Planter, bought this tract from his father for 50 pounds."

By the end of 1760 the white men had the upper hand. Strong

militia forces had laid waste the whole Cherokee country, burned the villages, destroyed the crops, and driven five thousand Indians into the hills to starve or submit. By November the Cherokees had had enough. They came to the council fire and a peace treaty was signed.

Daniel Boone lost no time in plunging into the mountains and forests with his rifle, though his family and his father's may have stayed in the safety of the East for some time. In this year he made his first trip across the Blue Ridge, guided by an old slave, and settled down in a small cabin which, before the Indian troubles, had been built for herdsmen grazing cattle in the summer.

He hunted also in eastern Tennessee and left a famous inscription carved in the bark of a beech tree on the banks of Boon's [sic] Creek. All his life he liked to leave these inscriptions, commemorating a good kill, fresh water, or just his presence in the country. This one reads:

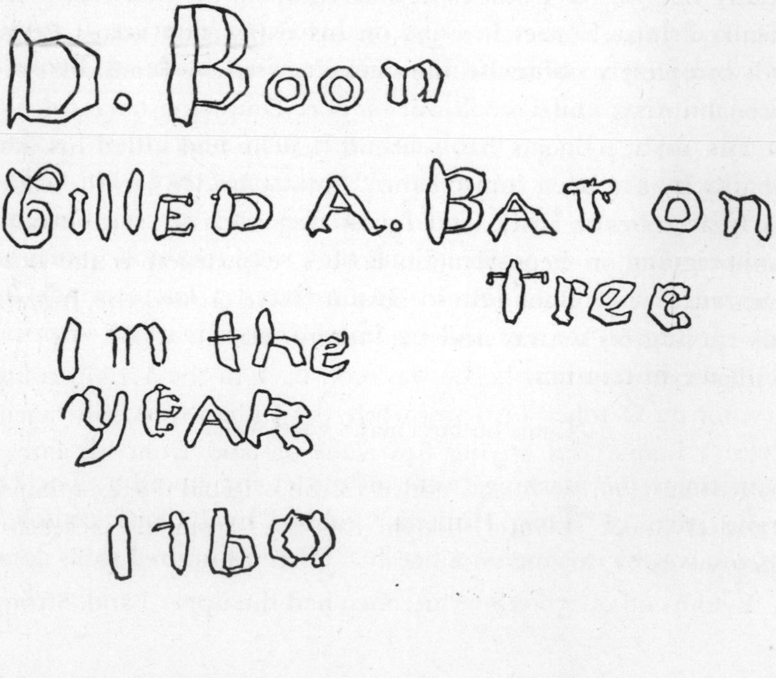

Thirteen years later he left almost the same inscription near Long Island, Tennessee:

D. Boon killa bar on this tree 1773

There has been much controversy as to the authenticity of these inscriptions, but there is no real ground for questioning them. Scores of similar Boone inscriptions have been recorded, always in lands where he is known to have traveled. They must be genuine, for the only alternative explanation is the existence of an industrious practical joker who ranged the wilderness carving fraudulent inscriptions without ever making a mistake as to the correct locale. The 1760 inscription was known as early as 1770. The tree still stood in 1853, and some years later it was photographed.

The long preservation of these bark inscriptions is, botanically speaking, not so remarkable as it seems. Attracted by their smooth surface, Boone invariably carved his records on beech trees. The beech grows slowly; and though expansion of the trunk ultimately stretched and distorted the lettering, it could not completely obliterate the deep carvings made by Boone's keen hunting knife.

The early pioneers habitually left such inscriptions, scores of which have been copied down. Sometimes they were meant as legal records. Early land boundaries and surveys were always marked on trees. Sometimes they were meant as guides to comrades who might follow. Boone traced a lost comrade by his carving on a tree; and he himself once marked a spring with the inscription:

Come on boys here's good water

Sometimes the markings were an outlet for emotion. The famous party of "Long Hunters," robbed by Indians, consoled themselves by carving on a beech: "Fifteen hundred skins gone to ruination," and adding their initials. Sometimes carving merely relieved the tedium of the wilderness.

Indians were not the only peril of that lonely frontier. White desperadoes were making nearly as much trouble as the Indians, for the frontier attracted people who were too bad for civilization as well as people who were too good for it.

The Cherokee wars had led to much disorder among the settlers themselves. Effective policing was nearly impossible, although local constables theoretically patrolled impossibly long hundred-mile beats through the backwoods. Horse thieves were active. Plundering of one kind led to plundering of another.

Eventually a band of desperadoes settled down to careers of professional crime in the Yadkin, carrying on their raids from a secret lair in the mountains. Two of the gang kidnapped a girl from the Yadkin settlements and rushed her into the wilderness, "designing to doom her to the basest of purposes." Several bands of settlers sallied out in pursuit.

Daniel Boone was with the band that found the girl—it was the first of his three chivalrous rescues of damsels in distress. The rescuers, following the trail as fast as they could, were amazed to meet the girl herself emerging from the underbrush. At their approach she had hidden till she could be sure who they were. Her abductors had quarreled—one can guess why—and in the excitement she had escaped.

Guided by the erstwhile captive, the vengeful little band pushed on to the kidnappers' camp. One man had escaped. The other lay unconscious where his partner had knocked him out and left him. He was seized and turned over to the authorities, but strange to say there is no further record of his case.

About a year later, stolen goods were found in the stack of fodder at one of the Yadkin farms. Forced to admit that he had been working with the criminals, the guilty farmer saved his own skin by agreeing to guide a party to the robbers' lair. Some miles in advance of the frontier the robber band had built a little stockade against a cliff, masking their fortifications among the trees and using a "natural chimney" in the rocks to aid their concealment. No trails led in—the band was careful about "making sign." They left no trail at all because they invariably approached their fort each time from a new direction.

Daniel Boone was in the party of settlers that pushed into the woods to the fort, rushed it, captured several of the robbers, and recovered a good deal of stolen property. Their guide was very nearly shot by the infuriated wife of one of the gang.

Even in these early days Boone's wilderness wanderings were probably more than mere hunting trips. In the market town of Salisbury, where sometimes he went on legal and other business, he met wealthy men of affairs. There was Richard Henderson, eminent in the local bar, for some years a justice of the colonial courts. Squire Boone had been one of the justices of the County Court of Pleas and Quarter Sessions before which Henderson practiced. There was Henderson's law partner, John Williams, and Henderson's friend, Thomas Hart, sheriff of Orange County. There was Hart's brother Nathaniel. Both of the Harts became lifelong friends and business associates of the Boones.

These were men of wealth, social position, power in the little society of the colony. All of them must have met Boone again and again about the law courts, and they lent sympathetic ears to the gaunt hunter's enthusiastic stories of the wild and wonderful lands whose fringes he had already touched on many a hunting trip and whose interior he wanted to explore. That would take capital. Boone was poor in those days; he had nothing but a local reputation; but he made an impression on these shrewd business men.

To what extent it was Boone who interested them, or how far they encouraged Boone's enthusiasm, no one will ever know. A stupendous idea, however, was slowly taking form in the minds of Boone, Henderson, and their friends. On the seacoast every ship that docked was bringing immigrants. From the populous East they made their way slowly to the mountains. The land was filling up. Some day, some day not very distant, the slowly spreading wave of immigrants was bound to top the mountains and spread out on the lands beyond. Every business man in the thirteen colonies had his eye upon that land. Establish some kind of title to those empty acres and you could sell them off at enormous profits to the settlers who were sure to come.

The Indians? Well, these were really the King's lands which merely happened to be claimed by "the Indian nations." It ought to be easy to prove in a white man's court that the Indian had no title. The only parchments that the red men had were deerskins.

The Indians would not take kindly to the idea. The first attempt at settlement would be dangerous. The forests were thick, every bush would hide an enemy. Wild animals abounded. Save for streams and narrow buffalo "traces" the forests were trackless. Successful land speculation meant finding the best lands first. To find them you needed a farmer who knew land when he saw it, a woodsman who could find his way in the wilderness, a scout skillful enough to stay alive with death about him everywhere. You needed somebody tough, brave, honest—and poor enough to risk his life for the chance of landed wealth. Well, there was Daniel Boone!

In 1764, hunters deep in the wilderness encountered him. Boone questioned them about the country they had covered.

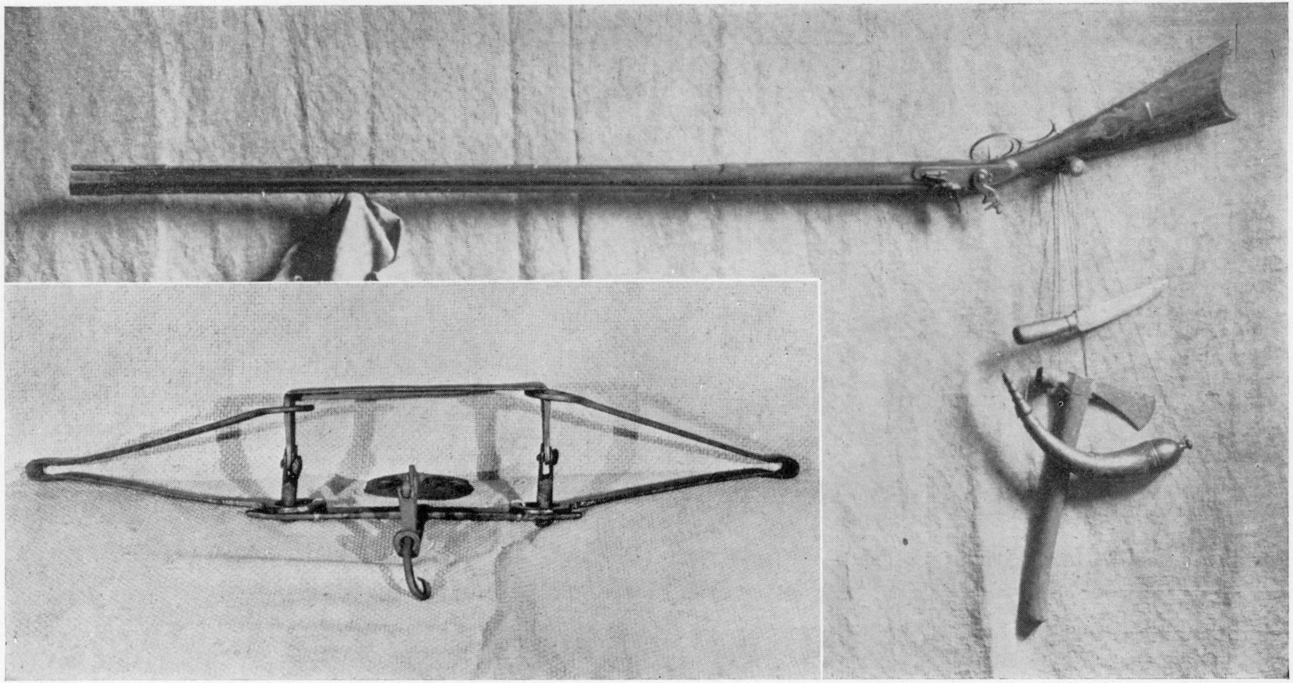

Photo Pictures, Inc. *H. Hesse*

DANIEL BOONE'S BEAVER TRAP AND ARMS

The beaver trap was made by Boone in 1796 and used in trapping with "Paddy" Huddlestone along the Kanawha River. It was presented to the West Virginia State Museum by Dr. J. P. Hale. The arms are now in the Filson Club, Louisville.

He made no secret of the reason for his interest. He was, he said, employed by Henderson and others to explore this country. That was the year when Daniel and Rebecca sold their farm and moved up the river, westward to the wilder country, closer to the mountains, closer to Kentucky.

It is no wonder that Daniel Boone's tree carvings were found far and wide in the country around the Yadkin. In the years that followed his marriage, he roamed the Yadkin, Clinch, Holston, Watauga Valleys again and again, both east and west of the Alleghenies. He knew the forests of North Carolina and what is now Tennessee. He crossed the mountains and penetrated to the borders of Kentucky and across, down the Big Sandy River.

He farmed only a little, but he hunted a great deal. For half a century or more he never missed a fall or winter hunt, except when all his time was occupied in fighting Indians. Hunting was the one thing he really lived for—long hunts alone, or with a few companions he could really trust, a matter about which Daniel Boone had high standards. The smaller the party, the better. They frightened the game less, and Indians were more easily avoided.

Hunting was more than a mere sport. It was a profitable profession. As Boone's nephew Daniel Bryan once explained to a curious inquirer: "It was not so much a ruling passion of Boone's to hunt, as his means of livelihood: His necessary occupation, from which he could not part & to which, & only it, he had ever been accustomed." True, farming helped to provide food for a pioneer family, but deer were everywhere. Venison was a staple article of diet on the frontier. A man could "hoppus" a deer to his cabin across his shoulders. Or he could "jerk" the meat in the sun, so that it would last almost indefinitely. Another way of preserving it was treatment with wood ashes and salt-peter. But all this was for family use. There was not much market for deer-meat.

Deerskins, on the other hand, were valuable articles of commerce, much used for making leggings and breeches. In the autumn, when the skins were in prime condition, a man who understood the woods and the ways of wild things could take a few pack-horses into the forests and return with far more wealth than any farm would produce.

A horse could carry up to 250 pounds—about a hundred dressed deerskins—over the rough wilderness trails. This was heavy packing. Four or five hundred skins was a fair season's hunting. According to the market and the quality of the skins, they brought anywhere from forty cents to four or five dollars apiece, and were classified as "bucks" and "does," the former being larger and more valuable. Americans still refer to dollars as "bucks," and think they are talking slang, when they are really echoing the business terminology of their ancestors.

Many hunters used to lie in wait at the salt licks, content to shoot such game as came to them. Others watched from trees. Even the women could hunt. Rebecca Boone, from one tree on the Yadkin farm, managed to shoot seven deer and—owing to a regrettable mistake—her own mare! Her more active husband preferred to range the woods, starting in the early morning or at the rising of the moon when he knew the deer were feeding. Dew moistened the dead leaves and twigs in the early morning and at night. It was easier to move noiselessly. He taught his sons the trick of moving up toward the animal while its head was down, browsing, and of freezing into immobility as it raised its head. The best rifles of the day had little range. A hunter had to get within about a hundred yards before he fired; and even moving up the wind, that was not easy.

As winter advanced the deer grew lean and their skins were hardly worth taking, but beaver and otter pelts then became prime. Some traders reckoned that a beaver was worth "a buck," or "two does," but as the pelts grew scarce the prices rose. Otter, too, were valuable; but Daniel loved beaver trapping almost as much as hunting deer, though to the end of his days he loathed the trapper's traditional diet of beaver tail.

The bait was simply a bit of twig rubbed with castor from the beaver's own glands. Attracted by the musky scent, the animals would swim up to touch it with their noses, holding their forepaws beneath their chins, and catch a paw in the trap. Their struggles dragged the trap into the water, they were pulled under by its weight and drowned. The trapper had only to haul in the trap and take the pelt. Otter were caught in the same way, but without bait. It was only necessary to put a trap at an "otter slide," where the animals habitually plunged into a pool.

It was cruel, but not much more so than Nature is herself. Pioneers who occasionally fed dead Indians to their dogs "to make them fierce," red hunters who tortured their enemies to death as part of a public ritual, and hoped to face the torture bravely themselves, could not be expected to worry much about the sufferings of dumb brutes whose pelts were worth money.

Farming in spring and summer, hunting in the autumn, trapping in the winter, Boone could make a living. The farm provided corn, fruit, vegetables, food enough for part of the season. Tobacco was a cash crop, everywhere accepted as the equivalent of money, but Daniel Boone rarely raised it. The forest provided the meat supply. Cattle were for milk.

A successful hunting and trapping season might bring in nearly a thousand dollars in modern currency, but there were expenses. A good "rifle-gun" was worth at least seven pounds, with powder-horn, shot pouch, and "patchen pouch" for wadding. A good hunter needed several—it was easy for rifles to get out of order in the woods. On long hunts one took a full set of gunsmithing tools along—a hand vise and bellows, files, and screw plates. Powder was expensive. Ultimately Boone learned to make it himself. A hunter could run his own bullets in his bullet molds, but lead was hard to transport. Traps and horses cost money.

And there was always the risk of robbery by the Indians. At least one British Indian agent encouraged the Cherokees to rob any trapper caught poaching on the tribal hunting grounds. The Cherokees usually felt sure that any hunter with a large supply of peltry must certainly be a poacher, and acted accordingly. An Indian robbery destroyed everything a hunter owned. It meant total loss of all his little capital of rifles, traps, and horses plus all his profits in pelts and skins, which presently adorned some distant wigwam village. There is no doubt that Daniel Boone sometimes made large sums by hunting and trapping, but sometimes, too, he came back from the woods stripped of everything he owned. It is easy to see why he was so often plagued by debt. Equipment had to be renewed or he could not hunt.

Hunting trips during these years carried him far and wide. He climbed the mountains and from the heights looked longingly out over the country beyond. It was, he thought, the most beautiful he had ever seen. Encountering other hunters, he dragged them, too, up the crags these wonders to behold. In 1760 he was hunting in the Holston Valley with Nathaniel Gist, son of Washington's famous scout. On this trip they had a great deal of trouble with wolves, whose dens were in caves adjoining the camp. The gaunt gray beasts, not yet so timid as they have since become, swarmed about and fought the hunters' dogs, killing some and crippling others. Eventually the two separated and came back by different routes, Boone passing near the spot where his first tree-carving was later found.

Once, Boone tried to break away from it all, give up the idea of western adventure, and settle in Florida. After the French and Indian War, East Florida had become a British colony. British settlers were encouraged to come in. In October, 1763, the new governor issued a proclamation offering a hundred acres to any Protestant immigrant. Friends from Culpeper County, Virginia, visiting Boone, told him of the proclamation. The tale of new lands stirred him, as it always did. His brother Squire, now twenty-one and only recently married, joined him and they were off with their friends, promising to be home for Christmas dinner.

In the main, however, Florida was a disappointment. It was wet and miry. Game was scarce. Once, friendly Seminoles saved them from semi-starvation, but they reached St. Augustine, explored the St. John's River, and according to legend Boone bought a house and lot in Pensacola. On the way homeward, Daniel paused to hunt, but as he had promised Rebecca, he stalked into the cabin exactly at dinnertime on Christmas Day.

And that was the end of it, for Rebecca objected. For the only time in their lives she said "no" to the spirit of adventure. She did not want to leave her family and friends. Rebecca won the argument: The house in Pensacola was never occupied. Boone and the long rifle went off to the woods beyond the Yadkin once again. A few years later, when it was a question of Kentucky, that was quite a different matter; the family and friends went along on the adventure.

Always eager to make hunters of his children, Boone began taking his son James on winter hunts as soon as the child was eight years old, teaching him the lore of the woods, the ways of the animals, the customs of the long hunters' camps. In the bitterest winter weather the child suffered from the cold. He was still so small that his father could button him up inside the capacious flaps of his hunting shirt to keep him warm at night. As he grew older, his father kept him in the woods three months at a time.

Later, in 1767, Boone hunted with Benjamin Cutbirth, husband of his niece, Elizabeth Wilcoxen, in the Watauga country, now part of Tennessee. Association with Cutbirth whetted his interest in Kentucky, for Cutbirth had been part of the adventurous group which penetrated overland to the Mississippi, probably the first to make the journey.

That same year Boone tried to emulate the trip. With one or two companions he pushed across the Blue Ridge and reached the headwaters of a branch of the Big Sandy on the eastern edge of Kentucky. Judging from its general direction that this stream would lead them to the Ohio, they pushed on until they were west of the Cumberland Mountains, and then, probably following a buffalo trace, stumbled on Salt Spring, near Prestonburg, in eastern Kentucky.

"Ketched in a snow storm," they camped for the winter and discovered that hunting was practically needless. The salt spring brought the game directly to their camp. Here Daniel Boone for the first time saw and killed a buffalo.

Doubtful whether it was worth while trying to push on into Kentucky through such hilly country, they turned back to the Yadkin and it was some years before they knew even the name of the stream on which they had wintered. Most of this hunting was safe enough, but you never could tell about the Indians.

Only his own presence of mind saved him from them on one occasion when he was hunting alone in eastern Tennessee near modern Jonesboro. Boone was rudely awakened in the night as he lay under his snow-covered blanket. Cherokees had surrounded his camp, and one brave pulled up the blanket to see who was under it. He recognized Boone, who woke just in time to stare into a copper-colored face and to hear its owner exclaim: "Ah, Wide Mouth, have I got you now?"

Boone saved himself (as he often did) by sitting up and being friendly. He shook hands all round, expressed pleasure in seeing his red brothers, exchanged bits of news, and was very well treated. None of which prevented him from putting as much ground as possible between his red brothers and himself at the first opportunity.

Life was well enough. He was doing right by Rebecca. He was supporting his family. But ever and anon he lifted up his eyes to the westward hills and found a perpetual lure. There are men who must know what is on the other side of the hill. Of them was Daniel Boone. When the sun sank behind the Cumberland Mountains it sank into mystery. A few white men had been there and had lived to tell the story, but even they had mostly skirted along the river banks or penetrated only a little way into the tangled forests. Boone remembered the tales he had heard of the lands beyond. There lay endless hunting, freedom, independence, wealth.

3. Goodbye to the World

FATE came plodding down the Yadkin Valley Road one day, leading a pack-horse. Fate had for the moment assumed the guise of a backwoods peddler, and his name was John Finley. It was nearly fourteen years since Boone and he had fled for their lives after Braddock's defeat.

There is no reason to suppose that the two men had ever met since. There was no particular reason why they should ever have met again; men scattered far and wide upon that wild frontier. And yet one day John Finley with his peddler's pack drew up at Daniel Boone's cabin door. He was just one more of those itinerant merchants who wandered with their moveable stores among the backwoods settlements, which were so nearly self-sufficing that a merchant with an ordinary country store would have starved to death. Still, there were a few things backwoods ingenuity could not produce; and frontier wives and daughters loved bright ribbons, fine cloth, odd knick-knacks as much as any other women.

Years later, in Missouri, Daniel's son Nathan remembered Finley; how he stabled his spare nags in the Boone stables; and most of all he remembered the yarns Finley spun beside the cabin fire. Kaintuck'—there was a land for you. Game in such abundance as no man dreamed of. A deer at every lick. Buffalo thick upon the traces. Herds so huge that a man had to be careful lest he be crushed to death in their mad stampedes. The ground rumbling with their hoofs. At the Falls of the Ohio, wild geese and ducks so plentiful there was no need even to kill them. All a man could eat were drawn by the current over the falls and thrown up freshly killed on the banks below. One might pick up enough fresh fowl for dinner any day.

And land—land such as a man might dream of. Well watered, lush and green, with fertile soil in all directions. Endless acres for the taking. A settler's paradise. A hunter's paradise, too, with deerskins at a dollar each.

Indians, of course. Danger to be outwitted. White man's brains and rifles against red woodcraft. But not too much danger. Finley had gone down the Ohio in 1767, landed on the Kentucky shore, received a hearty welcome from the Indians, and had gone inland on a hunting expedition with them. They were friendly enough—to traders. He set up his trading-post in the midst of Kentucky, exchanging "Indian goods" as fast as the delighted redskins could bring back the peltry. Then he had struggled back up the Ohio with his loaded canoe as far as western Pennsylvania, where he could change his pelts into good hard cash.

David Hall, an old pioneer, remembered those thrilling tales forty years after, when Kentucky had been won for the white man and there was only land to quarrel over: "A man by name of John Finley came to that country and informed the deponent, Daniel Boone and several others that he had been a prisoner [actually a trader, but perhaps a little of both] among the Indians and had been on the waters of the Kentucky River where there was a great advantage of profit to be made by hunting and trapping and directed us how to find said Kentucky River."

Finley wanted to go back into this land of swift and easy profits and he wanted to travel overland. But he could hardly hope to survive that dangerous journey without a skillful woodsman as "pilot." Was it pure chance that he ran into Daniel Boone? Did he remember him from Braddock's expedition? Did he hear his name mentioned in the western settlements of Pennsylvania? All three stories are told.

John Finley came at the turning point in Daniel Boone's career. In fact, he *was* the turning point. Daniel Boone was uneasy. The farm provided a living but not much more. Boone was in debt. Sometimes he was sued in the local court at Salisbury, where old Squire Boone had been a justice. The lawsuits meant new debts to Richard Henderson's law firm. A man could always hunt and there was comfort in that. But new settlers were coming in. He fretted as the land filled up. His heart was in the wilderness.

Social lines were beginning to draw tighter in North Carolina. Grafting officials oppressed the land-holders with false and fantastic fees. These were the years when the wild disorder of the "Regulators" grew in the backwoods as a protest; when a mob of them beat one unpopular attorney in the very courtroom and dragged another out of it by his heels; when Boone's friend, Judge Richard Henderson, had to flee from the bench; when the mob seized and ran the court to suit itself (leaving wild, profane abuse on the pages of its staid legal record, where the entries still remain), until at length the militia came to turn its arms against its own fellow-citizens.

The Regulators were completely crushed in a pitched battle at the Alamance, but their bitterness and discontent remained. Governor Tryon of North Carolina was brutal, domineering, bloodthirsty. He tried to bully the courts into executing more men. Families began to move as far west as possible, to get beyond the reach of such a government. The Watauga country, Powell's Valley, the Clinch Valley, the Cumberland country, received more and more settlers, on the very edge of Kentucky. Their minds as well as their eyes turned westward. Plenty of hardy, bitter men were ready to break with North Carolina entirely by the time Daniel Boone led the way to Kentucky a few years later.

Daniel Boone had no part in "the Regulation," but his Yadkin home was in the midst of the disturbances and he shared the general discontent. The hand of the royal governor was too heavy. Taxes were too high. Out in Kaintuck' a man could stand up.

No one realized better than Boone's friend Judge Richard Henderson how wide that discontent was. He had condemned some of the Regulators to death; but with the other judges he had stood out stoutly against the merciless governor's illegal effort to sway the court to needless severity. If Boone needed encouragement, this was the man to provide it. Boone had been served with a summons requiring him to appear in court at Salisbury in March, 1769. Henderson was there to defend him. John Stuart, Boone's brother-in-law, and John Finley went along to court. This was their chance to discuss their plans with Henderson.

The new country was a mystery; Finley knew nothing of trails overland. Cherokee war parties, however, attacked the Shawnees and other Indians north of the Ohio, and the route they followed was called the "Warriors' Path." Find the Warriors' Path and the problem was solved. Finley was not skilled enough to strike off into the forests. But Boone was a woodsman who could find his way anywhere. Why not go together?

Daniel and Squire Boone, their brother-in-law John Stuart, and Finley determined to visit this earthly paradise. They would need good weather—that meant a spring start. Squire Boone would stay behind long enough to get the crops in and, following in the late autumn or early winter, would arrive with fresh supplies just about the time the party needed them.

It was to be a hunting trip; the spice of adventure was in it;

but it was also a business enterprise involving a good deal of capital for a backwoods farmer—horses, lead, powder, salt, flour, blankets, camp supplies, plenty of traps.

Richard Henderson undoubtedly was somewhere in the background. He and Daniel Boone both attended the same session of court in Salisbury, the county seat, on March 16, 1769, a few weeks before Boone set out. Probably it was Henderson who supplied the capital. Boone is said to have been indebted to him already. But with deerskins fetching a good price and London clamoring for beaverskins there should be money in the venture.

And there was land! It might well be what Boone liked to call "a great speck," a profitable speculation.

They started from Daniel Boone's cabin on the first of May, 1769, with three other men as "camp-keepers"—Joseph Holden, James Mooney, and William Cool, or Cooley. These men seem to have been taken along as employees of the others—a practice which Boone followed in other hunting trips late in life. If all went well, Boone, Finley, and Stuart would have little time for pot-hunting and the preparation of skins. They would give all their time to hunting and exploration.

All six were mounted, and equipped with blankets or bearskins, a camp kettle, salt, tools, traps, and enough rations to last until they reached really good hunting grounds, after which they would have to live entirely off the country.

Finding the way proved easier than they had expected. At Martin's Station they passed the last settlements, only then being established. A "hunter's trace" which other white men had followed took them to Cumberland Gap. Here they touched the Warriors' Path. It proved to be plainly marked; there was no trouble keeping on the right route. Following the Warriors' Path for some distance, they bore westward and eventually camped near the headwaters of the west branch of the Rockcastle River.

The party moved rather slowly, probably hunting for venison on the way and perhaps beginning to hunt for hides from the very start. They could not at best make very good time, for the country was rough and wild.

Of the Indians they saw no sign. There probably were no Indians about, for Kentucky was only a hunting ground without permanent villages. By June 7 they had reached Station Camp Creek, still so called because they built their base camp here. Finley had formerly traded with Indians somewhere near this spot. As they had been traveling for some time in bad weather, they craved the comfort of permanent shelter. They set about constructing it.

Leaving the others to their hunting, Boone pushed on alone until he reached the summit of Big Hill, on the height of land between the Rockcastle and Kentucky Rivers. Here he could look down into the rich, level land, game-filled, fertile, beautiful, that he had come to find. Farther off, in the distance, the country seemed to change; but perhaps his eyes deceived him. It was too far off; he was not sure. Daniel Boone went back to camp.

It was now Finley's turn to push off alone. He was soon back with news that he had located the temporary Indian hunting village of Es-kip-pa-kith-i-ka, where he had formerly traded. The huts had been burned, but the stockade and the gate posts still stood. He was sure of the place now. Boone and Stuart went back with him to see it while the camp-keepers went on with their work.

Then Boone and Finley set off on a joint tour of exploration. After they had traveled for some time and had gone too far to get back to Station Camp, Finley was taken ill. Though he seemed to be in no danger, he was obviously unable to go on.

Providing him with food and shelter, Boone left him to recuperate alone and pushed on into the country north of the Kentucky River. Again he climbed a hill, and again scanned the landscape of "this terrestrial paradise." It was Boone's peak in Darien.

On the way back he found Finley well enough to move, and together they explored the Elkhorn Valley before returning to Station Camp.

The hunters now set to work in earnest, hunting in pairs. Each party went out in a different direction and brought their deerskins back to Station Camp at an agreed date after several days in the forest. One pair occasionally stayed in camp, preparing skins. Smaller temporary camps were scattered here and there. Still there was no Indian "sign," though the hunting party had been careless enough to make their station camp close to the Warriors' Path on which any hunting or war parties going that way would be certain to travel. They soon learned how unwise that had been.

The first attack came on December 22, 1769. Boone and John Stuart were following a buffalo trace through a canebrake, and were crossing a low hill near the Kentucky River, when they ran suddenly into a mounted party of Shawnees returning from a hunting trip in the Green River country to their homes north of the Ohio. Taken wholly by surprise as the Indians came bursting out of the canebrake, the two white men were seized without a chance to resist. They were ordered to take the Indians to their various camps. Tomahawks, suggestively raised, left no doubt what would happen if the white hunters were stubborn.

At the first camp visited, one of the camp-keepers was almost surprised, but Boone contrived to warn him and get him away into the woods while the Indians were still too busy gathering up their plunder to notice his presence. Thus warned off, the others lay low so effectually that the Shawnees seem never to have realized how many white men were in the party. The stores of skins in the outlying camps were trifling. While they were being robbed, the other four hunters should have been swiftly clearing the main stock of skins at Station Camp and getting the horses and peltry out of reach, relying on Boone and Stuart to delay the Indians as long as possible. But to Boone's dismay, when the Indians reached Station Camp all the horses and the stock of skins and peltry which six men had worked seven months to accumulate were still there.

"The time of our sorrow was now arrived," says Boone in the story of his adventures which he later gave to John Filson. He had staked everything on this trip—time, money, even his life. It was maddening to see all his profits and his little capital vanishing into the greedy hands of the raiding red men.

The delighted Indians gathered up everything of value in the camp, including rifles and ammunition. Then, with their two captives, the band moved off through the woods. The attitude of the Indians was that of any landed proprietors toward intruders. They seem to have had no intention of killing their prisoners so long as they offered no resistance. They were at peace with the English colonies. But they regarded the peltry as their own legitimate property because it came from their game. A sociologically inclined Shawnee later explained to a white friend that the game was the Indians' cattle, and killing it was downright theft.

Boone and Stuart were released unhurt after a few days. They were even provided with moccasins, a doeskin for patch-leather, a small "trading gun," and enough powder and shot to kill food for themselves on the way to the settlements.

The two were then told that they might go this time, but that if they again tried to hunt in Kentucky, they might expect the worst. Captain Will, on behalf of the Indians' hunting party, adjured the two white hunters: "Now, brothers, go home and stay there. Don't come here any more, for this is the Indians' hunting ground, and all the animals, skins, and furs are ours; and if you are so foolish as to venture here again you may be sure the wasps and yellow-jackets will sting you severely."

The words so impressed themselves on Boone's mind that he later dreamed he was being stung by yellow-jackets. The early settlers believed in dreams and premonitions. Boone interpreted this one to mean that he would be wounded by Indians. As it turned out he was right, and he named the stream on whose banks he had received the warning "Dreaming Creek." By that name Kentucky knows it still.

The two hunters shook hands with the Indians and parted.

The Indians quite definitely wanted the white men to get out of Kentucky and to stay out. They had dealt with Boone and Stuart as they usually dealt with poachers when they wished to be lenient. Boone's friend, Benjamin Cleveland, and hunters with him, caught by Cherokees while hunting beyond Cumberland Gap, were likewise robbed of everything they had, even their hats and shoes. But the Indians were careful to give them an old shot-gun and enough ammunition to provide food before ordering them out of the country. The chief known to the whites as Captain Dick, meeting another hunting party, directed the intruders to "his" river, where he assured them they would find plenty of game. A model of aboriginal tact, Captain Dick added a delicate hint: "Kill it, *and go home.*" White men had no business in Kentucky. When Captain Will robbed Boone and his companions, he doubtless thought he was being very kind to white trespassers who deserved a far worse fate.

Furious at their losses and by no means willing to admit the validity of Shawnee ethics, Boone and Stuart had not the least intention of going home. Boldly following their captors' trail, they were presently able to recover four or five horses. Stuart tried in vain to find his own horse, of which he was especially fond, and this delayed them and added to their danger. Nevertheless, they managed to get away undiscovered, and rode all night long, putting many miles between themselves and the Indians.

At dawn they paused to let the horses rest and feed. Boone stretched out on the ground to rest. Stuart had just bent over to tie his moccasins, when his ear, close to the ground, caught a rumble. He looked up hastily to see Captain Will and his band galloping over the hillock close behind, the sunlight glinting on their rifles. Before the white men could so much as mount, the Indians were on them.

Even under the provocation they had received, the Shawnees showed exceptional forbearance. Boone and Stuart bore two perfectly good scalps but the Indians offered no violence. Hugely amused at their failure to escape, they ejaculated, "Steal hoss, ha?" tied one of the horse-bells around Boone's neck and compelled him to caper about for their entertainment.

When the Indians were ready, they marched the two white hunters off to the north again, considerately informing them that they would be released as soon as the band had crossed the Ohio River. By that time the horses would be safe from further attempts at recapture.

A few nights later, however, as the party went into camp, Boone and Stuart bolted for the nearest canebrake. They could hear shouts from the Indians, who hastily made sure the horses were secure and then began to circle the brake, hoping to catch the prisoners as they emerged. Boone and Stuart, however, stayed in the tangles of the cane. This time they eluded pursuit and got safely away on foot.

Hurrying back to their camp, they found it abandoned. The other four hunters, giving them up for lost, had started back for the settlements. But they had not gone very far, and the other two soon overtook them.

Holden, Mooney, and Cooley had had enough. They wanted to get back to the settlements while they still had hair on their heads. Finley led them back, and as he disappears among the trees, he disappears also from history. It is said that he went north to Pennsylvania. He may have been the John Finley who was robbed of five hundred pounds worth of goods by the Indians a year or two later.

The hunters now exercised every precaution. It was not long before Daniel Boone had occasion for it. Just before or just after he and Stuart parted with the other four, while hunting, he saw strangers approaching through the trees. The leathery-skinned frontiersmen, in their wild dress, looked very much like Indians at a little distance and it was wise to take no chances. Boone made sure of his rifle and prepared for action. Then, doubtless from behind a tree, he sent out the usual challenge of the frontier:

"Hello, strangers! Who are you?"

Back came a welcome reply:

"White men and friends!"

He had blundered into his brother Squire, with a companion named Alexander Neeley, coming to keep the appointment made in the spring. They had found Boone's camp fire of the day before and knew that he was somewhere near. To them, there was nothing remarkable in this meeting in that almost trackless wilderness. The brothers were both skilled woodsmen; they had made an appointment to meet; and they had met. That was all.

Squire Boone had brought fresh horses, traps, and ammunition. The four went back to Station Camp, but they knew now it was too close to the Warriors' Path. They moved. The new camp is supposed to have been somewhere near the junction of the Red River with the Kentucky.

The hunters had one minor brush with the Indians, interesting mainly because it is responsible for the odd name of Lulbegrud Creek. Daniel Boone, who liked to read when he had the chance, testified later that his party "had with us for our pleasure" a book. It was *Gulliver's Travels.* They were whiling away a long evening in camp with Swift's account of Glumdelick and its inhabitants, the Lulbegruds, when Indians approached. When the hunters had driven them off, Neeley remarked whimsically that they had disposed of the Lulbegruds. Amused by this unexpectedly literary aspect of wilderness warfare, they gave the creek near camp a name from Swift. It is still called Lulbegrud Creek.

As winter advanced, though they still hunted for food, their main business was trapping. To cover as much ground as possible, the quartet divided. For safety's sake they still worked in pairs, but even this precaution did not long avail.

Daniel Boone and John Stuart were very close friends. Boone always asserted that he regarded Stuart as a brother—no idle expression in so closely united a family—and they usually hunted together. At length the two decided to separate, meeting every two weeks at their outlying camp. Stuart crossed to the south side of the Kentucky River in a small canoe that they had built.

He was never seen again.

His failure to return did not at first alarm Boone, since the river was badly swollen with rain and crossing was difficult. But when the water subsided and Stuart, who had a reputation for the precise fulfillment of agreements, still failed to return, Boone went over after him. He ranged the woods. He found Stuart's trail; he found a recent fire, he found his initials carved in a tree; but Stuart he did not find.

Five years later, however, when Boone was cutting the Wilderness Road to Kentucky, one of his men found a skeleton in a hollow sycamore at the Rockcastle River crossing, miles away. There was no sign of a rifle, but the powder-horn which lay with the body had a brass band with Stuart's initials, and by this Boone recognized the body of his hunting mate. The left arm was broken and the bone still bore the discoloration of a bullet, but there were no traces of other injuries and the skull showed no signs of the scalping knife.

Indians? Accident? Animals attacking a wounded hunter? No one will ever know.

Mortally wounded by the Shawnees, Stuart may have dragged himself to cover and then died silently. North American wild animals are not usually dangerous to man unless wounded or cornered—but Stuart was a hunter. Wounded only in the arm, he ought to have been able to reach the Kentucky's banks and shout for help—but Boone never heard him if he called at all.

Long after that someone found an abandoned trapline in the woods. Stuart's? No one ever knew.

Silent and mysterious always, the wilderness had struck. Once. It was to strike again.

In spite of Stuart's disappearance, the Boones continued their hunt. Men vanished often enough in the wilderness. For all they knew then, Stuart might be a captive of some roving Shawnee band, as Boone and he had been before. If so, he might escape this time as he had escaped twice already. There was no Indian war at the moment and he would escape torture—probably. If he was dead—well, men died violently, mysteriously, and often in the "dark and bloody ground."

Alexander Neeley, however, was not so philosophical. Violent death was common enough, though not so common as it was to become in a few years. But this death which struck from nowhere, so that a man vanished wholly, death inexplicable, unaccountable, implacable, unknown, was too much for him. The Boones were made of sterner stuff than he, and Neeley did not mind admitting it. He announced that he was going home, and started for the settlements, leaving the Boone brothers entirely alone.

Though they had declined to be driven out of the hunting grounds, the Boones were taking no chances they did not have to take.

Once it looked as if the Indians had found their camp. The Boones made a new one. They did their cooking at night, to conceal the smoke. The fire itself was sheltered so that no flame could be seen. They blinded the trail leading into their refuge. Part of it they concealed by walking some distance in a stream, a common Indian device. Where possible, they moved over fallen trees and smooth rocks which showed no trace of their passing. They broke the trail by swinging on the tough, dangling vines of wild grapes. And very close to camp they covered their footprints with leaves.

By May of 1770 ammunition was running low and a new store of skins was ready to go back for sale in the settlements. It began to look as if their Kentucky venture might still be profitable. Loading his pack-horses, Squire set off with the proceeds of their long hunt, promising to return with "a new recruitment of horses and ammunition."

He left his brother in absolute solitude in the forest, "without bread, salt, or sugar, or even a horse or dog." The last two were no great lack, for they would have been hard to conceal or keep quiet; and it had for some time been apparent that Daniel's life would have to be extremely quiet unless it was to be extremely short. As for bread and salt, early woodsmen often ran out of them, though they usually grumbled about it.

More serious was the lack of ammunition. Daniel had enough to keep himself in fresh meat and to keep off the Indians if they found him. But he had to husband his supply for emergencies. It was impossible to hunt on a commercial scale and lay in a new supply of skins, and it was too late in the season to trap. Instead of hunting he took to exploring. He toured Kentucky privately—very privately indeed, for Indian hunting parties were now all about. Boone always believed that they found his camp, but only when he was absent. They do not seem to have thought it worth while to waylay him, which would have meant lying in ambush for days at a time. Indians on the warpath would have done just that; hunting parties would not take the trouble.

When things looked dangerous, Boone retired to the thick tangles of the canebrakes—not always the nearest ones. Sometimes he made camp and built his fire in one place—then slipped off a mile or two and slept in the cane without a fire. Even a Shawnee does not go exploring canebrakes in the middle of a wilderness night. There was still no war and the Shawnees probably were not quite sure who he was and not very eager to find him. One stray hunter more or less made very little difference, though it would have been awkward if they had captured this stubborn white man for the third time after he had twice been told to go home. But so long as Boone could stay in the brakes he was safe. The cane, looking very much like a gigantic stalk of corn, grew to heights of ten, twenty, even thirty feet and its tangled masses might extend for miles.

Most of the Indians, whose signals he sometimes heard around him as he lay in the cane, very likely did not know he was there at all. Even when they found his camp, they may not have known it for a white man's. Few white men make camps like Indians; but Boone was an old hand in the woods, who had lived near Indians all his life.

After Squire left, he "passed a few days uncomfortably," and then seems to have been quite content. It was a year since he had seen Rebecca and the children. It would be almost another year before he saw them again. But Squire would carry news that he was alive and see that they were well cared for.

Meantime, he ranged the woods as far north as the Ohio River, and as far west as the Falls of the Ohio (Louisville), becoming thoroughly acquainted with the Kentucky and Licking Valleys. Boone was happy enough. This was the life he loved. The forest, game, freedom from social restraints, distinctions, taxes, inconvenient neighbors. He had "elbow room" in abundance. What more could a man ask?

Occasionally he saw Indians on the northern bank of the Ohio. The river was too narrow to make such proximity very safe, but in every case he escaped detection. On his way back to the Kentucky River he left the watercourses and struck off across country. Once he came upon an Indian fishing from a fallen tree which projected over a stream. But, as Boone used to tell the story in after years, "as I was looking at the fellow, he tumbled into the river, and I saw him no more." The implication was that Daniel at the moment was looking at that particular redskin over the sights of a rifle.

It was a favorite joke. His hearers did not always remember it exactly. Sometimes there were two Indians. Sometimes there was only one. But the essentials were always the same. Boone never explicitly admitted killing or even firing. But he "heard a gun crack and it sounded just like mine." Sometimes, more explicitly, it "sounded very much like Tick-Licker," his favorite rifle. And then "they tumbled in the water and I never saw them any more."

He used to remark of other Indians casually encountered in the forests, "While I looked at them they fell down and never crossed my path again." Never a killer and always rather well-disposed to the Indians, Boone had, as John Floyd once wrote, "very little of the *War spirit*. He never liked to take life and always avoided it when he could." He once told his son Nathan that in his whole life he was sure of having killed only one Indian and that was at the Blue Licks Battle. Sometimes he raised the score to three—never any more. In the heat of battle it was hard to be sure whether a shot went home. One fired as fast as possible and reloaded with equal speed. There is little doubt, however, that Boone was a bit too modest about his tally. He himself used to conclude with the remark: "But many was the fair fire that I have had at them."

On this occasion, he killed an unsuspecting fisherman solely because he feared for his own life if captured again. Then, since there might be other Indians about, he made a wide detour until he struck the mountains in the east, and "circled around to his camp."

Kentucky was an easy place to hide in. Like all limestone country, it is full of caves; and during these solitary explorations Daniel Boone found shelter in a good many of them. He lived in one cave in Mercer County and left another of his carvings on a tree near by—"D.B.—1770."

With this cave as a base camp, he explored Dick's River, and near its junction with the Kentucky had one of his most famous adventures. Wandering along the precipices which edge Dick's River, he suddenly found himself cut off by Indians on three sides with a sheer cliff on the other. It looked hopeless, but as he glanced desperately backward he saw that a sugar maple reached from the river bottom well up toward the summit of the cliff. Leaping into the tree top, he managed to catch the branches, break his fall, and let himself down unhurt amid a chorus of astonished "ughs" from the red men peering down from the cliffs above at a paleface who was melting into the landscape.

It was probably during this period of solitude that Daniel had another famous adventure. He had "killed a buffalo and thought to have a good breakfast." But he had frightened the entire herd, which stampeded toward the hunter. Boone escaped only by getting behind a tree and punching the terrified beasts with his rifle barrel as they rushed past. He once saved a group of companions from another stampeding herd by shooting the leader. Behind the huge carcass the white men crouched while the buffalo, dividing, rumbled harmlessly by, a great deal more frightened than the hunters.

Boone loved solitude. He also loved adventurous hunting of this sort. There was no reason why he should not have gone back to the settlements with Squire. The trip would have been safer and easier had the brothers gone together; and since he could not hunt in Squire's absence, Daniel could add nothing to their profits. But Daniel stayed. Was it just because he loved this solitary life? Or was there another reason? Those long exploring trips—were they pure love of adventure? Or was the Great Idea already bubbling in the woodsman's brain? Did he and Richard Henderson already have land speculation schemes afoot?

At all events, by the time he kept his appointment with his brother on July 27, 1770, at their old camp, no white man in the world knew the Kentucky area so well as Daniel Boone. He was ready to lead the settlers who were soon to follow.

Squire Boone had traveled to and from the settlements undisturbed, had sold their furs, paid off debts, provided for both families, and brought back new supplies. The two immediately moved farther east to begin hunting. According to legend, they moved down the Kentucky River, settled in a cave near the mouth of Marble Creek (Jessamine County) and then moved to another cave on Hickman Creek in the same county. Here the irrepressible Daniel carved his initials in the soft stone, but only a huge "D" survived.

Once they were alarmed to find their camp had been disturbed in their absence, but further examination showed the raider was a wolf. Trailing the marauder to its den they killed the mother and made an unsuccessful effort to bring up the cubs, which, as Boone later remarked to his eldest grandson, in spite of all he could do, remained wolves still. Another wolf, raiding the camp, ran off with Daniel's hat. In spite of delineations by imaginative artists, Daniel Boone disliked coonskin caps and always insisted on a hat. The loss of this one in the midst of the forest was a great annoyance; but a hasty shot brought down the wolf. Daniel recovered his headgear.

As autumn approached, Squire Boone made another trip to the settlements. This time he was so slow in returning that Daniel started east to meet him. On the way he came upon an aged Indian, left by his tribe to die. Touched by the old man's helplessness, Boone went back half a mile for a deer which he had killed and only partly eaten. This he carried to the old Indian and then left him. Not long after this, he saw a camp fire ahead. Approaching stealthily, he recognized his brother.

The two may have returned to the Kentucky River; but if so, it was for a brief time only; they soon went southward to the Green and Cumberland Rivers. Perhaps this was because the hostile northern Indians were now too numerous for comfort. Or it may have been because Daniel had seen what he really had come to see, and now wished merely to make a little honest money out of deerskins before embarking on the great project of his life.

Boone was in high spirits. He had seen and thoroughly explored the land he had dreamed of so long. Two consignments had been sent back to the settlements. Soon there would be a third, and then he could go home at last.

His high spirits led to an amusing incident which has found its way into the Boone legend. Another party, famous as the "Long Hunters" because of their prolonged stay in the wilderness, had been hunting farther south for nearly a year and a half. Returning, they reached the Green River country at about the same time as the Boones. According to a story widely told, they were alarmed one day by a strange sound in the forest near them. Veteran woodsmen though they were, the Long Hunters admitted they had never heard anything that remotely resembled it.

In the wilderness it is wisest to assume that anything unknown is dangerous. As one man the Long Hunters reached for their long rifles; and Casper Mansker, already famous as a woodsman, slipped silently off to investigate. It might be dangerous to follow up the mysterious sound, but it was not difficult, for it came steadily from the same direction. That was suspicious. Real woods sounds usually move about. Was this a new kind of Indian decoy?

Gripping his loaded rifle, Mansker dodged from tree to tree —and came upon Daniel Boone lying flat on his back on an outspread deerskin, all alone and singing cheerfully to himself. Indians or no Indians, Daniel felt happy that day; and like most men who live much alone, he had a habit of singing or whistling to himself. There are other tales of him, sitting alone by his camp fire singing to a gravely silent audience of rather puzzled dogs!

Leaving the Long Hunters, who did not return till August, he and his brother started back for their home on the Yadkin in March of 1771, their pack-horses loaded with the winter's peltry. By May they were near Cumberland Gap, and almost home; had in fact reached Powell's Valley on the outskirts of the settlements. Here they fell in with their former companion, Alexander Neeley, who after leaving them had made his way safely to the settlements and then, coming out with another hunting party, had lost himself in the woods and was in a wretched state. He had fired away all his ammunition in vain efforts to signal and had had nothing to eat except the meat of a stray dog.

After caring for Neeley's distress, the Boones hurried on.

They had camped for the night and were busy roasting meat for dinner when six or eight Indians appeared. Assuming a friendly attitude, the strangers shared the Boones' dinner. Then these not-very-noble red men proposed to trade their old rifles for the well-kept hunting arms of the Boones. When the brothers refused, the Indians fell upon them and took rifles, horses, skins, and everything else. The infuriated hunters offered resistance in spite of the odds but were overpowered, threatened with tomahawks, and driven off.

Going only a little distance, they hid, noted the direction the Indians took, and then, hurrying off to the settlements for arms and aid, gave chase. As they followed the trail of the robbers, the trails of other Indian bands which had been marauding along the frontier began to join in. The original band had evidently been much reinforced. That looked dangerous but the settlers continued to follow the trail, until one incautious fellow fired at a deer. As the Indians had now been warned of pursuit the party gave up and turned back. It was lucky that they did. An overwhelming force of Indians had been lying in wait for them only a little way ahead. That chance shot at a deer had saved them from a bloody ambush.

Even yet, the Boones were not quite done with their adventures. Continuing their journey home with one companion, they halted to rest in an abandoned cabin. It was not long before they discovered two Indians outside. All three white men fired together and killed both. Daniel and their companion took a rifle each as spoils; Squire Boone took their silver trinkets. This was their sole gain from the latter part of the expedition.

Just after their return a friend ran into Boone, still exasperated over his losses, and made a note of what he said: "I met Daniel Boone below the Holston settlements alone. He informed me that he had spent the two years preceding that time.

in a hunt on Louisa River [now Kentucky River], so called by all the Long Hunters; that he had been robbed by the Cherokee Indians of all the proceeds of this hunt."

Everything, even equipment, had now been swept away. After two arduous years in the wilderness, Daniel Boone was little if any better off than when he had set out with Finley and the rest. It was fortunate that Squire had been able to get at least two pack trains of skins and pelts safely back, but it was small reward for all they had endured.

At least he had explored Kentucky. The great idea was slowly taking possession of him: Kaintuck'—that was a land, now, where a man could really live. Daniel Boone knew. He had seen it—all of it.

4. First Attempt at Settlement

THERE is a haze over Daniel Boone's next two years. The second Indian robbery had left him with nothing to show for his winter's hunting and the capital outlay it involved. But with a farm and a rifle and some growing sons to bear a hand, it was pretty hard to starve in the backwoods. When the farming season was over, Daniel hunted as a matter of course. An old weaver in the vicinity had a famous pack of bear dogs, and the two chased bear in the mountains, coming home with their horses loaded down with bearskins. On one of these trips Boone went as far as French Lick on the Cumberland River, where he met French hunters who had come from the opposite direction, overland from the Mississippi.

By 1772 he was living in or near a hamlet called Sapling Grove in what is now Tennessee. Captain Evan Shelby, of Frederick County, Maryland, hard pressed by debt, had set up there as a store-keeper, with Daniel Boone as one of his customers. The entries in the Boone charge-account suggest that Rebecca and the children had come with him. Why else should a man be buying "17 pounds and half of Loaf Sugar"? In January, 1772, Daniel was buying "2 quarts of Rum"—plain evidence that the pious biographers of early days, who assert that Daniel never touched liquor, didn't know what they were talking about. Daniel himself later described to Audubon an incident in which the Indians took away his pocket flask, a queer thing for a teetotaler to be carrying about with him.

During these years Daniel was probably traveling from one Cherokee village to another, living in the wigwams, hunting with the braves, talking with the chiefs. He was sounding the Indians to see whether they were willing to sell Kentucky. He is said to have concluded very soon that they would hand the country over to the white men if the price were high enough. He interested Richard Henderson, whose brother later said that he had been "induced to attempt the purchase of Kentucky from the Cherokees, through the suggestion and advice of the late Col. Daniel Boone."

But at the moment Henderson was much occupied with his judicial duties. He was interested in the Kentucky project, but while he was in office he could do nothing; and he remained on the bench until 1773.

Boone grew impatient. He went back with Benjamin Cutbirth and perhaps with others for another look at the fertile land that haunted his imagination. Early in 1773 he occupied his old cave on Little Hickman Creek, in Jessamine County. As usual, he carved his initials—"D.B.—1773"—on the cave's walls. Boone grew impatient. He was as delighted with the country as before. He even selected a site for his future home. He decided to wait no longer upon Henderson, but to attempt immediate settlement.

On his return, he sold his farm and all the household goods he could not carry with him, and spent the spring and summer in getting ready, with the aid of Captain William Russell, the Clinch Valley pioneer. Henderson and his wealthy associates were not yet prepared to underwrite the venture. As far as they were concerned, the Kentucky scheme would have to wait.

But delay was dangerous. Already surveying parties were

drifting down the Ohio, poking the noses of their little craft up the tributary Licking and Kentucky Rivers, making friends with the Indians, finding out where the best lands lay. The McAfee brothers, James and Robert, met two other explorers at the mouth of the Kanawha River, early in June of 1773. They joined forces and traveled on together. Presently they met another party led by James Harrod, also seeking land.

By mid-August the McAfees, on their way home overland, "met Boon, preparing to move his family to Kentucky with forty other individuals." The news that three parties of land-hunters had already been in Kentucky must have stirred his eager spirit still more intensely. These men had already surveyed for themselves the best land they could find. How long would it be before others came? How long would it be before all the best land was taken up? Daniel decided to start at once.

To the end of his days, wherever Daniel Boone went there were always plenty of eager adventurers to follow. Even in these early days, the man's prestige was enormous. He had persuaded his wife's relatives, the Bryans, still settled on the Yadkin, to go along. They agreed to come by the shortest way and meet him in Powell's Valley. Boone rushed home to attend to last minute business; five other families joined him there. The Bryans met the little caravan as agreed, and the daring band of forty souls were off to the wilderness at last.

It was a desperate and dangerous adventure, with every man's hand against the adventurers. The royal government had forbidden western settlement. The Governors of North Carolina and Virginia were already alarmed at violation of the edict. No agreement at all had been reached with the Indians. They were sure to object violently, with all the legal right on their side. But Boone had determined to chance it. It was Daniel's scheme. And if he approved it, the others would go along.

The patient, fearless Rebecca was ready now as always to

follow her man where he chose to go. Daniel usually chose to go where there was likely to be a great deal of trouble; but—except when she objected to settling in Florida—Rebecca Boone never complained. Kentucky might be an anxious land for wives and mothers; but it could not be much worse than the lonely anxiety of a cabin on the Yadkin, with Daniel off among the canebrakes, redskins, and wild beasts in the green tangle of the forests. Marry a man with an itching foot, and a girl is bound to have anxieties. It was the common lot of the frontier woman. Better to go and share it with him.

That, after all, was life as the wives of all the pioneers knew it. Marry your man and then follow him. Bear his children. Feed him. Watch his cattle. Lend a hand with the farm at need. Milk, churn, weave, sew. Mold his bullets. Load his rifles when the shooting got rapid enough to demand it. Beat off the Indians yourself if need be. Watch your husband set out again and again into the forests, with death or torture or captivity always in prospect. Men, the great babies, must have their adventures; and perhaps—who knew?—there might be wealth at the end of it. Daniel had grown up in the richest farming land in the country, back there in Pennsylvania; and he was enthusiastic about landed estates in Kentucky.

They started in September, 1773. Daniel and Squire Boone had a fairly substantial force of riflemen to protect the women and children; and like all nomads they drove their livestock with them—milch cows, young cattle, swine, "intended to constitute the herd of the western wilderness."

Compared to these men and women, the later pioneers of the nineteenth-century covered-wagon days traveled in luxury. There was no road in 1773, only a narrow "trace" winding among the trees. Wagons were out of the question. Not for two years would the trace be even roughly cleared with axes. One rode if there were horses enough. Otherwise one walked.

Some of the difficulties were ludicrous and, to the twentieth century, hard to imagine; but they were none the less real. Goods, provisions, powder and lead went on the lone file of pack-horses, faithful, sure-footed beasts, that needed only a path (not always even that), able to dodge in and out among the trees or crash their way through cane and underbrush. The trouble with a pack train was that it was so easily stampeded. An Indian attack or a casual bump against a yellow-jacket's nest might scatter an expedition's horses, cattle, and equipment through miles of woodland, whence the beasts had to be rounded up, in constant danger from the Indians' rifles.

The argumentative powers required to persuade a recalcitrant cow on the way she should go through several hundred miles of wilderness were very considerable. "Who ever drives Cattle here ought to have patience in great abundance," wrote Boone's friend John Floyd ruefully, after his own first trip to Kentucky with livestock.

There were three mountain ranges to cross. The Cumberland Gap opened through the last range into Kentucky itself. In or near Powell's Valley, after the whole group was united, Boone decided that he needed more flour and farm tools and sent his son James back to Captain William Russell's to get them. The party was still fairly near the settlements, and the boy seems to have ridden off alone without thought of danger.

He found Russell easily enough and started back with Russell's son Henry, a boy of about seventeen, two slaves, and a couple of white workmen. Either because they lost their way or because the cattle lagged, they camped that night (October 10, 1773) on Walden's Creek, only three miles behind Boone and the main body. Probably neither group realized how near the other was. There was always a tendency for travelers to string out along the narrow paths they had to travel.

No one anticipated Indian trouble. Only the month before

the McAfees had returned without any difficulty except that of getting food. They had found the Shawnees and Delawares friendly enough. But the vastness and silence of the wilderness, the unaccustomed sounds that occasionally break it, are always just a little terrifying to those who do not know them well. That night, as they sat around the camp fire, they heard wolves, or Indians imitating wolves, howling in the forest. The howl of the giant timber wolf (though the beast itself is usually harmless enough) is one of the most startling sounds in all nature. It begins with barking like a big dog's, and then ascends in an ear-splitting crescendo up and up the scale, until it dies into an even more terrifying silence. The howls made some of the newer members of the party nervous, until someone remarked that in a short time they would be hearing the bellows of buffalo as well as the howls of wolves.

Reassured by the indifference of the veteran woodsmen, they spread their blankets and went to sleep. Just before dawn a party of Indians fired into them, shooting James Boone and young Russell through the hips, and killing most of the others. One man, who got away into the woods, was never seen again. A skeleton supposed to be his was ultimately found some distance from the scene, where he had presumably died of his wounds alone in the forest. One negro slave managed to slip into a pile of driftwood by the river. Here he lay concealed, a terrified witness of the horrors that followed.

The Indians settled quietly down to a little enjoyable relaxation before proceeding on their journey. The two boys, helpless with their wounds, were unable to move. The Indians had a great deal of fun torturing them to death. There was no time for a formal burning at the stake, but they did pretty well with their knives.

James Boone had recognized among the band Big Jim, a Shawnee who had often visited his father's cabin. He was a warrior of distinctive appearance. It was impossible to mistake him for any other Indian. Shivering in terror in his pile of driftwood, the negro heard James Boone begging his father's friend to spare his life. But the Indians were intent on torture. Again the hidden slave heard James Boone screaming for mercy, but this time the only mercy that he asked was to be tomahawked at once and allowed to die quickly. Again Big Jim refused. The torture went on, until at last the two boys died, their bodies slashed to ribbons, their nails torn out, their palms slashed in futile efforts to turn the blades of the Indian knives aside with bare hands.

That morning one of Daniel Boone's party had deserted. He had been caught stealing from a comrade, and though not sent back had been made to feel very uncomfortable. Slipping away before the camp was astir, he paused only to steal a few deerskins that Boone had left by the trail for his sons to pick up, and pushed on. He came upon the scene of the massacre just after the Indians had left. As he stood there staring at the horrible spectacle, Captain Russell came up from the other direction, on his way to join Boone's party. One man rushed ahead to warn Boone. Russell's party began to dig the graves.

Daniel Boone got his companions into safety in a ravine the moment the alarm was given, sheltering the women and children in a large hollow which running water had washed under the roots of a beech tree, posted sentinels, and prepared for attack. According to one story, the Indians never came. According to another, they attacked and were driven off, Boone himself killing one Indian and wounding another. But in spite of all the danger, Rebecca Boone sent back a linen sheet to cover her son and keep the earth from his body.

After beating off the Indians, Boone is said to have followed them down a little creek, returning at dusk to defend the camp. If this is true, the alarm lasted all day long. During the night, Indians were again discovered creeping up. The riflemen stealthily got ready and let them come within range before firing. Again the Indians fled.

Next morning Boone and some of the men followed them down-stream again and noted, with satisfaction, traces of blood. In spite of the darkness some of their bullets had gone home. Creeping on down the creek, they saw the Indians gathered around a fire. As the rifles cracked, they vanished.

The settlers were now too frightened to go on. Their cattle had been scattered. They suspected that larger war parties would be lying in wait for them farther on. They had already lost several men. Their courage failed completely, and the whole group started dolefully back for the settlements. At Snoddy's Fort the sadly shaken little company rested for a while. Then most of them moved on back to North Carolina.

The murders caused a tremendous sensation. They were, as a contemporary observes, "in every one's mouth." Indian murders were even then no rarity, but there was a peculiar horror about these.

Lord Dunmore, Governor of Virginia, remonstrated with the Indian tribes in solemn council, but it was difficult to fix the guilt. The chiefs shuffled, evaded. Eventually the Cherokees consented to execute one man, but the executioners only wounded him and left him for dead. Learning that the guilty warrior was still alive, the colony's representative, at considerable risk to himself, insisted that the chiefs themselves go and kill him. Eventually they did so. One other Cherokee was condemned to death, escaped, and was later captured and executed.

Some of the stolen horses and other property turned up in Pennsylvania, having been sold to traders by the Indians. The Shawnees later surrendered some of Captain Russell's books, which the murdered boys had been carrying. Why the Indians ever took them at all is a mystery.

The Indian murders led to a senseless act of retaliation by one Isaac Crabtree, either the same man who had been with the Boones or a relative. A group of peaceful Cherokees had come in to the North Carolina settlements to watch a horse race. They had had nothing to do with the murders, but the moment Crabtree saw the Indians he rushed at them and killed one before the astonished bystanders could interfere. He very nearly brought on an Indian war then and there. The Cherokees had consented to execute two of their tribe who had been involved in the murder of James Boone; but no one even tried to bring Crabtree to justice for this wanton slaughter.

The Boones, who were now without a home, settled down to what must have been a most unhappy winter at "Snoddy's on the Clinch." Daniel was beaten again. He had probably lost most of the money he had realized on the sale of his farm. But Daniel had been beaten before and he never stayed beaten very long. He intended to settle in Kentucky, and meantime he intended to live as near Kentucky as he could get. Captain David Gass gave the forlorn little family shelter, and they lived through the long winter, supported by what the Indians had left of their cattle and by Boone's long rifle.

A contemporary description preserves a picture of Daniel Boone at this time—one of a series that admirers left at various stages of his long life: "I have a distinct recollection of seeing Boone at my father's camp, on Reedy Creek, of Holston, in company with a tall young man named Crabtree, and some others—I think it must have [been] in 1773. Boone was dressed in deer-skin colored black, and had his hair plaited and clubbed up, and was on his way to or from Powell's Valley." To the end of his days, Daniel insisted on wearing his hair "clubbed up."

Boone made a solitary trip back to Powell's Valley in May of 1774 to visit his son's grave. Indian troubles were gathering and the trip was dangerous, but Boone would not be diverted. Logs had, as usual, been laid above the graves to keep the wolves off, but the ravenous beasts had pawed them aside and dug part way down. Boone opened the grave to make sure that the bodies (which he now saw for the first time) had not been touched, and then carefully covered them up again.

While he was finishing, a storm broke, so violent that it was impossible to move. As he waited for it to pass, the gloom, the howling of the wind, the dreadful associations of the spot where his son had been tortured to death to amuse the savages, brought on a fit of profound melancholy which he later described as the worst of his life.

When the storm had cleared, Boone moved a few hundred yards away from the graves, "hoppled" his horse, put a bell on the animal so that it would be easy to find in the morning, and camped for the night. He could not sleep, and as he lay awake watching the sky, which had now cleared, he distinctly heard Indians creeping up on his lonely camp.

Instantly alert, Daniel slipped away from his fire, quietly caught his horse, and drove it slowly along, stopping to jangle the bell now and then, as if the animal were moving about casually and grazing in perfect security. At a safe distance he silenced the bell and rode for his life, leaving the raiders to attack an empty camp. But for the storm which delayed them, they would probably have killed the father on the very spot where they had killed the son.

Stirring matters were afoot in Kentucky in the spring of 1774, and it is no wonder that the Indians were uneasy. James Harrod made a second trip, taking a large group down the

Ohio, up the Kentucky, and thence overland to the present site of Harrodsburg. Scattered here and there through the Kentucky woods were small parties of surveyors, still laying out the lands for the proposed grants to soldiers in the wars with the French and Indians.

They could hardly have chosen a worse time to visit Kentucky, for the Indians were aroused. Already disturbed by the westward trend of the colonists, they were still more excited by the arrival of surveyors; and they were lashed to fury by a peculiarly brutal murder committed at Yellow Creek, near the Ohio River. A certain Daniel Greathouse made up his mind to kill the family of Tahgahjute, a famous chief who had taken the English name of "Logan."

Logan had always been a friend of the white men, and was widely known among both whites and reds. Probably born near Sunbury, Pennsylvania, he had lived for a long time near Reedsville, in Mifflin County, on amicable terms with his white neighbors, and had then moved westward. Greathouse's atrocious crime turned an influential friend into an equally influential foe.

Going into the Indian camp as a friend one day, Greathouse quietly counted the band. White men under a certain Captain Michael Cresap, patrolling the Ohio when war seemed inevitable, had recently killed some other Indians; and a friendly squaw, fearing for Greathouse's safety because the Indians were aroused, warned him to go home.

Finding that there were too many Indians in camp for himself and his friends to deal with, Greathouse did go, but persuaded a few Indians to come over to the white settlement. Here he got them so drunk that they were helpless. In the group were Logan's brother and his sister, who was with child when she was murdered. All of these were shot, at least one was scalped, and it is said that the unborn papoose was stuck up on a pole. Two canoes full of warriors paddled over when they heard the shots, and many of these were also killed.

"Then," said Tahgahjute, "I thought that I must kill too." Greathouse, by his casual and purposeless brutality, helped to cause Lord Dunmore's war, which in the summer and early autumn of 1774 raged along 350 miles of frontier.

Aware that trouble was brewing, since there had been a series of killings all winter, Governor Dunmore wished to warn the surveyors in Kentucky. Captain William Russell, as a leading citizen of the Clinch Valley, was instructed by Colonel William Preston to select "two faithful woodsmen" to carry the warning. He chose Daniel Boone and his lifelong friend Michael Stoner.

Boone was the obvious man for the journey. He knew the country; he was living on the very edge of it; and there was little enough to keep him at home, especially as the militia were now mustering and he was certain to be called out.

"Mike Stoner, a large strong dutchman," was one of the numerous Pennsylvania Germans who had migrated with other Pennsylvanians. He was a good woodsman, and so muscular that legend said when he sat down to carve his name on a tree, he often did not bother to remove the pack, weighing two or three hundred pounds, from his shoulders. Russell reported:

> I have engaged to start immediately on the occasion, two of the best hands I could think of—Daniel Boone and Michael Stoner; who have engaged to search the country as low as the Falls, and to return by way of Gasper's Lick on Cumberland, and through Cumberland Gap; so that, by the assiduity of these men, if it is not too late, I hope the gentlemen will be apprized of the imminent danger.

"If they are alive," he also wrote, "it is indisputable but Boone must find them."

Boone received his first instructions from General Andrew

Lewis, soon to be the victor in the decisive battle of Point Pleasant, but these were countermanded by Dunmore, a fussy old gentleman who wanted to lay out the route himself. Boone was to "take the Kentucky and Meander to its mouth." This apparently meant that he was to follow the stream in all its windings. The governor wanted to make sure that he found somewhere in the valley the men he was looking for. No one knew just where they might be, as they had surveys to make at the Falls of the Ohio (Louisville), in the Kentucky River Valley, on Salt Lick River (Licking River), and along the Cumberland.

Shawnee war canoes were already blockading the Ohio River, so that the two men had no choice of route. They had to go overland along the very trace where Boone had just met with tragedy a few months earlier. Starting out June 27, 1774, Boone reached the new settlement of Harrodsburg, Kentucky, before July 8.

The diary which he kept during the trip has long since been lost; but one ludicrous episode of the trip remains, which illustrates the irrepressible pioneer humor that defied all perils. Like Homer's heroes, like epic adventurers in all lands and places, these men could laugh. No men ever traveled in greater danger than these two, but that did not prevent their pleasure in some innocent sky-larking. On the outward journey they came to a spot almost certainly identical with the future battleground of the Blue Licks. Here the salt-crazed buffalo had eaten the saline earth away to form trenches deep enough to conceal their huge forms. At one point, the animals had eaten from both sides so that only a thin wall of earth remained and in this there was a small hole.

As the two men approached, Stoner saw a buffalo licking the earth on one side, and said to Boone: "Shtop, Gaptain, and we will have shum fun."

Taking off his cap, the Pennsylvania Dutchman crept down

one side of the earth wall until he could thrust the cap suddenly into the face of the immense beast on the other side. The buffalo did not run, as Stoner had expected. Instead, it came charging straight into the thin wall of earth. As the horned head and shaggy neck burst through almost on top of him, the bulky Stoner scrambled for his life, yelling to Boone: "Schoot her, Gaptain! Schoot her, Gaptain!"

Seeing that the buffalo had stopped and that his frightened companion was in no danger at all, though still running, Boone rolled on the ground with laughter. Eight years later he was to carry his dying son in his arms across the very ground where now he lay and laughed.

At Harrodsburg Boone found cabins rising rapidly while Harrod and thirty-four men were also busily laying out the town. Each had been promised an "in lot" and a ten-acre "out lot." This was a bagatelle compared to the princely tracts Daniel Boone was later to claim, but at the moment it looked promising.

Daniel never could resist land, and he was nearly penniless. Indian war or no Indian war, he paused to register as a settler and confirmed his claim by building a cabin. The lot assigned him was next that of a certain Evan Hinton, and the two men met the demands of legality, and also saved time, by building a double cabin straddling the line. Boone never returned to claim it, but the double dwelling was known indiscriminately as Boone's or Hinton's cabin until the Indians burned it down in 1777. As a surveyor, Boone also helped lay off the lots.

In spite of the warning that he brought, Harrod's men stayed where they were until the middle of June. Then, after one man had disappeared and two others had been killed, the rest withdrew. Their buildings stood deserted but unharmed through the winter, and were occupied again in 1775 when Harrod returned to set up Harrodsburg permanently.

Boone and Stoner now "meandered" to the mouth of the Kentucky, pushed on to the Falls of the Ohio, and were back in the Clinch Valley after sixty-one days, having covered eight hundred miles of wilderness. They had found and warned part, at least, of the surveyors, most of whom got back safely, though a few were killed.

5. Public War, Private Treaty

LORD DUNMORE'S WAR with the Indians was already raging by the time Boone got back, bringing news of the surveyors and also news that on the return journey he had tracked a small party of Indians from Cumberland Gap eastward almost to the settlements. Commissioned lieutenant, Boone was directed to raise as many men as he could and start for the front. He had actually set out to join the main body of the colonial troops when a messenger overtook him with orders to return and aid in the defense of the frontier, where a series of small but bloody raids was spreading terror.

A brief memorandum by a supply officer—"Sept. 22d, Lieut. Boone, fourteen men, four days, three pounds of beef per day" —suggests a scouting party. Orders were to reserve beef rations for scouts and parties pursuing Indians.

He was in a few small engagements and was speedily promoted captain on petition of his neighbors. The settlers insisted on having a commander whose home was in the locality. Then, they thought, he would be sure to stand his ground and keep the Indians out. Promotion gave him command of three forts. His commander reported that "Mr. Boone is very diligent at Castle's woods and keeps up good order."

At this very moment Tahgahjute (Chief Logan) was leading a war party into the Clinch Valley, not far from Boone's command at Moore's Fort, close to his home. In spite of his vigilance, three of Boone's men were ambushed and killed by Logan's raiders. They had gone out to look at pigeon traps within three hundred yards of the fort and in plain view. At the sound of firing, Boone and a group of men rushed out to the relief, but found nothing save the usual war club, left by the bodies as a defiance. Boone pursued but the Indians had vanished. He was out again the next month under the command of Captain Daniel Smith in an effort to recapture stolen horses, but again the Indians got away.

In October General Andrew Lewis defeated the Indians at Point Pleasant. This practically ended the war, and Captain Daniel Boone was discharged from the militia, November 20, 1774.

The crushing defeat that the Indians had suffered made wilderness travel safer—indeed, the Earl of Dunmore has been suspected of bringing on the war mainly to open the way for a little jobbing in lands on his own account. If so, his schemes did him little good, for another land company was at last ready to begin operations. Though Dunmore, as Governor of Virginia, and Martin, as Governor of North Carolina, both fulminated against this enterprising group of business men, they were too late. Within a few months rebellion walked the land. Royal governors no longer mattered very much.

Richard Henderson's judicial duties had ended the year before. He was at last ready for his land scheme. Other colonies had been founded by "proprietors" acting under grants from the King. His Majesty had forbidden further settlements westward. Both the King and the Provincial Assembly had also forbidden treaties with the Indians by private individuals "with respect to his territory claimed by the Indian Nations in North America."

All this was, of course, perfectly well known to Henderson, an attorney and a former justice. It was his grandiose idea to disregard the royal proclamation, the necessity of a royal grant, and the laws of both Virginia and North Carolina. Perfectly aware that his measures would be opposed, he had tried to secure some shadow of legality.

There was an old decision by two successive British Lord Chancellors, which asserted that royal letters patent were not required "in respect to such places as have, or shall be acquired by treaty or Grant from any of the Indian Princes or Governments." Property rights, they had assured the King, were vested "in the Grantee by the Indian grants, subject only to your Majesty's right of sovereignty."

The "Indians" here referred to were East Indians from India, but the thing sounded legal, the authority was very high, and it might be possible to extend the principle. Copies of the decision had reached America as early as 1772. Various land companies thought it would be extremely interesting as a loophole in the law, if only they could make "Indians" mean American Indians. Henderson eventually procured a copy, though there is some doubt whether he knew anything about it until long after he actually had reached his agreement with the red men.

Henderson's Transylvania Company proposed to deal directly with the Indians for twenty million acres, set up a new, fourteenth colony, retain large tracts for their own estates, sell the rest to settlers, charge a perpetual quit-rent for every acre sold, and retain special rights in the government.

The idea was romantic, magnificent, feudal, and there might be a fortune in it. But it all sounded so queer to one North Carolina official that he wrote a contemporary: "Pray, is Dick Henderson out of his head?"

What the royal governors thought about it could just barely be printed. Governor Martin of North Carolina called it a "daring, unjust and unwarranted Proceeding," besides being "illicit and fraudulent" and "of a most alarming and dangerous Tendency," which would help the Indians "in annoying His Majesty's subjects." Worse still, "debtors and persons in desperate circumstances" would take refuge in the new colony "to the great injury of Creditors." And furthermore, said the sputtering governor, Kentucky belonged to the Earl Granville, anyhow.

Though Henderson may have tried to protect himself in London, his project certainly was a flouting of the royal governors. At any other period it would have been promptly suppressed—but not in 1775. The partners, in their agreement with each other, asserted that they would deal with the Cherokees "by the laws of England." They had to say something like that because the laws of both Virginia and North Carolina forbade anything of the sort.

Daniel Boone was hardly out of the army before he was traveling back and forth between the North Carolina settlements and the towns of the Cherokees, with whom he was by this time well acquainted. His lifelong friend Nathaniel Hart, one of the Transylvania Company partners, went down in person to "sound the Cherokees," probably acting on Boone's reports of a year or two earlier. Both Hart and Henderson visited the Cherokee villages in the autumn of 1774. It is said that Boone paid one final, exploratory visit to Kentucky in January of 1775.

By the time winter set in negotiations had gone so far that a Cherokee chief came back to North Carolina with Henderson "to make Choice of the Goods" which were to be paid for the land. A few days later the two returned to the Watauga country in modern Tennessee with an entire wagon train of "Indian goods" from Cross Creek (Fayetteville, North Carolina). Presently, from the woods, a Cherokee embassy emerged to examine

Mrs. F. R. Bissell

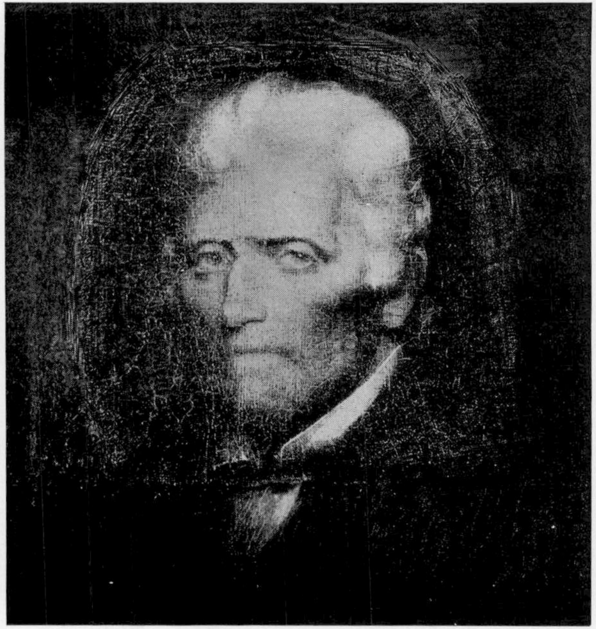

S. Bowles King

TWO PORTRAITS OF DANIEL BOONE BY CHESTER HARDING

After Boone's death, Harding painted numerous portraits of him, working either from sketches or from memory. This one, however, was according to tradition given to General Daniel Bissell by Boone himself.

This is the only portrait of Daniel Boone known to have been painted from life. Unable to get canvas, Harding used oilcloth. Forty years later, finding the portrait damaged, he cut out the face, here reproduced.

the tribe's prospective riches. The embassy included a squaw, to make sure the feminine viewpoint was represented.

By Christmas Richard Henderson, "for himself and Company," was publicly advertising for "settlers for Kentucky lands about to be purchased." By the next year the wily red men had a white attorney of their own and were ready for the treaty. The parties met at Sycamore Shoals, in the Watauga country.

Without waiting for the treaty, Boone was already concentrating a body of woodsmen at Long Island, in the Holston River, in preparation for the march into Kentucky as soon as agreement had been reached. This time he was going through. This time his settlement would be permanent.

Leaving his brother Squire in charge of the gathering woodsmen, who included old friends like Michael Stoner and Benjamin Cutbirth, Daniel went off to Watauga to attend the treaty-making. In his ghost-written autobiography, he says only that he "was solicited by a number of North-Carolina gentlemen, that were about purchasing the lands lying on the S. side of Kentucke River, from the Cherokee Indians, to attend their treaty at Wataga, in March, 1775, to negotiate with them, and, mention the boundaries of the purchase."

The laconic Daniel hardly does justice to the scene. He had himself journeyed about the forests, persuading the Indians to attend. More than a thousand Cherokees, big and little, braves, squaws, papooses, came to see the treaty made. They were led by their greatest chiefs. Knowing how important the negotiations were, the Cherokees had brought their shrewdest diplomat, Atacullaculla (Leaning Wood), a mere wisp of a man, old, tiny, delicately built, famous for his brains among both whites and reds. The white men humorously called him "The Little Carpenter," because they said he could put a treaty together as neatly as a carpenter joining wood.

There was Oconostota (Groundhog-Sausage), aged, withered,

and wrinkled as only an old Indian can be, the revered head of the nation, who had visited royalty in London, and whom the British recognized as "emperor." And there was also the redoubtable Tsiyu-gunsini (Dragging Canoe), a dour, distrustful fighting-man, who opposed the whole business with all the eloquence of an Indian warrior.

William Bartram, the famous traveler, who saw Ataculla-culla, described him as "a man of remarkably small stature, slender, and of a delicate frame, the only instance I saw in his Nation." But, added the admiring author, "a man of superior abilities."

An old settler later remembered Oconostota "with heavy and dul countenance, somewhat corpulent and weighed 180. he did not speak any english, but the traders who could converse with him, said that he was vary dul in point of interlect." On the other hand, "the Dragon Canoe, he was said to be vary large and coarse featured Indian fine with interlect and vary strong predjudices."

The Transylvania Company proposed to pay ten thousand pounds in goods, and someone had been shrewd enough to have this huge quantity of merchandise stored where the impetuous young warriors could see it. Before distribution among the tribe, it looked enormous; when it was parceled out, the Indians were disgruntled. One disgusted brave complained that his share was only a shirt that he could easily have earned in a day's hunting on the land they had given away.

Nevertheless, the treaty seems to have been fair on both sides. Someone who knew Kentucky well—obviously Boone, for there was no one else—had drawn the boundary carefully. The Cherokees seemed to have title to the land. The Iroquois had given up their claim in 1768, in the Treaty of Fort Stanwix. As they ruled the other Indians of the area by right of conquest, their cession seemed to end all claims but the Cherokees'. The British Government itself had, in the Treaty of Lochaber in 1770, acknowledged the Cherokee claim to this general area, or at least a good deal of it.

The tribe seemed entirely free to sell the territory if they wished. No one seems to have taken the least advantage of them. They not only had their own attorney, but the signature of "Thomas Price, Linguist" on the treaty guaranteed the accuracy of the translations. One of the men present later testified under oath that "the Indians understood all that was said by the said Henderson."

The negotiation was a long, slow business, which was not helped by the vigorous opposition of Oconostota and Dragging Canoe. Oconostota saw clearly enough the danger of a white advance beyond the mountains. "This is but the beginning," he said. ". . . The invader has crossed the great sea in ships; he has not been stayed by broad rivers, and now he has penetrated the wilderness and overcome the ruggedness of the mountains. Neither will he stop here. He will force the Indian steadily before him across the Mississippi ever towards the west . . . till the red man be no longer a roamer of the forests and a pursuer of wild game." Dragging Canoe was equally emphatic. Once the Indians broke off negotiations altogether. But at length Dragging Canoe stamped on the ground and said: "We give you from this place."

He took Boone by the hand, remarking: "Brother, we have given you a fine land, but I believe that you will have much trouble in settling it." It was Dragging Canoe, also, who made the famous remark that "there was a dark cloud over that country." No one dreamed how right the chief was, but all of the Cherokees warned the white men of the Indian tribes to the west and north of Kentucky. These, they said, were "bad people and when they came to war, would kill white people as well as red." All the red men "seemed very fond of Richard Henderson and often said they did not want him hurt."

The treaty was actually signed on March 17, 1775. There was a great feast and much merry-making. There was great slaughter of beeves and a mighty swigging of traders' rum. But feasting with the Indians apparently was not altogether to Daniel's taste at the moment. Undisturbed by dismal prophecies, he had left the council days before; and by the time the feast began he and his men had been traveling toward Kentucky for a week.

6. The Wilderness Road

BOONE'S men were assembled and ready to start when he arrived at "the Long Island" in the Holston River. There were thirty of them, all armed and mounted. There were his brother Squire Boone and his friends Stoner and Cutbirth. There was his old neighbor Richard Callaway. A certain Captain William Twitty had brought seven North Carolinians.

Though all were armed as a matter of course, they do not seem to have anticipated any more Indian trouble. Boone had just come from the signing of a friendly agreement and had left whites and Indians preparing to feast together. Their rifles were mainly to provide food. At the start, no one seems to have taken precautions of any kind against Indian attack.

On the tenth of March, 1775, axes began to ring. Daniel Boone and his men had started the Wilderness Road. They were all in high spirits. On the very first day they killed a bear and "had a fine supper," always a great help to the morale of any expedition. As Felix Walker, one of Twitty's men, later put it, with the immense satisfaction in rhetorical flourishes typical of the pioneer on those rare occasions when he took his pen in hand: "Every heart abounded with joy and excitement in anticipating the new things we should see, and the romantic scenes through which we must pass; and, exclusive of the novelty of the journey, the advantages and accumulations ensuing on the settlement of a new country, was a dazzling object with many of our company."

Their leader had special reason to be joyful, for he had left just in time to escape an importunate creditor, who on April 19, 1775, issued a warrant against Boone's property. The paper still exists with the words, "no goods" written across the back. A warrant issued for his arrest for debt bears the words, "Gone to Kentucky."

They passed through Powell's Valley, on through Cumberland Gap, and then began to enlarge the old Warriors' Path, blazing and clearing it as they went, for fifty miles. At the Hazel Patch they turned west, following a buffalo trace pounded hard and wide and deep into the soil by the endless herds that had followed it since time began. From Hazel Patch their Wilderness Road went on to the Rockcastle River, where the pioneers had to cut their way through twenty miles of dead brush. Then it ran along a buffalo trace for thirty miles of thick cane and reed, on through what is today Madison County, to the Kentucky River.

When, a couple of weeks after starting, they emerged from the underbrush and cane, the whole party were delighted with "the pleasing and rapturous appearance of the plains of Kentucky. A new sky and strange earth seems to be presented to our view."

They were now within about fifteen miles of the site of the prospective settlement, and they had met with no real difficulty of any kind. No one seems to have kept any kind of watch. Indeed, the impossibility of getting anyone to do sentry duty was greatly exercising Henderson, who, a hundred miles or so behind, was following hard on their trail.

On March 24, 1775, Boone camped for the night in the gently rolling forest country just outside the modern town of Richmond, in Madison County. The many small hills and tiny ravines offered perfect cover to any hostile force; and the next morning, as Boone's camp lay sleeping, there was a sudden volley from the woods, and Indians came rushing in, swinging their tomahawks.

Half awake and wholly terrified, the white men snatched their rifles and ran from the smoldering camp fire to the shelter of darkness and the forest. Once in safety, Squire Boone found that he had seized his jacket instead of his powder-horn and shot-pouch. Half naked, and with no means of defense, he crawled about in the darkness with his useless rifle until he could find his brother and borrow ammunition. Captain Twitty had been shot through both knees, so that he could not move. As the Indians burst into his tent to scalp him, his bulldog leaped at one brave, knocking him over. A second brave hastily tomahawked the dog. Then both vanished, leaving Twitty without further injuries. His negro slave Sam, hit by a rifle ball in the attack, leaped to his feet with one spasmodic effort, then fell dead into the camp fire. Felix Walker, though badly wounded, was able to join the scramble for the underbrush.

When the uproar at the camp had ceased, Daniel Boone gathered up his scattered men and went back. The Indians had gone, having stolen a few horses but nothing else. The expedition stood guard till broad daylight, but the attack was over.

Walker and Twitty were so badly wounded that travel was impossible. The others built a hasty log fort—long known as "Twitty's Fort"—and here they waited while Boone made simple medicines from woods plants and nursed the wounded men with what Walker describes as "paternal affection." Twitty soon died and was buried beside his negro slave. Rough stones, set in the ground, still mark their graves.

Three days later hunters out for provisions came upon "Samuel Tate's son," who told how his camp, at some distance from Boone's, had also been fired into. The little group had foolishly lighted a fire without posting guards and were busy with the usual nightly task of drying moccasins when the Indians shot into them. Two were killed. The rest scattered barefoot through the woods. The moonlit night and a late fall of April snow made it easy for the Indians to track them down. Samuel Tate himself escaped only by running down an icy stream, still called Tate's Creek in memory of the episode.

When Squire and Daniel Boone reached the scene, they found "two men killed and sculped." Boone at once sent word to other scattered parties to assemble at the mouth of Otter Creek.

His men were appalled. Kentucky was by no means so "pleasing and rapturous" now as it had seemed a few days earlier. The weaker spirits in Boone's party packed up and started for home. One man remained in the forest, still afraid to come into camp. As a woman slave of Colonel Callaway's went out to gather firewood one morning, she saw the poor wretch peeping from behind a tree, apparently unable to make up his mind whether whites or redskins remained in possession of the field. She ran back, screaming "Indians!", and threw the camp into turmoil. Boone caught up his rifle and got his men behind trees, yelling to them not to run till they saw him fall—which seems to have been the best he dared expect. At this point the hero in the underbrush announced his identity and came in.

When Felix Walker was well enough to be moved, he was put into a litter between two horses—one in front and one behind—and the party pushed on toward the Kentucky River. As they came into the river bottom, they caught a cheerful glimpse of Kentucky's wealth of game. A herd of two or three hundred buffalo were moving away from the licks around two sulphur springs, "some running, some walking, others loping slowly and carelessly, with young calves playing, skipping and bounding through the plain." Somewhat encouraged, the men set to work building shelter.

Meantime Henderson with other proprietors and a large party was painfully following some distance in the rear. Leaving only ten days after Boone, he brought his supplies along in wagons, improving Boone's roughly made road as he went along, until he reached the last settlement, Captain Joseph Martin's cabin in Powell's Valley, twenty miles east of Cumberland Gap. It was a kind of "jumping-off place" for Kentucky. While Boone was fighting the Indians off on the 25th, Henderson had peacefully "come to Mrs. Callaways." At Martin's he spent the 31st "making house for the wagons as we could not possibly clear the road any further," and tarried for nearly another week.

Other parties of settlers were following behind Henderson. On April 4 half a dozen recruits from Virginia caught up with him. They included a certain Abraham Hanks, uncle of Nancy Hanks, mother of Abraham Lincoln. On the way to Kentucky, Hanks lost his courage and turned back. On the way to the settlements again, he met still another group headed for Kentucky, changed his mind again, and reached Boonesborough after all, not far behind Henderson's party.

On April 5, while Boone and his men were hard at work at Boonesborough, Henderson got his pack train under way at last. There were endless discouragements. A hunter went out, and when he failed to reappear someone had to go and find him. Two pack-horses bolted into the woods. Word came that five people on their way to Kentucky had been killed by Indians. One traveler thereupon decided that he did not very much want to go to Kentucky with Henderson anyway, and "retreated back with his company and determin'd to settle in the Valley to make corn for the Cantuckey people."

As if this were not enough, the very same day came the messenger with Boone's letter describing the attack on his camp.

"My advise to you, sir, is to come or send as soon as possible. Your company is desired greatly, for the people are very uneasy, but are willing to stay and venture their lives with you." As for the Indians, "now is the time to flusterate their intentions and keep the country, whilst we are in it." He himself was indomitable. In spite of all these alarums and excursions, "this day," wrote Dan'l stoutly, "we start from the battle ground for the mouth of Otter Creek, where we shall immediately erect a fort."

The news spread through Henderson's party, and William Calk entered in his journal: "this Eavening Comes a letter from Capt Boon at caintuck of the indians doing mischief and some turns Back." Next day Henderson's cavalcade met "40 persons returning from the Cantuckey on account of the late murders by the Indians." The inimitable Calk observes that as Henderson's column "put up & Started Crost Cumberland Gap," they "Met a great maney peopel turning Back for fear of the indians but our Company goes on Still with good courage." The men they met were probably those who had deserted Boone, together with other adventurers who had rushed off independently to be the first to claim Kentucky land.

Discouraged by the news they brought, several more of Henderson's party instantly made tracks for Virginia. These cheerful souls also suggested that even the handful who remained with Boone would probably desert him before Henderson could get there with reënforcements. To make matters worse, William Calk and two friends went up a mountain and there "Saw the track of two indians & whear they had lain unter some Rocks."

Everything, Henderson noted, now "depended in Boone's maintaining his ground—at least until we could get there." At moments he expected to see Boone's face in every party of returning emigrants. Henderson determined to send a messenger ahead, for the grimly determined Daniel had sent word that he relied on receiving assistance.

Who was to make the solitary ride through these Indian-haunted woods, from which everyone else was fleeing? It was vital to let Boone know that Henderson had not been scared off and was on his way to support him. Henderson himself was still desperately afraid "lest Boon & the men with him should abandon the Country."

A certain William Cocke rather dubiously volunteered to go, but he made two conditions. Henderson must give him ten thousand acres of choice land, and he must have at least one companion. Henderson appealed to his whole company, offering a second ten thousand acres to anyone who would go with Cocke. With tears in his eyes, he exclaimed that he and the Transylvania Company were all ruined men if the Kentucky project failed. Still there were no volunteers. Cocke at length agreed, rather glumly, to go alone, "and if he escaped with his life, to perform the trust."

Cocke was even less enthusiastic at the prospect next morning when the time came to start. It was a dark, gray day, and he faced a ride of 130 miles, entirely alone, through wilderness where murderous Indian bands were known to be active and about which he had been hearing nothing but gloomy tales for days on end.

However, Henderson "struck whilst the iron was hot," no matter how doleful poor Cocke might look, and "fixed Mr. Cocke off with a good Queen Ann's musket, plenty of ammunition, a tomahawk, a large cuttoe * knife, a Dutch blanket, and no small quantity of jerked beef." Cocke carried with him, as Henderson confessed a few days later, "besides his own enor-

* *Couteau,* a word for the woodsman's knife, taken over from the French.

mous load of fearful apprehensions, a considerable burden of my own uneasiness."

All this perturbation was needless. There were no more Indians around. Cocke was not attacked and reached Boonesborough without difficulty. He was even able to communicate with Henderson by leaving notes along the road for him to pick up as he advanced, so that the proprietor was not surprised to find him safely with Boone when the two parties joined forces at last.

Fear is contagious, and it spread swiftly from the panic-stricken fugitives Henderson's party had been meeting. Some of Henderson's men simply deserted, slipping quietly away for Virginia. Others, as Henderson himself sardonically remarked, "saw the necessity of returning to convince their friends that they were still alive, in too strong a light to be resisted." Others went on because they were ashamed to go back.

But strange to say, rarely could anyone persuade them to stand guard, and all these terrified wights lay down to sleep in Indian country night after night, giving the Indians every opportunity to take them by surprise. William Calk's diary notes only twice, as something extraordinary, "we Keep Sentry this Night for fear of the indians," and on one of these occasions it was only "the forepart of the night."

It was another example of the same carelessness Boone had shown. Felix Walker thought that Boone had "conducted the party under his care through the wilderness, with great propriety, intrepidity and courage." But, he added, "was I to enter an exception to any part of his conduct, it would be on the ground that he appeared void of fear and of consequence—too little caution for the enterprise."

Carelessness and failure to provide security were to curse the first years of the new frontier. The first Kentucky settlers would neither reconnoiter if they could possibly avoid it, nor guard their camps if they could possibly sleep. Worn out by the exhausting labor of wilderness travel, they wanted rest more than safety, and were willing to run any risk to get it.

Some years later, after a series of Indian attacks should have taught caution, Colonel Daniel Trabue noted in a party which he accompanied into the forest the same casual attitude toward their own security: "As the weather was cold we made large fires, and our Dogs was all the sentry we had if they would bark one man would go around and see what it was." Only the cautious Colonel Richard Callaway provided ordinary military security. On his trip back from the settlements with an ammunition train in 1779, he "was very caucious in the wilderness kept up Sentrys every night, and marched in great order."

Henderson also wrote to his partners that "those who started in the morning with pale faces and apparent trepidation, could lie down and sleep at night in great quiet, not even possessed of fear enough to get the better of indolence."

They felt, he grumbled, that it was beneath their dignity "to be afraid of any thing, especially when a little fatigued. They would all agree in the morning, that it would be highly prudent and necessary to keep sentinels around our camp at night; but a hearty meal or supper (when we could get it) and good fires, never failed to put off the danger for at least 24 hours; at which time it was universally agreed, on all hands, that a watch at night would be indispensably necessary."

Neither wilderness, hardships, nor Indians could conquer Henderson's spirit and his rather sour sense of humor. He needed all his courage, for only once did he meet with any encouragement along that dreary way. He ran into the McAfee brothers. They had just finished a second journey to Kentucky and were on their way back to the settlements. But when they heard of Henderson's plans, they turned in their tracks and went to Kentucky again with him.

As the party approached Boonesborough on the 18th of April, they were met, as William Calk notes in his diary, by "4 men from Boons Camp that caim to cunduck us on." They brought extra pack-horses to assist the travelers and "excellent beef in plenty." Evidently Daniel Boone had already taken time for a buffalo hunt.

Henderson and his men passed the scene of the Indian attack at Twitty's Fort next day, and on April 20 "git Down to Caintuck to Boons foart about 12 oclock wheare we Stop." Here, according to the expedition's other diarist, they "were saluted by a running fire of about 25 Guns, all that was then at the Fort—The men appeared in high spirits and much rejoiced on our arrival."

It was a joyful moment for them all. Henderson had felt gravely responsible for the dangerous mission on which he had sent Cocke, and it was a huge relief to find him safe. The march out had been exhausting, with the horses worked to the limit of their strength, men tired and fearful, tempers snappish with strain and exhaustion, "one whole month, without intermission, traveling in a barren desert country, most of the way our horses packed beyond their strength; no part of the road tolerable, most of it either hilly, stony, slippery, miry, or bushy; our people jaded out and dispirited with fatigue, and what was worse, often pinched for victuals. To get clear of all this at once, was as much as we could well bear; and though we had nothing here to refresh ourselves with but cold water and lean buffalo meat, without bread, it certainly was the most joyous banquet I ever saw. Joy and festivity was in every countenance."

Henderson's own spirits did not remain so joyful after he had inspected his new domain. He found only a few rude cabins, without defense, though Boone's men had now been on the ground for weeks. Smitten with the land greed of the pioneers, they had neglected everything to survey land and establish claims.

Boone's hastily built structures near the spring were too small to house everyone, and their location on low ground was not satisfactory. In fact, it was dangerous. Sooner or later they were bound to be attacked. Henderson picked a better place for a fort a little farther up the river bank, and moved his tents.

In his diary, he sounds rather disturbed because "Mr Boone's company having laid off most of the adjacent good lands into lots of two acres each and taking it as it fell to each individual by lot was in actual possession and occupying them." As first comers, Boone's men proposed to be first choosers. But Henderson's followers, too, were infected with the land craze. Like the original party who had come with Boone, Henderson's men, too, wasted a great deal of time fussing about land. They spent nearly a week in running surveys, arguing about shares, drawing lots, arguing about that, and then drawing lots all over again—"at the end of which every body seemed well satisfied."

On the 26th, more settlers arrived and had to be shown land. Henderson held out "4 lots for the fort garden" in which he immediately "sowed small seed, planted cucumbers & c." It was already the end of April and high time to provide a future food supply, though his men must have worked heroically to get the land cleared so soon.

There were quarrels of some sort among the three partners in the land company who had made the trip together. Nathaniel Hart had behaved "in a very cold indifferent manner" about the fort site, admitting only that "he thought it might do well enough." Now he picked out land of his own and retired to it, announcing "that he would have nothing to say to the Fort, things were managed in such a manner."

"Cannot guess the reason of his discontent," noted poor Henderson in his diary. John Luttrell, the third partner, sided with Henderson, and, when he finally moved off to his own land, left two of his men behind to help make a clearing for the fort.

Work had hardly begun when in came the first of a series of unexpected and not always welcome visitors. One of the surprising things about Boonesborough was the amazing way in which people began to pop up in that wild country as soon as Henderson and his companions went to work. These visitors were Colonel Thomas Slaughter and Valentine Harman of North Carolina. As Boone told the story of these wanderers long afterward:

> When they came to the mouth of the Big Sandy they left the boat and took it on horseback—Harmon being a good Woodsman—They struck the Kentucky River about 1 mile above Boonsboro and came down to where we was at work building a fort about the 20th of April [the old woodsman's memory played him false: that was the day of Henderson's arrival] and they stayed with us two or three weeks, in which time they informed me of a Salt Spring they had found.

The pair were on their way up the river to Harrodsburg, where James Harrod was already at work on his settlement, whose future relationship to Henderson's Transylvania project was something of a puzzle.

Early in May, six or seven more men came in from the settlements. "They had heard nothing of our purchase, but merely set off to view the country." At first they seemed rather resentful at having been anticipated; but this wore off and they joined in Henderson's plans. Everyone was still busy on the fort when on May 3 a new complication arose. John Floyd came in from a camp on Dick's River, a little to the south, where he had left thirty men; and four days later came James Harrod from Harrodsburg.

Henderson's Transylvania Company had bought the land they occupied from the Cherokees; but Harrod and Floyd were actually settled on it. Possession is nine points of the law, but there was no law in Kentucky. What to do?

It would certainly never do to drive them off; and that would have been impossible anyhow. Harrod and Floyd had as many riflemen as Henderson, if not more. It was likely that Floyd would take a hostile attitude. He was a surveyor for Colonel William Preston, of Virginia, who had done his best to thwart Henderson's plans.

As for Harrod, he was "determined to live in this country." Driven out by Indians the year before, he had come back with about fifty men, mostly young and without families, to carve a fortune from the wilderness. Six feet or over, with jet-black eyes and hair, with a hot temper, usually under control, he was not a man to trifle with. Henderson had moments of gloom as he contemplated his own settlers—"a set of scoundrels who scarcely believe in God or fear a devil if we were to judge from most of their looks, words, and actions."

Could the three parties come to a peaceable understanding?

Luckily, everyone was in a conciliatory mood. It proved easy to reach an agreement. Floyd and Harrod stayed a few days, and then "took their departure in great good humor," while the Boonesborough men went on with their "plantation business."

There were various small incidents. A horse got lost. Henderson and Boone went off together to hunt for it. The bread supply ran out. The hunters had no luck. Once Henderson notes: "No meat but fat bear. Almost starved. Drank a little coffee & trust to luck for dinner." Later he speculates greedily on his chances for some fresh greens from the vegetable garden.

Four men got lost in the woods, and a search party went out. A few new settlers straggled in.

Elections for the new government were held May 20, 1775. Daniel Boone, Squire Boone, and Richard Callaway were among the six men chosen to represent Boonesborough. Three days later delegates came in from the other settlements that had been established at Harrodsburg and near it—"very good men and much disposed to serve their country," according to Henderson, who was beginning to take a more cheerful view of his associates.

Near the fort stood a huge elm, "in a beautiful plain surrounded by a turf of fine white clover, forming a green to its very stock to which there is scarcely anything to be likened." It was four feet through the trunk and the first branches began nine feet up.

Like George Washington and other land speculators of the period, whose papers are full of notes like this, Henderson had a keen eye for trees and canebrakes. He studied these attentively as the easiest clue to the quality of the soil in which they grew. (Modern ecologists, incidentally, do exactly the same thing.)

The circle of the elm's branches was a hundred feet in diameter. On a fair day it threw a shadow of four hundred feet and "any time between the hours of 10 & 2 100 persons may commodiously seat themselves under its branches." Here the delegates gathered to establish the new government of Transylvania. There was a great deal of oratory in the florid, eighteenth-century manner. Henderson himself addressed the convention in resounding style:

> You, perhaps, are fixing the palladium, or placing the first corner-stone of an edifice, the height and magnificence of whose superstructure is now in the womb of futurity, and can only

become great and glorious in proportion to the excellence of its foundation.

There were pages more of it. The proprietor suggested that the convention set up courts, organize militia, protect the game, and drive off intruding hunters—which was exactly the Indians' own idea! He also came out resoundingly against "vice and immorality," though how he expected his colonists to lapse into iniquity when there were no female vessels of sin for hundreds of miles (barring one or two negro slave-women) is a puzzle.

To Henderson's orotund periods, the settlers replied in the same vein:

> We received your speech with minds truly thankful for the care and attention you express toward the good people of this infant country, whom we represent. Well aware of the confusion which would ensue the want of rules for our conduct in life, and deeply impressed with a sense of the importance of the trust our constituents have reposed in us, though laboring under a thousand disadvantages, which attend prescribing remedies for disorders, which *already* call for our assistance, as well as those that are lodged in the womb of futurity. Yet the task, arduous as it is, we will attempt with vigor, not doubting but unanimity will insure us success.
>
> That we have an absolute right, as a political body, without giving umbrage to Great Britain, or any of the colonies, to frame rules for the government of our little society, can not be doubted by any sensible, unbiassed mind—and being without the jurisdiction of, and not answerable to any of his Majesty's courts, the constituting tribunals of justice shall be a matter of our first contemplation.

The two speeches are so much alike that one suspects Henderson of writing them both. The still loyal allusions to the British Government are interesting. Lexington and Concord had been fought. General Gage and his redcoats were having a rather bad time of it in Boston. But all this had happened since the Kentuckians set out. For all they knew, they were still loyal subjects of the King, though the ties of allegiance had been wearing a little loose even before they started.

On May 28, when the Reverend John Lythe conducted services under the great elm, he is said to have read the prayer for the Royal Family, for the first and only time on Kentucky soil. Next day came a letter describing "the battle at Boston," and within three years his Majesty's officers were leading Indian forces against Boonesborough.

The convention set up legal machinery, established courts, legislated against "profane swearing and Sabbath breaking," arranged for militia, and provided for the punishment of criminals, if any. One of the first bills brought in was Daniel Boone's "for preserving game." There had been trouble from the very first with the "great waste in killing meat. Some would kill three, four, five or ½ a dozen buffaloes and not take half a horse load from them all." Two or three hundred buffalo had been grazing near Boonesborough when the settlers arrived. Within six weeks "Fifteen or 20 miles was as short a distance as good hunters thought of getting meat, nay sometimes they were obliged to go thirty though by chance once or twice a week buffaloe was killed within 5 or six miles."

Boone got his bill through in short order. His committee reported the same day it was proposed. Squire brought in a bill "to preserve the range," and Daniel presented another bill "for improving the breed of horses." Kentucky was Kentucky from the very first—colonels everywhere, a wholesome interest in horseflesh, and, as soon as the corn began to grow, no lack of whiskey. Nor were romantic ladies long in arriving. Boone and Callaway brought out their daughters. Jemima Boone was so attractive that by the time she was fourteen Daniel had to discourage immediate matrimony. And as for the brunette

Betsey Callaway, a youth whose settlement her father's cavalcade passed on the way to Kentucky remembered Betsey and no one else when, as an old man of eighty, he sat down to write his recollections.

The new settlement was still a long way, however, from anything like completely democratic government. Henderson and the other "proprietors" retained the right to collect an annual quit-rent of two shillings per hundred acres on all land in Transylvania. Even when all the land was sold, the proprietors expected that they and their heirs would collect at that rate on twenty million acres for ever and ever. They also retained the right to appoint civil and military officers, and a few other special privileges. Daniel Boone was one of the committee which waited on them to ask that no new lands be granted to other settlers, except on the same terms that had already been accorded.

The feudal note was retained most clearly in a ceremony on the last day of the convention. Under the big elm, the Indians' attorney, John Farrar, handed Henderson a symbolical bit of turf. While both men held it, Farrar formally made delivery of seisin, and declared that Henderson was in full possession of the company's new domain.

By the middle of June Daniel Boone decided that the settlement was at last able to defend itself, and set off for the eastern settlements. He was in a hurry to get home. Rebecca had been with child when he started the Wilderness Road. It was nearly time for the baby to be born. With him went Colonel Callaway and a detail of men to bring back the salt that Henderson had stored at Martin's Station. Squire Boone soon followed. All three meant to bring their families back.

On June 8, just before Boone left, a dubious British visitor arrived—at least, later writers have regarded him with dark suspicion, though the settlers at Boonesborough gave him a cordial welcome. This was John F. D. Smyth, later a captain in the Queen's Rangers, a Tory corps. He was a friend of the Earl of Dunmore, Royal Governor of Virginia, who had been a bitter foe of the whole Transylvania project.

Smyth had been traveling through Virginia and North Carolina with a single servant. He had met Indians and made friends with them. It is quite possible that Dunmore had sent him out as a spy to see what was really happening among both whites and reds. He certainly displayed a suspicious interest in fortifications. None the less, he was taken into the life of the little community, conversed with Henderson, and stayed six weeks.

Then two more visitors from Virginia arrived. These were James Wood, member for Frederick County in the Virginia Assembly, and Charles Lewis of Augusta County, who said they had "called to view the settlement." They must have been eager indeed to view it, for they had traveled down the Ohio River with a big backwoods batteau, accompanied only by two Chickasaw Indians and three whites.

Were they Tories, too? Smyth represents the meeting as accidental, but he lost no time in deciding to journey on down the Mississippi with them to New Orleans. Once there, he hurried on to join Lord Dunmore.

Just why all these men were wandering down Indian-infested rivers while the Colonies were aflame behind them is a little hard to understand, unless they were engaged in some kind of espionage. River travel was not so dangerous as it later became, and it never was so dangerous as travel overland. One could keep well out in the wider streams and avoid surprise. But even so, the Ohio-Mississippi journey was not one to be undertaken without good reason.

While Boone was waiting for his baby's birth and his wife's

recovery, Henderson in Boonesborough was chafing at his failure to return.

"We are informed that Mrs. Boone was not delivered the other day," he and another partner write in a joint letter, "and therefore do not know when to look for him; and, until he comes the devil himself can't drive the others this way."

The prospective settlers knew and trusted Daniel Boone as they trusted no one else. And so the whole grandiose scheme of a new feudal empire in the West waited on a baby's birth in a rough settler's cabin on the frontier, with no aid but a neighbor's crude midwifery. In late June or early July little William Boone was born, but died soon after.

The frontier was no place to nurse one's grief. Daniel and Rebecca were on their way to Boonesborough some time in August.

Henderson returned to Oxford, North Carolina, that same month to consult his partners. They voted a present of two thousand acres of land "to Colonel Daniel Boone, with the thanks of the Proprietors, for the signal services he had rendered to the Company," and thanks to Callaway "for his spirited and manly behavior in behalf of the said Colony." No gift was made to Callaway directly, but his younger son was given 640 acres, the usual North Carolina grant and the largest that the Transylvania Company was going to make in the future.

In the end, Daniel Boone received not a foot of all this land. When the company's claim to the whole territory was voided, his claim vanished with theirs. Later, when the proprietors were given two hundred thousand acres as compensation, no one thought of granting any of it to the man who had opened the whole country. A much later map of Boonesborough shows that both Luttrell and Hart retained valuable tracts near the fort, and that there was also a "town claim" of 640 acres, but Daniel Boone owns none of this especially valuable land.

He had explored the country alone, established the boundaries, persuaded the Indians to make the treaty, opened the Wilderness Road, tended the wounded, stood firm when things looked darkest.

But people forget. That was the trouble all his life: People forgot.

Trouble was brewing for Transylvania. Denunciations by royal governors might not count for very much in the future, but the new democratically elected governors would not prove any more friendly.

The times were confusing. The King's governors were fleeing, or had fled, on all sides. The Declaration of Independence was still some months in the future. The Colonists in the East were not quite sure whether they were merely provincial Britons fighting for traditional British rights, or whether they were founding a new republic. Settlers in the Kentucky backwoods knew still less of what was happening. It was an awkward moment for land speculators who wanted to keep their titles clear.

As yet, Kentucky was not quite sure which side of the struggle it was on. The Transylvania Company contrived to balance water on both shoulders very adroitly. They sent a memorial to the Continental Congress, then sitting at Philadelphia. The proprietors of Transylvania, they explained, could not "look with indifference on the late arbitrary proceedings of the British Parliament. If the United Colonies are reduced or will tamely submit to be slaves, Transylvania will have reason to fear." They promised "assistance to the general cause of America," and expressed a hope "that the United Colonies will take the infant Colony of Transylvania into their protection."

So far, so good. These resounding phrases established their

loyalty to the American cause, in case George Washington succeeded. But suppose he didn't?

A special paragraph provided for that regrettable contingency: "The Memorialists by no means forget their allegiance to their Sovereign, whose constitutional rights and pre-eminences they will support at the risk of their lives. They flatter themselves that the addition of a new Colony in so fair and equitable a way, and without any expense to the Crown, will be acceptable to His Most Gracious Majesty, and that Transylvania will soon be worthy of his Royal regard and protection"—even if it had been founded in direct defiance of his Royal proclamation!

At any rate, British or American, the conquest of Kentucky was under way.

7. Life at Boonesborough

THE return of Daniel Boone and his family in late August of 1775 was the real beginning of permanent settlement in Kentucky. Wandering hunters could be driven off. Land speculators and adventurers might be harassed until they gave up and fled to safety in the settlements. Many of the fainter-hearted settlers could be frightened away, families and all. But there was a grim little remnant of Boones and Callaways, Todds and Harrods, Kentons and Logans, and bearers of other names famous on the frontier who sat stubbornly down to live in that land or be buried in it.

Boone and the others who brought their wives and children and all their pitifully small worldly goods to the wilderness, had given pledges to fortune. They had ventured all they had. There was nothing in the settlements for them to go back to. They had come to make their homes on lands where they meant to end their days.

Daniel Boone brought back with him a party of such settlers, besides twenty adventurous young men from North Carolina. He brought with him also a supply of salt, as well as ammunition, cattle, and dogs. His party traveled together as far as Dick's River, south of the Kentucky. Here they separated. Some went on to Harrodsburg. The rest, thirty in all, led by Daniel Boone, struck north for Boonesborough, where they arrived early in September. In Daniel's own words, they "arrived safe without any other difficulties than such as are common to this passage." And he added proudly: "My wife and daughter being the first white women that ever stood on the banks of Kentucke river."

What Rebecca Boone must have thought as the pack-horses topped the low pass in the southern hills and she looked down for the first time upon the great meadow where Boonesborough stood, is beyond conjecture. This was the promised land. This was the country for which Daniel had left her and risked his life year after year. This was the land from which he had returned again and again, each time bubbling with enthusiasm. This was the land that Daniel and Squire and John Finley had described as an earthly paradise, in many an enthusiastic evening by a Yadkin cabin fire.

Rebecca was used to the backwoods. Never in her life had she known the comforts so dear to women, and she didn't miss them. But the frontier as she had known it was after all a frontier which still touched civilization's outer edge. The Yadkin Valley was wild and rough, to be sure, but not too many miles to the east were colonial towns with courthouses, churches, merchants, doctors, parsons—some kind of contact with civilization.

Boonesborough was wholly cut off from the outside world. To reach it, she had ridden three hundred miles through unbroken wilderness without so much as a cabin or a trace of humankind.

What she saw, at the journey's end, as the weary horses dragged slowly down the hillside, was four or five rough cabins straggling along the river where the meadow joined it. A sixth cabin, Nathaniel Hart's, stood at some distance. There were a few cornfields here and there, and the remains of the garden that Henderson had planted in the spring. Around the meadow were the forests. Across the river a wooded bluff rose menacingly, giving any casually roving Indians a clear view of the cabins.

Nor were these wretched little shelters even fortified as yet. Henderson had talked about a "fort" in his diary, but he had never managed even to get a stockade built all the way around his proposed enclosure. Settlers arriving after the Boones in September found the cabins "not picketted in being open on two sides." Any enemy who wanted to could walk right in, though the cabins themselves were strongly built and close enough together to support each other by rifle fire. The stockade remained unfinished all winter and most of the following summer, at least.

There were no comforts or conveniences of any kind. It was hardly possible even to be cleanly. At the moment there were no other women at all, and it would be a long time before many came.

For this Rebecca had left the East. This was home. Here she would rear Jemima, her last unmarried daughter. Characteristically, Daniel hurried off to the woods for a hunt, or at least laid in supplies for one, as soon as he arrived. Henderson's account books show a charge against him for half a pound of powder and twelve pounds of lead on September 8, 1775.

Squire Boone came soon after, bringing with him the Bryan family, Rebecca's relatives from the Yadkin Valley, who had shared the Boones' disaster in 1773, but who still had faith in Daniel's schemes. On September 26 came Colonel Callaway, with his family and other settlers, including a certain William Poague, who turned out to be a valuable addition to the community. He was an "ingenius contriver," able to make piggins, noggins, and churns, for which the settlement had great need. This cavalcade also brought cattle, hogs, ducks, and chickens. The Cherokees were still so friendly that a band of them, meeting Callaway's party, divided part of a buffalo with them.

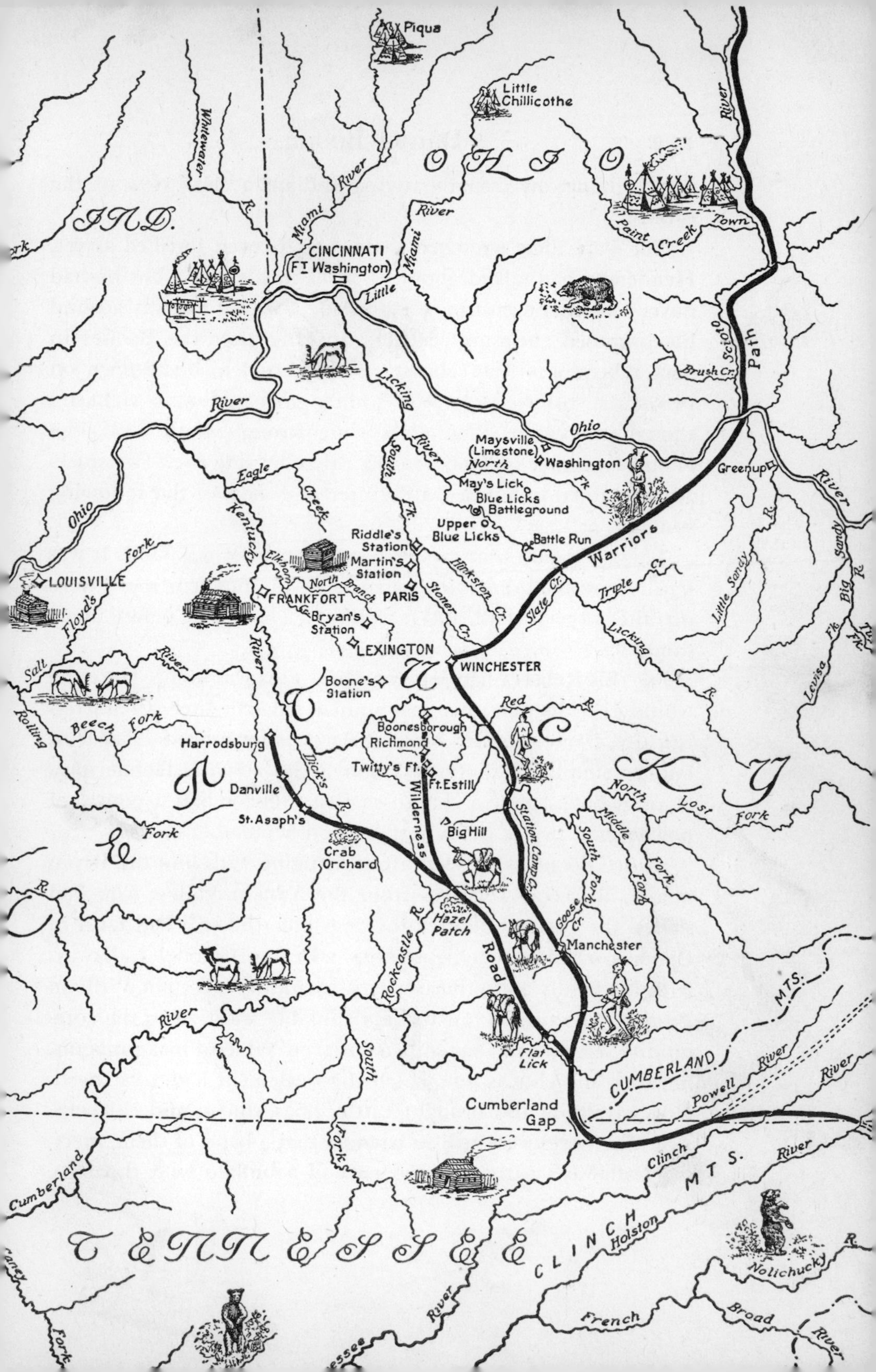

Piqua
Little Chillicothe
OHIO
IND.
Whitewater R.
Miami River
Little Miami River
CINCINNATI (FT. Washington)
Paint Creek Town
Scioto River
Brush Cr.
Path
River
Ohio
Licking River
South Fk.
Maysville (Limestone)
Washington
North Fk.
Greenup
River
May's Lick
Blue Licks Battleground
Upper Blue Licks
Battle Run
Warriors
Eagle Creek
Kentucky River
Ohio
LOUISVILLE
Floyd's Fork
Elkhorn
North Branch
Riddle's Station
Martin's Station
PARIS
FRANKFORT
Bryan's Station
LEXINGTON
Hinkston Cr.
Stoner Cr.
Slate Cr.
Triple Cr.
Little Sandy R.
Big Sandy R.
Levisa Fk.
Licking R.
WINCHESTER
Salt River
Boone's Station
Rolling Fork
Beech Fork
Harrodsburg
Danville
St. Asaph's
Dick's R.
Boonesborough
Richmond
Twitty's Ft.
Ft. Estill
Wilderness
Red R.
KENTUCKY
North Fork
Lost Fork
Middle Fork
South Fork
Station Camp Cr.
Big Hill
Crab Orchard
Fork
R.
Hazel Patch
Rockcastle R.
Goose Cr.
Manchester
Road
River
South Fork
Flat Lick
CUMBERLAND MTS.
Powell River
River
Cumberland Gap
Cumberland
Clinch
CLINCH MTS.
River
Holston
TENNESSEE
Nolichucky
R.
River
French
Broad
River
Fork

As general land agent of the Transylvania Company, Colonel John Williams, one of the proprietors, opened a land office on December 1, 1775, and there was a wild scramble for real estate. Already the danger of rival claimants to a single piece of real estate was showing itself. It was to cause Boone and other Kentuckians years of litigation and heavy losses. So intense, even in these early days, was the eagerness for land, that John Todd remarked: "I'm afraid to loose sight of my House lest some Invader takes possession."

During the next ten years Daniel Boone entered claims for well over ten thousand acres of land, while his brother Squire and other members of the family made claims almost equally lavish. At one time Daniel Boone's own land claims must have totaled something like one hundred thousand acres. Some of these were military grants with which Virginia rewarded soldiers in the colonial wars. Others were ordinary settler's claims under the land acts, fertile areas discovered on his wilderness journeys and marked off by tomahawk blazes on the trees.

The kind of writer who enjoys denigration of heroic figures, frequently endeavors to represent the whole Kentucky epic, and Daniel Boone's rôle in particular, as nothing but greedy speculation and land grabbing of heroic extent. It is certainly true that Boone wanted land and laid claim to land on a gigantic scale, as did most of the pioneers. To all these sturdy, independent souls, land that a man could call his own and walk over was the *summum bonum* of human existence. They agreed heartily with Henderson's "rapturous idea of property," and fully endorsed Colonel Callaway's opinion that "there is not any better way to make money than by land." One of their young associates, Nathan Reid, used to sit on a log in the wildest part of the primitive forest, discussing with a friend "the pleasure we should one day enjoy in the possession of boundless wealth. Spread out before us lay the finest body of land in the world, any quantity of which, with but little exertion, we could make our own."

But land was something more than a material possession, something greater than mere wealth. It was a symbol of a man's independence, something uniquely his own, carved by his own effort from the wilderness. Held captive by the Indians in Ohio, Daniel Boone was quick to note that the land there was so good as "to exceed the soil of Kentucky, if possible, and remarkably well watered." Simon Kenton, doomed to the stake by the Indians, had two thoughts in his mind, even in the midst of his peril. One was obvious: to escape the torture. The other was to own some of the "fine country"—in which at the moment he had every prospect of being burned to death. That same interest in land—good, rich land, something tangible and real—still remained to him as he lay shattered and broken in the dirt of an Indian village after having been beaten nearly to death in the gauntlet.

Freehold, land, estates a man could see and walk on, raise his crops on, use to endow the children that he got—that was what the pioneer wanted.

Daniel Boone was a poor man, the son of a poor father. He had a family to provide for; and when the land which he had risked his life to win through long and bitter years was to be had for the asking, he undoubtedly asked for some of it. His claims seem large in modern eyes. Actually, they were no larger than those of many another Kentuckian.

The settlements had agreed to warn each other instantly of any Indian "sign" discovered, and to aid each other if it came to a fight. The Cherokees to the south, who had been paid for the land, were friendly. Casual marauders were not a serious menace. Henderson, therefore, thought himself "secure against a formidable attack; and a few skulkers could only kill one or two, which would not much affect the interest of the company"

—a somewhat cold-blooded and capitalistic view of the matter.

So far, the Boonesborough settlers had had only nature to contend with. As late as June, while the Powell's Valley settlements in the east were convulsed with fear, Henderson still felt safe from Indians in his half-defended Kentucky cabins. Indians were certain to leave traces of their presence that a skilled woodsman could find, he wrote; and the skilled woodsmen with him found no such traces. In fact, one did not need to be a very expert scout. The "grass and herbage" were "so tender and luxuriant that it is almost impossible for man or dog to travel, without leaving such sign that you might, for many days, gallop a horse on the trail." The white men hunted on horseback. Any footprints, therefore, would be those of Indians. But there were no footprints. Not yet.

It was some time before stray Shawnee hunting parties observed with perturbation the presence of white men who showed every sign of making their settlements permanent. The news began to spread among the Shawnee villages north of the Ohio.

The settlers were fortunate in meeting with no attack during the warm campaigning weather which Indian war parties preferred. This was the time of the white men's greatest weakness, while the hasty cabins of the settlements were still without adequate defense and many isolated settlers were "cabining" all over the country in the blithest confidence.

The Indians did not at first realize what was happening. Not until December did word begin to go about among the wigwams north of the Ohio that the white man was in Kentucky in force. Whereupon so many scalping raids resulted that Boone later said the Indians seemed "determined to persecute us for erecting this fortification."

The attacks began just before Christmas, on December 23, 1775. Colonel Arthur Campbell, with two boys named Sanders and McQuinney, crossed the Kentucky River. They were so sure they were safe that they did not even take rifles along. The boys went on up the hill on the other side of the river. Campbell went two hundred yards upstream alone, and "took up a bottom"—that is, marked out a claim on river bottom land, which was certain to be fertile.

However safe they may have felt, keen and hostile eyes watching the fort had seen their coming. Lurking Indians were deliberately letting the unsuspecting white men walk deeper into danger. Ten minutes after they separated, there was a shot and a yell, and a cry was raised in the fort that the Indians had killed Campbell. The rescue party met him running for the landing, one shoe off and one shoe on, and learned that he had encountered "a couple of Indians," only about three hundred yards away.

When nothing further was heard of the boys, the fort became alarmed. Not only were these two in danger, but there were a dozen unsuspecting hunters scattered through the adjoining forests, engaged in the ceaseless pot-hunting on which Boonesborough depended for its food.

Daniel Boone hurried off with a party in pursuit of the Indians who had attacked Campbell, but found only two moccasin tracks. Since Boonesborough's hunters all were mounted, these had probably been made by the Indians. But the two boys had also gone out on foot and no one knew exactly where they might have wandered.

Toward nightfall the hunters began to straggle in, quite safe and entirely unaware of their danger. None of them had seen Indians and none had seen the boys. The search continued until, four days later, McQuinney was found lying scalped in a cornfield, three miles away.

Nothing was ever heard of Sanders again. Did he falter on the trail along which the Shawnees led their captives to their own country somewhere beyond the Ohio River? If so, one swift blow with a tomahawk ended everything and his scalped body was left to rot. Did he reach the Ohio country alive? Then he was either burned to death or he was adopted and grew up as an Indian, learning the lore of the forest, loving its wild life, and forgetting white man's ways. Many a white lad disappeared like that into the deep forest forever.

Next day fifteen rangers went out to scour the country thoroughly, urged on by an offer of five pounds for every Indian scalp they brought in. They picked up the "tracts" of six or seven Indians thirty or forty miles north of Boonesborough and heading toward Ohio. Then, quaintly says John Williams, the land agent, "we began to doubt there was a body of Indians about, who intended committing outrage on our inhabitants."

The raiders seem to have been a small group who had set out from the Shawnee country "to take a look at the white people on Kentucky" just before the treaty at Fort Pitt between the American commissioners and the chiefs of the western tribes. "King" Cornstalk, the Shawnee chief, when signing the treaty in October, had warned the American commissioners that this party from his tribe was out on the warpath and added that until they returned he could not be responsible for their conduct. He had, of course, no exact idea where they were and no way of reaching them. He added "that they might do some mischief, and that if any of them should get killed by the whites he should take no notice at all of it."

At worst, this had been a solitary raid. Daniel Boone was famous for absolute calm under all conditions. He and his veterans had seen Indian raids before and were not much disturbed. But the killing was enough to stir up a panic among the less experienced settlers, nervous in their isolation. Who knew how many other Indians might be lurking in the forests, or who would be the next to die? Kentuckians did not yet feel so sure of their own prowess as they felt a few years later when the war whoop was a familiar sound; when scalping raids were a familiar part of life's routine; when they had beaten off overwhelming Indian forces again and again.

Ammunition was already running low. Even for hunting, the powder supply would hardly last beyond March. If the Indians attacked in force, Boonesborough could not hold out. Actually, conclusion of the treaty with Cornstalk at Fort Pitt had for a time removed the danger; but no one in Kentucky knew of the treaty yet, and no one anywhere knew how far an Indian treaty could be relied on.

Settlers began to flee to safety in the settlements. There had been nine hundred land entries, laying claim to 560,000 acres. Five hundred people had come into Kentucky; but soon a scant two hundred were left. Only twelve women—including, needless to say, the dauntless Boone and Callaway wives and daughters—stayed with their men.

The settlers who remained were torn with dissension. Henderson and his friends had raised the price of land and claimed seventy thousand choice acres at the Falls of the Ohio, very nearly the best in the state. Early in 1776 Daniel and Squire Boone went with a party of hunters and surveyors to lay out Henderson's own holding there.

Many settlers resented such wholesale preëmption by the proprietors, for everyone was well aware of the future value of this site, which is today the city of Louisville. In December of 1775 or May of 1776, a remonstrance was presented to the Virginia Convention from "the inhabitants, and some of the intended settlers of that part of North America, now denominated Transylvania." The names of Daniel and Squire Boone and of Richard Callaway were conspicuously absent. They had been among "the few adventurers who went to see the country last summer [1775], overawed by the presence of Mr. Henderson."

The petitioners, "anxious to concur in every respect with

our brethren of the united colonies," doubted the validity of Henderson's original title to Cherokee land. If they were right, every land title in Kentucky was worthless and had been worthless from the start. The petitioning settlers further viewed with alarm "the late conduct of those gentlemen in advancing the price of the purchase money from twenty shillings to fifty shillings sterling, per hundred acres." Bad as those extortionate terms might be, there was worse: "they plainly evince their intentions of rising in their demands as the settlers increase, or their insatiable avarice shall dictate."

Some practical and politically minded gentlemen at Harrodsburg sent in another petition, asking that Kentucky be made part of Virginia. They also hinted delicately "how impolitical it would be to Suffer such a Respectable Body of Prime Rifle Men to remain in a state of Neutrality" merely for the sake of "a Certain Set of men from North Carolina stiling 'emselves Proprietors."

All Harrodsburg indignantly entered into an agreement to apply for no more land grants until the earlier and cheaper terms were restored. In May, 1776, as the dispute grew bitter, John Floyd wrote hysterically that "the Harrodsburg Men have made a second revolt & Harrod & Jack Jones at the head of the Banditti—God knows how it may end but things at this time bear but a dull aspect—they utterly refuse to have any Land Surveyed or comply with one of the office rules."

Henderson and Company met the rising tide of doubt as to validity of their Cherokee title by agreeing not to ask any money for lands already occupied, until September, 1776. By that time, they hoped, the matter would be legally decided in their favor. But they did issue a proclamation warning new settlers off disputed lands, and they brought pressure to bear both upon the Virginia Convention and on the Continental Congress. One, or perhaps both, they hoped, would support the Company.

Instead, the Virginia Convention adopted a resolution condemning all land purchases from the Indians without state authority, while Congress remained wholly unresponsive.

It was the beginning of the end for Henderson. The only authority he could now hope to claim would have to come from the home government in London. At best, that authority was doubtful, and if America became independent it would be wholly impotent. The Transylvania Legislature—which had begun with such a flourish when Henderson reached Boonesborough in 1775, and which was to have assembled again in 1776—never held another meeting.

So far as the settlers themselves were concerned, these legal problems could be peacefully adjusted sooner or later, but the Indian danger could not. The new American government was working with all its might to keep the Indians quiet, but British emissaries were equally diligent. The Indians themselves were slow in taking sides. It was rather pleasant to keep the white men pleading.

The Delawares on the Wabash soon sent word to their brothers the Long Knives at Harrodsburg that the British and Kickapoos were holding a council. Delaware chiefs would attend to learn their plans. "If their Brothers of the Long Knife * would send a man they could rely on, they would on their Return inform 'em of the same & they were Apprehensive the Kiccapoos would strike their brothers ye Long Knife."

James Harrod, who could take a hint, went off to see the Delawares at once "to converse with 'em on ye same." It was not long before these same friendly Delawares were fighting with the British.

Perhaps the Kentuckians, too, might at this stage have joined

* The Indians very early began to call the Virginians "Long Knives" or "Big Knives," and the name was eventually applied to all Americans. Though it is commonly supposed to be derived from the cavalry saber, it is more probably derived from the big hunting knives carried by the early woodsmen.

the British side in the Revolution. The British later hoped to win them over, and very nearly did so. After all, Washington and the rest were in illegal revolt against constituted authority. But the Indian danger was imminent, deadly, and obvious; and the British made the fatal mistake of trying to terrorize Kentuckians. They helped the Indians in their effort to frighten the Long Knives away.

For a time the British and the Indians succeeded in producing an almost hopeless situation. In July of 1776 Colonel William Russell, Daniel Boone's associate in the ill-fated expedition of 1773, was advising the complete abandonment of the Kentucky settlements. Cut off from the other settlements by hundreds of miles of Indian-haunted forests, Kentucky seemed unable to defend itself; and it was nearly impossible either to reënforce settlers living at such a distance or to supply them with munitions.

8. Three Kidnapped Daughters

IN spite of all the talk about Indian wars and in spite of the December murders, Boonesborough had begun to feel fairly secure again in the early summer of 1776. Farther to the north, a few settlers had been killed, but Daniel and Squire Boone had come home from their surveying at the Falls of the Ohio without hint of danger. Daniel himself lived in an unfortified cabin by the river, and it is said that a few other settlers had even built cabins on the other side.

Everything seemed so safe that on Sunday, July 7, after the usual Bible reading, a party of three young girls went for a paddle on the river. Jemima Boone was suffering from a "cane stab" in the foot. It was not an infrequent injury, since the stubble of broken cane was sharp, and young girls and even grown women rarely wore shoes in the summertime. Jemima wanted to soak the wound in the cool water of the river, and Betsey and Fanny Callaway went with her to paddle.

These three were the belles of Boonesborough. Betsey, sixteen, was engaged to marry Samuel Henderson. Jemima and Fanny, though only fourteen, already had serious suitors eager to marry them. Daniel Boone was at the moment enacting the rôle of stern parent, opposing the marriage of so young a girl to Flanders Callaway, a nephew of Colonel Callaway.

A great many youngsters clamored to go along on the boat ride; but young ladies with suitors felt much too grown up to bother with small-fry. With the ineffable dignity of adolescence, they left the smaller girls weeping on the bank and set off. They had been willing enough to take Nathan Reid, a dashing young man lately arrived from Virginia; but at the last moment Nathan was too busy.

Daniel Boone himself is said to have seen them on their way and then to have strolled off on one of his solitary rambles. If that is so, he did not go far, for it is quite certain that he was soon back in the cabin with his moccasins off, taking a quiet Sunday afternoon nap.

The two Callaway girls paddled about safely enough, with Jemima Boone steering and dangling her bare foot in the river. The current carried them slowly downstream until they were about a quarter of a mile below the fort, and then drew them toward a steep cliff on the other side of the river. One of the Callaway girls suggested going ashore to gather flowers on the bank opposite the settlement; but when Jemima Boone remarked laughingly that she was afraid of "the Yellow Boys," they prepared to turn back.

Not being very skillful or very strong, they had trouble with the canoe and, according to some stories, got stuck on a sandbar. Struggle as they might, they could not control the canoe, and "it would go to the other shore despite of their hearts."

The cane came down so close to the water's edge here that its branches hung over into the river. It was an ideal hiding place for five warriors, who had been watching the fort and who, observing the girls' struggles, had quietly waited to see if they might not drift within reach.

The band included some Shawnees, who seem to have met the Cherokee chief, Hanging Maw, in the forest. He had come north along the Warriors' Path to stir up the northern tribes against the white men who were encroaching on the common hunting grounds. Apparently they had come down to reconnoiter Boonesborough, more or less under Hanging Maw's leadership, before going back to Ohio to hold a council and discuss plans for attacking it. There was no war as yet and no special reason for taking prisoners. The tribes had not formally cast their lot with the British. But no Indian was going to neglect a chance like this.

As they silently waited, the boat drifted nearer and nearer. The girls' futile struggles with the paddles only brought it closer. When they had drifted into shallow water a few yards from shore, the Indians pounced on them. One ran waist-deep into the water and, seizing the canoe by the "buffalo tug" at its prow, tried to haul the craft to shore. Little Fanny Callaway, the smallest of the three, whacked him over the head with the paddle until it broke. Betsey, too, struck out with her paddle as hard as she could, until the other Indians made signs that they would upset the canoe unless they stopped.

The little white squaws were then easily overpowered, dragged through the shallow water to shore, and then, under cover of a densely wooded ravine, rushed to the hills which edge that side of the river. Their screams were instantly silenced by the threatening flourish of knives and tomahawks. One warrior seized Betsey Callaway by the hair and threatened to scalp her if she made another sound. After that, the mute threat of the tomahawks was enough to keep them quiet.

When the Indians reached the hilltop, Jemima Boone, who was not Daniel Boone's daughter for nothing, announced that she would not go another step. They could kill her if they wanted to, but her bare and wounded foot was a good deal worse than death. The Indians at first threatened, but the fourteen-year-old girl was stubborn. Refractory prisoners were casually tomahawked in most cases; but the American Indian has a gentle way with children, always, and these girls were little more than children. Besides, Hanging Maw when not upon the warpath was a kindly soul, indulgently inclined. Bowing to the inevitable, he and his braves provided moccasins for Jemima and for Fanny Callaway, both of whom were barefoot. Then they cut off the long skirts of all three at the knees, so that they could travel more easily, and let them make wrapped leggings out of the scraps as protection against the underbrush and brambles through which they would have to go.

Recognizing Hanging Maw, whom she had seen at her father's cabin, probably in the Watauga country, Jemima Boone told him who she was. The chief, who spoke excellent English, asked if the other two were her sisters.

"Yes," lied adroit little Jemima, hoping they would get better treatment if the Indians thought they were all daughters of Daniel Boone. Acquaintance with the Shawnee brave, Big Jim, had not saved her brother from death by torture three years before, but Hanging Maw was a less sinister individual. In any case, women were rarely tortured.

The Cherokee chief was mildly amused. Rare was the Cherokee who got the better of the white hunter, "Wide Mouth."

"We have done pretty well for old Boone this time," said he, laughing.

The wily savages as usual divided their party going through canebrakes, so that the trail would be hard to follow. They forced their captives to do the same thing, and even to walk down little streams to hide the trail completely. Where possible, the Indians traveled on the barren tops of ridges, where they left less "sign" than in the lush vegetation of the lowlands.

The Indians treated the girl captives well enough, vastly better than an ordinary group of white soldiers would have treated them. They shared the hard, dry, smoked buffalo-tongue which was their only ration, chatted freely, and explained that they were on their way to the Shawnee towns. They called their captives "pretty squaws," but—true to the honorable Shawnee tradition—made no attempt to offer familiarity.

The war party camped that night not far from the present city of Winchester, Kentucky, after covering some ten or twelve miles. Each girl was then pinioned for the night with thongs at the elbows and set against a tree, since it was impossible to lie down when bound in this way. One end of the thong was tied to the tree and the other held by a sleeping Indian. The three were placed far enough apart so that they could not reach each other, while the Indians sprawled on the ground in a circle around them. Jemima Boone, who had a penknife in her pocket, tried to reach it and cut herself and the others loose while the Indians slept, but it was no use. All night long they sat there, each girl lashed to her tree, wondering what the morning would bring.

As soon as it was light, Hanging Maw started his band off northward as fast as he could, the girls still full of confidence they would be rescued—a confidence that dwindled as the day passed with no sign that rescuers had found the trail.

By leaving as much evidence of their passing as they could, the quick-witted daughters of the pioneers aided the pursuit which they knew would do its best to follow them. Betsey Callaway, the only one with shoes, managed to dig her high wooden heels into any damp earth, and especially into the mud at buffalo wallows, as plain evidence that a white woman had passed that way. They managed to lag behind the Indians whenever possible and contrived to break a good many twigs. When the warriors asked suspiciously what they were doing, the girls replied innocently that they were tired and were helping themselves along by grasping the bushes. The explanation was not a conspicuous success, but in spite of the Indians' vigilance they broke enough twigs to leave marks on their hands.

"I saw the blisters on the little fingers where the bushes

pinched them," a somewhat sentimental Boonesborough youth afterward reported.

Once the Indians detected Betsey Callaway in the act of breaking a twig. They threatened her with their tomahawks, but they never noticed that she was slyly tearing off bits of her clothing and dropping them on the trail. One fragment of her white linen handkerchief even had the name "Callaway" marked on it. Eventually, the Indians knocked the wooden heels off her shoes to keep her from leaving marks, but the dauntless little sixteen-year-old continued to leave the imprint of her shoe-sole.

Jemima Boone made her sore foot the excuse for frequent falls, accompanied by loud screams intended for any white ears that might be listening in the forest. The Indians hushed her by waving their knives and tomahawks, but it was not long before the girl prisoners found another way of disturbing their captors. Encountering a stray pony in the woods, the Indians put Jemima Boone on it, hoping to hurry up their march. Sometimes the other two also rode.

Children of the frontier, these young girls knew all about horses. They did what they could to make the pony troublesome and then tumbled off at every possible excuse. Laughing heartily, the warriors would pick them up and put them back. When they continued to fall off, the joke rather wore out. An Indian mounted and gravely tried to teach them to ride. It was no use. They fell off almost as frequently as before.

They were, of course, taking desperate chances when they annoyed the Indians in this way. If the good-natured Hanging Maw had not been the most tolerant Cherokee ever heard of, the three of them would have been tomahawked a dozen times over. Except for bruises, however, no one was hurt except Betsey Callaway, who was justifiably bitten by the outraged pony. Finally the harassed Indians decided that since the pretty squaws were still falling off the pony nearly as fast as they could be put back, the party would make better time without a mount. They turned their horse loose again and went ahead with their captives on foot.

The Indian kidnappers had been so quick and clever that, according to one story, the girls were not even missed until milking time. Then a hunter, probably one of their suitors, who had gone out to meet them, gave the alarm. According to other stories, their screams were heard at once, but they were too far down the river for help to reach them, as they had taken the only boat.

There was intense excitement in Boonesborough. Daniel Boone leaped from the bed in his cabin, seized his rifle, and raced for the river bank, without even waiting for his moccasins. No one had ever seen him betray so much agitation. It was hours before he even missed his footgear, and even then only when a friend reminded him. Samuel Henderson, Betsey Callaway's betrothed, who was shaving at the moment, doubtless with an eye to his fiancée's return, had rushed out rifle in hand with one half of his face shaven and the other still bristling. He never had a chance to even up his countenance until the girls were safely back, three days later.

Efforts at rescue were delayed at the very start, because the Indians had been careful to set Boonesborough's only canoe adrift, and the riflemen had no way of getting across the Kentucky River without wetting their powder. The intrepid John Gass had to swim over for the canoe, expecting invisible Indians to begin sniping at him from the bushes at any moment. No one had any idea how strong the raiding band were nor where they were. While Gass swam, the rest of the Kentuckians lined the bank and covered the other shore with their rifles. But there was no need of precaution. The Indians had long since gone.

When Gass towed the canoe back, Boone took five men over

the river and examined the other shore. A mounted party had already ridden downstream, crossed by the ford, and were working upstream from there. Boone divided his men so as to find the trail as soon as possible. With John Gass and Samuel Henderson, he himself started downstream toward the horsemen. John Floyd led another party upstream. As Boone, finding no tracks, was turning back, Colonel Callaway rode up with his mounted party. It was John Floyd and his men who actually picked up the Indians' trail.

Callaway wanted to ride straight after them, feeling sure that his mounted men could ride them down easily enough. He was probably right. But Daniel Boone pointed out that the Indians would certainly keep one warrior traveling well in their rear to give the alarm if the pursuit got close. He would hear the approach of horsemen and the Indians would instantly tomahawk their prisoners to prevent recapture. This actually did happen to another woman prisoner in that very year. They agreed that Callaway should disregard the trail entirely and ride off at full speed for the ford across Licking River, where he would lie in ambush. Meantime, Boone's party would follow the Indians' trail, or its general direction, with the utmost caution.

It was now so late that there was little hope of following more than a few miles. Floyd's men went as far as they could, and Boone soon overtook them. As they consulted, a dog began barking in the woods. Slipping silently toward the sound, they came upon nine strange white men building a cabin. The Indians had passed without molesting them and apparently without even noticing their presence. Boone and his party halted here for the night, ready to start early Monday morning.

They had rushed after the Indians so hastily that they were still wearing their long, Sunday-go-to-meeting pantaloons, precious garments reserved strictly for the Sabbath and exceedingly awkward for wilderness travel. Worse still, they had no food, and it began to look as if there would be a long chase. John Gass, the man who swam the river for the canoe, made his way back to Boonesborough in the black night of the forest and returned before morning with breech-clouts, leggings, hunting shirts, and more ammunition, as well as a supply of jerked venison, which was the only provender the housewives of Boonesborough could supply. He also brought moccasins for Daniel Boone, who had been dashing about the woods in his bare feet for hours and by this time needed them badly.

Three of the cabin-builders now joined the pursuit, and they pushed on as soon as there was daylight enough to see the trail. For a time it was easy to follow, and they even noted the exact spot where the Indians had camped. Beyond their camp, however, the warriors had slipped by separate paths through the thickest canebrake they could find. The trail had simply vanished.

Boone soon gave up the attempt to find it again. He knew that every minute counted and he felt sure that the Indians were making for the Shawnee camps on the Scioto. Remarking that it was no use to follow the trail very closely, anyway, until the Indians had gone farther and become less cautious, he led his men swiftly and silently for thirty miles northward along the general route the kidnappers were taking, and then turned at right angles until he crossed the trail itself. Boone and his men knew they were going in the right direction. Even though they were not trying to follow the Indian trail, they frequently crossed it and recognized the "sign" the girls had left. Betsey Callaway's lover could look down in the mud and see her footprints. The suitors of the other two girls could catch similar "sign" that their intended wives had passed that way, en route to become slaves and concubines in some smoky wigwam in a squalid village forever.

After resting for the night when there was no more hope of following the trail, the pursuers were up and away at dawn. Knowing the country of old, Daniel Boone remarked that he was sure the Indians would cross a stream which they were then approaching, only a short distance ahead. They found the crossing within two hundred yards. The moccasin prints were still fresh, the water still muddy. Boone had been right again!

Since the Indians had now covered thirty-five miles without any sign of white pursuers, Boone believed they would be less cautious. It was time now to stick doggedly to their trail. The band still made some effort to evade pursuit, for though they followed the Warriors' Path most of the time, they broke off every now and then for a little while into one of the numerous buffalo traces running parallel with it.

Their precaution was useless. Boone was by this time too close to be shaken off. In a little while his party passed the freshly slaughtered carcass of a buffalo from which only the hump had been cut. It was so fresh that blood was still oozing. Again Daniel ventured a prophecy: The Indians, he said, would halt and cook at the next water. Again Daniel was right. The Indians did exactly what he had expected.

Moving silently ahead, Boone's men came on a small snake the Indians had paused to kill. It was still wriggling. Ten miles farther on the white men came to a small stream. The trail did not cross. Instead, it disappeared entirely. There was no "sign" of any kind on the other bank. This meant that the Indians had taken the precaution of wading down the stream for a while to break the trail before halting. Their trail did not go on. They must be very near. They were probably within earshot.

It was about noon. Boone was sure the raiders were concealed somewhere near at hand cooking a meal. For the third time he was right.

Now came the ticklish part of the rescue. As they went along,

Boone and his men had discussed the danger that he had already pointed out to Callaway. The prisoners might be tomahawked the moment the Indians saw the rescuers. The Boonesborough men made ready for quick action at the finish. In the lightest whisper, Daniel Boone gave his orders. They must exercise the utmost caution. They must approach in dead silence. When they came up with the Indians, no one was to fire until he got Boone's signal. The surest way to save the captives was to pour in a sudden volley and then charge into the camp.

The party divided. Samuel Henderson and one group went downstream. Daniel Boone and another group went upstream. Within two or three hundred yards, they found the Indians, "up a little creek that puts into Licking [River] just above Parker's Ferry," not far from the Blue Licks.

The raiders believed that they had by this time distanced any possible pursuit. Even the prisoners had begun to agree with them and had nearly given up hope of rescue. Actually, however, the pursuit had been much swifter than the Indians dreamed. While Boone's men were closing in from the south, Colonel Callaway's band were already lying in wait, some miles ahead to the north. The Indians could not escape unpunished. Saving the girls was the real problem.

As Boone's men crept up to the outskirts of the camp, the warriors had just kindled a fire and were getting ready to cook. Betsey Callaway sat leaning against a tree. The two younger girls lay with their heads in her lap. Only one Indian—the guard lounging near the girls—had his rifle with him.

The other Indians were all busy. One was gathering wood. One was forcing a spit through the buffalo hump to get it ready for cooking. Hanging Maw had gone to the stream to fill the kettle. They had posted a sentry on a small mound in the rear, exactly as Daniel Boone had predicted; but the brave had just strolled down to the fire to light his pipe and get materials for mending his moccasins. He had left his rifle behind him. The unhappy warrior had chosen the worst possible moment to do it, for within a few seconds John Floyd's rifle was drawing a bead on him from the underbrush.

The leading white man was within thirty yards of the Indians before he saw them. He turned silently to wave the others on. As he did so, the Indians caught sight of him. The two sides had seen each other at almost the same moment, but only Boone's men were armed and ready. Seeing that Boone's plan for surprising the Indians with a sudden volley was now impossible, the leading rifleman fired instantly, hoping to drive the Indians away from the girls. Boone and Floyd fired also, and one other man got a shot in before the Indians vanished. Floyd's shot knocked the sentry sprawling into the fire; but Indians build small fires and he was not too badly hurt to reach the canebrake.

Fanny Callaway was idly watching the warrior who was putting the buffalo meat on the broiling stick. There was not a sound in the woods around her. Suddenly, she saw blood burst from a shot wound in the Indian's breast, and then heard a sudden sputter of shots.

"That's Daddy," cried Jemima Boone, as the rifles crackled.

"Run, gals, run!" yelled the rescuers.

The three girls jumped up, screaming with joy. One Indian paused in his sprint for the canebrake to throw a tomahawk which just missed Betsey Callaway's head, and it is said that the others threw knives. Seeing what might happen, Daniel Boone roared an order to the girls:

"Fall down!"

They threw themselves on the ground obediently, but were too agitated to stay there, and bounced up as the white men rushed yelling into the camp.

It was an exciting few minutes. Betsey Callaway was nearly brained by one of the rescue party who took her for an Indian.

He saw a very dark brunette, wearing a red bandanna, short skirts, and leggings, rise from the ground as he charged. He was just bringing the butt of his rifle down on the girl's head when Boone caught his arm.

"For God's sake, don't kill her," he panted, "when we have traveled so far to save her from death."

Boone and Floyd felt sure their shots had gone home, but the canebrake was too thick around them for certainty. There was a hasty crashing and rustling in it as the Indians fled. Then silence. All of the kidnapping warriors were gone. Some were without moccasins, knives, or tomahawks. The only firearm they had saved was one small shotgun. It was practically impossible to find an Indian in a canebrake, and the white men let them go. In any case, says Floyd, "being so much elated on recovering the three poor little heart-broken girls, we were prevented from making further search."

Boone and Floyd were almost certainly right about the Indians they shot. There was blood on the ground where each target had been, and two of the band did die of wounds. One of them, says legend, was the son of Chief Blackfish of the Shawnees. But at least one of the others certainly got back to Shawnee country alive, and Hanging Maw returned to the Cherokee villages, where he lived to a ripe old age. After his death, a startled Congress received a petition asking for a pension for his squaw! Ironically enough, Hanging Maw had in the meantime achieved a reputation as the white man's friend.

At the American post of Fort Randolph, far to the northeast, Captain Matthew Arbuckle heard that three girls had been kidnapped. He sent a stern message to the Shawnees demanding their return. Since the tribe was still formally at peace with the Big Knives, a Shawnee chief, brother of Cornstalk, the head chief himself, returned with the American messenger. He gave assurance that the girls had already been retaken, and made false promises of peace for the future.

Years afterward an old pioneer wrote out an account of the fight which is a fair sample of many contemporary versions: "the seckond day just before night, Boon arrived in sight of the smoke ascending from the fire where the Indians had taken up camp. he vary cautiously creeped up within gun shot of the camp without being seen by the Indians. they were busy cooking, the girls were laying down. Boon and his men fired on the Indians at the same time and rushed on to the camp hooping and hallowing, the Indians were so much frightened that they immediately fled."

The girls described the Indian marauders as Shawnees and Cherokees. All spoke good English and said they were taking their prisoners "to the Shawnee towns" in Ohio. Floyd thought a captured war club was of Shawnee make, and the girls remembered a few native words which some amateur philologist identified as Shawnee.

The victors paused to examine the battleground.

"At yonder bush," said Daniel Boone, pointing, "I fired at an Indian."

Some of the men went over to look and found a rifle and some blood. There was more blood by the camp fire, where Floyd had also hit his man. The Kentuckians found two small shotguns which they smashed as worthless, but they were well on their homeward way before the girls remembered that the Indian sentry had left his rifle on his knoll. Nobody wanted to go back for it, and it was left to rust.

Since the kidnappers had told their prisoners that there was an Indian band at the Blue Licks and another on the Kentucky River, it was desirable to get back to Boonesborough as soon as possible. But everyone was exhausted, the girls by the discomfort of two nights tied up to trees and the speed with which the Indians had forced them along; the rescuers by the even greater speed with which they had followed. Boone therefore made camp for the night after covering a relatively short distance.

Next day, entirely unmolested, they set out for home. Encountering the stray pony again, they stopped to catch it, and the girls who had pretended to so much trouble in staying on its back rode home to Boonesborough with no difficulty at all. There was a good deal of jesting at Samuel Henderson's expense. With several days' growth of beard on one side of his face and three days' growth on the other, he was by no means a romantic object. But Betsey Callaway didn't mind—she married him within a month.

Just as they reached the hill along the river opposite the fort, not far from the place where the three girls had originally been kidnapped, Colonel Callaway's mounted band rode up. After watching the Licking River ford and finding nothing but the tracks of one retreating Indian, they had correctly decided that the girls must have been rescued by Boone's men, and had ridden home.

It all ended happily. The cane stab in Jemima Boone's foot, the original cause of the fatal canoe ride, had miraculously healed during her captivity. The Indian band at the Blue Licks which Hanging Maw had mentioned never appeared. The other band along the Kentucky River did little damage. Boonesborough gave itself up to rejoicing.

The anxious fiancés of the rescuing party made sure of their brides by getting married as soon as they could. Betsey Callaway had been kidnapped on July 7. She was married to Samuel Henderson on August 6. The bride's wedding finery was nothing but a dress of Irish linen. The bridegroom, having ruined his hunting shirt saving his bride from the Indians, had to borrow one to be married in. There was no magistrate, and

Squire Boone, as a lay preacher, officiated at the first wedding in Kentucky.

Old Colonel Callaway had his doubts about it all. There was no way to get a marriage license, the courthouse being several hundred miles distant. But he could not quite bring himself to divide lovers who could always argue that the Indians might catch the bride again. He had Henderson to thank in part for the fact that Betsey was not already the compulsory bride of some redskin in Chillicothe. He gave his consent, but only after young Henderson gave bond to have another ceremony performed by less doubtful authority as soon as possible. The dutiful couple complied with his wishes.

The other two girls, being only fourteen, were married to their admirers the following year, Jemima Boone to Flanders Callaway; Fanny Callaway to John Holder. Both bridegrooms had assisted in the rescue. Daniel Boone had had his own doubts about Jemima's suitor, but he withdrew them all after the share Flanders Callaway had taken in the pursuit of Hanging Maw. That worthy chief, quite unintentionally, had helped the course of true love on its way.

The kidnapping of the girls made a tremendous sensation on the frontier and even in the eastern settlements. "Shortly after the affair happened it was noised about on the frontier settlement and all the settlers were extolling Boon to the vary skies for the prowess and bravery he displayed." Contemporary letters frequently mention the episode, and James Fenimore Cooper based an episode in *The Last of the Mohicans* upon it. Indeed, his famous character Leatherstocking bears a suspicious resemblance to Daniel Boone at all times.

Hardly had Boonesborough settled down to the routine of everyday frontier life once more, when startling news arrived from the East. The Colonies had declared their independence. America was a nation and Kentucky was part of it. A traveler brought with him a copy of the *Virginia Gazette*. The Declaration of Independence was read aloud from its pages, cheered, and celebrated with a bonfire. Soon there was a new flag fluttering in the forest.

9. "Year of the Three Sevens"

THE kidnapping was the most spectacular, but not the only, evidence that Kentucky's Indian troubles had fairly begun. It was not long before several hunters failed to return. The cabin of David and Nathaniel Hart was burned, and five hundred apple-tree scions, which had been carried through the forests from Virginia, were ruined by raiding Cherokees. Two men were killed near Licking River.

Worse still, ammunition was beginning to run low. The Transylvania Company had previously supplied it, but the Company's days were obviously numbered, and the new state government of Virginia had little ammunition to spare. The Chiswell lead mines in Virginia were working furiously, but Washington's army used up most of the powder and shot that could be produced.

Even before the girls were kidnapped, George Rogers Clark and John Gabriel Jones set off from Harrodsburg to Virginia, determined to persuade the state government to supply powder and lead for defense and do something about the land-title question. They had a desperate trip, taking turns on the only horse fit to ride, both of them suffering from "scald feet," while every now and then they could hear somewhere in the woods shots which could only come from Indian hunters. Not once did they hear the sound of a white man's rifle which, with its heavier charge, had an easily distinguishable report. They found

Powell's Valley settlements partly burned and Martin's Station abandoned. At length they met a party of white travelers, who mistook them for Indians and made ready to attack, but, discovering the mistake in time, helped them on their way.

The Virginia officials, having a first-class war on their hands, were dilatory. But Clark was a blunt and emphatic person. He told the Virginians that a land worth having was also worth defending, and he got his powder—five hundred pounds of it. Meantime, on September 7, 1776, Colonel Arthur Campbell sent a little ammunition overland from the Holston Valley for Daniel Boone to distribute. He sold it to the people, charging six shillings for powder and ten pence a pound for lead. One pound of powder was reserved for official use by scouts.

The Virginia militia sent the five-hundred-pound consignment to Pittsburg and Clark took it down the Indian-haunted Ohio River. Finding the Indians too close for comfort, he hid the ammunition on islands in several different places near Limestone (modern Maysville, Kentucky). Then, taking his boat a little way down the river, he and Jones set it adrift and started overland to get pack-horses.

Clark went on to Harrodsburg, while Jones and a party of ten men went back for the ammunition, were ambushed by the Mohawk chief Pluggy on Christmas Day, and lost several men. But the Indians did not find the powder on which the safety of the settlers depended.

Four days later (December 29, 1776), Chief Pluggy and his band attacked McClelland's Station, which stood them off, being at the moment the best-fortified post in Kentucky. The chief was killed. His warriors hung about for two days, then started north to their villages.

Simon Kenton and an equally adventurous friend trailed the band lately led by Pluggy, deceased, to the vicinity of Limestone, where they found the place at which the Indians had crossed.

Hardly more than a boy, Kenton was already one of the most daring and skillful of wilderness scouts and hunters. According to a legend long current in Kentucky, he and Boone once approached a wilderness ford from opposite directions. Each discovered the other's presence at the same moment. Neither recognized the other for a white man. They maneuvered for shots all day long, with such consummate use of cover that neither was able to recognize his friend until the end of the day. True or false, the legend shows the high opinion Kentucky's connoisseurs of woodsmanship held of each man's skill.

Relying on his adroitness and knowing where Clark had hidden his powder, Kenton lingered long enough in this dangerous country to make sure the store of ammunition was safe and then hurried home with the news. A force of thirty men went out and brought it in. They wished to return by a short cut along the Warriors' Path, but Kenton, always cautious when there was no need for desperate chances, warned them not to try. The powder was too valuable to risk. They took the longer way back in safety.

Though they had been victorious and though the Indians were plainly gone, the settlers of McClelland's Station knew well enough the redskins would soon be back. Deciding that their station was too exposed, they withdrew while they were still safe, and took refuge in Boonesborough on New Year's Day, 1777. Their despair was an appropriate beginning to the desperate and bloody year which was remembered ever after as "the year of the three sevens." It was only a little while before the settlers at Hinkston's Station (later called Riddle's, or Ruddle's, Station) also gave up the struggle.

The discouragement of these people proved contagious, and when they set out for the East, ten Boonesborough men decided the risks in Kentucky were too great and went with them. This reduced the strength of the little fort to thirty riflemen. Seven stations were abandoned within a short time and two or three hundred people left for the settlements. Boonesborough, Harrodsburg, and Logan's Station (St. Asaph's) were now the only settlements on the Kentucky frontier.

The abandonment of the weaker settlements had its bright side, however. It concentrated the settlers in three strong forts instead of leaving them scattered in a great many weak ones. And the departure of the more timid pioneers left behind an iron breed that would not be defeated.

"I want to return as much as any person can do," wrote John Floyd, "but if I leave the country now, there is scarcely a single man who will not follow the example. When I think of the deplorable condition a few helpless families are likely to be in, I conclude to sell my life as dearly as I can in self defence, rather than make an ignominious escape."

There would soon be need of this gallant spirit. Raids like Hanging Maw's were somewhat unofficial—just aboriginal high spirits. Pluggy's raid had been more serious, but his band was too weak to do much harm. The other attacks had been nothing but casual raids for scalps and plunder. But the Shawnees and other northern Indians had now gone over to the British side. Armed and equipped from royal arsenals, aided by royal officers, they would soon be ready to take the warpath in force.

Kentucky was now organized as a single large county of Virginia. Following the British model, it had a county lieutenant as civil head and was defended by an organized county militia. John Bowman became the first official Kentucky Colonel, though Daniel Boone had previously held this title, apparently by Henderson's authority. One of the two majors in the new militia was George Rogers Clark, soon to become the military hero of the West. Daniel Boone, James Harrod, John Todd, and Benjamin Logan were captains. Hitherto, each settlement had had a chief of its own selection. Now these same leaders were to hold commissions by state authority. These were the men who bore the brunt of the savage Indian fighting of the next few years, compared to which the earlier Indian fights seemed insignificant.

Kentucky was developing a military organization none too soon. Captain Daniel Boone had hardly been commissioned when more Indians began to arrive. By early March the first really strong war party was lurking in the vicinity of Boonesborough, watching the white men and biding its time.

There had been wrath among the wigwams when Pluggy's disconsolate warriors returned with news of their chief's death. The White Peril was getting serious. Mkahday-wah-may-quah, or Blackfish, war chief of the Shawnees, now took the warpath in earnest, with a couple of hundred men, intent on wiping out all these Kentucky settlements at a blow before they were large enough to be dangerous.

The warriors reached the deserted settlements just as Simon Kenton and a few others set out from Harrodsburg to get some flax and hemp that had been left behind. One man, riding ahead, saw Indians moving among the empty cabins and turned back to give warning to the rest. But he was not quite quick enough. The Indians had seen him, too, and the white men had to ride for their lives.

Kenton had been ordered to take part of the flax to Boonesborough, but that was now impossible. As his men slipped back through the woods he saw so many signs of a large war party that he sent the others to Harrodsburg to help defend it, and himself rushed off to warn Daniel Boone. Kenton reached Boonesborough after two dangerous days in the woods, too late. Blackfish and his braves were already there and had killed two unsuspecting settlers. Kenton, with his usual mixture of cold daring and equally cold caution, hid on the edge of the clearing at Boonesborough, because he thought the Indians might try to pick him off as he crossed the open space to approach the fort. When he did reach the gate, the two bodies were just being brought in.

Meantime, near Harrodsburg, a sugar-maker and some friends were attacked. Young James Ray had taken several men over to his brother William's sugar camp, where they were drinking the fresh sap. They heard some sounds in the woods, but, supposing they were caused by animals, paid very little attention. No one dreamed Indians were anywhere near. But Blackfish's warriors had seen the white men and were creeping up. Suddenly forty or fifty of them appeared only a few yards away. The white men, some of whom were not armed, scattered in all directions. The Ray brothers stayed together as they ran, until it was obvious that William could not hold out. His brother James panted a suggestion that he surrender. Instead, William turned back to fight and was captured.

James Ray slipped behind a tree, slashed off his leather leggings while a dozen Indians dashed past him, firing harmlessly into a tree-top where they supposed he was concealed. Emerging, Ray dashed for the fort, distancing the fleetest of the Shawnees after a hot pursuit.

Meantime, a certain William Coomes, at work near by, ran over to see what the trouble was. He took along his shotgun, which, after the usual Kentucky fashion, he had given a name—Beelzebub. Coomes almost ran into the arms of fifteen Shawnees, but he saw them in time. He and Beelzebub dodged quickly behind a tree, while the warriors rushed into a cabin to look for him. While they were still inside, Coomes slipped into the branches of a fallen hickory whose yellowing leaves blended with his leather garments. Here he lay concealed while the Indians dragged in William Ray, wounded. Ray was tomahawked and then scalped, while Coomes watched from the fallen hickory. Once a warrior sat down on a log so close that Coomes could all but touch him. At another time, as he told the story afterward: "A great tall yellow fellow steped up in front of and stared him in the Eyes for two or 3 minutes, He said dad drabit I was a great Mind to let Belzabub off at him."

Toward evening the Indians left, but Coomes stayed in hiding, afraid to move.

James Ray covered four miles in thirty minutes, reaching the fort at dusk. The alarm spread instantly. Families outside picked up and scampered for the stockade after sundown. Among them was Mrs. Squire Boone, who was living in a cabin near Harrodsburg while her husband was in North Carolina on business. The men who had gone with Kenton for the flax arrived late the same day without encountering Indians.

Everyone had "forted up" safely, but there was a terrific scene between the impetuous Hugh McGary and the hot-tempered James Harrod. McGary roared that the commander had neglected necessary precautions. (Like every other commander in Kentucky, he had.) The dispute grew fiercer. Both men raised their rifles. Mrs. McGary thrust her husband's rifle barrel to one side. In the end they agreed to go out with thirty men and see whether any of the Ray party were still alive.

They found William Ray's body, so horribly mangled that it could not be identified.

"See there!" said one. "They have killed poor Coomes."

"No," came a voice from the tree-top. "They haven't killed me, by Job! I'm safe." Coomes crawled out.

Next morning, smoke was rising from a workshop outside the fort, and a party which went out to investigate saw a rifle leaning against one of the cabins. A moment later Indian rifles blazed from ambush and the party retreated with only one man wounded, after killing and scalping an Indian, whose body they took back to the fort to show the women their prowess. The Harrodsburg settlers were always rugged souls—it is they who are credited with feeding dead Indians to their dogs "to make them fierce."

With William Ray's mangled body as a ghastly warning, Harrod hastily put his neglected defenses in order. He had not yet set up palisades in the gaps between the cabins. Everyone worked through the night to build the stockade and they finished just in time. Blackfish attacked on the 18th and 28th. Once the Indians almost killed Mrs. Squire Boone, who was outside gathering chips. Bullets struck the gate of the fort as she slipped through to safety.

The baffled Blackfish eventually withdrew from the vicinity of Harrodsburg, leaving a few warriors as usual to hang around, steal, kill, and in general give the settlers something to worry about.

They could get fresh meat only by sending a hunter out before daylight to hunt at a great distance, returning with his game after dark. James Ray, seventeen years old, was the only man in Harrodsburg skillful enough to do this with impunity. He used to ride away from the fort at full speed, so as to give lurking Indians a difficult target, travel about twelve miles, hunt, butcher the deer while holding his bridle over one arm, load it on the horse, and ride back. He always galloped the last quarter of a mile and regarded the final spurt of one or two hundred yards as the most dangerous part of the dangerous journey. Even at night Indians had a chance to shoot him as he crossed the clearing. Other hunters who tried to do the same thing disappeared.

One man was scalped within a hundred yards of the fort while his family watched from the stockade. Another settler, cut off from Harrodsburg by the Indians, took refuge in Boonesborough for two weeks. Then, after he had been given up for

C. Frank Dunn

The "Ann McGinty" blockhouse and a corner of the stockade.

C. Frank Dunn

A pioneer interior.

HARRODSBURG RESTORED

dead, he walked into his cabin one day as if nothing had happened, casually inquiring of his wife: "How are you by this time, Nancy?"

At Boonesborough, parties of Indians were seen frequently. Luckily Daniel Boone had commenced new fortifications after the capture of the girls and, though work on them had lagged for a time, he had strengthened his defenses a good deal during the winter.

Boone had learned much about the value of reconnoissance since he had led Henderson's advance guard into Kentucky in '75. He now kept sentinels alert at the fort. Each of the three settlements had two scouts in the forest constantly. These six men patrolled as far north as the Ohio and moved east and west along its banks. They were usually able to warn of the movements of large parties of Indians; but small war parties could slip up almost to the forts themselves and lie in ambush until victims approached. Eventually Boone was forced to divide his meager force, now only twenty-two men, into two reliefs, who took turns soldiering and farming.

Between assaults on Harrodsburg, Blackfish tried his luck against Daniel Boone on April 24. It was the first attack in force on Boonesborough and the first of many encounters between the two men, who to the end of their battles retained a certain queer, half-chivalrous liking for one another.

Boone's permanent scouts, Simon Kenton and Thomas Brooks, failed to observe the approach of the Indians. Some forty to a hundred of Blackfish's Shawnee warriors arrived unexpectedly, hid, and succeeded in decoying most of Boonesborough's fighting men outside. There was some suspicion that Indians were about. The cows had stood at the head of the lane that morning, snuffing and showing signs of uneasiness, and would not go out to pasture. This was usually a sign of Indians. Squire Boone's

"Old Spot" was particularly sensitive to their presence and often gave the alarm in this way.

Nevertheless, two men had left the stockade at sunrise. Indians fired on them from the woods and then gave chase. One poor fellow was overtaken, tomahawked, and scalped within sixty yards of the fort; but Kenton, who was standing at the gate with a loaded rifle, ran out and shot the Indian at close range. The noise brought Daniel Boone and nearly a dozen others charging to his aid. As they came, Kenton saw another Indian drawing a bead on Boone and fired just in time to down the redskin. The Indians cleverly retreated far enough to draw the white men along the lane, away from their fort. Then a great many more warriors rushed into the lane in their rear, cutting them off.

"Boys, we have to fight!" exclaimed Boone, as he saw them come screeching up. "Sell your lives as dear as possible."

There was nothing for it but to fall back fighting and try to shoot, smash, club and cut a way through the Indians. Boone yelled an order to charge for the stockade:

"Right about—fire—charge!"

That meant one shot apiece and then a savage hand-to-hand with clubbed rifles against knives and tomahawks. Kenton managed to reload twice during the scrimmage, and looked up from his powder-horn to see Boone down with a broken ankle, while an Indian was preparing to finish him with a tomahawk. Again Kenton fired at the crucial moment and for the second time that day saved Boone's life. Still another brave rushed up to take Daniel's scalp. Kenton knocked the Indian down with a clubbed rifle. Then, picking the wounded man up in his arms, he dodged through the Indians and back to the stockade.

The women of Boonesborough had been looking on from the fort. As they watched Kenton's approach, they suddenly saw a girlish figure dart from the gate, out on the battlefield. It was Jemima Boone. She had slipped unobserved away from the other women and was now proudly helping Kenton carry her father in.

Safely inside the gates, the laconic Daniel expressed a qualified approval. Too badly wounded to leave his cabin, he sent for Kenton, then only twenty-one:

"Well, Simon, you have behaved like a man today; indeed you are a fine fellow." It was an accolade.

Boone's old comrade, Michael Stoner, was also hurt in this skirmish. Shot through the arm, so that he could no longer hold a rifle, he made for the fort—but not before he had picked up the loaded weapon with his one sound arm and handed it to another man, profanely adjuring him, in his Pennsylvania Dutch accent, to shoot "one of tem Got tamn yellow rascals."

Captain Billy Bush, seeing how badly he was hurt, tried to help him, but Stoner cried: "Oh Push! Push! don't make so big a mark. We was too big a lump to shoot at."

Bush let him stagger on alone and paused to load. He had just poured in his powder and had a bullet ready in his mouth, when he saw some Indians loading, reflected that he was a fool to make a target of himself, and ran for the fort. The Indian bullets struck so near him that the pebbles they threw up cut his legs.

Daniel Boone was temporarily out of the fighting—the old wound ached, on bad days, ever after—though neither a broken bone nor a gunshot wound was any great matter on the frontier. Blackfish and his Indians, having failed to carry the fort, hung about for a while, stealing what they could. Then they went back to Harrodsburg. On May 23 and 24 they made two more attacks. The first was kept up until eleven at night. The second began next morning and went on until midnight, when the band drew off after several attempts to set the fort on fire.

Through all the danger, flames, and uproar, Daniel Boone directed the battle from his bed.

His brother Squire, just back from the settlements, went out from Harrodsburg on May 26 "to hunt Indians" and found one too many. As his party slipped through the woods, they saw that Squire had lagged behind to search for moccasin tracks, and called to him:

"Boone, come on!"

A moment later Squire heard another call of "Boone!" This time it came from one side. He walked straight to the place. Ambushed Indians shot him and escaped unseen.

He had barely recovered from this wound when in September he was wounded in another fight. A group of men who had gone out to shell corn were attacked by Kickapoos. Squire, after firing a shot, had retired to some high weeds for shelter while loading. An Indian, running in to scalp another man, discovered him when the two were only ten feet apart. Squire got a glancing tomahawk blow on the head, but the Indian lost his tomahawk, just as the white man drew a small, silver-hilted, three-edged sword—the pride of his life—and ran it clear through the warrior. Seeing that the hardy savage was still full of fight, Squire grasped him by the belt and hauled him closer and closer till the swordblade protruded fourteen inches from his back. Both men were dripping blood. After a desperate effort to get Squire's hunting knife, which was too slippery with blood to grasp, the Indian, still gripped by his adversary, backed to a fence, broke loose, climbed over, and fell dying, breaking the sword short off as he fell. Squire later told his son that it was "the best little Indian fight he ever was in—both parties stood and fought so well."

As the Indians left Boonesborough after their final attack, one of Logan's scouts, lurking in the forest, saw them go. Observing that they were heading toward his settlement, he slipped back through the forest and was barely able to give the alarm before the war party appeared, May 30. Logan, finding his ammunition running low, slipped out at night, made his way to the Holston settlements—either alone or with Harrod as a companion—and was safely back in ten days.

Indians were heard outside Harrodsburg imitating owls and using the gobble of the wild turkey as a decoy. This familiar ruse failed, but James Ray had to sprint 150 yards to the fort on one occasion, only to find the gates closed and the Indians so close behind that the settlers dared not open up. Ray dropped behind a stump just outside the wall with the bullets kicking up the dust around him, while his anxious mother watched his predicament from a loophole. After four hours of this, Ray had an inspiration and called to the others inside: "For God's sake, dig a hole under the cabin wall and take me in."

There was a sound of spades busily plied. Then the earth opened beside him and he crawled gratefully into it, under the logs, and to safety within the stockade, while the bullets thudded against it.

On July 4 the indefatigable Blackfish again attacked Boonesborough, concentrating his forces and keeping up the siege for two days. During this attack the Indians burned an old structure, now empty, variously known as Fort Boone and the Little Fort, from which the settlers had moved when the new stockade was finished.

Reënforcements finally began to come in. Colonel John Bowman brought one hundred Virginia militiamen. William Bailey Smith had gone back to North Carolina and on his own authority enlisted forty or fifty mounted riflemen, mostly former friends and neighbors of the Boones. These men arrived in July, too late for most of the fighting, but their presence helped to scare the Indians off. Smith had his men open ranks as they marched into Boonesborough, with a distance of six feet, head-to-tail, between their horses. Watching Shawnee scouts were deluded into reporting the arrival of two hundred men—four or five times their real number. Thus reënforced, the Kentuckians took the offensive and again went out looking for Indians. When snuffing cattle gave the alarm at a turnip patch near Harrodsburg, white men silently surrounded an ambush that had been laid for them. They drove off the Indians, and captured fifteen "bundles," as the Indian packs were called.

It had been a desperate struggle; but in spite of that George Rogers Clark enters in his diary at Harrodsburg, July 9: "Lieut. Linn married. great Merriment."

Blackfish, meditating by a hidden camp fire somewhere in the forest, had at length concluded it was no use and, for the time being, retired. There were no more assaults in force. The Indians were content to hang about and "practised secret mischief." They had not driven Boone and his settlers out, but they had burned cabins, destroyed crops, forced the abandonment of various settlements, killed a number of men, and created a real food-shortage which would grow more serious later in the year.

It was too late to start new crops, but Boonesborough was agreeably surprised to find that, though the new cornfields had been laid waste, the old cornfield of the year before had spontaneously produced seven bushels an acre from natural seeding. This field the Indians had overlooked. The incident gave rise to the famous remark that Kentucky soil, planted and cultivated, produced twenty bushels an acre; merely planted, ten bushels; not even planted, seven. In spite of this fortunate chance, however, food was scarce. In December one settlement reported that it had but two months' supply of breadstuff and commented significantly on the number of widows and orphans. Even the news of Burgoyne's surrender, in October, 1777, which reached Kentucky during the winter, was no reason for supposing that Indian raids would cease.

All in all, Blackfish need not have been discouraged.

10. Prisoner of the Shawnee King

IN January of 1778, Boonesborough's salt supply began to run short. Salt was one of the most pressing needs of the pioneers. They had to have it for curing meat and hides, and they enjoyed it as one of the few condiments that added flavor to their monotonous diet. To be left in the wilderness without bread or salt was one of the few hardships of which they ever complained, and Boonesborough at the moment had eastern militia wintering there who were probably complaining very loudly indeed.

Daniel Boone took a party of some thirty men, lashed the station's salt-kettles, which had been especially sent out as a gift from the Virginia government, on pack-horses, and set out for the Blue Licks. These salt springs were a central point on the forest traces on the Licking River, a tributary flowing north into the Ohio River in northeastern Kentucky.

Boone's salt-makers were to camp at the Licks for about a month and were then to be relieved by a new party. These reliefs were to continue until a year's supply of salt had been sent to the station on pack-horses, which were the only kind of transport that could negotiate the narrow wilderness paths. But Captain Boone did not keep his fellow-settlers at Boonesborough waiting till a pack train could get through. A special messenger rushed back with the first small sack of salt his men could make.

Fortunately they were living in a country where nature provided salt in abundance. Far below their feet, imprisoned in rock and sand, lingered the waters of prehistoric seas. Rainwater, seeping down through many strata, forced the salt waters to the surface, where they bubbled out in those salt and sulphur springs common in all limestone country. There were innumerable springs of this sort, large and small, throughout Kentucky, scattered ten to thirty miles apart.

These were the "licks"—so called because the deer and buffalo, eager for salt, licked up the impregnated earth. These animals, like the mammoth and the mastodon before them, had found the springs long before the white man came, perhaps even before the red man. Mammoth and mastodon had crowded around the salt licks, where even the earth was full of the mineral they craved. "Big Bone Lick" took its name from the disjointed skeletons of the huge beasts which millennia before had died there, caught in the marshes into which their gigantic bulks sank easily and fatally. They had perished in such numbers that a man could walk for several hundred yards without touching ground, stepping from one huge bone to another.

The pioneers gazed upon the remnants of these enormous carcasses with wonder but accepted their presence without much speculation. The huge vertebrae made comfortable camp seats. They were neatly rounded to accommodate the appropriate portion of the human frame weary with much hunting. They were also a convenient rest for the poles from which camp kettles swung above the fire. The big bones were just one of the benefits the wilderness provided, and the hunters accepted them without troubling their heads over fossil lore. A few were sent back to Virginia for the edification of the philosophic Mr. Jefferson, and others to France for the great Cuvier to study.

It was fairly simple for Daniel Boone to make salt. The settlers merely had to go to the springs, fill their kettles with salt water, and boil it down. The mineral mixture that resulted contained a good many things besides sodium chloride, but salt predominated and the iodine mixed with it was very good for them, though nobody suspected it. Iodized salt is a modern invention, but sea water is full of iodine, and the settlers, willy-nilly, ate iodine with their home-boiled product.

The labor of salt-making was prodigious. It took 840 gallons of this weak brine to yield a single bushel, though very fine springs were said to give a bushel for every eighty gallons or even less. But the work was worth doing. A bushel of salt was worth a cow and a half.

Salt-making was not merely laborious, it was also dangerous. The Indians knew quite as much about the salt licks as the white men. Red man-hunters watched the licks for scalps as eagerly as white pot-hunters watched them for game. Salt-making parties like Boone's had to go out in force, ready to defend themselves at any time.

At first there was no trouble. Boone's salt-kettles bubbled merrily for some weeks, and several horse-loads of salt had already been sent back to the station, in charge of three men. It was about time for the relief to arrive, and the thoughts of the salt-makers in the lonely little camp began to turn to their homes and families in Boonesborough. They had been undisturbed for some time and had begun to feel entirely secure. The Indians usually kept close to their villages in Ohio during the bitter weather. That was why winter was the best time for salt-making—warm work, anyhow. Furthermore, the Indians had been very badly beaten only a few months before, and it did not seem likely that they would be returning to Kentucky before spring at the earliest.

Early in February Daniel Boone went out to scout, hunt, and follow his trapline for beaver. The camp had to be supplied with meat; there was beaver sign in the Licking River and Hinkston's Creek. Pelts were valuable, and Daniel Boone was never one to scorn an honest dollar. The salt party kept three scouts in the woods at all times. Boone was to reconnoiter in one direction, while his son-in-law Flanders Callaway and a companion were operating in the other.

In winter the buffalo left the licks and sought areas where plenty of cane had grown. As there were no canebrakes near the salt camp, Boone made a wide swing of five or six miles to find game and to make sure his reconnoissance included country well out to the flank. Toward evening he loaded his pack-horse with buffalo meat and headed home for camp through a blinding snowstorm, hardly able to see or hear anything in the forest on one side or along the river on the other.

He had been leading his burdened horse slowly along the river bank and had just passed a narrow place where the upturned roots of a fallen tree left barely room to squeeze through. The Shawnees were on him before he was aware. Boone noticed that his horse seemed nervous. He glanced back quickly. The Indians were right behind, thirty paces away, having hidden behind the fallen tree to let him pass. The best accounts say that he was attacked by four braves at once. All accounts agree there were too many Indians for comfort. The warriors were scouts from a Shawnee war party, sent toward the Blue Licks to see if anyone was there. They had stumbled upon Boone by accident.

Daniel snatched at his knife, hoping to slash the thongs of green hide—"buffalo tugs"—that held the load of buffalo meat on the horse, scramble up, and ride for his life. But after using the knife to skin and clean a buffalo, he had thrust it back into the sheath covered with blood and grease. It had frozen fast, and its greasy hilt was so slippery that his hands, also greasy, could not get grip enough to pull it out.

He dropped the bridle and ran, leaving the horse to shift for itself. One Shawnee stayed with the game. Two more opened out, one on either side, to flank the fugitive. A fourth slashed off the load, mounted Boone's own horse, and proceeded to ride him down.

It was no use trying to hide. His trail in the snow was plain to follow.

There was a lively chase for half a mile and then, as Boone dodged through the wintry forest, the Indians drew closer and bullets began to sing about his ears. Indians were notoriously poor shots, but the range was now getting very short. Spurts of snow and bits of flying bark warned him. Then, at a few yards' range, a bullet cut the thong of his powder-horn. Boone had a charge in his rifle, but he would never get a chance to reload if he fired it.

Daniel knew Indians, and he also knew when he had had enough. He did not believe the bullets so far had been meant to kill, but only to warn him. The next shots would be aimed to kill. He halted in his tracks. No chance of escape was left. He prepared to surrender to his red brothers.

Slipping behind a tree, he placed his rifle in front of it as evidence that he would not resist. The braves came up, laughing, disarmed him, shook hands warmly, and marched him off.

The Indians were naïvely delighted with their capture. This was no ordinary white man, but the great hunter himself, long known to them by reputation. They all set off together for the Indian camp on Hinkston's Creek, not far from the Blue Licks.

As they came into camp, Boone stared in amazement and horror at what he saw. In a sheltered part of the valley blazed a fire thirty or forty feet long, and around it sat a party of more than a hundred Shawnee warriors, fully armed. Boone looked quickly at their faces. All were painted for war. The chief approached, a short and sturdy warrior, past middle age.

It was Blackfish. The war chief himself had taken command of the party. This, Boone must have realized instantly, was no ordinary raid.

As he looked around, he saw that not all were Indians. With the warriors about the fire were several white men, hardly distinguishable from redskins in their rough woods dress. Worse and worse. White brains were directing red savagery. There was Charles Beaubien, a French-Canadian whom the British employed as Indian agent. There was Louis Lorimier, French-Canadian trader, whose post in Ohio was a center for the Shawnees and who had enormous influence in the tribe. Worst of all, here were the "white Indians," George and James Girty, brothers of the notorious Simon whose mere name spread terror along the American frontier.

There was even a negro slave named Pompey, who later in the year was to fight with the Indians at the long siege of Boonesborough. According to one account, the negro had escaped from the Kentucky settlements and joined the tribe voluntarily. More probably, he had been captured in some raid and held as slave by the Indians, who often kept negroes and sometimes traded in them.

Boone must at first have supposed he had been captured by an isolated raiding party of a few adventurous warriors. As he looked at the savage group stretched out by the fire or rising curiously to see the prisoner, he knew the full extent of the danger.

The presence of white men showed that the attack had been carefully planned and encouraged by the British. The band was strong enough to overwhelm Boonesborough in a few hours. It might even be able to capture the other settlements, surprising them one by one. Boone was calm as usual as the painted warriors led him up to Chief Blackfish, but behind the quiet blue eyes his brain was working furiously.

"King" Cornstalk, the great chief of the Shawnees, had been treacherously murdered by irresponsible American soldiery while in an American fort on a mission of peace only three months before. The Shawnee war party was now out to take revenge on the nearest and weakest of the Big Knives' settlements. Indian justice demanded revenge—it did not matter on which individuals vengeance fell so long as somebody belonging to the offending tribe of the Big Knives suffered. The British had astutely taken advantage of Shawnee indignation to spur the Indians on. Hence the unusual venture on the warpath in midwinter, contrary to all custom.

The distinguished prisoner received a hearty, if somewhat sardonic, welcome. The Indians shook hands, uttered the usual * greeting, "How d' do," or "How d'y," patted him on the back, made much of him, and laughed mightily over his capture.

Among the chiefs who gathered about him Boone recognized the leader of the band who had captured him nine years before. and boldly greeted him by name:

"How d' do, Captain Will?"

Captain Will was greatly surprised, but when reminded of his earlier captures showed no resentment at Boone's previous escape. Instead, he shook hands once more, with increased cordiality. Thereupon all the warriors who had already shaken hands did it all over again with the utmost gravity.

This friendly reception meant nothing in particular. Sometimes it was merely an ironic prelude to torture and death at the stake. In this case it may have been entirely sincere, for there was always a faintly chivalrous note in Daniel Boone's warfare with the Indians. He hated killing. He was never cruel

* All the early documents give this form of the greeting. Later, the Plains Indians made it simply, "How." In Minnesota and Ontario the modern Ojibway still use the greeting, "B'joo," an obvious adaptation from the French of the early explorers.

himself (there is no record that he ever took a scalp), and he was never the victim of cruelty. The Indians admired him, were invariably pleased on the rare occasions when they outwitted him, were delighted to have caught him this time, and later obstinately refused to give him up, even for cash. Daniel Boone was as good a woodsman as any of them, and a far better shot. Such men were valuable in any camp. The Shawnees regarded him as a prospective ornament to the tribe and made no secret of their plans.

With the negro Pompey as interpreter, Blackfish explained that his band was going to attack Boonesborough, and then inquired who the men at the salt springs were. His scouts had by this time discovered them. Seeing that his first attempts at evasion did no good, Boone admitted the salt-makers were his own men. Blackfish blandly announced that he would go down and kill them right away.

Daniel Boone did some quick thinking. The fortifications at Boonesborough, he knew, were in their usual bad condition. According to one story, a whole side of the stockade was still missing and there were only two blockhouses. With nearly thirty men at the salt camp and the relief already outside the fort on the way thither, the almost empty settlement would hardly be able to resist assault. The settlers, entirely off guard, could be taken by surprise and easily killed. Even if the Indians spared their lives, the very best that could be expected was a long march with helpless women and children through bitter weather, with prolonged captivity at the end for those who did not die of hardships, torture, or the tomahawk.

The salt-making party were now some distance away, and the Indians were not at the moment heading in their direction, but Blackfish's scouts had seen them. Boone's little party would probably also be taken by surprise, just as he had been himself.

On the other hand, there was still a chance to save Boonesborough. The Shawnee was an intrepid daredevil, but Indian nature is rarely persevering, especially in cold weather. Give the warriors one small success to boast about, and they would very likely decide they had done enough and go quietly back to Ohio.

With the friendliest air he could assume, Boone told Blackfish he would himself go with him and persuade the young men to surrender. Blackfish must guarantee that they should not be tortured or forced to run the gauntlet. The latter ceremony was usually inevitable whenever a new captive was brought into a village.

Boone further explained that it was too cold to move the women and children now; but in the spring it would be easy enough to take them to Detroit. Blackfish agreed, but added that if Boone failed to persuade his salt-makers to surrender, his own life might be the penalty.

Next morning the war party set off. By noon they were within two hundred yards of the salt-makers and had entirely surrounded them without being discovered. Boone was then sent down a hill toward them through the snow, under surveillance of warriors following a little way behind him but near enough to shoot in case of treachery.

The spring had been flooded with fresh water for some days and the salt-makers, unable to work, were resting quietly in camp. Boone's absence occasioned no uneasiness. Scouts or hunters were likely to stay in the forest for days at a time and the other two scouts were also still out. Seeing men approaching through the woods, the salt-makers looked up from their blankets, supposing it was the relief coming in from Boonesborough. Then, seeing Indians, they leaped for their rifles.

"Don't fire!" yelled Boone. "If you do, all will be massacred."

GOVERNOR HAMILTON BUYS SCALPS

A unique Revolutionary propaganda print now in the possession of Earle R. Forrest.

Hurriedly he explained: "You are surrounded with indians and I have agreed with these Indians that you are to be used well and you are to be prisoners of war and will be give up to the British officers at Detroyt where you will be treated well." A militia lieutenant had been left in command. Under his orders, the salt-makers formed a circle and stacked arms. A larger circle of warriors then emerged from the woods on all sides, surrounded them, and ordered them to sit down. Including Boone himself, the haul of prisoners was either twenty-seven or twenty-eight, two salt-packers and two scouts being absent.

The Indians now held council to determine whether they should kill their prisoners in spite of promises. There was no possible excuse for such treachery; but it was exactly what the American soldiers had done to Cornstalk, and the war party had come out to avenge his murder. They proposed to spare no one but Boone. He would be useful at Boonesborough in the spring.

White, red, and black sat down together in the council. For two full hours the solemn debate proceeded, as warrior after warrior rose and spoke, for mercy or for death. The negro Pompey, sitting by Boone, translated for him, but in so low a voice that the other prisoners could not hear. With no knowledge of Shawnee, none of them had the least idea that their lives depended on the outcome of the ceremonious Indian council. The white agents whom the British had sent along sat silent through it all, but Daniel Boone was permitted to make the closing speech. Sixty-six years later, one of the salt-makers repeated what he remembered. It was not a speech likely to be forgotten:

"Brothers!" said Boone, as Pompey turned his words, sentence by sentence, into Shawnee. "What I have promised you, I can much better fulfil in the Spring than now; then the weather will be warm, and the women and children can travel from Boonesboro to the Indian towns, and all live with you as one people. You have got all the young men; to kill them, as has been suggested, would displease the Great Spirit, and you could not then expect future success in hunting nor war; and if you spare them they will make you fine warriors, and excellent hunters to kill game for your squaws and children. These young men have done you no harm; they were engaged in a peaceful occupation, and unresistingly surrendered upon my assurance that such a step was the only safe one; I consented to their capitulation on the express condition that they should be made prisoners of war and treated well; spare them, and the great Spirit will smile upon you."

This was the first speech the startled prisoners had understood, and now for the first time they realized the peril they were in. The war club passed from hand to hand as the vote was taken, under the eyes of the captives. Fifty-nine warriors dashed it into the ground, as a vote for death; sixty-one let it pass as a token of mercy. There is a story that they let Boone vote. The group of reckless, brutal young braves who wanted blood had lost. Blackfish, who had allowed Pompey to translate for Boone, had won. The older chiefs seemed to approve.

All had turned out exactly as Daniel Boone had hoped. The Shawnees were entirely satisfied. Here was a big haul of prisoners and plenty of glory—plenty of profit, too. Prisoners were useful as slaves and could be sold to the British for cash. Why go on to Boonesborough through the snow and risk a hard fight for nothing, when they could now slip safely back to Ohio with prisoners, much glory, and no losses?

Boone is said to have pretended conversion to the British side. The pretense would have been credible enough, for even Simon Girty had served for a time with the Americans before joining the British, and Boone himself had been a Colonial officer under the British flag in 1774. He could point to the surrender of his men as proof of his conversion, and he painted an alarming picture of Boonesborough's strength. The fort was far too strong, he said, for any war party of this size to think of capturing. Why not let it alone for the time being, and return later with a larger band?

Blackfish was greatly impressed. When he actually did come back, six months later, he brought four or five hundred warriors.

In vain did their white comrades urge the Shawnees on to the attack, while Boone and the other prisoners listened in an agony of suspense. Charles Beaubien was disgusted with Boone's success. He doubted that the garrison of Boonesborough was any stronger than his own band. With Boone's large party absent, he argued, it was probably weaker. Capture would be easy.

Beaubien was entirely correct. But "the Savages could not be prevailed on to attempt the Fort, which by means of their prisoners might have been easily done with success," as the British lieutenant-governor at Detroit, Henry Hamilton, later complained. He did not know that it was Boone who had thwarted his whole enterprise.

Boone had, in fact, played his part altogether too well. He convinced the Indians and thereby saved the settlement. Blackfish probably expected that with his prisoner's intervention he could eventually take the town without even fighting for it. But what deceived Boone's enemies also deceived some of his friends. There was no chance for Boone to take his own men into his confidence. They had no knowledge of his plans. And his devious play-acting roused suspicions of his loyalty.

Once the retreat with the prisoners had been decided on, it was promptly carried out. Three hundred bushels of salt were thrown away. Then the war party filed off to the north through the white and silent winter woods, with their prisoners under close and careful guard.

Having been accepted as a friend, Boone was eager to keep up the pose. He joked and made friends with the warriors, and there may have been some surly and suspicious glances from the other whites at a leader who had first made them surrender to the redskins and now seemed to be on the best of terms with his savage captors.

Since there had been no fighting, there were no wounded. Since the prisoners were all seasoned woodsmen, there were no weaklings or laggards. There was, therefore, none of the usual dreadful tomahawking and scalping of prisoners who were unable to keep up with the rest of the party. Once they had agreed not to kill their prisoners, the Indians kept their bargain and, according to their lights, treated them well. When, in the division of the burdens, a warrior tried to make Daniel Boone carry a heavy brass kettle, he refused. When the brave insisted, Boone knocked him and the kettle down together, and was immediately protected by Blackfish.

They had barely reached camp that night, however, when Boone noticed warriors clearing a path in the snow. He inquired of Pompey what it was for. As he had suspected, the Indians were getting ready for the gauntlet. Boone went straight to Blackfish with a protest and a reminder of his promise, only to be met with:

"Oh, Captain Boone, this is not intended for your men but for you."

Blackfish was right. In his eagerness to protect his companions, Daniel Boone had quite forgotten to stipulate that he, too, should be exempted from the gauntlet, something every new captive normally must go through, even when the tribe intended to spare his life. Blackfish was offering his prisoner the honor of running the gauntlet among warriors only. Most captives were dragged to the villages and compelled to sing at the tops of their voices as they approached. Thus warned, the entire population—squaws, children, old men, and any warriors who happened to have stayed behind—seized clubs, sticks, stones, hatchets, deer's antlers, or anything else that seemed likely to hurt the prisoner, and raced out to help belabor him.

It was, as a brave once explained, "a sort of how do do." It was also a useful way of sorting out the stronger and braver captives from the weaker and more timid. The weak would not survive, and a timid man who hesitated stood a good chance of being beaten to death; but a bold man who dashed fearlessly through his tormentors was reasonably sure to escape with minor injuries. Practical purposes aside, the Indians found the gauntlet vastly diverting. It was their idea of innocent merriment.

Boone surprised the warriors by zigzagging from side to side, escaping the worst of the ordeal. When one man stepped squarely into the path, hoping to get in a good blow, Boone butted him in the chest with his head, knocking the eager redskin sprawling amid shouts of Shawnee laughter. Once the gauntlet was over, the band crowded around to offer congratulations on his courage, and Boone remained a prime favorite.

Boonesborough discovered its loss almost at once. The other two scouts, returning to the empty camp, at first thought the salt-makers had wearied of waiting for the relief and had gone back to Boonesborough. Kindling a fire, they prepared to camp for the night. But they soon discovered an Indian bow, some arrows, and moccasin tracks. Then they observed that the precious salt had been thrown into the snow. Leaving the remaining salt-kettles where they lay, they rushed off by night to warn the advancing relief, whom they found in camp. Hearing their story, the relief party made for the fort at full speed. The intrepid Simon Kenton with a few companions hurried off after the Indians. The trail was easy to follow, for the snow was "half leg deep," but Kenton's handful of men could not attack so large a force.

News of the capture of so many men spread rapidly through the settlements. A friend wrote to George Rogers Clark on March 7: "Came an Express from kentuckey here and informed me of Capt Daniel Boone with Twenty Eight men being taken prisoners from the Salt licks on licking Creek without Sheding one drop of blood." A party of settlers on their way to Kentucky turned around and went back to the states when they heard what had happened.

No news came back from the captives. Kenton had found no bodies. There were no signs of fighting. The wilderness had swallowed a forlorn little handful of Kentuckians. That was all.

After weeks had passed with no news of her husband, Rebecca Boone gave him up for dead; and about May she joined the families of the other missing men on the lonely and dangerous way back to the North Carolina settlements. Jemima, now married to Flanders Callaway, remained behind. It was natural enough to suppose Daniel Boone was dead. He had been captured before and had escaped. The Indians were likely to remember that and kill him in revenge. It is said that Rebecca finally learned he had been taken to Detroit; but that news was no guaranty of safety; and with it all trace of him ended.

The war party and its prisoners made fairly good time back to Ohio, considering that game failed, leaving them with nothing to eat but slippery elm and white oak bark, and that they were loaded down with plunder; but it was, as Boone later remarked, "an uncomfortable journey in very severe weather."

Several Indians had their ears frozen; and the prisoners, being tightly tied up at night, suffered a great deal.

Ansel Goodman, one of the party, thus described his own treatment, which all the others must have shared: "The night after he was taken, his arms were tied behind him, a rope or Buffaloe's Tug tied fast around his middle and then made fast to an Indian on each side of him, and the one around his arms was made to go around his neck and tied fast to a tree, and in that position he had to sleep upon the snow, a little while before he reached the Indian Town he was compelled to strip himself, and was entirely naked, his arms again made fast and a load of Bare meat packed upon him. It was a heavy load Indeed he was packed heavily from the time he was taken untill he arrived at the town."

By February 18, ten days after the capture, they were at Little Chillicothe, an important Shawnee town on the Miami.

There was wild rejoicing when the war party came in. So large a number of prisoners was almost unheard of. There had been nothing like it since Braddock's defeat. In spite of the agreement, all the prisoners—except Boone, who had already done so—were compelled to run the gauntlet. Ansel Goodman had to "dance like the whites" to amuse his captors. There was a great war dance and sixteen prisoners were selected for adoption into the tribe.

On March 10 Boone and ten other prisoners were taken to Detroit by forty Indians with Blackfish at their head. The warriors wanted to collect their pay from the British, who had encouraged them to go on the warpath. Several prisoners, whom they did not want to adopt, were to be sold.

The Americans firmly believed that the British paid for scalps, and one contemporary deposed on oath: "that all the Indian Warriors are liberally Rewarded for every Trip they make against us; & that all the Squaws and Children receive plenty of Cloathing from them, & Rations when at Detroit." Some time after Boone's captivity another man wrote: "The Custom of giving goods in small portions at Du Troit to Indian Warriors is laid aside; the rule now is for them to go into the Magazines (when they Come with a scalp or prisoners) and take what they Can Cary at one Load." It is certainly true that Lieutenant-Governor Hamilton, who directed the raids on Kentucky, did receive scalps from the Indians when he met them in council. But on this occasion, all prisoners were handed over alive and unhurt.

Boone met and made friends with the lieutenant-governor. The British official felt a certain pity for these unfortunate white captives, helpless in the hands of the savages. After all, both sides were of British blood, however divided by the Revolutionary struggle. Boone himself testifies that he was treated "with great humanity." Hamilton offered the Shawnees one hundred pounds for him, intending to parole him and let him go home—an offer which the Indians instantly refused. Though it was an immense sum for a prisoner, Blackfish and his braves had other plans. They let the British have some of their other prisoners, but according to Hamilton himself, "took Boone expecting by this means to effect something."

They did, however, let Hamilton "borrow" him for interrogation. Boone had the malicious satisfaction of giving the British at Detroit their first reliable information of Burgoyne's surrender. So far, the isolated post at Detroit had heard only rumor.

"It was a well known fact in Kentucky before I was taken," he said, answering Hamilton's question, "that Burgoyne and his whole army had surrendered to Gen. Gates."

The startled Hamilton called the news to his military secretary in an adjoining room: "Capt. Boone says it was well known in Kentucky before he was taken."

Hamilton urged Boone not to mention it to the Indians, but—

"You are too late, Governor," answered the imperturbable Daniel. "I have already told them of it."

Failing to secure Boone as their own prisoner, the good-natured British officers tried to lend him "a friendly supply for my wants," but he refused their offers with simple dignity, saying he could never hope to repay "such unmerited generosity." He did accept a horse, saddle, bridle, and blanket from Hamilton's army supplies, as well as some silver trinkets for Indian trading; and he demonstrated his ability to make gunpowder, "having been shut up in a room with all the materials." The British also gave him clothing, but unfortunately Blackfish decided that they fitted him rather better than they fitted Boone, and his prisoner was in no position to insist on keeping them.

This kindness from the enemy may have been sincere enough, but there was an element of policy in it. Boone is said to have shown Hamilton his old British commission as a militia captain which he carried about him for just such emergencies. He kept on dropping tactful hints that Kentucky was not irrevocably wedded to the American cause; and his hints seem to have been taken seriously by the British and also, unfortunately, by some of the American prisoners. It was strange to see their leader so cordially received by the Indians and made much of by the British. There were whispers.

After about ten days at Detroit occupied in reports to British officers and distribution of rewards for services rendered, the Shawnees started back to Little Chillicothe, taking their famous prisoner with them. They went by a roundabout way, visiting the Delaware, Mingo, and Shawnee villages, while Blackfish gave the warriors of the various tribes instructions for his expedition against Boonesborough, when the warm weather came.

When they reached home again, they found that the first of Boone's fellow prisoners had escaped from the Shawnees' clutches. This was Andrew Johnson, who had been left behind in the Indian camp. By pretending to be a mere simpleton, Johnson disarmed suspicion. He was so small that the Indians were by no means sure he was quite grown up. He pretended to be afraid to leave camp; he pretended to be gun-shy; when persuaded to shoot he invariably flinched at the report, missing not only the mark but the tree in which it was set. Convinced that he was a mere fool, the Indians would ask: "Pequolly [Little Shut His Eyes], which way Kentuck?" Pequolly always pointed in the wrong direction. The Indians laughed contemptuously and ceased to watch him, never dreaming that Little Shut His Eyes really had eyes far wider open than their own.

Pequolly stayed with the Shawnees long enough to attend a war dance. Then, while the excitement was at its height, Little Shut His Eyes slipped quietly into the forest completely equipped for travel with his tribal "father's" rifle, tomahawk, knife, powder, lead, and blanket coat. Being in reality an excellent woodsman and now completely outfitted, he had no difficulty in making his way swiftly to Boonesborough.

The honest Shawnees were dreadfully agitated. Pequolly, they said, was a little fool. He would surely die in the forest unless they found him. They searched three days for his trail. It was in vain. They inquired of Boone whether Pequolly could possibly survive the trip. Boone, diplomatically, was not at all sure.

Pequolly's Shawnee father was greatly concerned for his son's safety. The fault, he said, was all his own. He had recently scolded Pequolly. He had been too severe, and that had made

Pequolly run away. The good old warrior was extremely sorry about it.

Johnson brought Boonesborough its first reliable news of what had happened to the salt-makers. He also brought the Kentucky settlers their first accurate information of the whereabouts of the Shawnee villages. Within a few weeks Pequolly was back with five companions, raiding the homes of his late captors, stealing horses and taking scalps. The scalps were vengeance, but the horses were badly needed in Kentucky, for the Indians had stolen nearly all the settlers had. Johnson's raiders were exultant over bringing seven back with them.

When the vengeful Johnson led the first party of Kentucky raiders against them, the Indians had no idea they had been attacked by white men. It was night when the retaliating Kentucky band ran into their first Indian camp, where Blackfish and a few others were living temporarily. As the rifles poured their fire into the astonished red men, Blackfish called, "Huy! Huy! We are Shawnees," supposing that one of his own war parties was making a mistake.

When the fire continued in spite of that, the Shawnees took to the woods and escaped. But even when they had come back and looked the ground over in daylight, they still supposed they were the victims of hostile Indians of some other tribe.

Then a Shawnee warrior, scouting toward Boonesborough, saw white men traveling homeward with stolen horses. He recognized Pequolly among them and brought word to Blackfish. The Big Knives had found the Shawnee country and had taken the offensive.

Daniel Boone himself later remarked that the worst mistake the Indians ever made was to take the Boonesborough prisoners back to their home camps. The Shawnees were quick to realize the danger that had now arisen. Before Johnson's raid the northern Indians had been mysterious plagues, emerging mysteriously from the forests and vanishing with equal mystery into them again. Pursuit was difficult. No one knew where their camps were, and it was impossible to carry the war into the Indians' own country and destroy their bases, as Clark, Boone, and Logan did a few years later. Now the Shawnees' troubles had really begun. There were a number of Kentucky woodsmen with accurate knowledge of the red men's territory and an active interest in evening up the score.

There were two or three other escapes during the year, but for the most part the prisoners were watched so closely or had been taken so far north that there was little hope of getting away. One even reached Lake of the Woods, far out in Minnesota. Seven who escaped from the British at Detroit were recaptured, put in irons, and sent to prison in Montreal. Thence they at length escaped to Connecticut. Others spent years among the Indians. Joseph Jackson took the Shawnee name of Fish and enjoyed Indian life so much that he refused to come home even when the Revolutionary War was over. He was strongly suspected of bearing arms against the Americans in various campaigns, but he returned to American territory in 1799. Later, however, he rejoined his Shawnee friends along the Mississippi.

As soon as Boone and Blackfish got home from Detroit, the Shawnees began the adoption ceremonies that were to transform Captain Daniel Boone, of the Virginia militia, into Sheltowee, or Big Turtle, a Shawnee warrior in good and regular standing in his tribe, son of the great war chief Blackfish himself. One gets an idea of the high esteem in which the Indians held Boone from the fact that this powerful chief wanted him as a son and, after the adoption ceremonies, really treated him as such. Blackfish even unbent enough from the habitual reserve of an Indian chief to comment admiringly on the fleetness of foot with which James Ray had outrun his best warriors at Harrodsburg the year before.

The adoption was lengthy, ludicrous, and unpleasant. Says the biographer Peck, who had many conversations with Daniel Boone, "the hair of the head is plucked out by a tedious and painful operation, leaving a tuft, some three or four inches in diameter, on the crown, for the scalp-lock, which is cut and dressed up with ribbons and feathers. The candidate is then taken into the river in a state of nudity, and there thoroughly washed and rubbed, 'to take all his white blood out.' This ablution is usually performed by females. He is then taken to the council-house, where the chief makes a speech, in which he expatiates upon the distinguished honors conferred on him, and the line of conduct expected from him. His head and face are painted in the most approved and fashionable style, and the ceremony is concluded with a grand feast and smoking."

11. Sheltowee, the Ingrate

DANIEL BOONE was now a Shawnee, but his fellow tribesman did not have such implicit faith in the efficacy of their own magic as to trust him completely. When he left camp, he was likely to see someone lurking along his trail. Once, when Blackfish gave him permission to turn his horse out to grass, he was secretly amused to see that the old chief had posted armed Indians to watch him from concealment. Worst of all, his little Indian sisters were set to watch him, and there is no vigilance like a child's.

Boone was careful to show every sign of contentment and went quietly about the Indian camp, whistling to himself as he usually did at home, "apparently so contented among a parcel of dirty Indians." He was, in fact, living the life he loved best. Some of his fellow prisoners were amazed and disgusted.

Blackfish and his squaw treated him with invariable affection, addressed him as "son," made no distinction between him and their two real children. They had recently lost a son—killed, it is sometimes said, by Boone's own men in the rescue of the kidnapped girls—and Boone had now, by tribal ritual, taken his place. The other two children were little girls. One, Pom-me-pe-sy, was an ill-tempered little creature of four or five; the other, Pim-me-pe-sy, an agreeable little girl of one or two, whom Boone helped care for. With the silver trinkets Hamilton had given him he bought maple sugar from other Indians and brought it back for Blackfish's children, who tried to speak English and call it "molas'."

Sheltowee was much indulged. Sent to chop trees, he blistered his hands and complained to Blackfish that this was no work for a warrior. In Kentucky a warrior had servants to do that kind of thing. The chief amiably relieved him of future tasks of the sort. When Boone voluntarily went out to work in the fields, Blackfish assured him he need not do so; his own squaw would have corn enough for both families when Rebecca came from Kentucky to live with the Shawnees. Sometimes the war chief drew maps in the soil and explained the local terrain to his son, who in turn dilated on the valuable arts of civilization that the Kentuckians would contribute to tribal prosperity.

Boone afterward reported that "the Shawanese king took great notice of me, and treated me with profound respect, and entire friendship, often entrusting me to hunt at my liberty. I frequently returned with the spoils of the woods, and as often presented some of what I had taken to him." The "king" was probably Moluntha, Cornstalk's successor as tribal chief; but he might have said the same thing of Blackfish.

While Sheltowee was preparing for escape, he was at the same time joining heartily in the target shooting and other sports of his fellow braves. Blackfish's squaw, whose attachment to him greatly touched her white son, was careful to warn him that he must let the Indians beat him. Sheltowee himself remembered well enough what had happened in North Carolina in his early youth, when the Catawba brave, Saucy Jack, had grown jealous of his marksmanship. Though exhibiting his strength and skill, he was careful not to excel the others, or at least not often enough to arouse ill-feeling. He noticed "in their countenances and gestures, the greatest expressions of joy when they exceeded me; and, when the reverse happened, of envy."

Though Big Turtle was allowed to hunt for the camp, wise old Blackfish was shrewd enough to dole out a measured and limited quantity of powder and lead before each trip. Sheltowee either had to show a reasonable amount of game or return ammunition.

As Boone came and went on these expeditions through the woods around the camp, he was wise enough to make no suspicious movements. He had already detected the favorite Indian device of giving a prisoner apparent freedom but watching him secretly. He did, however, with infinite pains, slowly build up a secret hoard of lead and powder, cutting bullets in two, using only half of each, and firing with the lightest possible powder charges at small game. He also hid away some jerked venison.

His ability as a gunsmith stood him in good stead. In emergencies when rifles were used as clubs, the stocks often broke, and the ability to repair them was rare and valuable, especially among Indians. A Kentuckian once remarked of another that he "was neither the biggest fool or the wisest man he knew, but he stocked a gun well."

Boone repaired one rifle successfully. When the admiring Indians clustered round to watch, he used to turn unexpectedly in his seat. The long barrel would swing around suddenly and the watchers had to leap out of the way swiftly to save their shins. It was just Daniel's little joke, but the Indians never dreamed of his amusement.

As soon as he was done, the Shawnees gave him the lock and barrel of another to repair for them, and he set to work. Boone now had firearms, of a kind, for his escape, together with the little store of ammunition he had saved and three or four bullets which the Indians had given him for "setting" the rifle he was repairing. Not much, but better than nothing. He tucked the bullets in his shirt flap and waited.

He even made jokes about escaping, and in doing so persuaded the simple red men that he possessed the gifts of a really powerful medicine man. One day when the warriors were less observant than usual, he managed to draw the bullets out of their rifles. (It was an old trick which he had played as a boy in Pennsylvania.) Then he told Blackfish he was going home.

"No you ain't," said Blackfish. "If you attempt it, I'll shoot you."

Boone set out and at forty yards invited the astonished warriors to shoot him if they could. Thoroughly convinced by this time that he really was escaping, they all fired, while Sheltowee made a great show of catching invisible bullets in a leather apron. Then he walked quietly back, shaking out of his garments the bullets he had taken from the rifles earlier:

"Here, take your bullets—Boone ain't going away."

Sensation in the audience.

Boone was also sharing the hardships of the tribe's nomadic existence. At one period the food supply of the Shawnee camp ran so low that they had to kill and eat their dogs, and when these were gone existed for ten days on a decoction of the inner bark of white oak, "which after drinking Boone could travel with the best of them." When at length they killed a deer, no one ate, but all partook first of a jelly made of the entrails. Boone swallowed his share of the vile mess but "his stomach refused it." Finally, he was able to keep down half a pint "with wry face and disagreeable retchings," which greatly amused the still starving Shawnees. They told Boone he might eat now, but "if he had done so before this treatment he would have died." A venison feast followed.

In June the camp moved to salt springs on the Scioto River,

north of the Ohio, where for ten days Sheltowee made salt for his red brothers. The spring was a Shawnee secret. The Indians had opened the rocks to bring water to the surface and had then fitted a round flat stone over the opening to hide it. But now Sheltowee was a member of the tribe. It need not be concealed from him.

During this time a war party had been out, engaged in an attack upon Donnelly's Fort on the Greenbrier River and Fort Randolph at Point Pleasant, in West Virginia. Just after Boone and the rest of Blackfish's family got back from their salt-making, these warriors returned after a sharp defeat and immediately began to plan the long-discussed attack on Boonesborough to retrieve the disaster on the Greenbrier. It was to be a very large war party. No one who, like Boone, was living in the camp, and knew Indians, could mistake the meaning of all the bustle.

If Boone was ever to escape, this was the time. Blackfish probably expected to use him as a guide and interpreter in attacking Boonesborough, and may even have hoped that Boone would again oblige him by persuading his fellow-settlers to surrender. But on June 16, 1778, the Shawnee camp looked for its fellow tribesman, Big Turtle, in vain.

His actual departure was not very spectacular. While off on a bear hunt, the Shawnee band stirred up a flock of wild turkeys. The usual way to hunt wild turkeys was to scare them into trees and then pick them off at leisure. As the men scattered in pursuit, Boone found himself alone with the squaws and children, who had been left with the salt-kettles and camp gear. He knew it would not be long now before the war party descended on Boonesborough. This opportunity seemed as good as any likely to offer. He waited till he knew by the reports of their rifles that the Indian hunters were occupied.

Then he walked over to his horse, cut the lashings, and tumbled off the kettles.

"My son, what are you doing?" cried his Shawnee mother.

"Well, mother," said her adopted son calmly, "I am going home. I must go and see my squaw and children and in a moon and a half I shall bring them out here to live with you."

"You must not go," cried the scandalized old squaw. "Blackfish will be angry."

When the kindly old woman warned Boone that he would certainly die in the woods, he confessed that he had arms and ammunition, bade her a friendly farewell, mounted, and rode off, leaving the squaws screaming at the tops of their voices to give the alarm.

Using the beds of running streams to obliterate his tracks, the escaping prisoner rode all night and all the next morning until his horse gave out about ten o'clock, dripping sweat and unable to go farther. Turning it loose in the forest, Boone went on afoot, breaking his trail when he could by running along fallen trees. Distancing his pursuers, he covered the 160 miles to Boonesborough in four days, eating only one meal besides his jerked venison.

After crossing the Ohio, he stocked his rifle with a bit of wood that happened to fit the breech fairly well. Having nothing else, he lashed the rifle together with thongs, as was sometimes done on the frontier. It was good enough to shoot a buffalo, when he was close enough home to dare risk the report. Later, he twice made deposition to the fact that he halted in his flight at a spot in Mason County where a buffalo road met the forks of three branches of "Johnson's Fork," and there "roasted some meat, and got some drink near the mouth of the branches." He enjoyed the feast, but even in his hunger he remembered to save the tongue, a great delicacy, for his eight-year-old son, Daniel Morgan Boone, whom he hoped to see in a few hours.

His journey was an amazing record of endurance and self-reliance, though not quite so amazing as represented by some of the early biographers, who quietly eliminate the horse, forget about the hidden store of jerked venison, and either say outright, or strongly hint, that he made the entire trip on foot.

Crossing the Ohio was an adventure in itself, or would have been but for an astounding bit of luck. Hardy woodsman though he was, Boone was not a strong swimmer. The Ohio is not a wide river, but the fugitive reached it in time of flood. As he ranged hastily along its northern bank, never knowing when Indians might appear, he found an old canoe, very likely hidden there by some war party who expected to use it at their next crossing. It had a hole stove in one end, but Boone plugged it and got safely across.

According to another story, he made a raft and, putting his rifle and clothes on it, swam the stream. Still another story makes it "a Buckeye chunk."

Once across the Ohio, Boone was in familiar and relatively safe country—in no more danger than on any of his hunting trips, and it was but a short distance to Boonesborough. He paused for his first rest, and made an "ooze" of oak bark for his scalded feet.

Weary, bedraggled, Daniel Boone limped along over the last miles of forest, bearing his gift for his child and eager to see his wife. There was excitement in Boonesborough as the exhausted fugitive appeared.

Only Jemima was there to greet him. His family was gone, his cabin empty. Its humble furnishings were already somewhere on the Yadkin River. When Daniel and Rebecca saw each other again, they discovered that she had turned her horse in at the Bryan cabin on the very day he had returned to their own cabin at Boonesborough.

Nothing was left, or so it seemed to the disconsolate Daniel as he stood looking at the rough logs, the cold, blackened fireplace, the empty pegs. Even the cat was gone. A deserted home is always depressing; but imagine returning to an empty and deserted log cabin after four months of captivity in Indian wigwams, after four days of peril in the wilderness, after hunger, cold, thirst, and constant danger! And imagine bringing home a buffalo tongue, through all that, to please a little boy, and then finding no little boy.

As he stood looking at the emptiness, Boone felt something rub against his leather leggings. He glanced down. Rebecca had forgotten the cat. Living as a stray among the other cabins, it had recognized its master and come home. It knew him. It rubbed purring against his legs. Boone sat down. The cat jumped into his lap.

Neighbors crowded around to console him, bringing so much to eat that one of his friends feared he would die with gorging. Sternly, he took everything eatable away from the exhausted man and fed him on nothing but broth till he was sure he had recovered.

There may have been some black looks, too. Wives and relatives and friends remembered the men still in the power of the Shawnees. It was hard to forgive a loss like that and easy to hold one man responsible. No one knows what tales of Boone's fraternizing with the Indians Andrew Johnson had brought back.

But after all, the man was a tower of strength. The news spread: Daniel Boone was back. From Harrodsburg, Colonel John Floyd wrote to a friend in the settlements: "Capt Boone has runaway from the Shawanese & arrived with abundance of news." North of the Ohio, back in Chillicothe, Blackfish postponed his attack. He knew well enough what kind of news Sheltowee would carry. The settlers would have warning, now. After all his planning and trouble, his attack would have to be delayed. Wearily, he sent word to Governor Hamilton. He needed further instructions.

There were times when the war chief of the Shawnees was not entirely pleased with his adopted son.

Boone had returned in the very nick of time. In spite of the raid at the Salt Licks, the frontiersmen had continued to neglect their defenses. The fort was still in bad condition—so bad that when Daniel Boone arrived it probably could not have been defended at all. The wooden palisades had gone to pieces. The Indians could almost walk in whenever they pleased. Like most of the early Kentucky forts, it had no adequate water supply within the stockade; and the gates and the two blockhouses both needed repair.

Looking back from the safe and comfortable life of the twentieth century America they helped create, the Kentucky settlers seem incurably slack in the very matters on which their lives depended. Again and again the Indians surprised them easily. Twice, they just climbed over the walls of sleeping forts and started scalping! In the midst of hostile Indian country, close to the Warriors' Path, the settlers let their forts get out of repair. Stumps were allowed to stand and weeds to grow up around the stockade, offering cover under which the Indians could creep up, and denying the defenders a clear field of fire for the long, brown Kentucky rifles. The weeds could have been cut down easily enough and the stumps leveled off—but no one ever troubled.

The settlers' indifference to water supply inside the stockade seems strangest of all. Boonesborough did have an old well, but it gave very little water. Few of the others had even that.

They depended on springs outside the palisades, on chance rainfall caught on the cabin roofs and run into water-barrels. Everyone knew that these frontier forts had to be ready to shelter not only the settlers but their thirsty horses and cattle whenever danger threatened—as it invariably did threaten several times a year. But the Kentuckians, inveterately American from the very first, always took a chance on defense and hoped for the best.

When, however, one considers the pitifully small numbers of the Kentucky settlers and the arduous and immense labor they faced daily, one begins to understand why so many important things were neglected. They had, in the first place, to clear the virgin forest. Then the trees had to be cut into lengths, some hundreds of yards of deep trenches had to be dug, the logs "up ended" to serve as palisades, and the trench filled in. Cabins had to be built and furniture improvised. Nails and screws were scarce. Iron was too heavy to pack over wilderness trails; and everything had to be pegged together or logs cut to dovetail. Where a modern carpenter swiftly drives a nail, these men had to whittle pegs and bore holes to receive them. Then the rank forest earth—a tangle of roots, stumps, and stones—had to be broken to the plow and the crops started, somehow. The crops were likely to be destroyed by Indian marauders at any time, but the effort had to be made and the chance of destruction taken. Crops and game and a few wild fruits were the only source of food supply. In addition, firewood had to be cut, dried, and brought in against the winter.

Often, all this had to be accomplished with only half of the men at work. It was quite usual for men outside the fort to take turn-and-turn-about—one standing guard while the other labored. Sometimes, even so, the Indians were adroit enough to slip up and kill the guard quietly before attacking the worker.

As for water supply, it was obvious that one ought to find a spring and build a fort around it; but this was rarely practicable. The land around springs was usually too marshy for a stockade. To sink a well with nothing but picks and shovels was a tedious operation, and the frontiersmen held the old belief that underground water ran only in well-defined streams which they had no way of locating. The usual practice was to build on high ground, as near a spring as possible, and carry water into the fort every day. Rain barrels helped a little.

A prolonged Indian siege could have starved out or parched out any settlement at any time; but Indian sieges usually lasted a day or two at most. The Indians were too impatient for real siege operations, and they always ran the risk that a relief would come up from other stations, catching them between two fires. Given a few days' time, Kentucky could, in the latter part of the Revolution, raise a force of six or seven hundred rifles, quite enough to deal with any Indian war party; and the various settlements were swift, brave, and generous with their aid to one other.

The Indians preferred to surprise a station when they could. If surprise failed, as it usually did, they tried to carry the fort by assault, meantime laying waste crops, killing cattle, and burning cabins outside the stockade. Assaults on a well-defended stockade were nearly useless without artillery; and it was almost impossible to transport the field guns of that day over wilderness trails—only once did the British contrive to bring them in.

Assault having failed, the next step in Indian tactics was to decoy the settlers outside the walls; and if this final stratagem did not at once succeed, they withdrew, to strike somewhere else.

A relatively small water supply was, therefore, usually sufficient. If the settlers could hold out for two or three days, they were safe from any ordinary Indian attack.

But the approaching attack on Boonesborough was not ordinary. The war party that Boone had seen preparing in Chillicothe was the largest yet sent against the Kentucky settlements. Every man Boonesborough could get would be needed in the defense. George Rogers Clark had taken a good many riflemen for his campaigns farther west. For the time being, this meant that men were scarcer, and the Kentucky settlements weaker, than ever.

Though Rebecca had long since returned to the Eastern settlements, her husband did not follow, but remained in Boonesborough where he was so badly needed. He sent a call for help to the settlements on the Holston River, themselves far enough away to be comparatively safe. From close at hand, Benjamin Logan sent fifteen men, cutting his own force at Logan's Station down to a bare twenty-four, and Harrodsburg also sent a small force.

There was as yet no thought of any course but fighting it out to the bitter end. The settlers repaired and strengthened their fort and made ready for the coming ordeal. They even began a new well inside the walls, but with typical frontier recklessness abandoned it as the days wore on and there was no sign of Indians. The sheer good luck of getting rain storms at the right time was all that saved Boonesborough from the consequences of this folly.

The neglect was partly caused by the urgent necessity of strengthening the fort. Only two corners had projecting blockhouses enabling the defenders to enfilade the front of their own walls if the enemy got too close. These two, by firing in two directions each, could actually rake all four of the walls, but four blockhouses were really needed. Daniel Boone promptly got his men to work on the palisades and set them to strengthening the two blockhouses already built and erecting two more. He carried their walls up two stories, with defenses on the second story to the height of a man's head. There was no time to roof them.

A small group of riflemen went north as far as the Licking River and brought back the salt-kettles which Boone's party had abandoned six months before and which had been too heavy for the Indians to carry off. A party had previously gone out to hide them. It was no small task, for it took two men to lift one of the huge, flat, iron vessels.

While preparations for defense were in progress, Simon Kenton brought word of Clark's capture of the British post at Kaskaskia; and from beyond the mountains came the joyful news that the King of France had sent his fleet to aid the Revolution.

Everything was quiet. The riflemen saw no Indians. Scouts roamed the forests and sentinels at last stood guard by night, but there was no trace of an enemy.

Had the fickle red men given up their plans entirely? Was Boone's escape, together with the warning which the Indians knew he must have carried, enough to discourage them for good?

At this juncture, on July 17, 1778, came William Hancock, another of Blackfish's prisoners.

Hancock, a poor woodsman, had taken nine days for the journey that Daniel Boone had made in four. He had started with three pints of dried corn, but he had almost no clothes left on him and arrived so nearly dead that Boone and others nursed him for three days. Exhausted, lost, and discouraged, he had lain down to die. Glancing up, he saw his brother's name carved on a tree, recognized a place where they had formerly camped together, realized that he was only four miles from Boonesborough, and staggered on. He was so weak that when he reached the north bank of the Kentucky River opposite Boonesborough he could barely make himself heard on the other side.

Hancock brought news that after Boone's escape the Indians had postponed the expedition against Boonesborough for three weeks, but nine days of the time had already expired.

Hancock had actually been at Old Chillicothe during the council which preceded final preparations for the attack, had seen the presents sent to the Indians from Detroit, and had talked with the British officers who brought them. The Indians had said they were bringing four hundred men and four field guns. Unless the settlers consented to join the British, they would either batter down the walls with the cannon or else starve them out by siege warfare, supporting themselves meantime on the settlers' own cattle.

The Indians were coming, then!

"If men can be sent to us in five or Six Weeks," says a letter to the Virginia military authorities, written in another's hand but signed by Daniel Boone, "it would be of infinite Service, as we shall lay up provisions for a Seige. We are all in fine Spirits, and have good Crops growing, and to intend to fight—hard in order to secure them." He expected the Indians, he added, "in twelve days from this"—that is, about the end of July. Virginia immediately began plans to send relief.

But still no Indians came. It was now six full weeks since Boone had escaped and the fort was quite ready to give a good account of itself. Was it possible that Indian scouts, seeing its strength, had carried back word of the preparations? Was it possible that the attack had been abandoned after all?

It did not seem likely, but the daring Boone proposed to do a little preliminary raiding on his own account. He might find out something important.

There was a good deal of argument about this expedition. Colonel Callaway thought it was the wrong thing to do, and he had his own doubts about Boone's motives, which were in fact mixed, though they never included the treachery Callaway feared. As Trabue reports his arguments, Boone insisted that "the indians would certainly be their in a few Days but they would have time to go against some indians that lived not far over the Ohio and if a few men would go with him he would conduct them to this little Camp and as these indians was rich in good horses and beaver fur they could go and make a great speck and get back in good time to oppose the big army of Indians." The prospect of "a great speck" was too much for the frontiersmen. Callaway lost both the argument and his temper, and the stubborn Daniel had his way. No wonder there were mutterings that "it was the nature of Boone" to be "foolhardy."

At the head of a tough little band of thirty, prepared to live on the parched corn they could carry and the game they could kill along the way, he set out for the Indian country. Beyond the Blue Licks a third of his men lost courage and went back to the fort, but the rest rode on. With Boone were Simon Kenton and Alexander Montgomery, scouts and woodsmen as skillful as himself.

Behind, in Boonesborough, sulked the suspicious Colonel Callaway, who thoroughly disapproved of the whole undertaking, and who had probably for some time entertained lingering doubts of Daniel Boone's loyalty. As a matter of fact, he need not have been so suspicious, for higher authority in the East distinctly approved of Boone's latest exploit. "A Capt and 11 men from Kentucky went within 5 miles of Chillacotha lately undiscovered, and return'd safe," wrote Colonel Arthur Campbell to a colleague, suggesting a similar incursion from the East while Blackfish was busy at Boonesborough.

Boone's was a reconnoissance in force, amply able to take care of itself, large enough to cope with any ordinary band of marauders, and yet small enough to evade a larger one. They crossed the Ohio in safety, either leaving their horses on the Kentucky side or swimming them across, and then, painted like Indians, pushed on toward the Scioto Valley, where Daniel Boone had made salt for Blackfish.

In the midst of these scenes of their leader's captivity, they stumbled on one small group of Indians in camp and decided to attack during the night or in the early morning. When the time came, however, the others declined to go, and Boone slipped up to the camp alone. A dog began to bark. An old Indian rose in his blankets and called to it. As he did so, Boone could see the glitter of a silver half moon on the warrior's breast. He aimed at this and killed him. The rest, supposing they were attacked in force, fled to the underbrush, while Boone slipped quietly back to his companions. A little later they fell in with an Indian war party of thirty warriors—part of the force gathering to attack Boonesborough. There was a desperate little wilderness battle, in which the Kentuckians, without loss on their side, killed one Indian, wounded several more and captured three horses with all the Indian baggage.

The Indians were first discovered by Simon Kenton, who was, as usual, scouting ahead. Moving silently through the woods, he was startled by the tinkling of a bell and took cover. As he did so, two Indians appeared, one riding a small pony, the other following on foot. As Kenton watched, the man on foot sprang suddenly upon the horse behind the rider, and both Indians burst into a roar of laughter.

Kenton let them come within range and then dropped both with a single rifle shot—one dead, the other badly wounded. As Kenton ran up to get their scalps, he heard something rustle in the cane and looked up to see two more Indians aiming at him. Dodging the two shots just in time, he hid in the vegetation. It was not thick enough to hide him long from the warriors, who soon began to hunt, though in some portions of Boone's march it had been so thick that the men could hardly get through and had to take turns breaking it down. At this moment Boone and his men appeared and after some brisk firing drove off the Indians. They could not carry off the body of the Indian Kenton had killed. Kenton scalped him.

The Kentuckians were now within four miles of Paint Creek Town. Kenton and Montgomery went ahead cautiously until they could peer into the village from the underbrush, and then reported to Boone that no warriors were there.

Boone had seen enough. From the absence of the Paint Creek braves, it was evident the Indians were gathering in force and that could mean only one thing. His party turned and headed for the fort at full speed, leaving the two scouts, Kenton and Montgomery, alone in the woods in hostile territory, living on what they could find, watching the Indians and seizing every opportunity for a little bushwhacking. If Indians could skulk in Kentucky, these hardy scouts could do a little skulking of their own in the Shawnees' Ohio country.

To avoid discovery, Boone's men had done no hunting, and had been for several days without fresh meat. Deciding hungrily that by this time one shot would make very little difference, they killed a buffalo and feasted. They finished it unmolested; but as they took up the homeward journey, they discovered the place from which two Indian scouts had been watching everything.

12. Blackfish Lays Siege

BLACKFISH and his Shawnee warriors had actually started on the warpath while Boone's band was hovering near their villages. But in spite of the pitched battle that had been fought, the Shawnees seem to have had no idea that the white raiders were still out. Neither do they seem to have hurried to reach Boonesborough before the white men could get back. Moluntha, "the Shawnee King," certainly knew that Boone's party had been in the Ohio country, because a day or two later he told Boone so.

The Indians were a large body of warriors and large bodies of troops always travel slowly. They crossed the Ohio near Cabin Creek in the vicinity of modern Maysville, went on to the Upper Blue Licks, and then followed the old buffalo trace towards Boonesborough. On September 5 Boone and his men slipped past them in the woods at the Lower Blue Licks and reached the fort at Boonesborough without being molested, bringing full information. One man's feet gave out and he lingered a day in the woods with one companion, returning safely the next night.

Knowing that the enemy would arrive at once, Boonesborough spent its last night of peace in final preparations, cleaning and repairing rifles, molding and trimming bullets—slow business, since the molds made only one or two at a time—and filling all available vessels with water.

Boone himself reckoned the enemy's numbers as 444 Indians and twelve Frenchmen—that is, French-Canadians. He was probably right, for on August 17, 1778, the British Lieutenant-Governor Hamilton who had sent out the expedition officially reported "at least 400 Indians assembled to attack the Fort of Kentucke where Captain Boone was taken last year," while there were other large war parties on the Ohio. The Indians were led by Boone's foster-father, Blackfish, war chief of the Shawnees, with the French-Canadian Lieutenant Antoine Dagneaux De Quindre, of the Detroit militia, as aide. A certain Isadore Chêne went with them as interpreter for the Wyandots and Ottawas, and they were also accompanied by Peter Drouillard, a trader who later rescued Kenton. Other Indian chiefs were Moluntha, who had led many raids into Kentucky; Catabecassa (Black Hoof), who had been at Braddock's defeat; and Blackbird, the Chippewa chief, who later left the British side and joined the Americans.

With the warriors came a pack train. They had all the ammunition they could possibly need, and soon made lavish use of it. The Indians had been armed and even provided with war paint by the British Army. A report of Hamilton's from Detroit in this very month lists eighty pounds of rose pink and 550 pounds of vermilion. Indians liked to be brilliant, but this was enough to daub up a small army. A more sinister item in the same inventory is "150 doz scalping knives." Even Blackfish's army could not use them all.

Boone's patrol rode into the fort on September 6. The Indians, close behind them, camped that night on the north bank of the Kentucky River. Early in the morning they slipped across at a place not far from the fort but safely screened from view, still pointed out as Blackfish Ford. Getting the neighboring ridge between themselves and Boonesborough, they moved down under its shelter and then crossed under cover of the trees and

COLONEL RICHARD CALLAWAY
From an early silhouette.

underbrush until they were fairly near the fort. It was a model bit of minor tactics for infantry.

The Indians seem to have had no very bad intentions in the beginning. Throughout his life they cherished a queer, half-humorous fondness for Daniel Boone. They had refused a huge sum for him at Detroit, and as Boone himself said, during his captivity he had "had a great share in the affection of my new parents, brothers, sisters, and friends," as well as the "entire friendship" of the chief Moluntha, now with the warriors surrounding the fort. Even after several more years of warfare the four Shawnee braves who later cornered Boone unarmed in his tobacco shed and could easily have killed him, treated the affair as an enormous practical joke—the American Indian always had a keen sense of humor. They merely tried to catch him again and take him home with them.

In the main, Blackfish and his men had kept the bargain made when Boone's party of salt-makers were captured. None of the prisoners had been killed or tortured, and Boone had received the signal honor of adoption by Chief Blackfish himself. What more, from the Shawnee point of view, could a reasonable man's heart desire? It is mortifying to have your beloved tribal kinsman show you a clean pair of heels and run away. But the Shawnees seem still to have believed that their adopted brother—at least subconsciously—loved them after all, even if he had had the bad taste to escape.

Lieutenant-Governor Hamilton himself believed that he could persuade the Kentuckians to leave their homes and their allegiance to the American cause and come to Detroit as faithful subjects of the King. Considering how nearly Kentucky did come to breaking away from the Union a few years later, after the Revolution, this was not a wholly vain hope; and it accounts for the friendly attitude of both sides as the siege began.

The Indians were first seen about ten o'clock. Daniel Boone

was outside the stockade, rifle in hand, and his nephews, Moses and Isaiah, sons of Squire Boone, were watering horses. Seeing men in the distance, the little boys supposed they were the expected reënforcements and were just about to ride out to meet them when their uncle warned them that these were Indians and sent them inside the stockade.

The long line of Indians straggled into view over the hill, displaying the British and French flags. Making no further effort to conceal their presence, the invaders immediately sent their English-speaking envoy, the negro Pompey, into the clearing with a flag of truce. The black messenger climbed on the cornfield fence and waved his white flag as he hailed the fort, asking if Captain Boone were there. The Shawnees had rather expected him to get lost and die in the woods, though a white man living with them had been sure that he would go "straight as a leather string, home."

The settlers let Pompey hail again before they answered. They did not want to appear too eager. But when he called once more, Boone himself answered, "Yes."

His presence once recognized, Pompey shouted that Hamilton expected Boone to fulfill his promises and surrender peaceably. The Indians had letters from the lieutenant-governor, and they wanted Daniel Boone to come out and get them.

The leaders inside the stockade took hurried counsel together and then yelled across the stockade to Pompey that no one would come out; but that he might bring the letters up to the stockade if he wanted to. At this, Blackfish himself called to Boone from some distance, addressing him as his son Sheltowee, and asking him to come out.

Boone agreed to meet him at a certain stump, walked out to Pompey and was taken to the chief. The Indians spread a blanket for Boone to sit on and then clustered around him. As the watching settlers saw them close in, they concluded in despair that "Boone was gone."

But Blackfish was still friendly. He and Boone shook hands like the best friends in the world, and blandly asked after each other's health. It was now about three months since they had met.

There was a certain strain in the conversation:

"Well, Boone, how d'y?"

"How d'y, Blackfish?"

"Well, Boone, what made you run away from me?"

"I wanted to see my wife and children so bad that I could not stay any longer," said Sheltowee gravely.

"If you had only let me know," replied Blackfish, "I would have let you go at any time, and rendered you every assistance."

It was no time for Sheltowee to express incredulity. He did, however, at length venture to ask Blackfish why the Shawnees had not fought more stoutly when surprised in a minor skirmish a few weeks before. Blackfish said nothing, but clapped his hands in quick repetition to imitate rifles. The white men's fire had been too fast.

Blackfish handed over a letter and proclamation from Hamilton, urging surrender, warning against the folly of resistance, pointing out that Indians were hard to control and reminding Boone that resistance would probably end in a massacre. Boone explained to Blackfish that he had been away so many months that he was no longer in command. He told the Indians that "there great virginia father had sent them a bigger Captain since there frend Boone had been with them; and that he wold not surrender the fortress, notwithstanding there friend Boone wished them to do so."

Going back to the fort, Captain Boone presently emerged with Major William Bailey Smith, elaborately attired in scarlet uniform and "macaroni hat" complete with ostrich plume. This, as the simple red men could see, was indeed a commander. But still there was no final agreement.

Blackfish remarked at some stage of the conversations that his warriors were hungry. The woods were full of deer, but Boone, knowing perfectly well that the Indians would take what they wanted anyway, kept up his friendly pose. He told his "father" to let his warriors help themselves to the station's provisions.

"There, you see plenty of cattle and corn; take what you need, but don't let any be wasted." Both now retired, and the Indians fell upon the supplies.

Inside the fort there was little debate. Daniel Boone offered to do whatever the rest decided. Being no longer in command, he had no intention of taking the whole responsibility of decision on himself. The Indians were getting angry. They could not be put off with negotiations much longer. They had promised to take the Kentuckians safely to Detroit and would probably do so. But that meant surrender. If Boonesborough resisted and lost, there would be a dreadful massacre of women and children. There were obvious advantages in yielding, and if Daniel Boone presented them to the anxious little council, he did no more than his duty.

Boonesborough, however, was unanimous for battle to the death and no surrender. Colonel Callaway sputtered indignantly that his family at least was not going to grow up among the Indians. Squire Boone, the pious Hardshell Baptist, said "he would never give up; he would fight till he died." The rest were of the same opinion.

"Well, well," remarked Daniel philosophically, "I'll die with the rest."

But however willing to fight, all realized the value of delay. Virginia had been getting reënforcements ready for weeks. No one knew how soon help might arrive. They must negotiate with the Indians as long and as slowly as they possibly could.

Daniel is said to have brought back word from Blackfish that to make peace all the officers must go over to his camp, out of sight (which meant out of rifle range) of the fort. Callaway vehemently opposed the idea, and it was finally agreed that the Indian chiefs would have to come up somewhere near the stockade.

Even to the stoutest heart it all looked pretty hopeless. Boonesborough was very weakly defended. There were only thirty men and twenty boys, including a few pack-horse drivers who had recently come in as temporary visitors. There were a number of women, including Boone's daughter, Jemima Callaway, and his brother Squire's wife, and a number of children; but there was no need to worry about Rebecca. She had been safe in the settlements for some time.

Though the settlers anxiously debating behind their log walls did not know it, the trusting aborigines had already been grossly deceived by a quick-witted Kentucky prisoner with the added virtues of a really good liar. Captured not long before, he had elaborately persuaded Hamilton that each of the Kentucky forts had lately been reënforced with three companies of seventy men each! Hamilton had passed this apparently important, but completely false, information along to his red allies.

The half-dug second well was badly needed now, when hands to finish it could not be spared from the loopholes; but the Indians made no effort to interfere with the bucket-carriers, who went from the fort to the Lick Spring for Boonesborough's usual water supply. The horses of Boone's reconnoitering band, who had returned just ahead of the war party, were safe within the stockade, and to the delight of the settlers the Indians let their livestock alone, killing only what they needed. Some of the cattle came up to the fort for milking as usual at sundown, and were brought inside. Under cover of darkness a few bold spirits slipped out and brought in vegetables from the garden, which had been planted just outside the stockade, where it could be temporarily protected from marauders.

Boone, Callaway, and Major W. B. Smith went out to meet Blackfish, Moluntha, the Canadian commander, De Quindre, and some twenty warriors. Boone, like other frontiersmen, had at least a smattering of Shawnee, and De Quindre probably spoke English, but the interpreter Chêne was retained. Later Boone and others were confused by the two French names, and Boone's ghost-writing biographer, John Filson, got the idea that a wholly imaginary Duquesne was the French commander —an error followed by a good many writers, though the British documents since revealed make the whole thing perfectly clear.

The situation was slightly embarrassing to Sheltowee. Both Blackfish and Moluntha, "the Shawnee King," had shown him special kindness until his escape a few weeks before. To make matters worse, somebody had killed Moluntha's son "the other day, over the Ohio," and the grim old father now reproached Boone for it. Indians were always killing or getting killed in the woods, and there is no telling who was really responsible for this brave's death. Boone had just returned from this very country; but the only Indians his men had killed had been an old Indian killed by Boone, and Simon Kenton's victim. Boone was able to assure Moluntha that he personally had had nothing to do with it. But Moluntha replied: "It was you, I tracked you here to this place."

Nevertheless, a panther-skin was spread on a log for the ambassadors to sit upon, and warriors courteously held branches over their heads. Blackfish displayed a wampum belt in three colors—black for warning, white for peace, red for war—and ended his speech with the words, "I come to take you away easy."

Major W. B. Smith remarked that it would be hard to transport so many women and children.

"I have brought forty horses," said Blackfish, "on purpose for the old people, women and children to ride."

Boone asked for the rest of that day and all of the next to consider the matter. It was agreed that the Indians would stay beyond a line thirty yards from the fort, and the whites would not carry arms outside the stockade. Blackfish assured Boone there would be no wanton slaughter of their stock. An escort of warriors accompanied Boonesborough's negotiators homeward, as far as the line agreed upon.

Blackfish gallantly presented seven smoked buffalo tongues for the women, and though some suspicious settlers feared they were poisoned, the meat turned out to be perfectly good. At one time Blackfish even suggested that he and some warriors would like to see Boone's squaws, but Sheltowee replied gravely that white squaws were very much afraid of Indians. It was all very handsome and quite unlike the usual methods of Indian raiders. They were very friendly out there, strolling in the clearing together, with the rifles covering every move from the fort and with Indian rifles just as ready back in the underbrush.

The Indians had been outmaneuvered in this backwoods diplomacy. They had practically admitted that they had no artillery which, though it had never yet appeared in Kentucky, was always feared. Furthermore, if Blackfish really had brought forty horses to take away women and children, he had brought far too many. Evidently, then, he had a wholly exaggerated idea of the numbers in the fort. Believing the tales of that unidentified but admirably plausible Kentucky romanticist who had been captured not long before, the war chief of the Shawnees supposed that the force inside the walls was very nearly equal to his own, besides being well protected behind a strong stockade, newly repaired. The Kentuckians had beaten off his warriors easily enough the year before. Their boldness, in the face of a large Indian force, spoke for itself.

The Kentuckians encouraged the delusion. Colonel Callaway had quietly staged a sly little masquerade. Women, children, even the slaves were dressed up, armed and kept moving about inside the fort. Great numbers of heads, or at least hats, were perpetually popping over the stockade or bobbing about behind it; and a man with a head, two hands, and two or three hats is as good as Cerberus when the copper-colored census-taker has to observe from bushes across a clearing over which rifles will soon be cracking.

All the hats and hunting shirts in the settlement were pressed into service and it is said that dummies were rigged up to make the showing more impressive. The big fort gate was kept wide open to let the Indians see the fictitious multitude. Pompey seemed unduly eager to get close to the fort. He might easily have found out too much and had to be warned to keep his distance or he would be shot.

There were several other reasons why the peace proposal, remarkable though it was, could not be regarded as wholly insincere. Hamilton had shown Boone a great deal of kindness in the preceding March, he certainly bore him no personal ill-will now, and rather imagined the surrender was already prepared. The Indians had been much impressed by George Rogers Clark's success in first capturing, and then winning over to the American side, the French settlers around Cahokia and Kaskaskia, who were on friendly terms with the redskins. As John Bowman wrote to Clark in October, one reason why the settlers at Boonesborough were willing to negotiate was that "Hearing that the Indians gladly treated with you at the Illinois gave them reason to think that the Indians were sincere."

There was a good deal of changing sides about this time. Two of the enemy's leaders were about to go over to the Americans

—the Chippewa chief, Blackbird, now with the force outside Boonesborough, and the Canadian Beaubien, who had helped capture the salt-makers at the Blue Licks. In Detroit the British governor knew that many of his French subjects were inclined to make friends with the Americans and entertained justifiable suspicions of some of the British. It was easy to change sides, since the revolting Colonists were quite as British by blood as the King's faithful subjects and sometimes members of the same families.

Some Kentuckians eventually joined the Detroit Militia. On the other hand, part of the Detroit Militia deserted to the American side, and Hamilton later declared that "secret treason" had ruined his government at Detroit. Things were all very mixed-up out there in the backwoods, where the hard task of survival was the main problem.

Blackfish's proposal was one of the most amazingly generous ever made by an overwhelmingly strong force to an enemy one sixth or one eighth their number, but it made much more sense then than it makes after the lapse of a century and a half. The Indians were probably far more sincere than the whites. They never dreamed of the rejection of such favorable terms, and they really did want their adopted brother, Big Turtle, to come back to them.

Blackfish remained impressed by the glowing prospects of white coöperation with the Shawnees that Boone had drawn while a captive. Moreover, he still did not suspect how much stronger his own force was. He probably never found out.

Preparations for battle went on swiftly inside the stockade, while outside everything was peaceful. Powder was served out, flints were picked, rifles cleaned, bullets molded—women and children working with the men. The night passed with sentries alert in the blockhouses and men dozing by their rifles, but not an Indian appeared. If Blackfish's men kept watch over the fort, there was not a sign of their presence.

The following day was equally quiet; but at evening came the white flag again, followed by the impassive chiefs. Boone himself told them the bad news. The Kentuckians were "determined to defend the fort while a man was living." Gravely the chiefs moved to one side to discuss this unexpected reply. Then they returned with a proposal equally unexpected. Through the interpreter, De Quindre insisted that they had come on a peaceful, not a warlike, errand. Lieutenant-Governor Hamilton had ordered them to avoid bloodshed. Allowing the cattle to enter the stockade was evidence of their pacific intentions. Even if the Kentuckians did not wish to return to Detroit, it might still be possible to negotiate a peace treaty. Why not have still a third meeting to draft it? If nine of the Kentucky leaders would sign, the Indians would withdraw, and they would all live as friends thereafter. This, as Boone remarked, "sounded grateful to our ears."

When negotiations were resumed next day, the same atmosphere of friendliness prevailed. By this time all the negotiators were well acquainted. As John Bowman wrote a month afterward, two days were "taken up in this matter till they Became Quite fimeleyer with one another." In spite of that, the settlers distrusted all Indians enough to make sure that the peace conference should meet, not inside the fort as the Indians ingenuously proposed, but in the hollow of the Lick Spring, only about eighty yards from the stockade and easily swept by rifle fire from it.

Here the negotiators gathered around a cloth-covered outdoor table, Indians, British, and Americans. A clerk took down the decisions. It was all very formal. The British union jack (and, for some queer reason, the flag of France, then fighting on the American side) were displayed by De Quindre. Boonesborough possessed an American flag by this time, but there is no record the settlers brought it along.

Only eight of the Kentuckians, instead of the nine stipulated, appeared at the council table: Daniel and Squire Boone; the suspicious Richard Callaway and his nephew Flanders (Daniel Boone's son-in-law); William Hancock, like Boone an escaped prisoner; Boone's old associate Stephen Hancock; Major William Bailey Smith, later historian of the siege, and William Buchanan. At the stockade, masqueraders were showing themselves in great numbers for the benefit of Blackfish, De Quindre, and a large number of Indians who now emerged from the forest.

There was a prolonged discussion. The Indians showed the white negotiators every hospitality. Skins were spread as seats. Food and drink from the British commissariat at Detroit were provided, a subtle temptation for the pioneers, who had enjoyed nothing of this sort for years. There was much conversation, in the course of which Squire Boone, the preacher, created a sensation by mendaciously remarking that George Rogers Clark, the terror of the Indians, was on his way to Boonesborough with a large army.

After a day of this curious combination of war, revelry, and diplomacy, an agreement was reached. It was to be signed the next day. Blackfish stipulated that eighteen warriors should attend him, so that all the villages represented in his army would also be represented at the conference. Boone and the others objected in vain. Blackfish was adamant on this point. Otherwise, he explained, the Indians could not be induced to regard the treaty as binding. The settlers did not dare bring an equal number, for it was not safe to risk having half their forces surprised outside the fort. They retired knowing that they would be outnumbered more than two to one when the treaty was signed.

The Indians may have been sincere in their first offers; Boone and the pioneers never had been. They had merely been playing for time under a cloak of friendship and eagerness for peace from the very start. Now it was the Indians' turn to try a little duplicity. A number of signs increased the settlers' suspicions. Toward evening Blackfish was seen walking around the fort at a little distance and surveying it carefully from every angle. From the Indian camp came the sounds of the war dance. It was a queer way to prepare for the signing of a peace treaty.

During the night braves crept down to the hollow by the spring and took cover amid the weeds, which at the end of summer were rank and tall enough to hide a good many of them. Others hid rifles near the treaty grounds. In the morning some cattle, probably scenting Indians, were seen uneasily hanging about the fort. When the visible warriors were told that the "white squaws were afraid to go out to milk," the Indians, anxious to oblige, courteously helped drive the cows up to the fort, where they were promptly secured for the rest of the siege.

Meantime, the women of Boonesborough were busily preparing a feast for the negotiators. The idea was to give an impression of abundance, as if Boonesborough were provisioned for a siege of any length. But after dinner the extra tables, the pewter plates, the knives and forks were carried back to the fort.

Diplomacy began again. All were unarmed, but Boone and the rest had thoughtfully laid their loaded rifles just outside the gate. Inside, every porthole held a rifleman, and the blockhouse nearest the treaty-makers held a special party of picked marksmen. The suspicious white negotiators had left orders to fire if they waved their hats. The riflemen were not to look for individual targets but to "fire into the lump." The chances were two to one they would hit Indians.

The distrustful Boonesborough men noted uneasily that this time Blackfish was accompanied, not by the older counselors who had been with him previously, but by young and vigorous warriors. When the Kentuckians pointed this out, the chief had the effrontery to insist that they were the same warriors who had come the day before.

Blackfish proposed that they should "make a lasting peace and forever bury the tomahawk and live as brothers." Boone replied laconically that he "was willing." To everyone's astonishment, Blackfish then offered them six weeks to leave the country! When this was refused, he inquired:

"Brothers, by what right did you come and settle here?"

He was reminded of the Watauga treaty with the Cherokees, of which he pretended never to have heard. Turning to a Cherokee standing near, the Shawnee chief inquired if this were true. Assured by the Cherokee that it was, Blackfish was somewhat taken aback.

"Friends and Brothers," he said, "as you have purchased this land from the Cherokees and paid them for it, that entirely alters the case; you must keep it and live on it in peace." He then proposed the Ohio River as a boundary and the cessation of all hostility. The settlers were to come under Hamilton's authority and take the oath of British allegiance. To this the settlers agreed.

A warrior carried around the "pipe-tomahawk," half hatchet, half peace-pipe, the blade for war, the pipe for peace. Gravely each Indian negotiator took a puff or two as it went around the circle. Boone was instantly ablaze with new suspicion. Familiar with Indian ways, he noted that it was offered only to Indians, not to white men. One of the white men drew up the articles agreed upon. Blackfish said he must announce the agreements to his braves, and stepping to one side delivered a loud and vigorous harangue in Shawnee, largely into space, as few Indians were visible. His elocution was much admired by the listening whites, though none of them understood more than a few words. His voice, someone later remarked, was "like old preacher Vardaman's."

When he came back, the chief made an extraordinary proposal. It was, he said, "usual with them, in making friends, to shake hands; but when they made a long and lasting peace, they caught each other by the shoulders and brought their hearts together." As there were more Indians than whites, each white brother should shake hands with two Indians at once. Blackfish obviously was adopting a custom to suit his own purposes. But it is not so surprising as it now seems that the Kentuckians fell into the trap. The suggestion was suspicious, of course, but it was not much more suspicious than most of the proceedings of the last three days, and the Indians so far had kept faith scrupulously. After all, they had just concluded a peace treaty.

Rather reluctantly, each Kentuckian held out both hands. An Indian, apparently in the best of humor, seized each hand of each pioneer—two to one. Blackfish himself approached his son Sheltowee and interlocked his right arm with Boone's left, laying his other hand on the other arm, while another Indian also took hold of him. It was instantly apparent that something was wrong, for the grips tightened into a good deal more than a mere handclasp or embrace.

"Go!" cried Blackfish.

At a little distance a warrior pulled a rifle from under his blanket and fired a signal shot into the air. Each pair of warriors tried to drag their particular "brother" over the high, steep banks of the Kentucky River, where they would be under cover and could be dealt with at leisure.

But the pioneers, their nerves taut with suspicion, "began to dispute the matter though unarmed." Colonel Callaway, who had been the most suspicious of all, was the first to break away, and the others shook themselves loose eventually, though "they had a dreadful scuffle." Major Smith, having broken loose, seized one of the Indians with whom he had shaken hands. But as he did so, a ball from the fort killed the warrior and they fell together, Smith on top. He picked himself up unhurt and made for home. Daniel Boone sent Blackfish sprawling, as he shook himself free, and the startled Indians seem to have thought that the chief was dead. For a crucial moment their fighting slackened. The warrior who had carried the pipe-tomahawk around—it was the only weapon at the scene—struck at Boone, but the blow landed between his shoulders as the prospective victim was bending over. He suffered only a slash on the head and a wound on the back. A second blow with the tomahawk missed Boone but hit Major Smith, "who was that instant passing rapidly by." Squire Boone, in his excitement, threw the warriors off "as so many little children." He ran a few steps, was hit by a bullet that knocked him down, picked himself up and made for the fort again. He did not reach it until the gate had been slammed and barred, but he and another man got in by a cabin door, previously designated and guarded for just such emergencies.

It was a lively few minutes. All the negotiators ran for the stockade as soon as they could break away and get in a blow or two. They waved their hats madly as they ran, in the agreed signal. The fort was blazing with rifle fire. From the underbrush Indian rifles blazed an answer, while between the running men the bullets whistled.

Except Squire Boone, all escaped without injury or with slight wounds. One negotiator could not get back into the fort at all. He spent the rest of the day outside on his stomach, earnestly hugging the ground behind a good thick stump. He had no rifle and could not defend himself. The Indians either did not know he was there or could not reach him in the face of the covering fire of the sharpshooters in the blockhouse, who knew he was outside well enough and could probably see him, but could not go out to his aid. With bullets flying in both directions, there was nothing for the distracted diplomat to do but lie low, keep the stump between himself and the Indians, and pray they would not get around on one side and pot him from the flank. Only when darkness fell was the poor fellow able to worm his way to the gates and safety.

Inside the southwest blockhouse, one William Stafford had beguiled the tedium of his wait during the negotiations by drawing a bead upon an unconscious warrior seated on a log not far from the council. As Stafford fingered his trigger and thought what a fine mark the unsuspecting brave would make, the Indian signal gun cracked and the scuffle commenced. Stafford pulled the trigger and the warrior fell dead.

The Indians were equally ready. On the upper log of another blockhouse, a certain Ambrose Coffer was stretched, lazily surveying the scene and quite unaware that Indian rifles were trained upon him from the underbrush. As the fight commenced, fourteen bullets went through his clothes, but he tumbled into the blockhouse unhurt amid the unsympathetic jeers of his rapidly firing comrades.

There was a great deal of noise. The Indians gave the war whoop. The frontiersmen shouted defiance back. Terrified women and children screamed and cried. Dogs began to howl and bark. The cattle stampeded round and round the fort enclosure. Matters were not helped by the panic of Boonesborough's Pennsylvania Dutch potter, Tice Prock. Instead of joining the riflemen, he fled into Squire Boone's blacksmith shop and hid under the bellows. Mrs. Richard Callaway chased him out with a brush, in spite of the poor fellow's shrieks of "Py sure, I was not made for a fighter!" Her husband, seeing there was no hope of getting him to fight, set him to digging the well deeper, and poor Tice dug away with alacrity in an earnest effort to get as much earth as possible between him and the bullets as fast as he could.

Presently, however, things quieted down a little, though some rifles went on cracking till dark. Once the Kentuckians were inside the fort, there was very little to fire at, though the Indians watched the portholes and tried to fire into each one that opened. It was useless to rush the palisades, or at least the Indians soon concluded that it was after one or two attempts, not knowing how few the defenders really were.

At the first lull in the firing, Daniel Boone took advantage of the opportunity to cut the bullet out of his brother's shoulder. Squire had managed to fire two shots, with a little help in loading his rifle. No longer able to load at all, he retired to bed in his cabin, valorously taking along a broad ax. This he stood by the bedside, hoping to get in a whack or two before he died if the Indians broke in. Then Daniel and the others had their own wounds dressed and the excitement died down until the Indians attempted a charge, which was quickly repulsed.

Seeing that their steady fire on the fort produced no results, the Indians eventually scattered flax along a fence leading up to the walls and set it on fire, hoping to ignite the wooden palisades. The settlers ran a trench under the wall and out to the fence. Thus sheltered, men crawled out and pulled down part of the fence connecting with the stockade. One night an Indian crept up to within fifteen paces of the fort near this point. London, Colonel Henderson's negro, crawled out into the ditch and fired at the flash of the Indian rifle. Something had gone wrong with their priming, however, and both flintlocks simply snapped without firing. For some time each man aimed at the sound. They went on snapping their locks at each other until the Indian rifle "fired clear" and killed London.

Blackfish now tried stratagem. In the forest quiet, the people in the stockade could hear the sounds of ponies and pack-horses being caught, saddled, and loaded. Orders were loudly bawled from the thickets nearest the fort. They were mostly in Shawnee but many frontiersmen knew something of the language. During the night all the Indians who could find hiding places crept up as close to the fort as they could get. Just before dawn, while it was still too early to distinguish anything clearly, the whole Indian force—or so it was meant to seem—retreated with a great deal of noise.

It was all just a little too obvious. The red man could drift through the woods with no more noise than a scalped ghost, as the Kentuckians knew only too well. The noisy departure was all a most un-Indian-like proceeding—particularly the steady tooting of a bugle which for some reason De Quindre had brought along, and which now sounded steadily, growing fainter and fainter as the retreating column drew farther and farther off into the hills. Then the Indians slipped silently back.

These far from subtle maneuvers would hardly have deceived a child. They did not for an instant deceive the suspicious Boone listening intently behind the log fortifications and peering cautiously over the upright logs and from the loopholes. Usually there was a strong temptation to rush out at the first assurance that the Indians had gone. The interior of the stockade, especially when cattle, hogs, and horses were penned in with men, women, and children, was uncomfortable, unpleasant, and crowded. Food was scarce and monotonous, water scanty, sanitation deplorably crude. People got on one another's nerves, what with noise, sleeplessness, anxiety, pain, and danger.

The natural thing was to let the stock out to fresh pasture and water—two things no raiders could destroy—as soon as the enemy disappeared. The settlers were always eager to see what had happened to their crops and cabins outside the stockade. Usually they took the precaution of sending out scouts or small patrols to search the woods and make sure that the Indians were really gone, for even after a real withdrawal small parties of scalp-hunters were likely to lurk about, hoping to kill a man or two, or capture a woman or boy here or there.

This time, however, De Quindre and Blackfish had completely overshot the mark. The settlers were so contemptuously sure the withdrawal was a feint that they did not so much as open the gates or risk sending out a scout. Silence—the menacing silence common in Indian wars—came down upon the clearing. The two parties of Indians lay waiting. Behind their defenses, the Kentuckians waited too—white patience against the red man's.

It was the white men who waited longer. After a little while the Indians realized that their stratagem had failed, and the clearing again blazed with their rifle shots. All day long the Indians fired at every chink and cranny in the Boonesborough defenses. One man was wounded because two logs had not been closely joined. All day long the frontiersmen blazed back at every stir in the underbrush or at every stump that could shelter a redskin.

So far, the invaders had achieved precisely nothing. Now, however, a new sound arose amid the firing. From the shelter of the steep river bank, where the Kentucky fire could not reach, woodchoppers could be heard at work. It sounded as if roots were being cut. Then the sounds changed, and in the clear water of the Kentucky River a broad muddy band appeared. The water upstream remained clear. Downstream the muddy water extended farther and farther, its upper end remaining always at the same spot. Over the edge of the bank, a watcher caught sight of a cedar pole which waved back and forth in a curious way. It looked, he reported, as if it were being used to loosen dirt.

The Indians were digging. The Detroit militiaman, De Quindre, was about to introduce European siege warfare on the frontier. The Indians were obviously running a mine from the river bank to the stockade. Just what they would do when their mine reached the fort was not so obvious. They might dig under the wall and let it collapse of its own weight. They might try to bring their mine up in the middle of the stockade and rush in. More likely, they intended to bring in powder and blow it up, or to build an immense fire against the logs and burn them. After the siege, huge torches made of poles and rails covered with inflammable flax and hickory bark were found lying ready.

Since it was important to see what the enemy was doing, the settlers constructed a rude watchtower out of such lumber as they could find, and pushed it up on the roof of the cabin which Richard Henderson had used for a kitchen when the fort was built. The cabin's stout log construction could easily carry the weight; the timbers of the watchtower were thick enough to turn bullets; and it went up without casualties.

From the protection of its upper story the lookouts could now peep over the edge of the steep banks and they instantly confirmed the garrison's worst fears. They could actually see the fresh earth being dumped into the river. Day and night reliefs of riflemen watched from the tower, but the Indians were too sheltered to be picked off. Pompey, the negro, occasionally bawled out a demand for surrender, or engaged in an exchange of bad language with the men in the blockhouse.

The only thing to do was to countermine; and a group of amateur engineers set to work. About three feet wide and very deep, the countermine began in the cabin under the watchtower and ran under the other cabins along the river wall of the fort. Under the blockhouse the whole floor had been dug out to a depth of four feet, so that there was plenty of room to shoot Indians as fast as they emerged. The Indians' minehead would inevitably run into this, or at least come near enough to be detected—in fact it was not long till each side could hear the other digging.

The Indians would have to emerge—if they did emerge—from a long narrow passage, one at a time. There would be a lively skirmish, but they could be dealt with as they came out of the mine, if enough men could be spared from the walls. They would probably attack through the mine and on the surface at the same time.

To advertise to the enemy what they were doing, Boone had the garrison ostentatiously throw the excavated earth out over the stockade. He rigged a box in ropes for the purpose. Captain John Holder picked up all the biggest stones as they were dug up and with murderous intent hurled them over the bank where the Indians were lurking. There were roars of protest from the warriors who, with much profanity, bade the settlers "fight like men, and not try to kill them with stones like children." One of those solemn, humanitarian females who are always about at the wrong time adjured him: "Don't do so Captain, it might hurt some of the Indians, and they will be mad and have revenge for the same."

Digging trenches, as any soldier knows, is the most exhausting labor known to man, and the hot September weather made the task none the easier. The siege dragged on. Each side tried to pick off the other's men but everyone kept religiously under cover.

Jemima Boone showed her usual courage, moving fearlessly about the fort with ammunition and food for the men at the loopholes. Eventually, while standing at the door of her cabin, she was hit by a spent bullet in what accounts of the matter euphemistically describe as "the fleshy part of her back." She was not much hurt, the bullet being extracted by a mere tug on the cloth it had carried into the wound.

The fire of the Indian sharpshooters, who could look down

into the stockade from the hills, became annoying, and the settlers cut doors from cabin to cabin, so that it was possible to move under cover almost the whole way around the stockade. Occasionally the Indians killed cattle with their plunging fire from the hilltops, but this merely increased the supply of fresh beef. Sad to say, however, "Old Spot," adored pet of Squire Boone's family, who often gave Indian alarms, was wounded in an anatomical area highly embarrassing to an industrious cow; but with prayerful nursing she survived and dwelt among the Boones to a ripe old age.

Settlers got hurt pretty regularly, but few were killed; and a bullet wound was common enough in those days. Boone is credited with a remarkable shot, very likely fired from the watchtower. The Shawnees' negro, Pompey, had been industriously sniping from a tall tree, and was doing his best to pick off people moving within the stockade, over which, from his lofty perch, he could fire easily enough.

"You black scoundrel," muttered Captain Boone as he raised "Old Tick-Licker," his heaviest rifle, which fired a one-ounce ball, "I'll fix your flint for you!"

At the crack of the rifle, Pompey came tumbling out of the tree, dead. When the siege ended, his was the only body found. The Indians had hidden or carried off their own dead, as usual, to prevent scalping, but no Shawnee cared in the least what had happened to the black body or woolly scalp of a negro slave. Dead or alive, a warrior's honor was safe if he still had his scalp. The bodies of Indians scalped by the whites were simply left to rot in their disgrace, but Boonesborough men secured no scalps during the siege. It was hard enough to save their own.

As Virginia Militia, the Kentuckians flew the new American flag. Its small staff had been lashed to a tall pole set up in the stockade. After several days' firing, the Indians managed to shoot the small staff to pieces, and there were war whoops from the underbrush as the flag fell. Since the pole had no halyards, the Boonesborough men had to take it down entirely, lash the flag on again, and raise the pole anew with a defiant answering cheer. The flags of the attacking forces, displayed about three hundred yards from the fort, were never brought down.

On the seventh night Indians slipped up near enough to hurl lighted torches against the stockade—a daring venture on their part, since the torches had to be carried well within rifle range; and prancing about in the night with a lighted torch where Kentucky riflemen could see it was distinctly bad for the health. Most of them sailed harmlessly over the stockade and cabins into the open square of the fort where they could do no damage. Blazing arrows accompanied the torches. Some were wrapped in the inner fiber of the shellbark hickory, which is full of oil and burns readily. Others were filled with powder and ignited by a piece of punk which served as a crude kind of time fuse. The torches were made of bundles of this bark, an inch thick at the tip and extending loosely along the shaft to a thickness of four or five inches. The arrows were smaller bunches of the same material. Shooting from the high bluff across the river, it was fairly easy for the Indians to drop them on the cabin roofs. At times the torches, fire arrows, and flashes of rifle fire made everything so bright inside the fort that the settlers could see "to pick up a pin."

Toward the end, Boonesborough's water supply was nearly exhausted. Squire Boone had unbreached some old muskets and inserted pistons. These improvised squirt-guns would throw a pint to a quart of water on the cabin roofs, and were distributed to the women for use if the cabins took fire.

One way of getting fire arrows off the roof was to go up with a broom and sweep them off, taking the chance of being silhouetted against the light and shot. Since the shingles were secured by a single peg each, they could often be torn off with one jerk. Sometimes they could be punched off from inside the cabin.

But there was no safe way of reaching the torches that had been thrown against the wooden stockade on the outside. To put them out meant going outside, and Indian rifles were ready for just such a move. John Holder was the only man who took this desperate chance. Looking down from a blockhouse, he saw that a torch had landed against a cabin door which was already blazing to the top. Dashing along the stockade, he burst into the cabin, wrenched open the outer door, and doused it with a bucket of water, swearing like a demon.

Alas for John! He had escaped death from Indian bullets but trouble awaited him within the stockade. Mrs. Richard Callaway, a dauntless but very pious lady, had heard his oaths. She scolded him soundly for daring to use such language in her hearing. It was, she said, a time fitter for prayer than swearing. The agitated Holder swore in return it was at least no time for prayer.

When the torches were at their worst, it looked for a few minutes as if all were lost. If the stockade took fire, the settlers would have no choice but to rush out into the arms of the savages. Even if only a part of the stockade was burned, a storming party of Indians could burst in and end matters with the tomahawk. Despair settled down. The Kentuckians waited.

Behind the Indian lines three white men were lurking and watching all that went on. Simon Kenton and Alexander Montgomery had come back from their scouting trip too late, and found themselves cut off. They might have gone on to Logan's Station, only forty miles away; but they were used to hanging on the outskirts of Indian camps; and throughout the siege they hovered behind Blackfish's band, waiting for the chance that never came, to slip through into the fort, or to strike a blow outside where it would do the most good.

Quite unknown to them, a certain William Patton was also concealed behind the lines. His home was in Boonesborough; but he had been in the woods when the Indians arrived and had come back too late. Finding Indians all around the fort, he settled down in the woods. In the daytime he would slip off to distant hills and watch the fighting, "and sometimes in the night he would approach tolerably near." He was close at hand on the night the Indians attacked with firebrands; and finally, convinced that Boonesborough was taken, he slipped off to Logan's to give the alarm there.

His story is recorded by Daniel Trabue, who was in Logan's Station at the time: "The Indians made in the night a Dreadfull attack on the fort they run up to the fort a large number of them with large fire brands or torches and made the Dreadfullest screams and hollowing that could be imagind Mr Patten thought the Fort was taken he came to our Fort to wit Logans Fort and informed us Boonsbourough was taken and he actuly Did hear the Indians killing the people in the fort They took it by storm &C he heard the women and children & men also screaming when the indians was killing them we beleaved every word he told as he was known to the people to be a man of truth."

As a reporter, Mr. Patton left something to be desired, but he had an undeniable flair for vivid detail. From a comfortable armchair and the distance of a good, safe century or so, it is easy to laugh at his imaginings. From the underside of a wet bush on a rainy night, after a week in the woods, with the scalp very loose on your head, with several hundred murderous fiends yelling, torches flaring, and rifles banging just in front of you, these things were a little less funny. And it is probable that he did hear women scream, children cry, and men yell. It was one of Boonesborough's livelier nights.

As the settlers watched in blank despair, the fires blazed—but only for a little while. They slowly dimmed, then flickered out. A period of misty, rainy weather had set in during the last few days of the siege. The wood was so damp from the drizzle that it would not burn.

But the digging still went on. There was a good deal of tart conversation about it across the battlements.

"What are you doing down there?" a rifleman would call from his station.

"Digging a hole," a warrior would grunt. "Blow you all to hell tonight. May be so? And what are you doing?"

"Oh, as for that, we are digging to meet you and will make a hole large enough to bury five hundred of you sons of bitches."

In the stable outside the fort was a stallion, brought in to improve the breed of frontier horses. The Shawnees slipped up and shot the animal. After that, there was a great deal of aboriginal humor:

"White man keep a horse in the house!"

"Go and feed the horse!"

"The horse wants water."

"Go take him to the river."

Sometimes the blockhouses yelled back taunting inquiries of their own. What had become of Pompey? Everyone knew well enough he was dead.

At first the replies were evasive. Pompey had gone for more Indians. Pompey had "gone hog-hunting"—after the settlers' swine, which roamed the woods. One brave called:

"Pompey ne-pan." (Pompey is asleep.)

Finally, toward the end of the siege, they admitted:

"Pompey nee-poo." (Pompey is dead.)

It was just another of those little Shawnee jokes. The two words were near enough alike for a pun.

Another brave carried his love of derision to lengths which offended Boonesborough's ideas of decorum. After a few pot shots from the steep hill across the river, he would climb out on the limb of a tree, stoop, take down his breech clout, and present his copper-colored stern to the white men, at the same time making an extremely indelicate suggestion.

He did it again and again, while Boonesborough fumed—not much shocked but very angry indeed. It was no use shooting. Everyone blazed away at the warrior but it was a waste of ammunition. He was always just out of range, up hill and across a river ninety yards wide.

Finally someone loaded an extra large rifle with an extra large charge and waited. The first shot missed. But the warrior was so pleased with his little joke that he tried again. The second shot brought him down. After that there was no more strip-teasing.

From start to finish there was an odd good nature about this curious siege. Equally strange was the unusual persistence of the Indians and, quite as remarkable, their willingness to do manual labor for several days at a time.

It was Squire Boone who undertook to improvise artillery. A century later Bulgarian peasants, fighting their Turkish oppressors, were to make cannon from the trunks of cherry trees. Kentucky's amateur artillerist made two cannon barrels from black gum trunks, anticipating the Bulgarian model, and wrapped them with an iron wagon tire. One burst when tried, but Squire loaded the other up with twenty or thirty one-ounce rifle balls; waited for a promising target; trained it finally on a group of unsuspecting aborigines one foggy morning and let drive.

"It made a large Report equal to a Cannon the Indins squandered from that place much frightened." In fact, "it made them skamper perdidiously whether they was hit with the bullets or whether it was the big loud Report it was uncertain." It was, at any rate, consoling to see them scamper.

Unfortunately Squire's mastery of interior ballistics was a little weak, and at the next shot the barrel burst. Thereafter, there was much Shawnee repartee across the stockade, and taunting Indian yells of:

"Fire your wooden gun again!"

"Fire your damned swivel."

Nevertheless, the Shawnees are said to have been uncertain just what had happened, and to have feared that when their mine was completed they might find Squire and his howitzer looking grimly down it.

Matters were growing serious in Boonesborough. There was dissension and distrust among the leaders. Little food was left. Over a week of work, heat, anxiety, loss of sleep, the strain of perpetual vigilance had worn the people down. Through the ground the guards in the station trench could hear the steady thump-thump as the approaching enemy dug away the last few feet of earth. The relief from the Holston Valley had not appeared.

The rainy eighth day of the siege faded into a black, rain-swept night in which the guards could watch the clearing only by fitful lightning flashes. No one proposed surrender but no one in that wretched, isolated little camp had any expectation of more than a day or two of life.

All through the night the settlers waited. It was so dark that the Indians could easily creep up undetected. The rain drowned any warning sounds. At any moment the explosion of a mine might blow open the gate. The Indians might burst through their tunnel and into the fort. Or all this might be merely a feint and scaling ladders might be rushed to the stockade and hundreds of yelling braves come pouring over.

The night was quiet, soggy, miserable, and anxious. The rain ceased and the guards noted in the stillness that the familiar sounds of digging in the tunnel could no longer be heard.

At camp a few Indians still hung around and there was an occasional shot. When the sun was an hour high, even these were only reports in the distance. What did that mean? Was this another trick? Was this the lull before the storm?

Instead, it meant salvation. The steady rainfall had soaked the earth above the rude mine and many sections had caved in. To the Shawnees it was the final blow. The disgusted warriors gave up. Some say the siege had lasted nine days. Others say eleven. At any rate it had broken all records for Indian warfare in Kentucky.

During the morning, scouts emerged from the fort and cautiously reconnoitered the woods. This time it was true. The enemy were really gone at last; and at noon the gates were opened. The half-starved cattle were let out to grass. The settlers themselves strolled about the clearing to stretch their weary legs after nine days of siege.

Around the portholes of the fort, Indian bullets were embedded to form a thick leaden incrustation. Some had fallen out and lay on the ground outside. Since lead was precious, the British ammunition was scraped up and melted down again into American bullets. Boone himself said that the frugal pioneers picked up 125 pounds of bullets, not counting what remained stuck in the logs.

As they rejoiced, out of the woods emerged Simon Kenton and Alexander Montgomery—but it was only a few days before Kenton was off again, this time to be captured by the Indians and be sold by them to that very Peter Drouillard who had been with the besiegers.

Having done the best they could for Boonesborough, the volunteers from Logan's Station started home. There Captain Benjamin Logan—who had taken Patton's story at its face value—was getting ready for what was coming. He knew well enough whose turn was next if Boonesborough were taken. "He said there was little doubt but the Indians would come to our Fort," according to Daniel Trabue, who was looking after supplies for him at the moment.

Logan ordered the women and children "to bestir themselves and bring in the fort rosting years punkins fill their vessils all full of water." In a short time there was corn in every house and all the pails, tubs, pots, kettles, and even the churns were brimming with water. Then this indefatigable officer bethought him of the permanent store of provisions and inquired of Trabue, his commissary, who later reported the story. When Trabue replied that he had ample supplies for a siege, Logan insisted: "Let me see." When he had seen, he commented: "You have got a good quanity but it is uncertain how long we might be besieged and I think you had best go out to the big lick and Drive some cattle up and we will stop them up in the fort as we may need them if you will go I will send men with you."

"I certainly will go," replied Trabue, and was just starting with six or eight others when Logan called after him: "Stop I am afraid for you to go I will go by my self. go back in the fort I will hunt the cattle & Indians alone I will keep in the cane the whole way."

An hour later he was back with a broken arm and two or three other wounds. Indians—apparently stragglers from Blackfish's band—had caught him in the cane. Next day the cattle came running to the fort with arrows sticking in them; but the settlers were afraid to open the gates lest the Indians might rush in, and the poor cows had to take their chances outside.

With his commander wounded, Trabue had his doubts about morale and "very frequently would go around the fort and look at the rest of the people—they were a couragus people but yet I will say they all looked very wild you might frequently see the woman a walking around the fort looking and peeping about seeming that they did not know what they was about but would try to incourage one another and hope for the best."

Next day wild figures appeared. The settlers "could not see only the front of them." They were in Indian file.

"Yes yes the indins is a coming," someone shouted.

Women ran to the loopholes to look out. Some of them cried: "Lord have mercy on us yonder they come."

There was a long stillness. Then a woman cried again:

"It is our boys."

The Logan's Station detachment was moving in from Boonesborough with the news of victory. Someone went to the shattered Logan with the news. Says Trabue: "Capt Logan smiled for the first time since he was wounded if ever I had seen people glad it was at that time." Since Beowulf, the Anglo-Saxon has been given to understatement.

It was not long until the Holston Valley militia reached Kentucky. They had arrived too late for the siege, but Boone had asked for them in five or six weeks and they were on time or nearly so. There was still plenty for them to do. Dour Presbyterians of the Cromwellian breed, they were all for smiting the heathen hip and thigh, and wanted to start out after Blackfish. But a council of officers from Boonesborough and Harrodsburg assembled at Logan's Station and finally decided against the plan. Instead, they used the Holston men to drive off the scattered marauders who lingered behind the main war party, trying earnestly for scalps and loot.

Blackfish and most of his warriors moved north toward the Ohio River in complete leisure, regretfully convinced at last that their brother Big Turtle really did not care to join the tribe. They seem to have had no fear of pursuit—may even have hoped for it as a last chance to draw the Kentuckians forth from their defenses. But Kentucky was too weak to give chase.

On their way home the disconsolate warriors ran into Ansel

Goodman and George Hendricks, two of Boone's salt-makers, who together with one other prisoner, Aaron Foreman, had taken advantage of the warriors' absence to escape. Hendricks was recaptured. The other two escaped. The warriors consoled themselves by punishing Hendricks severely for running away.

Last of all comes the bill. There is, in the Virginia State Archives, a small account book dealing—still in pounds, shillings, and pence—with militia affairs. It reduces the epic story of Boonesborough to two entries:

(1777) Decr 2. Boone, Capt. Daniel; for pay & rations of his Comp^{y} Kentucky Militia, *per* acco^{t}. [£]713.19.4

(1778) Nov. 26. Boone, Major Daniel, for horse hire & powder for Boonesborough garrison, *per* acct & Cert, [£]123.3

13. Treasons or Stratagems?

THE siege was hardly past when the jealousies or suspicions among Boonesborough's leaders, which had barely been glossed over while the Indians were on the other side of the palisades, broke out openly. The Callaway and Boone families had been friends and neighbors for a long time. Colonel Richard Callaway had been one of the first settlers in Kentucky. He and Boone had worked together from the beginning. Their daughters had been captured by the Indians while out for a boat ride together; and the two fathers had jointly directed the rescue, each heading one of the two parties. The success of Boone's men and the failure of Colonel Callaway's may not have improved the colonel's temper. The links between them had, however, been drawn still closer when young Flanders Callaway, the colonel's nephew, married Jemima Boone.

But in spite of these years of friendship there had been bitter dissension and dark suspicion during the siege. Colonel Callaway had fiercely objected to the Paint Creek expedition and to what he thought Boone's foolhardiness, or worse, in leaving the fort to parley with the enemy. Boone, to be sure, was personally acquainted with Chief Blackfish and Chief Moluntha, and Callaway had not the privilege. But the parley had actually gained three days' time—a success which probably increased the good colonel's ire.

Even though it had proved an eventual success, Boone's insistence on negotiation had very nearly ended in getting eight of the leading men of Boonesborough killed or captured at a moment when every rifle counted.

Worse still, there were grave suspicions of Boone's loyalty. They were cruel, and they were unjust; but they were very natural, especially in the gossipy atmosphere of a small and utterly isolated frontier community, with little to talk about save Injuns, crops, and each other. After the siege, when the Injuns had gone and the crops were all destroyed, gossip flourished. Talk about disloyalty at Boonesborough seems to have been widespread. It is worth noting that old William Clinkenbeard, an early settler at Strode's Station, who had lived in Boonesborough for a while, used in his later years to murmur mysteriously about the "Tories" there and does not even mention the name of Daniel Boone.

It was bad enough for Boone to let himself be captured, but he had even guided the Indians to the salt-makers' camp and had compelled his own men there to surrender without a fight. True, Boone explained that he did this only to lure the Indians away from Boonesborough. True, he actually had lured the Indians away. True, too, that an attack at that time would certainly have ended in a massacre.

But the other captives at Detroit and Chillicothe had seen him made much of by the Indians. Everyone had seen the friendship and esteem that Blackfish and Moluntha showed him. Later they had seen him received by the British with similar marks of friendship.

The wily old hunter really had deceived Hamilton into thinking that Kentucky was nearly ready to come over to the British side. "By Boone's account," the lieutenant-governor excitedly reported, "the people of the frontier have been incessantly harassed by parties of Indians they have not been able to sow grain and at Kentucke will not have a morsel of bread by the middle of June. Cloathing is not to be had, nor do they expect relief from the Congress—their dilemma will probably induce them to trust to the Savages who have shewn so much humanity to their prisoners, & come to this place before winter."

Just what Daniel Boone hoped to gain by these tales is not clear now. He may have thought that British belief in Kentucky's weakness would induce Hamilton to send out relatively weak war parties. He may also have thought that if Hamilton had any hope of winning the Kentuckians over peacefully he would cease sending war parties altogether. There is no question that Boone's ingenious tales did secure a delay which made it possible to get Boonesborough ready for defense. If the others had been as active as he, it would have been ready a couple of months before the Indians arrived.

But all these sinister tales were carried back to Boonesborough by the little stream of escaping captives who found their way to Kentucky both before and after Boone's own escape.

When the Indians arrived, Boone was naturally the first man they asked for. They had quite definite hope that he would persuade the Kentuckians to surrender but there is not a scrap of evidence that he ever counseled anything of the sort—and his enemies would never have missed the chance to bring out such discreditable evidence if it had been possible. When Colonel Callaway objected to going outside to negotiate, Boone was evidently one of those who overruled him. Callaway was naturally irritated, particularly when it turned out Boone had been right all the time.

No one will ever know what bitter recriminations passed when the negotiations that Boone insisted on had failed; when the time that they had gained proved too short for relief to arrive, after all; when defeat and a horrible death for every living being in the fort seemed imminent from moment to moment; when husbands thought in agony of the fate of their wives and their children; and when the little group of leaders debated anxiously the last, hopeless expedients that might possibly save their lives.

It was no wonder that when it was all over the finger of an evil suspicion pointed at the man who had lived four months with the enemy; who was an adopted member of their tribe; who was the "son" of the chief who had commanded the attack and a friend of the "hair-buying general" himself.

There was some ground, too, for suspecting Toryism. Americans were a puzzled race in those years. Washington and his army were technically rebels. They had taken up arms against their sovereign lord, the King. Many other Colonists had loyally and legally taken up arms on the King's behalf, and others were in silent sympathy with the royal cause. Rebecca's family were mostly Tories, some merely as sympathizers, some as active soldiers of the King against his Colonists. Her relative, Samuel Bryan, had just returned from Kentucky when he was killed fighting for the King. It was even said that Daniel Boone had never wished to fight on the rebel side, that he had gone to Kentucky in 1775 to avoid the revolutionary struggle then impending.

As the war dragged on and the tension grew, the lot of Tories in the East became more and more unhappy. Many of them in the states bordering on Kentucky sought refuge from their troubles on the frontier, where fewer questions were asked. A still larger Tory immigration came later. By 1780 many of the settlers could hardly be driven to arms and many, when captured, quietly took lands in loyal British territory and calmly settled down as subjects of the King again.

How much of this Tory attitude existed in Kentucky in 1778 there is no telling, but the charges against Boone grew out of the realization that such a situation was developing. As early as 1777 the British had tried some highly modern propaganda methods. During the attacks on Logan's fort a man was killed and scalped at the gate. When the Indians were gone the defenders found beside the body a bundle of proclamations by Sir Guy Carleton, British commander-in-chief in Canada, addressed to Kentuckians in general and to Clark and Logan by name. They promised pardon, lands, equal rank and equal pay for all who would join the Canadian forces. If they yielded, the Kentuckians were promised that Indian attacks would cease.

Logan cannily gathered the papers up and stowed them away without divulging their contents—"for what reason is not known," observes John Bradford naïvely. It all helps to explain Lieutenant-Governor Hamilton's credulity as he listened to Daniel Boone's tales, and Colonel Callaway's suspicion as reports of them came in. Worse still, Boone is said to have remarked that while he was with the Indians, "he could hear from Boonesborough every week." He probably meant that Indian scouts watched the fort steadily, as was easy enough from the high hills across the river; but the remark could be twisted into suspicious evidence of treason within the fort itself.

There was nothing for it but a formal trial, on which Colonel Callaway and Captain Benjamin Logan insisted. Courts-martial were not infrequent in the loosely organized and unruly frontier militia, and Boone himself, as a militia officer, sometimes sat as one of the judges. Unfortunately, the records of this particular trial have vanished from the archives, having probably been removed and destroyed by some well-wisher eager to clear the defendant's reputation.

Daniel Boone's good name actually suffers very little if at all from the episode, if we may judge from the only account of it that has come down to modern times. Colonel Daniel Trabue, who knew Boone and was "present at his Tryal," wrote down a full account in his reminiscences. The charges were preferred by Callaway and Logan and the two, as Trabue naïvely remarks, were "not pleased" by the acquittal which immediately followed. Boone was charged: first, with leading the Indians to the camp of his salt-makers and compelling their surrender; second, with encouraging the reconnoitering expedition to invade the Indian country before the siege of Boonesborough; third, with being "willing to take all our officers to the Indian camp to make peace out of sight of the fort"; and fourth, with being "in favour of the british." "All his conduct proved it," according to Callaway, who thought that "he ought to be broak of his commyssion."

But "Boon insisted otherwise." He had indeed, he admitted, urged the salt-making party at the Blue Licks to surrender; but "the reason he give up these men at the blue licks was that the Indians told him they was going to Boonesborough, to take the fort Boon said he thought he would use some stratigem he thought the fort was in bad order and the Indians would take it easy he Boon said he told the Indians the fort was very strong and had too many men for them that he was friendly to them and the officers at Detroyt and he would go and show them some men to wit 26 and he would go with them to Detroyt and these men also and when they come to take Boonesborough, they must have more warriors than they now had Boon said he told them all these tails to fool them he also said he Did tell the British officers he would be friendly to them and try to give up Boonesborough, but that he was a trying to fool them."

Boone might have added that the Indians outnumbered the salt-makers four to one and that the Indians were sure to find the salt-camp anyway. Blackfish was only a few miles away, and the Blue Licks were on a much traveled warpath, though Colonel Callaway contended that the war party was "not going towards the men" at the moment Boone was captured. It was a point on which Callaway could not possibly have any first-hand knowledge, since he was thirty or forty miles distant at the time.

If Boone had not acted as he did, Blackfish's war party would probably have captured Boonesborough and scalped the very men who later held the court-martial, besides surprising and killing both the salt-makers and the relief party which was just leaving Boonesborough. As a result of Boone's adroitness, no salt-makers were killed, and the relief party was able to get back to shelter. Thanks wholly to him Boonesborough was attacked, not when it was weak, but months later when it had plenty of warning, was in good repair, and—as the event proved—well able to stand a siege.

There is no doubt that Boone had discussed joining the British with Hamilton; and poor Chief Blackfish had apparently lent too credulous an ear to the guileful Daniel. That Boone ever really contemplated treason is a ridiculous idea, disproved by all his years of faithful service. That he worked a legitimate ruse of war for all it was worth is likely enough. But traitors do not carry warning.

Callaway's suspicion was largely due to William Hancock, who had been captured with the salt-makers and had escaped after being held in the Shawnee camps and also in Detroit. There he had seen the deference paid Boone by the British. It was he who brought back the wild rumor that Boone "had agreed with the British Officers that we would come with the Indians, and that the Fort should be given up. That the people should be taken to Detroyt, and live under the Jurisdiction of his gracious Majesty, King George III."

It was a foolish tale—military treason is hatched a little less publicly than that, and casual prisoners of war like Hancock are not taken into the secret; but it helps explain the suspicion that arose later when Blackfish and his warriors really did arrive with precisely such a proposal as Hancock had predicted.

Boone "told the same tale that Mr. Hancock had stated, only said he was Deceiving the British Officers and Indians. That he was now come home to help his own people fight, and they must make that preparatione that they could."

There is no record that Boone even troubled to defend himself against the charge of negotiating with the Indians "out of sight of the fort." He had actually met them well within sight of the fort, and the suspicious Colonel Callaway had gone along. Treating with the Indians had delayed the siege three days and everybody knew it. Callaway was either influenced by personal animosity or he was too ready to believe the wild gossip that Hancock brought home.

The court-martial found Boone not guilty, a reasonably obvious verdict; and he was further vindicated by prompt promotion to the rank of major.

It is not unusual for an officer with a clear conscience, whose conduct is being gossiped about or called in question, himself to demand a court-martial in order to clear his name. To take a very modern instance, such was the action of the unfortunate German lieutenant-colonel of the general staff who ordered the retreat from the Marne. At least one of Boone's idolaters has pretended that Callaway and Logan really pressed the charges out of pure good nature. They knew, according to this version, that gossip was going round and they wanted to scotch it at once and see their old comrade's name kept clear.

There is not a particle of evidence for this bit of charity. Trabue, who was there, heard the evidence on both sides, and saw the participants in the court, is quite definite that Callaway and Logan were disgusted by the acquittal. One of the women used to say that "Boon never deserved any thing of the country." One of the Bryans summed it up by saying simply that "Boone was blamed by a few—but when tried acquitted."

Once cleared of the charges, Daniel Boone hurried off to the settlements to find his wife and family. He was so quick about it that he was actually on the way before all of the relief had come in, and he met part of these troops on the Wilderness Road.

What did Boone think of it all, as he made his way eastward through the forests?

No selfish motives had kept him at Boonesborough. His own family was safe in the settlements. There was plenty of time before the Indians came. If he wanted to join the Tories, he could easily go to North Carolina and join them there. But his first loyalty was to the settlers who had trusted him and followed him to Kentucky. With them he would stay and with them he would die if necessary.

His reward was charges of treachery and a court-martial at the hands of these very people. It was not the last time that he was to feel the ingratitude of his friends, but it was the first and perhaps the bitterest. In later years his children often repeated his stories and opinions, but to this episode they seem never to have referred. At least once Boone discussed it with a kinsman. Otherwise he kept silence.

But just after the siege, before his return to North Carolina, he wrote a letter to his wife denying the charges of Toryism in language so profane that the blushing Rebecca took her scissors and snipped the bad words out. It had been alleged that he was a Tory and had taken the oath of allegiance to the King. It was not true: "God damn them they had set the indians on us," runs the only sentence of that emphatic letter that has been preserved. Rebecca was shocked; her Daniel rarely swore.

It was all over, so far as Daniel Boone was concerned. There was comfort in his acquittal—no ordinary verdict of "not guilty," but a complete exoneration by his friends and neighbors, an exoneration made more emphatic by his immediate promotion. His accusers were not promoted. Daniel harbored no malice. He gave still more heroic service to Kentucky. He risked his own life and his family's lives again and again.

The last word may well be Simon Kenton's: "They may say what they please of Daniel Boone: he acted with wisdom in that matter."

14. Red-Skinned Raiders

BOONE found Rebecca and the children living comfortably enough in a small cabin near that of William Bryan, Rebecca's brother, who had married Boone's sister. Soon after Daniel's return they moved to the dwelling of Rebecca's father, but it was not long before they were off again to Kentucky.

It had been difficult for news to get back to the settlements during the fighting with Blackfish; but a letter or two had been sent East before the siege began, announcing Boone's escape. Friends may have sent the word on to Rebecca. She was very likely expecting her husband when he walked in with the story of his escape, of new laurels in the defense of Boonesborough, of the charges against him, of his triumphant acquittal, of his promotion.

All the rest of the winter of 1778-79 and all the summer of 1779 Daniel and Rebecca remained in the East. No one knows quite what Boone was doing in this period. In the "autobiography" he himself says merely that "nothing worthy of a place in this account passed in my affairs for some time." The Virginia authorities must have wanted first-hand reports from Major Boone on the situation in Kentucky, on the British defenses at Detroit, and on the location of the Indian villages. Some have conjectured that Rebecca's Tory family pleaded with him to stay out of Kentucky and succeeded in delaying his return.

Because of this prolonged absence in the East, he missed Bowman's attack on the Shawnee villages in the spring of 1779, the first serious effort of the Kentuckians to carry the war into the enemy's country on a large scale. Four companies, about two hundred men in all, surprised Little Chillicothe one foggy night. The Shawnees were very weak at the moment. Louis Lorimier, with Chiefs Black Stump and Yellow Hawk, had taken four hundred warriors to settle on the Mississippi. Most of the warriors at Chillicothe fled. The women and children huddled into the council house while twenty-five men and fifteen boys fought as best they could, encouraged by the conjurer Assatakoma. Joseph Jackson, one of Boone's salt-makers who was still a prisoner, was hastily bound to prevent his escape and lay helpless listening to the fight.

Blackfish brought up reënforcements but was mortally wounded by a rifle ball that ranged along the thigh from the knee upward. For a time the grim old chief wanted to surrender, hoping that white medicine might save his life. Bowman withdrew after a few hours, however, having destroyed cabins and crops and taken a large drove of horses. There was no surrender, and Blackfish died of infection a few weeks later.

There was great excitement among the Indians and hasty appeals were sent to other villages for help. "Girty is flying about," says a white officer's report. But by the time reënforcements were ready Bowman had reached the Ohio, where boats met him and ferried his men across.

In October of 1779 the Boone family started back to Kentucky with two of Daniel's brothers and with a large group of immigrants, many of them from the Yadkin country.

Either with this party or with one that soon followed came Abraham Lincoln, grandfather of the President. He is said to have come on Daniel Boone's advice; and the story is plausible enough, for the Boone and Lincoln families had intermarried and had been neighbors in Pennsylvania and probably also in Virginia.

"It was like an army coming out," said a man who saw the cavalcade. "The[y] would be camped for ½ mile, all along in a string." It was a dangerous way to camp, but there were no attacks. Bowman had seriously damaged the Shawnees. It would be some months before they were ready to take revenge. The immigrants brought cannon with them—two "swivel guns," a personal gift from a North Carolina friend to Daniel Boone. Several horses died on the journey, however, and the heavy guns had to be left behind at the ford of the Cumberland River, where they lay for years. They remained as good as ever, for the artillery of that day was made of bronze, which does not rust, but no one could spare horses to get them to Kentucky, no matter how much they were needed.

Colonel Callaway had also been in the East, serving as Kentucky County's representative in the Virginia Assembly. He, too, started back with a pack train, forty men, lead, flints, and a little powder. "Men were very easy to get to go with the powder and lead," says Colonel Daniel Trabue, "as they wanted to see the country and get the land."

It was not a company which the Boones would have found congenial. After the court-martial Boone and Callaway met very little. Just as Boone set out, he and Callaway were both made "trustees" of Boonesborough, but refused to serve.

The other branches of the Callaway family were not estranged. At least, Daniel and Rebecca lived and traveled with Flanders Callaway in later life. But there is no record of any further friendly relationship with Colonel Callaway himself during the rest of his brief life.

Proud, sensitive, disinclined to quarrel, Boone did the only thing he could do. He moved away from the settlers he had led to Kentucky, and from the town whose site he had chosen for his home when all Kentucky was a wilderness. He had a land claim a few miles north, near what is now Athens, Kentucky, and here he set to work building a new settlement of his own, Boone's Station. He lost no time in doing so. A traveler inquiring for him at Boonesborough that same autumn was told that Boone had gone "to settle a station," and following, found him hard at work.

Much had happened since Daniel had last been in Kentucky. The white men had temporarily the upper hand. Even before Boone's capture, George Rogers Clark had sent spies straight into the British garrisons and after receiving their reports had made an incredible march through the wilderness. His men came through very much alive and captured the British posts of Kaskaskia, Cahokia, and Vincennes during the summer. Hamilton, hurrying down to attack them, had recaptured Vincennes and then had been besieged in his own fort and compelled to surrender, February 25, 1779. An amazed Indian band returning from a raid on the settlements had walked straight into the arms of the victorious Americans to be captured and promptly tomahawked.

While Daniel Boone was still in the East, Hamilton had been sent overland as a prisoner and was sputtering indignantly in a Virginia dungeon. Boone is said to have visited him before setting out for the frontier again.

There was now good reason for hurrying back to Kentucky. Since the Transylvania Company had collapsed, the settlers' claims to its lands no longer held. The Virginia government was sending out a special land commission to hear all claims and determine which were valid. It had authority to issue certificates for four hundred acres where a settler's right of occupation was established, and a preëmption right to one thousand acres of land adjoining each claim. The settlers were to pay the state ten shillings for each one hundred acres, plus ten shillings to the clerk for a certificate.

Hearings began October 13, 1779, and thereafter the commission moved about from one fort to another, awarding lands to the settlers in each. It held several sittings at Boonesborough, and Boone established what then appeared to be perfectly good claims to fourteen hundred acres for himself, another fourteen hundred for Israel Boone and one thousand acres for George Boone, besides appearing on behalf of six other settlers. In all, the commission issued certificates for 3,200 claims. It looked as if the vexed question of land titles had been laid to rest at last.

But for Daniel Boone the land title settlement was only the beginning of more trouble. Early in 1780 he set off for Virginia to buy state land warrants, which had to be secured before surveys of new land claims could proceed. The original warrants of the Transylvania Company had now been worthless for some time, and all land would in future have to be held from the State of Virginia. Bitter cold had kept an army of land speculators in the East during the "hard winter" of 1779-80, but Nathaniel Hart's friends there warned him in the spring that the speculators would soon be arriving. Everyone in Kentucky wanted to get warrants as soon as he could.

Boone is said to have carried about twenty thousand dollars of his own money. Part of it he had raised by selling the Kentucky land he already owned to get funds to buy warrants for more land. Nathaniel Hart gave him £2946.10 of which Boone was to give Mrs. Hart as much as she needed, up to three hundred pounds, spending the rest for land warrants. Many of his other friends gave him such funds as they could scrape together. Altogether he must have had in his saddlebags between forty and fifty thousand dollars. It was all currency. There was no way to get checks and bank drafts.

However skillfully he could elude the wily Shawnee, Daniel Boone was no match for the still wilier rogues of civilization. With one companion, he halted for the night at an inn in James City, Virginia. When the two men went to sleep, they

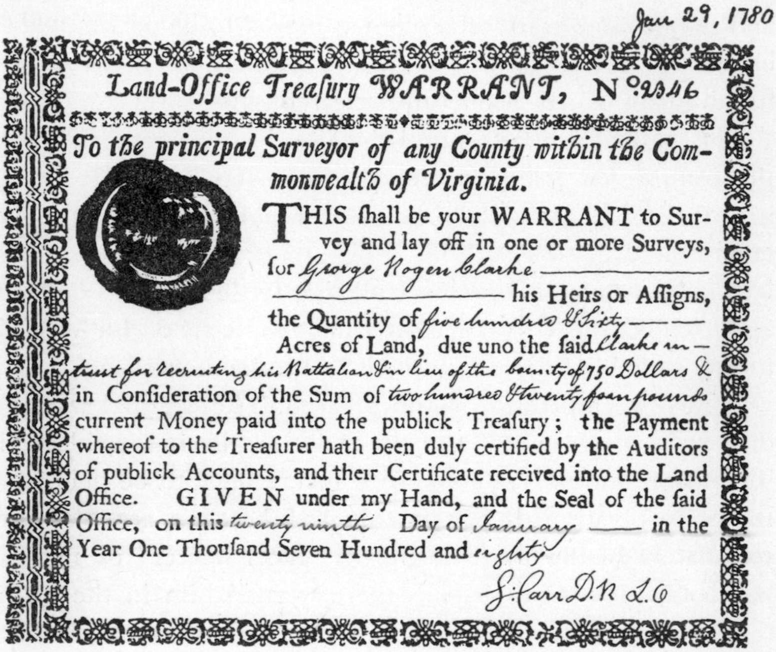
Jan 29, 1780

Land-Office Treaſury WARRANT, No. 2346

To the principal Surveyor of any County within the Commonwealth of Virginia.

THIS ſhall be your WARRANT to Survey and lay off in one or more Surveys, for George Rogers Clarke —— his Heirs or Aſſigns, the Quantity of five hundred & Sixty —— Acres of Land, due uno the ſaid Clarke in trust for recruiting his Battalion & in lieu of the bounty of 750 Dollars & in Conſideration of the Sum of two hundred & twenty four pounds current Money paid into the publick Treaſury; the Payment whereof to the Treaſurer hath been duly certified by the Auditors of publick Accounts, and their Certificate received into the Land Office. GIVEN under my Hand, and the Seal of the ſaid Office, on this twenty ninth Day of January —— in the Year One Thouſand Seven Hundred and eighty

J. Carr D.R.L.O

A VIRGINIA LAND WARRANT

Issued to George Rogers Clark. Reproduced by permission from the Durrett Collection, University of Chicago Library.

carefully locked the door and placed the saddle-bags at the foot of their bed. All his life long Daniel believed that his father, who had died in 1765, appeared to him in dreams. If the old Quaker appeared angry, it boded evil; if he was smiling and cheerful, all would be well. "Each time when captured, robbed or defeated he thus dreamed unfavorably about his father," he used to tell acquaintances.

If ever a son needed ghostly admonition and warning it was

that night, for disaster hovered in the darkness. When the two men woke in the morning the bags were gone, and the door was unlocked. Boone's papers were scattered about, his clothing had been thrown into the garden, and the saddle-bags had been dropped at the foot of the stairs.

A search of the inn revealed a little of the paper money hidden in some jugs in the cellar. None of the rest was ever found nor was it possible to identify the thief.

The victim himself always believed that the theft was planned by the landlord and actually carried out by an old woman who hid in their room before they entered and then crept out to rob them in the night. Presumably both travelers had been drugged. Otherwise it is hard to imagine why the alert woodsmen, used to waking at the slightest noise in the forests, failed to hear the movements of the thief.

It was the old story: Success, the landed wealth of which he dreamed his whole life through, again lay just within his grasp. Then it was snatched away once more, as it always had been in the past, as it always was to be in the future. He had been rich the night before. Now he was "destitute"—it was his own word—once more.

Worse still, he had lost a great deal of money which was not his own. The loss was widely felt and criticism was inevitable, but the Harts, who were the heaviest losers, remained his friends. Thomas Hart wrote on August 3, 1780:

> I Observe what you Say Respecting Our looses by Dan[l]. Boone I had heard of the misfortune Soon after it happen'd but not of my being a partaker before now I feel for the poor people who perhaps are to loose even their preemptions by it, but I must Say I feel more for poor Boone whose Character I am told Suffers by it, much degenerated, must the people of this Age be, when Amoungst them are to be found men to Censure and Blast the Character and Reputation of a person So Just and upright and in whose Breast is a Seat of Virtue too pure to

> admit of a thought So Base and dishonorable I have known Boone in times of Old, when Poverty and distress had him fast by the hand, And in these Wretched Sircumstances I ever found him of a Noble and generous Soul despising every thing mean, and therefore I will freely grant him a discharge for Whatever Sums of mine he might be possest of at the time.

Thomas Hart meant what he said. He proved his faith in Daniel Boone's integrity a few years later when he went on a joint promissory note with him for £118.9.8—well over five hundred dollars. Boone continued to act as his agent and they did business together for years afterward. His brother, Nathaniel Hart, was equally generous. "I am to lose the money Boone was robbed of," he wrote, "except he recovers it by suit."

That never happened, and the Harts never demanded restitution of their money.

Other losers were not so charitable. They demanded satisfaction and Boone managed eventually to pay them off in land. Though no written record of their indignation has come down, some at least cherished rancor for decades afterwards.

Some of Boone's friends later secured their lands by satisfying the court that their land papers had disappeared when Boone was robbed. John Snoddy proved in 1781 "that he was possessed of a pre-emption for one Thousand acres of land in the County of Kantucke that he sent the same along with Daniel Boone and it was lost and that he never received a Warrant for the same."

Meantime, the captured Hamilton's successor as lieutenant-governor at Detroit, the Tory Major De Peyster, was planning simultaneous attacks on the Americans in Kentucky and the Spaniards along the Mississippi. He went at it on an ambitious scale, as his bills from the traders who supplied his "Indian goods" show. One of them about this time is for £42,989. Another is for £12,185. The stores which he thus collected included:

750	lb vermilion	....	£750
8000	" powder	....	£2000
14,975	ball, lead & shot	....	£1,123
476	dozen scalping knives	....	£428
188	tomahawks	....	£119

Then, as if to make sure that the Indians were sufficiently bedizened with their favorite color, there is an additional quantity of vermilion paint, 1,206 pounds, worth £1,206. No wonder vermilion is listed as "Merchandize absolutely necessary for the Savages depending on Detroit"!

As an incitement to war, De Peyster was merely supplying free and in unusual quantities the same goods that the white Indian traders had supplied in exchange for furs in time of peace. A contemporary list of "Goods Suitable for the Indian trade" includes vermilion paint, "New Pinsilvania Rifles," and "Scallping knives good blades & solid handles."

Skilled and experienced British agents went out from Detroit to rouse the Indians, whose rapacious demands for presents were worrying the army officers. They knew they had to retain the good will of the red men at any cost. The Indians knew it too; and it was a situation of which they took full advantage.

According to De Peyster's plan one expedition was to go down the Mississippi and drive the Spaniards from St. Louis. Another would assail George Rogers Clark in Kentucky. It was to attack his fort at the Falls of the Ohio, create as much trouble as possible, and make sure that the Americans were kept too busy to aid the Spaniards.

This second expedition was commanded by Captain Henry Bird of the Regular Army. It was to have two cannon with a detachment of British "bombardiers" to fire them. No more nonsense with futile Indian sieges, torches, fire arrows. Smash the stockade with solid shot, pour the Indians into the breach, and end the whole thing out of hand with tomahawk and scalping knife.

Both the Spaniards and the Americans learned all about it in plenty of time. Lieutenant Abraham Chapline, who had been captured by the Indians in October, 1779, saw the preparations at Sandusky, escaped on April 28, 1780, and reached the Falls of the Ohio on May 19. He reported the route of the proposed British advance and the alarming fact that they were bringing artillery. His news was promptly relayed to headquarters and was known in Virginia by early summer.

The same news was brought in by George Hendricks, one of the men captured with Boone two years before, who had already escaped once and been retaken.

Bird had already left Detroit on April 12, more than two weeks before the prisoners escaped, but he was forced to move slowly. He was having troubles of his own, transporting artillery up shallow rivers in canoes, and then portaging the guns over wilderness roads, with so few pack-horses that they had to make several trips back and forth over the portages.

His Indian allies were first late at the rendezvous and then mutinous. In fact, the British themselves were worried about Bird's personal safety at their hands, and General Haldimand, commander-in-chief in Canada, expressed concern over "the Fickleness of the Indians and their aversion to controul."

On May 31 Alexander McKee, expert in handling the northern Indians, caught up with Bird. Next day a band of three hundred warriors joined him and on June 5 there was to be a general rendezvous of all the tribes, coming from various directions, on the Ohio. On June 13, however, Bird was still delayed at the mouth of the Miami River, waiting for the Chillicothe chiefs, though in the meantime a third band had brought his force up to seven hundred.

When the expedition got under way again there was more trouble. The Indians flatly refused to attack Clark, and insisted on going down Licking Creek and attacking the small settlements just beyond. These forts, they explained, were so far north that they were a serious threat to the Ohio villages. Bird accordingly started up the Licking, only to be delayed by low water. By June 20 Alexander McKee with the Indian advance guard had reached the northernmost settlement, Ruddle's Station. He arrived before daybreak. Surrounding the fort, he tried to keep his savages in hiding until the artillery could catch up.

A few settlers came out during the morning to cut grass; and the sight of scalps was too much for the Indians. They fired and gave the alarm. The little fort defended itself vigorously until noon. Then a light field-gun arrived and had already fired two rounds when the six-pounder came up. This went into battery in plain sight of the startled Kentuckians. It was now a matter of minutes before their stockade would be pounded to pieces, opening the way for Bird's hundreds of Indians. Defense was hopeless. For the first time in history a Kentucky fort surrendered.

A week later Indian scouts approached the next fort, Martin's Station, a few miles farther on. They intercepted two expresses, belatedly going out for aid, and brought one in alive. By ten o'clock next day (June 28, 1780), the Indians were all around the place and the captured messenger was sent back to the fort with Bird's demand for surrender. There was no hope. This little garrison gave up, also. Two other forts, whose settlers had left everything and fled, were burned.

The excited Indians were now eager to go on, but Bird, seeing how badly they were getting out of hand, insisted on retreating. His real motive was probably humanitarian, but some of his prisoners were killed in spite of his efforts, and Kentucky execrated him as an "inhuman wretch." He had several hundred captives, many of them women and children. British regulars honestly tried to avoid atrocities—and the Indians would soon be wholly out of hand. Many of his warriors were from the northern region around the Great Lakes. McKee was influential among the Shawnees, but there was no handling these other redskins.

After the first surrender, "the violence of the Lake Indians in seizing the Prisoners, contrary to agreement, threw everything into confusion, however the other nations next morning returned all they had taken back into Capt Bird's charge."

At Martin's Station Bird insisted that the Indians deliver all prisoners with at least a suit of clothes left them, and then quietly told the Kentuckians to put on as many clothes as they could wear, one suit above another. In spite of that, prisoners were knocked down and stripped. When the prisoners were removed under a guard of white troops, the Indians were indignant. "The great propensity for Plunder again occasioned discontent amongst them, and several parties set out towards the adjacent Forts to plunder Horses."

The expedition started back to Canada with its captives, loaded down with their own household goods. Most of them reached Detroit alive. Behind them lay an abomination of desolation created by the Indian raiders. Some time later a hunter stumbled by accident on the site of Ruddle's Station and saw: "Little wheels, plough irons, blacksmith's tools, feather beds ripped open, etc., scattered about there," where once there had been peaceful farms and homes.

But not all the prisoners were downcast by any means. A good many of them had not been ardent patriots to begin with. Some were just settlers who wanted land and happened to find it in Kentucky. Others were Tories who had been driven out of the Eastern settlements for their loyalist convictions. Lieutenant-Governor De Peyster wrote to an army officer: "The Prisoners daily brought in here are part of the Thousand Families who are flying from the oppression of Congress." These families were not looking for more trouble in the backwoods; they kept their loyalist principles quiet. But when they found themselves out of Kentucky and in British hands again, these somewhat faintly held convictions came to the surface, and they went over to the British readily enough.

"I don't believe we have more than two Families really Rebels," reported Bird. Most of his prisoners, he thought, were "good Farmers with extreme industrious Families who are desirous of being settled in Detroit with some Land. They fled, they say, from persecution, & declare if Government will assist them to get on foot as Farmers, they will, as Militia, faithfully defend the country that affords them protection."

It is not quite fair to call these people turncoats. Some of them had already openly refused to take the oath to Congress. But it was surely carrying matters a little far for thirteen of the Kentucky prisoners, immediately after their capture, to join the Detroit Rangers who had captured them.

However, some of this protestation of loyalty to the British Crown may have been as hollow as Boone's had been two years before. One of Bird's prisoners, Captain William Hinkston, had given up his settlement after the Indian troubles of 1776, and had returned with his family in 1780, just in time to be captured. In conversation with Bird, he intimated (like Boone) that he had British sympathies. But three days after capture he had (also like Boone) escaped.

Such escapes as Hinkston's, immediately after capture, were extremely difficult because the Indians were still alert. In the Shawnee villages the captives had a little chance. They could steal firearms and so get food on the long journey home. Without a rifle there was very real danger of starving to death in the forests, and some people nearly did starve. Of four hunters who blundered into Bird's expedition just about the time Hinkston escaped, one was killed and two were captured. The fourth, who got away, had either lost his rifle or did not dare to fire it. He wandered seven days in the woods with nothing to eat but "part of a squirrel which he took from a hawk" before he stumbled into Boonesborough, "the poorest object you ever see." Hinkston's willingness to face such hardships is evidence enough of his loyalty.

Persons who were known to have gone over to the British side had their Kentucky lands confiscated by the Americans. It was too soon to be sure about the loyalty of the captives who had been carried off by Bird, but about one man there could be no doubt. Alexander McKee, who had helped Bird bring the Indians down upon Kentucky, was still a Kentucky landholder with a claim of two thousand acres on the south branch of the Elkhorn, which he had held since 1774. It is small wonder that the indignant Kentuckians now prepared to seize his lands.

Bird, McKee, and their redskins were scarcely out of the country when Daniel Boone was one of a jury of escheat, sitting at Lexington July 1, 1780. Under a recently enacted Virginia law, the estates of Tories could be seized and sold for the public benefit. The jury was "sworn and charged to say whether John Conolly and Alexander McKee be British subjects or not within the meaning of the Act of Assembly entitled And [sic] Act Concerning Escheats and forfeitures from British Subjects' and in case they should find them to be such then diligently to enquire after a[nd] true presentment make of all Such estate both real and personal that they were possessed of on the 4th July 1774. Or at any time since."

Dr. Connolly, a notorious Tory, was in the well-known Tory corps, the Queen's Rangers. McKee had just been giving a pretty convincing demonstration of his own loyalist sympathies.

Boone and the other jurymen decided that they both were British subjects, and "after the 19th of April 1775, the said John Connolly and Alexander McKee of their own free will did Depart from the said States and Joined the Subjects of his Britanick Majesty." Each man lost his land. McKee's property was eventually devoted to public education by the state and to this day still helps to educate Kentucky youth at Transylvania University.

If the Indians had had their way, Boonesborough would have been one of the next stations attacked, but after Bird's withdrawal life went along fairly peacefully.

George Rogers Clark, in general military command in the West, was quick to retaliate. By the end of July orders were out for a rendezvous of Kentucky troops on the Licking, preparatory to another raid on the Shawnee villages. As Logan marched north to join Clark, a deserter slipped away to the British, who thus had plenty of warning. Bombardier William Homan, of the Royal Regiment of Artillery, was greatly distressed because the Americans advanced so fast he could not withdraw the guns which had compelled two stations to surrender. The Indians had left him only one horse. However, he "drew the Gun a considerable way into the Wood, not near any Road and digged a hole & buried it so securely, that no one could even suspect of such a thing being concealed there. The smaller Ordnance, loose shot, and shells & c we concealed in different parts of the Wood."

Boone and the other commanders brought their men up soon after Logan and the concentrated force of about eight hundred men moved across the Ohio. They had left Kentucky dangerously empty behind them but outlying settlers had been concentrated at Bryan's Station and the Indians were busy enough defending their own country. Chillicothe was burned again together with other towns. There were some atrocities. The Americans killed a squaw "by ripping up her Belly & otherwise mangling her—they also opened the graves of the Indians that had been buried several months, and scalp'd them." By August 9 they were on their way back to Kentucky, beating off pursuing Indians.

There were minor Indian troubles all year long. Colonel Callaway and Pemberton Rawlings, whom Boone had refused to join as trustees of Boonesborough, had been surprised in March, 1780, just a mile and a half from the town. Callaway had been given a concession for the ferry across the river at Boonesborough, and had gone out to cut timber and build his boat. He was instantly killed. Rawlings, badly wounded, ran a quarter of a mile before he was caught, tomahawked in the back of the neck, and scalped. Two negroes with them were captured and never heard of again. A fifth man got away. Poor Callaway's body was scalped, stripped, mangled, and rolled in the mud. Rawlings, still alive when found, lived only a few hours. In the Shawnee towns Joseph Jackson, one of the prisoners captured with Boone's salt-makers two years before, saw Callaway's scalp as the triumphant warriors brought it in. He "knew it by the long black and gray mixed hair."

Just after Callaway had been killed, William Bryan, Jr., a relative of Daniel Boone by marriage, went out to look for his horse, heard the sound of its bell, walked toward it, and was killed. Indians had caught the horse, tied it up, hidden, and waited for a white man to come after it.

Some of the terror of those days lingers in a dilapidated scrap of a pioneer diary, now among the Bryan family papers. It was probably kept by Morgan Bryan, another of Rebecca's relatives. Yellowed, faded, and torn till it is barely legible, the fragile old paper tells this series of horrors in a few matter-of-fact entries:

> March the 8 day
> Cornal Callway & pmbrton Rollans scalped the 9 day William Bryan Junr kiled the 9 day some Indians seen near lexanton & the 10 day Capt Ridel fort atacked the 11 some of our peoppel went to asist them 12 John Marton's Station the 7 John Denton wounded 13 Sam'l Grant & Squire [Boone wounded?] the same day James—& William Marshil fired at [i.e., by Indians] by our station The same Evening three Men fird at three Indians and made a Discovery of Many more Same day Benjman Coppe Thomas Todd & one Simmons Chased by a number of Indians with in one mile of our Station and got in to Lexanton & 29 men Came to pursew the Indians Same night We sent 3 men & they met in the way . . . shot til—14 in the moring 70 men turned out in purseut of the Inndins.

In August there was a small attack on Holden's Station, said to have been directed by Simon Girty and the indefatigable Alexander McKee.

Daniel Boone himself had three narrow escapes during the year. Hunting south of the Kentucky River with a party of twenty-five others, he detected the approach of Indians early one night. Under his directions the group hastily built a fire and rolled up their peltry in blankets to look like sleeping men. Then they retired to the underbrush and waited. At dawn the Indians fired on the camp and rushed in, only to be met by a volley from the white men safely hidden in the thickets.

Boone always did a good deal of solitary scouting. He had a habit of sitting silently at work—darning his hunting shirt, mending his leggings, molding bullets—while others talked. Just as silently he would disappear.

"And now," loungers by the fire would remark, "we shall know something sure; for old Daniel's on the track." Later a gaunt, solitary shadow would slip into a cabin door, and Boone would be back with word of a new band of raiders, or with news that the woods were clear.

On one of these solitary tours between Boonesborough and the Blue Licks he turned east of the direct route and went down Slate Creek. He soon ran into Indian "sign." Working cautiously along for several miles of level forest, he reached a spring on a slope above the creek, still quite unmolested.

As he paused here for a drink, a rifle cracked in the woods and a bullet knocked the bark off a tree above him. Boone leaped into the bushes before there was time for another shot. He ran down the slope, crossed the creek, and slipped silently downstream through the cane on the other side, where he waited in ambush. Two warriors soon appeared.

As Boone had expected, the Indians had also worked down to the creek and were hunting for him there quite unaware that he now had at least one of them at his mercy. One of them —that was the trouble.

Daniel was in a quandary. No matter which Indian he shot, the other would see the puff of smoke and kill him in the act of reloading. Boone decided to make one shot do for two. Aiming stealthily from the canebrake, he drew a bead on the leading warrior and waited for the other to come in line. The instant the Indian did so, he fired. One warrior dropped, shot through the head. The other was hit in the shoulder. The wounded brave dropped his rifle and ran. Boone crossed at leisure, picked out the better rifle, threw the other one into the creek (where it was later found), and continued his journey to the Blue Licks.

In October of 1780 Daniel and Edward Boone went "on a tower to the Upper Blue Licks" to boil salt. On the way home they paused to let their horses graze and Edward idly sat down to crack hickory nuts on the stones. A bear wandered by within range and Daniel fired. His shot was not instantly fatal. The wounded animal vanished down a little stream with the hunter in pursuit. Edward stayed with the horses, still cracking nuts and not keeping a very sharp lookout since there had been no sign of danger.

The bear dropped after a short run and Daniel Boone had just reached the carcass with an empty rifle, having carelessly failed to reload, when suddenly he heard shots behind him where he had left his brother. Then silence. Then the sound of a dog following his own trail. Realizing that Edward was either dead or a prisoner and that he could do nothing for him now, Daniel slipped into the nearest canebrake.

He eluded the Indians easily enough; but the dog caught up. Every time Boone turned on it, the animal ran back toward the Indians, then came yelping after him, a sure guide to his pursuers. To make matters worse, Boone had dropped his ramrod and was wearing new shoes, which grew so slippery that he could hardly keep his feet. It looked as if he would be unable either to defend himself or escape.

But keeping a sharp eye out as he ran, he saw a stalk of cane about the right size, snapped it off, used it as a ramrod, and waited for the dog's next approach. As the brute came on again he shot it and then, changing his course abruptly, moved silently on into the fastnesses of the cane. There was "a horrid yell" from the Indians as they came upon the dead dog. But the pursuit ended.

Emerging from the cane at last, the fugitive dodged quickly behind a tree and reloaded. Then he waited silently to see if any Indians came out of the canebrake on his trail. There was no sound and no sign of further pursuit. No Indians appeared. The red men had given up their man hunt.

Edward lay dead in the forest. They found his body next day, with the entire head cut off.

Daniel got back to Boonesborough, after losing his hunting knife, collected a party, and started out in pursuit of the Indians, whom he trailed as far as the Ohio. On the way back, Daniel and some of his relatives stopped to hunt as usual. They had done their best. Death was tragic but common. Meantime the settlement had to have venison.

Just after this, in November, 1780, Virginia divided Kentucky County into the three new counties of Fayette, Jefferson, and Lincoln. Within the next few months, Daniel Boone was chosen county lieutenant, lieutenant-colonel of the militia, sheriff of Fayette County, and representative in the State Assembly. He was also made one of the deputy surveyors.

It was the peaceful duties of a legislator which brought him once more into the enemy's hands. By April of 1781 he was back in the capital as Fayette County's representative in the State Assembly. Cornwallis' troops advanced and the legislators withdrew to Charlottesville. Sir Banastre Tarleton, the famous Tory leader, made a sudden raid on the town, drove in the small American detachment guarding a ford and was sweeping into Charlottesville with 180 dragoons and seventy mounted infantry before anyone realized what was happening. John Jouett, a Virginian who had been in Kentucky, gave the alarm and the legislators scattered. Thomas Jefferson, looking down from his hilltop of Monticello, saw the red uniforms and vanished hastily through the back door and into the woods. Boone was imperturbable as usual. He, Jouett, and others paused to load a wagon with public records, waited a little too long, and found British troopers riding toward them.

They turned their horses calmly and proceeded out of town at a leisurely walk, letting the British troopers ride up to them without the least concern. Unimpressed by Eastern fashions, Boone was still "dressed in real backwoods stile." The innocent Tory dragoons had no idea that the blue-eyed, fair-haired, quiet-spoken, and entirely unimpressive figure in buckskin and homespun jogging along beside them was one of the most redoubtable fighters in the Virginia militia.

Everything went well. The two would probably have shaken hands with their pursuers and parted amicably had not Jouett grown nervous. By this time he had had all he could stand of the enemy's society. He attempted to make their parting at the next cross-roads seem natural by remarking casually:

"Colonel, this is our road."

The British officer pricked up his ears.

"Ah, a Colonel, ha?" he cried. "You are just such prisoners as we want."

The troopers marched them both back to Tarleton, who by this time had rounded up "some of the principal gentlemen of Virginia," plus a member of the Continental Congress. According to his own account "the gentlemen taken on this expedition were treated with kindness and liberality," but much depends upon the point of view. Boone was confined in a coal house and, as everything was damp, emerged next morning in very grimy condition. He is said to have whiled away the waking hours of his confinement by singing to himself as usual.

After Tarleton had rejoined Cornwallis the prisoners were released on parole. There is a story, however, that Boone was not paroled but escaped. Indeed it is doubtful whether any ordinary troops could have kept a prisoner who had already escaped from the Shawnees twice.

The exact facts as to the alleged parole are rather mysterious. Certainly Daniel went back to his Indian-fighting, parole or no parole, the following year. He may not have given his word at all. Or he may have given it merely not to bear arms against His Majesty's forces. One of the Tory Bryans, said to have been campaigning with Tarleton, may have intervened on Boone's behalf.

The legislators who escaped the raid resumed their lawmaking at Staunton, but Boone's name does not reappear on the records of the session. The British were still holding him on June 17, and the legislature adjourned on the 23rd. He had no chance to return. It is said, however, that at the next session objection was raised because he had taken a British oath.

While Daniel was absent in the early part of 1781, Rebecca bore a son; and two of their daughters, who had married very young, also had babies at nearly the same time. When the new father-grandfather returned, he was presented with a row of all the babies available and challenged to identify his own. Family tradition avers that he picked the right one. It was probably this innocent domestic prank that accidentally set afloat the cruel story about Rebecca's alleged illegitimate child.

No one knows where he spent the summer, but he was back in Boonesborough near the end of August. In September he made a trip up the Ohio and thence overland to the old home in Pennsylvania, which he had left as a boy in 1750. James Boone's family records have the entry: "1781. october 20th then Daniel came to see us the first time." He was sitting in the legislature again from November, 1781, until January, 1782, but he does not seem to have been very assiduous in his duties. In December the House ordered the sergeant-at-arms to take Daniel Boone and other absent members into custody.

By his prolonged absences in the East Boone escaped the new series of minor but bloody Indian raids that plagued Kentucky in 1781. At Bryan's Station the Indians killed the sentinel who stood guard over a man plowing corn and another man taking his horse out to grass. The settlements along the Green River were attacked and women and children carried off. As Colonel Benjamin Logan closed in on the Indians with the pursuing party a twelve-year-old girl prisoner exclaimed to her mother, "There's Uncle Ben!"—and was instantly tomahawked.

Squire Boone was forced out of his recently built station. He had left Boonesborough in 1779 and gone to the Falls of the Ohio to settle, then in 1780 had moved south to his land near Shelbyville. The first attack, in May, 1781, was led by Simon Girty. Squire himself rushed out half-dressed. As he happened to be wearing that rare garment, a white shirt, Girty was later able to boast that he had made Squire Boone's shirt-tail fly. In spite of that minor triumph, the Indians retired, leaving Squire with three wounds, including a broken arm which, when it healed after being roughly set by amateurs, turned out to be an inch and a half shorter than the other.

In September Squire at length decided to abandon his settlement and make for Linn's Fort, not far away. Indian scouts saw them, and about noon attacked from ambush. Handicapped by women and children, the white men fought off their pursuers as best they could, but a number were killed and it was dark before the survivors straggled into safety. Ten-year-old Moses Boone ran for his life with the rest, but presently stopped to defend himself. One of the men, George Yant, turned, beheld the valorous little figure, and asked what he was doing.

"I'm pointing at an Indian that is trying to kill me," said the child.

"Why don't you shoot him?"

"My gun is wet and won't go off," returned Moses.

"Where is he?"

Moses pointed to a claybank:

"There he is."

At this moment the Indian's painted face peered over. Yant fired and, as the warrior rolled dead into the stream, told Moses to run.

"What shall I do with my gun?" asked the boy.

"Throw it away," cried Yant. It was a bitter blow but eventually the boy did so and reached the fort in safety.

Men who went out to retaliate on the Indians were ambushed. Raiding Hurons and Miamis attacked Floyd at Long Run. The British Indian agent, Alexander McKee, urged another attack on Boonesborough, but the Indians refused. At Christmastime some Pennsylvania settlers were ambushed near White Oak Station, a mile from Boonesborough.

Most of this bushwhacking served no military purpose whatever. The British were slowly losing in the East. Cornwallis had been shut up on the Yorktown Peninsula. The war was really over, though no one knew it; but Kentucky had still to endure some of its harshest years.

15. The Year of Blood:

SIEGE OF BRYAN'S STATION

SEVENTEEN HUNDRED AND EIGHTY-TWO has been called Kentucky's "year of blood." One blow after another fell, now here, now there, until the more timid settlers again packed up for departure and Daniel Boone himself was on the verge of despair. Prisoners, escaping from the Indian camps in the early spring, brought word that trouble was brewing. Even before they began to arrive, it had been predicted "that a very formidable army of English and Indians would come Quickly," and "that every Preparation was making for that purpose."

The British and Indians had been making vigorous preparations at Detroit all winter, and each side was now keeping a close eye on the other. All through the early spring hostile scouts had been watching the Kentucky settlements. In August the British commander at Detroit sent in an intelligence report: "Mr. McKee informs me that the people of Kentuck are night and day employed in moving their Families and Effects to a large Settlement called Bryant's Station, where they hope to remain in security." Another reconnoissance had confirmed the report. At the same time, Caldwell had gone down to the Ohio and was there awaiting still further reports on the Americans.

The Indians had been infuriated by the Americans' cold-blooded massacre of ninety-six unarmed and unresisting Christian Indians at the Moravian Settlement of Gnadenhütten, news of which had been carried back by reconnoitering bands to the chiefs in the home camps on the Ohio. The Shawnees in Ohio were neither Christian nor unresisting, but they had a fellow feeling for their red brethren who were.

They took revenge in June, when they smashed a force of nearly five hundred Pennsylvania and Virginia militia under Colonel William Crawford on the Sandusky River in Ohio, and burned the white commander at the stake.

Crawford died hard—he was two hours in the fire, succumbing only after he had been scalped alive and live coals had been poured on top of his head. The incident became famous, both because Simon Girty, the "white Indian," sat by to enjoy the fun and also because it was better reported than most such tragedies. Dr. Knight, Crawford's fellow-captive, watched the spectacle, with Girty's assurances ringing in his ears that he would soon follow Crawford to the stake; but he managed to escape and wrote a famous narrative of the whole grisly episode.

The year's Indian troubles in Kentucky had begun, however, long before Crawford's disastrous expedition. Spring came quickly that year, but it brought no joy to the dwellers behind the log stockades. As early as February the fine mild weather brought down Indian war parties.

In March the settlers in Boonesborough watched the river grimly. What they saw was only a little thing; but it was a sign of violent and horrible death waiting for someone. Three logs were floating down the river past their wooden battlements. To inexperienced eyes the floating timber meant little enough; but to the keen-eyed woodsmen it could mean only one thing. No white man's hand had fastened those logs together, for there were no white settlements upstream. Somewhere farther up the Kentucky River, Indians were crossing. Which of the settlements would the raiders make for?

They soon found out.

Hitherto most of the Indian fighting in Kentucky had been with Shawnees, coming in from the North. The Cherokees in the South were quiet—at least they made little trouble for Kentucky. But now the savage Wyandots, who had been forced west in inter-tribal warfare some years earlier, had buried the hatchet with their red brethren and were moving east again. In March twenty-five of them passed Boonesborough—probably the very Indians whose raft had given its silent warning to the settlement downstream. Boonesborough was ready and the war party of the Wyandots passed harmlessly by; but at Estill's Station they caught a young girl outside the stockade and gleefully killed her within sight of the fort.

In May Captain Estill led his men out in pursuit of Indians—probably of the same band. He caught up with them and was killed in a bitter fight from which only a few of the white men escaped alive.

By August the Indians were everywhere. From the thickets along the Ohio River to the north, they had at first viewed apprehensively the "row-galley"—armed with artillery and propelled with many oars—with which George Rogers Clark tried to patrol the river and keep the war canoes from paddling over. Clark had discovered that "open small boats will by no means answer the purpose of Cruising on the River as they are often liable to be ambuscaded when they come near the shore, or in narrow parts of the River." His "Gallie" had four-foot bulletproof gunwales, with additional hinged gunwales that could be pulled up and "Raise her sides so high that she can Lay within pistol shot of the shore without the least danger." Daniel Boone grudged Clark the men that had to be detached to build his galley and other defenses, knowing how much they were needed in his own part of Kentucky.

It was the white man's first effort at naval warfare in these wild streams. Clark's galley could catch and sink any canoe it sighted; but the trouble was, it never sighted them. The Ohio was only a quarter-mile wide, and the galley had to patrol a couple of hundred miles of it. It was easy enough for the war parties to lay up canoes or rafts in the bushes and make the short dash across when the river was clear. Clark needed a fleet to make the Ohio into a real defensive line for the Kentucky settlements and for that he had neither men nor artillery. In the East, Washington and his Continentals were too hard pressed to spare him either; and not even a whole fleet on the Ohio could have stopped war parties slipping over from the perfect security of the forest on the Ohio bank to the equal security of the forests in Kentucky.

The white settlers should, of course, have kept small armed patrols—or at least pairs of scouts—perpetually reconnoitering through the forest, ready to give the alarm when they ran into a war party. Such arduous and dangerous service might have cost a few lives, but skilled woodsmen in small parties could usually escape easily; and a patrol's traditional duty is to run away, not to fight.

The Kentuckians knew all this well enough. The trouble lay partly in their inbred aversion to standing guard, and partly in their small numbers. They were settlers, not soldiers; and defense, though necessary, was incidental. Their crops, which often had to be tilled by half the men while the other half stood guard; their hunting—a main source of fresh meat; building and guarding their little forts; and the hundred tedious labors of primitive life which city folk take for granted, because they are done for them—all these things were even more needed than reconnoissance. The Indians might or might not come. If they came, they would be dealt with. Meantime, every night the cows had to be milked.

A kind of reconnoissance was, however, occasionally attempted. At this very time Colonel Todd's militiamen had been excused from all other duty. In June Captain Robert Patterson took forty men from Kentucky to meet Clark's armed galley on the Ohio.

A relatively unimportant but amusing incident of the march arose from the appalling language of an impulsive youth named Aaron Reynolds. Now forced marching through forest country in the insect season does not bring out the best in human nature. One is frequently wet and tired. Muscles ache under heavy burdens. The ground is cold and damp to sleep on—the rheumatism that afflicted the pioneers, as it had afflicted their raiding Anglo-Saxon forebears a thousand years earlier, testifies to that. The strain of perpetual watchfulness and perpetual danger tears at the nerves. Mosquitoes, blackfly, and other pests add their touches of irritation, which find vent in violent speech. And anyhow, the frontier was never a place for the mealy-mouthed.

This Aaron Reynolds, however, had a talent for profanity remarkable even in that day and place. Among the mighty swearers of the backwoods, he stood out as a mightier swearer still. Hard men listened with amazement to the impressive language that poured out of him in his moments of emotional exaltation during the more uncomfortable episodes of an uncomfortable march. The forty rangers do not seem to have minded at all—in fact, they very likely enjoyed the pyrotechnics; but Captain Robert Patterson, a gallant fighter but a pious soul, was much annoyed.

Commanding officers in more modern armies rarely allow themselves to be annoyed for very long by their subordinates. There are ways and means of swift and summary suppression. But the fighting men of the Kentucky frontier could not be handled by any such methods. They thought themselves quite as good as their officers, and were frequently right. Furthermore, they expected to be just friends, neighbors, and equals of their commanders if they returned unscalped from an expedition. Such discipline as existed in these desperate little bushwhacking forays was therefore strictly *ad hoc,* and very little of that.

It all grated upon the nerves of Captain Robert Patterson; and where discipline failed first and diplomacy was a bad second, Captain Patterson tried bribery.

Kentuckians, both regenerate and unregenerate, have from the earliest days had a keen appreciation of hard liquor. Captain Patterson was a pious soul but he did have a little jug along. He promised his insubordinate warrior a quart of the best if he would swear no more.

The effort seems to have been rather a strain upon Reynolds. When the little band at the end of their dangerous march stood at last on the banks of the Ohio, the Captain declined to make good. Since the agreement, he averred, Reynolds's language might have been somewhat milder than before, but it had hardly been mild enough to earn a whole quart. The indignant Reynolds swore that his language would have graced a bench of bishops, and his fellow Indian-fighters, standing in military array before their commander, shouted their approval from the ranks. They may have hoped for a dividend from Reynolds—fluids of all sorts were getting scarce after their long march.

At any rate, Captain Patterson bowed to the views of his troops (except for the commander of H.M.S. *"Pinafore,"* no captain has been so complaisant since) and regretfully produced the quart, which he had carried all the way through the forests and cherished for his own use.

Reynolds triumphed, but it was to be a matter of only a few weeks before he proved that the vocabulary of iniquity was not his only talent. Patterson was to have good reason to admire the man he had rebuked.

By August the Indians were raiding in force at Hoy's Station.

They prowled around just long enough to cause alarm and capture two boys, and then—sure of pursuit, which was exactly what they wanted—started slowly for the Ohio. This raid was really nothing but a feint, carried out by about seventy warriors to draw the settlers in that direction, while the real attack came down at Bryan's Station. Captain Holder gathered up such men as he could find, all mounted, and rushed off, gathering others as he passed McGee's and Strode's Stations (near Winchester), meantime sending out expresses to summon men from the various stations. Daniel Boone left others in charge at Boone's Station, and rushed over to Boonesborough to turn out his men there.

Holder caught up with the Indians at the Upper Blue Licks. As his men reached the river, they could see in a sand-bar on their side of the stream the footprints of the captive boys who had been forced to run footraces to amuse the warriors. Broiling-sticks lay all around. The Indians cared so little about the pursuit that they had paused for a cooked meal and some relaxation with their captives. They had broken camp just a little ahead of their pursuers—the other side of the ford was still wet from their feet—and a rear guard had probably been watching Holder's approach for some time. As the white men stared, the Indians themselves appeared, lounging along two different trails, as if they were dividing their party.

The ambush was too obvious, as a certain John Fleming pointed out. But Holder and the rest insisted on a fight. The whole party crossed the river, and divided on the other side so as to chase both bands of Indians. They had no means of knowing which band had the prisoners.

Three quarters of a mile farther on, Holder's men saw a solitary Indian ahead of them running for dear life. They gave chase—and ran straight into the ambush that had been prepared for them about 150 yards above the mouth of what is now called Battle Run Branch.

The Indian chief, whoever he was, was a sound tactician. He had slipped his braves into cover on the edge of a ridge with the stream in front of them. They were invisible and hard to attack, but they could fire straight into the white men as they rode up.

Fleming, who had warned of ambush, was wounded at the first volley. More men, who had dismounted farther to the rear, ran up on foot, but the Indians were too many, and the whole group swung slowly back to the ford to keep from being surrounded. The other party—led by a man who was not named Michael Cassidy for nothing—heard the fight and started for it.

Fleming, shot in the hip, had found refuge behind a log where he was more or less sheltered and where the Indians did not notice him. But just as Cassidy arrived an Indian ran forward swinging his tomahawk. Fleming, too badly wounded to get up, shot him from the ground. Just then a second Indian appeared, and Fleming, unable to move and now with an empty rifle, yelled to Cassidy to shoot. Cassidy shouted back that his rifle was empty, too.

But the Indian didn't know that—as the agitated Fleming pointed out with some annoyance. Cassidy, taking the hint, advanced belligerently with a perfectly useless rifle, and the Indian—who apparently also had an unloaded rifle!—fled.

By this time, Holder's half of the party had been driven off and every Indian in sight was concentrating on Cassidy's men, who withdrew, carrying Fleming and other wounded men dumped over their horses like so many sacks. The first man or two across the river halted on the bank and held back the arriving Indians with rifle fire until the rest could struggle across.

One wounded man was too badly hurt to travel, even in a litter. Hiding him in the bushes, the others promised to come back the next day bringing milk, which was the one thing the poor devil craved. When they came next day, they found that in the feverish thirst which gunshot wounds produce, he had crawled to the creek for water. But they shook their heads when they saw that the water he drank ran out of his wound, as did the milk they gave him. He was dead before the litter had gone more than two or three miles.

Tradition says that Battle Run Branch ran blood for days afterward—a very doubtful tale as there were no white men around to see; but it is apparently quite true that bullets could be picked out of the trees there for the next half-century. As a rescue, Holder's expedition was a total failure. He had not even seen the prisoners, though they survived and later returned to Kentucky.

The raid at Hoy's Station deceived Daniel Boone and all the other settlers, as it had been meant to do. A war party of seventy Indians was big enough to be alarming, and no one dreamed that they were a mere detachment from an approaching force four or five times their number. Each little fort made ready to send its quota for the relief expedition, which was to pursue and punish the raiders.

In Boone's absence a mounted detachment gathered at Boone's Station under William Ellis. Bryan's Station gathered its Indian-fighters and in the South Colonel Benjamin Logan began to assemble nearly five hundred militia.

It was always dangerous to call out any large number of a station's fighting men. In order to get enough Indian-fighters to relieve an endangered stockade somewhere else, the home fort had to be stripped of its best men and left with only old men, boys—that meant very young boys—and the dauntless frontier women to keep watch, prevent surprise, and drive the Indians back with the accurate fire of the long Kentucky rifles. Food might run short if there were no hunters to range the woods, and a very small band of Indian raiders could easily destroy a whole season's crops if not promptly driven off.

In the absence of the men it was more dangerous than ever to go out to the spring for water or to bring in the crops. Often there was nobody left to patrol the woods and give warning. The Indians sometimes struck in small parties at several settlements at once, or attacked one after another in quick succession, feeling for a weak spot. When the siege of one station was lifted, it might mean an attack elsewhere and no one knew which little wilderness settlement would come next. The defenders did not always dare march away to relieve a neighboring town even after they had beaten the Indians off from their own, for it was a favorite Shawnee stratagem to withdraw ostentatiously and then slip stealthily back, hoping to waylay the defenders as they emerged into an imagined security.

On this occasion Daniel Boone practically stripped Boonesborough of its defenders, knowing that Logan's large force would be passing that way in a day or two. Boonesborough could hold out for a little while, at worst. Logan would scatter any Indians indiscreet enough to attack it. In the meantime Boone's own forces seemed badly needed farther north. And badly needed they were—though not quite where Daniel Boone thought. At least he was right in believing he could leave Boonesborough unguarded without danger. It was not even harassed.

The Indian wiles that had failed in the siege of Boonesborough four years earlier very nearly succeeded this time at Bryan's Station. The feint at Hoy's just missed being successful. Wholly unsuspected by Daniel Boone or his fellow commanders, the most formidable British and Indian force that had ever entered Kentucky was working swiftly southward. With anything like proper reconnoissance its large numbers should have led to its detection by American scouts. In mid-July the British leaders, Caldwell and McKee, with some fifty white rangers and about three hundred Indians, left Wapatomica (in northwestern Ohio) to destroy the fort at Wheeling, on the upper Ohio. They had gone only a day or two when runners burst into Wapatomica with the news that George Rogers Clark was coming with a large force and with artillery, always the nightmare of a frontier commander. The chiefs at Wapatomica, in terror, sent runners to recall Caldwell and McKee. They caught up with them on the Scioto; and after some argument with the Lake Indians, whose homes were not threatened, they returned. The two ranger officers and the three Girty brothers now gathered eleven hundred Indians at Piqua, Ohio, with a reserve of three hundred only a day's march away, and waited for Clark.

It was a false alarm. Clark was nowhere near, though excited scouts swore they had seen his army. When the invaders failed to appear, the Indian forces began to melt away. Those who remained insisted on raiding somewhere, and set out to attack Kentucky. The force included Caldwell, McKee, Captain Matthew Elliott, with Simon and George Girty, three hundred Wyandots and some other Indians.

At the Shawnee town of Old Chillicothe they paused for council, and Simon Girty made a famous speech:

> Brothers: The fertile region of Kentucky is the land of cane and clover—spontaneously growing to feed the buffalo, the elk and the deer. There the bear and the beaver are always fat. The Indians from all the tribes have had a right from time immemorial, to hunt and kill unmolested these wild animals, and bring off their skins—to purchase for themselves clothing, to buy blankets for their backs and rum to send down their throats, to drive away the cold and rejoice their hearts after the fatigues of hunting and the toil of war. [Great applause.]
>
> Brothers, the Long Knives [i.e., Virginians] have overrun your country and usurped your hunting grounds. They have

destroyed the cane, trodden down the clover, killed the deer and the buffalo, the beaver and the raccoon. The beaver has been chased from his dam, and forced to leave the country. [Palpable emotion among the hearers.]

Brothers: The intruders on your land exult in the success that has crowned their flagitious acts. They are planting fruit trees and plowing the lands where, not long since, were the canebrake and the clover field. Was there a voice in the tree of forest, or articulate sounds in the gurgling waters, every part of this country would call on you to chase away these ruthless invaders, who are laying it waste. Unless you rise in the majesty of your might and exterminate their whole race, you may bid adieu to the hunting grounds of your fathers—to the delicious flesh of the animals with which they once abounded—and to the skins with which you were once enabled to purchase your clothing and your rum.

After their council the Indians moved down the Little Miami, crossed the Ohio—undiscovered and not even suspected—and moved up the Licking River along the traditional war road. With them they brought some of the people taken the year before at Ruddle's and Martin's Stations, to watch the butchery of their former friends and neighbors. Why the Indians burdened themselves with these Kentuckians during their approach is a mystery. There was always the danger that one of them might escape and carry warning. Why take such a chance? Perhaps the captives were to serve as guides. Perhaps they were to persuade their compatriots to surrender. Perhaps they had changed sides. Certainly no one will ever know the truth of the matter now.

At Bryan's Station no one had the least suspicion that an attack impended. The men were already assembled and engaged in last minute preparations before marching to the relief of Hoy's. Getting ready for battle was a slower business than preparing for a hunting trip. The patches which held the bullets were oiled with extra care. The "necks" which the molds left on the hand-made bullets had to be filed down with precision. Otherwise a bullet might stick in the barrel. If that happened the only thing to do was to unbreach the rifle. As there was no time for gunsmithing in the heat of combat, a jammed bullet meant one man and one rifle out of the fight at the very moment when they were needed most. Locks were oiled so that the hammer fell easily. Flints were picked till they were sharp. Otherwise the lock would merely snap and the rifle miss fire. While this was going on, Bryan's Station kept its gates barred. They were never opened. Suddenly the settlers became aware that the Indians were all around them. How they found out is a mystery. Not an Indian showed himself. And yet Bryan's Station knew its danger.

There is a story that an express suddenly dashed in with warning. Who sent him? No one knows. It is doubtful that he even existed. It has been surmised that one of the Kentucky captives broke away from the Indians and gave warning. How? There is no record that any of them were seen, even after the station was besieged.

But the gates stayed closed, and riflemen manned the loopholes. The cattle were still pasturing outside the fort. There was no time to bring them in and it would have been sure death for men to go into the woods after them. Worse still, there was no water in the fort and the only spring was some distance outside the stockade.

Bryan's Station at this time was a fortified parallelogram two hundred yards long by fifty wide, with the usual blockhouses at the corners. Forty cabins were arranged at intervals within the stockade, which formed a common rear wall. The stockade itself was made of sharp pointed logs twelve feet high. As usual, there were two gates.

The fort stood on a hillside overlooking a little creek. The high ground around it was roughly cleared and gave the riflemen the field of fire they needed; but it was August and a hundred-acre field of tall corn near the fort offered concealment to the enemy. The buffalo trace was lined with trees; fields of hemp, weed, and stumps provided more cover for the Indians, and along the creek the canebrake was so thick and so tall that a man on horseback could hide in it. A few cabins stood outside the walls—to be abandoned in time of danger like the present.

Inside the stockade forty-four riflemen were filling their powder-horns, their bullet bags, and their "patchen pouches" of wadding. The women were pouring molten lead into the molds for extra bullets.

Hidden by trees and underbrush from anxious eyes at the loopholes, the Indians divided. One small group crept down into the cover along the creek. The main body slipped silently into the canebrake and weeds close around the all-important spring. The settlers were now hopelessly cut off from either water supply though the Indians had no means of knowing their advantage. The hot August sun would soon be parching and the Indians would certainly try to fire the cabins and stockade.

But as yet the sun had not risen and the Indian chiefs were not quite certain what lay before them. If the relief from Bryan's Station had already started for Hoy's, the silent stockade must be nearly empty and perhaps it could be rushed. If the men were inside, the invaders still outnumbered them six or ten to one (accounts of the numbers involved vary widely), but there was little to be gained by trying to rush a twelve-foot log wall with forty-four of the finest marksmen in the world shooting from cover while their women reloaded spare rifles behind them. Even in twentieth-century war, aimed rifle fire is still the deadliest thing there is; and these men were habituated to the rifle from childhood, holding it a disgrace to shoot a squirrel anywhere but in the head except when they amused themselves by the still more difficult art of "barking" the branch under the little animal and bringing it down stunned though untouched. They were less particular, but quite as accurate, when they fired at Indians.

Before daybreak a negro was attacked. A few Indian scouts were seen on the prowl, and at the crack of James McBride's rifle—traditionally the first shot of the siege—one of them fell. Girty the "white Indian" and his companions still hoped that whoever was left at Bryan's might imagine the dead scout belonged merely to some small raiding party such as were always slipping into Kentucky and lurking around the settlements. After all, one dead Indian was nothing unusual.

Thomas Ball and Nicholas Tomlinson—two men, in the desperate hope that one at least would get through alive—rode out into the woods, knowing their danger but hoping to reach Lexington. Once there, it would be easy enough to bring up Boone's and Logan's men. Miraculously, as it then seemed, both men survived. The Indians saw them but let them pass undisturbed. They were unwilling to betray their presence and hoped to finish off the station quickly and be gone before relief came.

The gates had hardly slammed shut behind the messengers when the water problem arose. The women, cooking four days' provisions for the troops the night before, had used up every drop. The Indians had arrived so early that the day's supply had not yet been brought in. If the men went out, they would be doing exactly what Girty and Caldwell wanted. They would all be shot down and the fort would be left undefended. The thing to do was to be as natural as possible. The women of Bryan's Station would go out to the spring this morning as they did every morning, unconcernedly pretending to see nothing and to fear nothing.

There was some trepidation when this scheme was first proposed. One or two women suggested that they were no more bullet-proof than men. But it was the only way and eventually it was decided that all the women in the fort should go, lest favoritism be shown to any. The whole group knelt inside the stockade to pray for safety. Then these women of the pioneering breed put on their sunbonnets; slipped off their moccasins because they thought they could run faster without them in case of need; gathered up their piggins and noggins; and took along their gourds, because the spring was so shallow that the water had to be dipped up gourdful by gourdful.

They went out at intervals, "stringing along, two or three together, as naturally as possible"—and, as one of them said, "a paler-faced crowd of women was never seen." One little girl in her 'teens kept ahead of her mother, hoping to serve as a shield if the Indians fired.

Slowly the little procession strolled down the hill, covered for part of the way by rifles held just inside the loopholes, but soon beyond range. There was a pause, and probably a good deal of cheerful feminine chatter at the spring. It was a gallant bluff, for Indians were all around them. Under one clump of bushes a hand clasping a tomahawk was visible. Farther on a pair of moccasined feet protruded slightly.

At the fort, inside the gate, stood the long row of moccasins where the women had left them. Husbands, fathers, and sweethearts could look at them and wonder if they would ever again be worn. At the loopholes the men clutched their rifles and watched in agony. Each man had two or three rifles, loaded and ready.

Prone in the underbrush the savages peered in amazement—or more probably in exultation. This was success beyond their hopes. The Kentuckians could not possibly suspect the presence of a large force, or these defenseless women would never have casually emerged from safety intent upon the ordinary day's routine of the pioneer housewife.

Let the women alone. A squaw is always useful about camp. They all would be prisoners later in the day.

More slowly the burdened line of women came up the hill. Grown women carried two pails each. Little girls trotted beside their mothers carrying a piggin or a noggin apiece. Now they were in range again, under the protection of the Kentucky rifles. At least they would not be killed or tomahawked out of hand. That was some comfort.

But they could still be shot from cover; and hundreds of rifles would be blazing at them in an instant if the Indians suspected what was really happening, guessed that the fort was being provisioned under their noses. The bodies would lie out there in the cleared space, the watching husbands knew, the long-haired scalps safe only so long as rifles enough still spoke from the loopholes to keep the scalping knives away from the dead.

These things were not good to think about.

The women were drawing closer and closer to the fort. No sign of haste or alarm, now. That would be fatal. If the women could only play out the gallant little farce, could only go on acting their parts to the end! Now they were nearly out of range from the underbrush and close in under the wicked brown muzzles held just behind the friendly loopholes, not a barrel showing. Now at the gate.

Birds were raising their usual early morning chorus. The creek beyond the fort burbled a little. Otherwise the unearthly silence of the great woods brooded unbroken over forty-four men about to fight for their lives, some hundreds of savages eager for scalps and plunder, and fifty white invaders accompanying the savages, whose thoughts in that moment are beyond speculation.

Through the wooden gate the women and little girls filed slowly in. The timbers grated shut. Bars thudded into place.

They set the water down. Men looked at their women and women looked at their men. Someone must have drawn a long breath, and there may even have been a little kissing.

Outside nothing showed; inside nothing stirred.

Birds cannot sing forever and the silence came down again. Somewhere back in the forest the captives from Ruddle's Station waited to see whether their own fate would be reënacted.

The morning drew on in utter silence. Girty finally grew tired of waiting for the men within the station to open the gates and start off, leaving the fort undefended. On the other side of the fort, opposite the spring side, a small party of Indians appeared. These were decoys intended to draw the Kentuckians out of their defenses in pursuit, or at least to bring all riflemen to the wrong side of the stockade while the hundreds of Indians hidden in the underbrush rushed it from the other side. It was the old device that had tricked Boone and Kenton a few years earlier, but the Kentuckians were used to it now.

Though well aware of what was being planned, the apparently gullible men of Bryan's Station swung open the cabin "outdoors" giving through the stockade in the rear, and a feeble little party of thirteen ran out, firing desperately, drawing a return fire from the Indians, and making as much noise and excitement as they possibly could.

From the underbrush on the creek side, near the spring, Girty and the hundreds of concealed savages heard the fighting. They had no idea how many men the fort contained. The thirteen on the other side were out of sight and they were trying to sound like a great many more than they actually were. For all the attacking party of Indians knew, they really were the entire garrison. None of the attacking savages suspected that twenty-nine riflemen were silently waiting for them on the spring side of the fort, or that the thirteen men in the sally party were by this time running for the stockade with all their might, ready to add their rifles to the twenty-nine. Four of the cabins' "outdoors" had been left wide open for their retreat.

The war whoop rose from the underbrush and up the hill from the spring, led by Girty, came the naked horde, painted in red and black, waving incendiary torches.

Back and forth along the wall of logs flickered and crackled rifle fire. The Indians were many and had to attack on a narrow front so that the riflemen standing under cover had easy target and plenty of it, while the Indians had to shoot on the run with nothing to aim at but a few loopholes. The frontiersmen, with two or three rifles apiece and the women loading for them, could deliver a volume of fire that was appallingly swift and deadly.

A scattering of Indians reached the fort and managed to set fire to a few of the cabins outside. But it was useless to try to climb a twelve-foot stockade raked by fire from the blockhouses at each corner, with the further prospect of axes and clubbed rifles for any daring brave who succeeded in scrambling across.

The attack melted away, the Indians taking to cover; and, except for the dead and badly wounded, the hillside lay empty. But the danger had not vanished with the Indians, for the burning cabins were sending a shower of sparks over the station whose dry timbers seemed likely to take fire at any moment. From their concealment the Indians watched in exultation. At any moment the settlers might be forced out by fire. But suddenly a stiff east wind sprang up and turned the stream of sparks away from the fort. The station was safe for the time being. If the messengers had managed to get through the Indian lines, relief would soon be on the way—and best of all, it was clear that Girty and Caldwell had no artillery.

The Indians were keeping up a more or less steady fire on the stockade, hoping to pick off the marksmen one by one. It was not a very successful effort—a whole day's shooting by several hundred Indians killed exactly two Kentuckians.

So steady was the settlers' fire that the Indians could not get near enough to use their torches a second time. Instead, they shot flaming arrows in the usual hope of setting fire to the dry cabin roofs. All the men were needed at the loopholes; but whenever a fire arrow landed on a roof, a little boy was sent up to throw it down and to pour on water which his mother handed up. Being small, the youngsters could still find some shelter even on the roofs. Since the roofs sloped in, this was not so dangerous as it sounds; and there is no record that any of these intrepid urchins were injured. A fire arrow landed in a cradle without harming the baby Richard Mentor Johnson, who grew up to be ninth Vice-President of the United States.

One little girl ate her breakfast from a pewter plate. By lunchtime she had nothing to eat from. Her plate had been melted down and was flying across the clearing in the form of bullets.

Once during the siege little Betsy Johnson ran up to her mother, who had led the procession to the spring, crying:

"Jake Stucker has just killed an Indian!"

"Pshaw," replied the mother. "What's one Indian?"

There was indeed an embarrassing surplus of Indians outside at the moment, but relief was on the way. Though the settlers did not know it, their messengers had both survived. By this time Girty knew it well enough, and knew what it meant, too. He had failed to surprise the fort. He had failed to rush the fort. He had failed to set the fort on fire. From the loopholes the rifles cracked viciously whenever an Indian showed himself. At any time, now, Boone, Logan, and Todd would be moving up with the militia. Girty prepared to ambush the relief, which would have to come in along the trace leading from Lexington to the northeast gate of Bryan's Station.

The messengers had reached Lexington without difficulty. They knew that the militia had already been called out, and they hoped to find them, like their own force at Bryan's Station, waiting the order to march. But the Indian feint at Hoy's Station had served its purpose. Major Levi Todd and the Lexington men were already on their way to Hoy's. Riding after them, the messengers came up with Todd's force at Boone's Station, where Captain William Ellis's troopers were waiting. Boone himself was still at Boonesborough.

Back along the trail they had come, now pounded Todd's thirty riflemen afoot and Ellis's horsemen, sixteen or seventeen in number. It was two o'clock in the afternoon before they reached Bryan's. By that time the Indians had ceased firing and a strong band had slipped along under cover of the brush on the creek bank and were hopefully waiting in ambush.

As the relief approached the station, there was an absolute hush. Not an Indian was to be seen. The fort lay peaceful in the middle of the clearing and there is no record that the defenders saw the reënforcements or tried to signal.

Todd and Ellis were not in the least deceived. They knew Indians, and they knew an ambush when they saw one—or rather, when they saw nothing, they knew what to expect. They decided to let the horsemen ride hell-for-leather straight at the gate, while the men on foot pushed around through the tall August growth of the hundred-acre cornfield, wholly under cover.

Ellis was one of those powerfully pious men who are sometimes remarkably handy in a rough-and-tumble. He had led the "travelling church" into Kentucky. He now led his handful of cavalry straight into and straight through the Indians' trap. They rode, if not into the jaws of death, at least into the best imitation of hell that the very considerable ingenuity of the American Indian could provide. For a hundred yards they ran the gauntlet of the fire from the ambushed warriors, while the men at the fort, hearing the uproar and then seeing them emerge, got the gate open.

Incredibly, every man and every horse came through without a scratch. Indians were proverbially bad marksmen; a galloping horse is not a really good target; and with the single-shot firearms of the day most of the Indians got only one chance at them. But legend also says that they got through because of "the great dust that was raised by the horses' feet." The experience of the World War and after shows that smoke screens do reduce the accuracy of rifle fire almost to nothing. It was August and the buffalo trace was dry enough for sixteen or seventeen horses, ridden at a mad gallop, to produce a very fair screen.

The men in the cornfield did not fare so well. Unseen by the Indians, they had slipped through the corn in safety until near the fort. At this moment they heard the burst of yells and rifle shots that greeted the horsemen as they dashed through the ambush. Unhesitatingly they rushed back—to the rescue, as they thought. Actually, they were just in time to run into an overwhelming mob of angry Indians and to see Ellis and his men vanishing into the fort, which they themselves might have reached easily enough if they had kept on as agreed.

Luckily, the Indian rifles were mostly empty when the handful of white men appeared on foot. There was an instant and tremendous stir with ramrods and powder-horns among the red men, but they kept a respectful distance from the menace of the loaded Kentucky rifles, as the whites melted discreetly backward into the maize, firing as little as possible.

The watchers in the fort, waiting for them to break out of the cornfield and dash across the clearing for the gate, suddenly heard an ungodly rumpus in the corn. It was not clear then and it never will be clear now just what did happen in that cornfield. There was much yelling, the flashing of many tomahawks, and a violent waving of the tassled cornstalks; but there was almost no shooting. One lucky shot knocked down James Girty, brother of Simon, but he bounced up again unhurt. The blow of the bullet had knocked him off his feet; but to the universal disgust of all Kentucky his life was saved by a piece of leather, stolen from the station vat, which he had wrapped around his powder-horn.

The watchers from the blockhouses waited vainly for their rescuers to emerge from the tangled green of the cornfield. The sounds of combat slowly faded. The rescuers were in full flight for Lexington, leaving two dead men behind them.

It was evident to Girty and Caldwell by this time that the fort could not be taken. It had some sixty rifles now, instead of forty-two, and forty-two had already proved quite enough to keep the Indians at bay. Girty decided to try diplomacy.

Working his way through the hemp, he reached a big stump within five yards of the fort, and in the deadly stillness hailed its defenders. Many of the Kentuckians knew him personally, for he had served as a scout against the Indians in Lord Dunmore's War, and he had been on the American side at the opening of the Revolution. Remembering this, Girty told them who he was and "said he had no doubt a plenty of us knew him." From his stump Girty then shouted a summons to surrender, explaining that he had large forces with him and expected artillery in the evening. If Bryan's Station surrendered now, he would protect the settlers. If they waited till the artillery blew down the stockade and the Indians stormed it, the warriors would be roused to fury and no one would be able to control them.

There was a sickening silence in the little fort. They knew well enough what had followed when British artillery had been emplaced before Ruddle's and Martin's Stations. They remembered the corpses along the trail to the Ohio. Girty's talk about artillery might be bluff. On the other hand, if he did have artillery coming up through the forest, they all were doomed and they all knew it.

Then up rose Aaron Reynolds, the mighty swearer. Either he had reformed, or the display of his vocabulary upon this occasion has been inadequately recorded for an appreciative posterity. This time there were ladies present, and the listening heroines of Bryan's Station may have cramped the famous Aaron Reynolds style. It looked at the moment extremely probable that he and the ladies and everyone else in that forlorn hamlet would be scalped before nightfall. Simon Girty, if he ran true to form, would probably do his share of the scalping; but in the meantime Aaron Reynolds contemplated Simon Girty's proposal and Simon Girty himself with repugnance and he meant the world to know it.

Setting one barrel on top of another within the capacious stone fireplace of a cabin near Girty's stump, he was able to poke his head out the top of the stone chimney. Thus sheltered, with only his head exposed, he enjoyed very much the same security as a turtle. He presented almost no target in case of a treacherous shot, and he could duck into the safety of good stone walls in an instant.

From his protected perch he gave free rein to his emotions. He owned two good-for-nothing dogs, bawled Aaron. He had named one Simon and the other Girty. That soldier of fortune replied in an injured tone that this was serious and no time for joking; but Aaron Reynolds was irrepressible. The Indians might bring on their artillery, he shouted, and be damned. (That mild expletive is the only profanity recorded.) Kentucky was coming to the rescue. "If you and your gang of murderers stay here another day, we will have your scalps drying in the sun on the roofs of these cabins." Warming up as he went along, Reynolds added that while they had plenty of powder and lead "to beat such a son of a bitch as Girty," still all they really needed was switches for the "yellow hides" of his Indians.

Bryan's Station was delighted. There was a huge guffaw as Girty heatedly invited Reynolds to come outside and say them words. Morale had improved tremendously.

"Girty," says a contemporary, "took great offence at the levity and want of politeness of his adversary."

Captain John Craig, the commander, managed to get in an official word at some time during the conversation and called over that there would be no surrender. From behind his stump in the clearing, the "white Indian" snarled back his regrets. It was too bad. Bryan's Station would certainly be captured in just one more day, and then—

At that moment Aaron Reynolds turned his dog on him. Girty retired.

All night long the white men stood to their rifles. Sometimes a rattle of shots brought them leaping to the loopholes, but there was no real assault, and toward dawn the silence of the forest settled down again.

The sun dragged up out of the trees. There was the smoke of endless camp fires to show where the Indians had been. But there was no attack. Only silence.

And then a horse galloping and a rider in buckskin waving his hat. The relief was coming in. The messenger dashed up to the fort yelling:

"They are gone! The redskins are gone!"

16. The Year of Blood:
DEATH AT THE BLUE LICKS

NEXT day Daniel Boone led in the men from Boonesborough, and other contingents came in from Lexington and Harrodsburg. Scouts out looking for Indian "sign" had seen enough to show that the enemy had retreated from Bryan's Station, northward along the buffalo trace. Nowhere in the woods was there sign to indicate that any of the savage warriors had lingered behind.

There was a bustle of hurried preparation in the fort all morning. A council of war debated whether to pursue the Indians at once, with such force as they had; or to wait until Colonel Benjamin Logan could come up with four or five hundred men from the southern settlements, when they would be in overwhelming force. Major Hugh McGary of the Lincoln County militia was for waiting, but he was ridiculed as timid. Colonel Todd pooh-poohed his advice. One lost day would enable the Indians to get across the Ohio into safety. John Craig, who had been in command during the siege, insisted they now had enough men to catch and defeat the Indians. It looked as if Craig ought to know. Todd thought the Indians' numbers were exaggerated—and anyhow, "the more the merrier."

At noon they marched, the men of Bryan's Station, Lexington, Harrodsburg, and Boonesborough—well under two hundred in all, but confident that Logan would be coming up with reënforcements in a day or two. They were marching, had they but known it, to the last pitched battle of the American Revolution. Meantime, Bryan's Station lay silent in the wilderness, guarded only by its women and its children.

The scene, as Boone and the rest marched out of the fort, was enough to make any man long for revenge. Everything outside the stockade that would burn was in ashes. Leather had been stolen from the tanning vat. Dead cattle, hogs, and sheep lay where they had been slaughtered, already rotting in the August sun. The Indians had cut meat from some, but many had been killed solely for the sake of destruction. The hemp had been burned, the potato vines pulled up, the cornstalks broken down. It was part of the effort to make Kentucky uninhabitable for the Americans; it was also exactly what the Kentuckians had done in many an Indian village; but no one thought of that.

No finer fighting men ever faced an enemy than the leathery frontiersmen who looked around at the desolation, gripped their rifles, and rode on. Daniel Boone was now approaching fifty but his age meant nothing—he was to roam the woods for thirty years to come. It was now thirteen years since he had first entered Kentucky. He knew every brook and creek, every buffalo path and ravine, every hiding place for a deer, a hunter, or an Indian. Captured by the Indians two or three times, he had lived among them and knew the queer processes of the red man's brain, and he had won a kind of grudging admiration from them. The Shawnees never quite got over hoping that Sheltowee would join the tribe again, some day, and settle down to the life of a sensible Indian. Boone had already lost a brother and a son, both killed by Indians, but he was risking his family's blood as well as his own again today. His son Israel Boone, his nephew, a son-in-law, and other relatives by marriage marched with him.

The other two commanders were John Todd, veteran of the

battle at Point Pleasant, one of the men in Henderson's original legislature at Boonesborough in 1775; and Stephen Trigg, who had come to Kentucky as one of the court of land commissioners and had remained as an Indian fighter. Like Boone, each of these was lieutenant-colonel of his county militia, and theoretically in command of its troops. Sometimes the command was very theoretical. Even after a council of war the three commanders could not get their orders obeyed!

These Kentucky woodsmen were fierce but not especially enthusiastic fighters. They wanted lands, homes, and security; and they were perfectly willing to fight anyone—British or Indian—who interfered. But except for a few adventurous spirits like Kenton, they found no zest in the business. They cared so little for military display that only one officer carried a sword. Colonel Todd, as commander, had borrowed Daniel Boone's, the only one in Kentucky. It was lost next day in the battle, but was later fished out of the Licking River and identified.

The strict obedience—intelligent but unquestioning—which is the soul of an army was wholly alien to everything in the settlers' wild independent life. There was no magic in a commission. Under the system which gave every little hamlet a full quota of company and even field officers, at least a quarter of the expedition held commissions anyway. The less than two hundred men who started off on Girty's trail were "commanded" by no less than three lieutenant-colonels, enough for a modern infantry regiment of three thousand. They were men highly respected in their communities, and experienced in wilderness war, but that did not in the least mean that they could get their orders obeyed by their unruly troops. If discipline failed, there was nothing to do but fall back on mob impulse.

When Girty, Caldwell, McKee, and their Indians gave up their attack and slipped away from Bryan's Station, they had gone quietly into camp at the ruins of Ruddle's Station, which had been looted and burned twenty-two months before. The prisoners who had been brought back to Kentucky slept that night amid the ruins of their homes.

The Indians had plenty of food, for as McKee later officially reported they had "killed upwards of 300 hogs, 150 head of cattle, and a number of sheep." As they had also captured some horses, there was no difficulty in carrying supplies.

They were careful to guard their rear against the retaliation that they knew would follow, but their night's rest was undisturbed. Not until next day did the pursuit even get under way. Breaking camp at their leisure in the morning, the retreating invaders moved on to the Blue Licks. They had been traveling very light, and one hundred Indians, leaving the war party at Ruddle's Station, "went after their things they left at the Forks of Licking."

The rest, impudently blazing the trail behind them so that the pursuing Kentuckians might make no mistake about their route, took the shorter way to the Blue Licks, where they went into camp on "ground advantageous in case the enemy should pursue us." Scouts lingered along the trail behind, especially about the Blue Licks, watching for the pursuit which by this time was not far off. In the early morning one of them brought Caldwell news that the Kentuckians were only a mile away.

At this point the main Licking River bends through three quarters of a circle around a hill. Just behind the crest of the hill were two ravines filled with a tangle of fallen timber. It was perfect cover and Caldwell decided to ambush the Kentuckians right there. The Indians at first objected that the Blue Licks were an important hunting ground. They were afraid a battle might frighten the buffalo away. Eventually Caldwell persuaded them. The main body of warriors wriggled into the fallen trees where they were completely invisible, and a few others remained in sight on the hillside. It was an ideal position for an ambush, with water around them almost everywhere, cutting off the Kentuckians once they had crossed, and yet with a clear line to the rear for the Indians themselves. Retreat would be easy if the Kentuckians turned out to be more numerous than reported. It would be hard for the white men if the Indians won.

On the trail behind, the white pursuers pushed on in brash confidence, very bold and very sure of themselves—all but one.

Daniel Boone was doing some thinking. The leisurely Indian retreat, the failure to conceal the trail, the obvious confidence of the retreating invaders, what did they mean? Had the Indians wished to escape, they could have traveled at twice the speed they were making; or they could have broken up into many small bands which, scattering in all directions, would leave no trail whatever.

Just what were the redskins planning? Daniel Boone had his suspicions. Was this the same trick that had failed at Boonesborough and at Bryan's Station? An attempt to draw the white men out of their defenses into ambush?

Out there, somewhere in the woods ahead, what was Simon Girty thinking? Bryan's Station had been so magnificently defended that there was no hope of immediate capture. Very well, then. Retreat. Draw the whole Kentucky force out into the wilderness. Catch them on unfavorable ground and destroy them all.

Caldwell's Wheeling expedition had barely got started; his attack on Bryan's Station had been a failure; but he still had a chance to wipe out half the fighting men of Kentucky in a single smashing blow.

As the Kentucky pursuers moved swiftly through the forests, more and more unpleasant reflections of this sort kept passing through the mind of Daniel Boone. He had carefully counted the Indian camp fires, and "concluded there were at least 500 Indians."

The abandoned camp of the night before at Ruddle's Station looked as if the Indians were stronger than the Kentuckians supposed. Why hadn't they hidden their camp fires? The warriors would have scattered if they wanted to escape pursuit; instead, they kept together. Their trail ought to have been concealed, all traces of passage hidden, footmarks few and far between, taxing the observation of the keenest scout. Daniel kept his sharp blue eyes on the ground and did not in the least like what he saw. Anybody could follow a trail like this. Discarded equipment lay along the line of march. Tomahawks had blazed the trees. The only reason for blazing a trail is an expectation it will be followed. Did these Indians *want* to be followed?

Lieutenant-Colonel Daniel Boone was increasingly uneasy. The more "sign" he saw the less he liked it. Boone knew his Indians; and this was not the way fleeing Indians ought to act.

At sundown the Kentuckians halted and the plan of battle was explained to everyone. They might encounter Indians any moment now. Half the men were to ride their horses straight into the Indian line. The rest, on foot, were to follow close behind, attacking at close range when the cavalry charge had broken the enemy.

After a short rest they mounted again and pushed on through the darkened forest until midnight. Then they went into camp near the present town of Ellisville in Nicholas County. They had covered thirty-three miles from Bryan's Station that day.

The Indian camp was only three or four miles away, but neither side knew where the other was. The Kentucky camp was not harassed in the night, and if the Indian scouts found it at all, they sent no message back.

Early in the morning the Kentuckians pushed on, with a

screen of five scouts ahead of them. As these men came over the hill-top looking down into the river and across the valley, they saw two Indians walking back and forth on the opposite ridge. Nothing else was in sight and everything seemed visible, for the hills had been gnawed bare by buffalo hungry for salt. The scouts halted and waited for the rest to come up.

When Todd arrived, he took one look and sent back along the column for Boone. Daniel approached with the remark, "Colonel, they intend to fight us."

"How do you know?" asked Todd.

"They have been for some time concealing their number by treading in each other's tracks." He pointed down to the ground at their feet, where the Indian trail wound forward through the forest. "Don't you see they are doing so?"

Boone, who had known this part of the country for years, suggested that they cross the river higher up and then strike the trace again in the high ground to the north. That would take them around any possible ambush. He was overruled, and the whole cavalcade blundered down to the Blue Licks ford beyond which, on their hill, the Indians waited in cheerful anticipation. A medicine man, after due incantation, is said to have learned from the Great Spirit the night before that the white men would soon be at the river and would offer battle.

As the Kentucky advance guard came down to the river bank, they could still look across and see a few Indians moving on the hill a mile beyond the stream. Had they caught up with the enemy? Or were these merely stragglers?

The Kentuckians again halted for council. Somewhere in the rear Logan must now be hurrying after them with four or five hundred rifles. With such a force they would be overwhelming. But would the Indians wait to be overwhelmed? Delay might mean their escape. It might also mean that the Kentuckians would be attacked instead of attacking.

Daniel Boone proposed delay. He knew the country only too well. He had passed here with Michael Stoner in 1774. Near this very place, six years before, he had been captured by Blackfish's warriors, and a few years later had driven off two Indians single-handed. Along the hill in front, they could see for a mile, and it was true that all seemed clear. But over the crest and out of sight, two ravines ran from the hill down to the river. It was a likely spot for an ambush, and Boone pointed this out with emphasis.

Two volunteers splashed their horses across the river, rode for a mile and a quarter, and returned to report they had seen nothing. It was what in modern military parlance is called "negative information"—a notoriously treacherous thing. If you have seen the enemy, well, you have seen him. But if you have not seen him, there is always the uncomfortable possibility that he is there all the same, and you have just overlooked him.

For two scouts to ride alone into enemy country is a nervous business. The best of scouts is never without a thought of his own skin and its safety. The two volunteers had not looked quite so carefully as they thought, nor had they seen so much as they thought. Some hundreds of Indians, keeping close to the ground and using cover as only Indians can, were in the very area they had reconnoitered—or said they had reconnoitered. Simon Kenton, who could live undetected for days at a time on the outskirts of an Indian village, might not have been so easily deceived; but Kenton was far in the rear, toiling ahead with Logan and the reënforcements. Boone would have done better, but his place as a commander was with his own men.

The early morning quiet was still unbroken, that treacherous quiet which was so often the prelude to bloody massacre. Only a few Indians had been sighted—smoking their pipes!—and they had offered no resistance; but the Kentucky commanders were still unsatisfied. With their men in a circle around them, Todd asked Boone's opinion.

Boone insisted that there were three to five hundred Indians (his official report afterwards said four hundred or more) in ambush in the ravines just ahead. No matter what the scouts reported, he knew the ground and he knew Indians. He proposed that half the Kentuckians move upstream, cross near Elk Creek, and attack one ravine in flank, while the rest attacked from some other position.

It was the soundest kind of modern tactics—a holding attack combined with an attack in flank—but even that might not have succeeded in such wooded country. The two attacks would have to be absolutely simultaneous to be successful and Todd might have to wait for Logan to come up before he had enough troops for such an enveloping movement.

Not a sound came from the warrior-packed ravines. Boone's advice might have been heeded even yet. But an ill-timed remark about McGary's courage, made by someone or other at Bryan's Station a couple days before, still rankled. McGary had been in favor of waiting for Logan then. But now he wanted to fight, and he wanted to fight in a hurry. Boone warned him that the horseshoe bend where they stood was the worst possible ford. If he really insisted on crossing, there was a really good ford two miles downstream.

McGary sneered something about cowardice.

Boone, nettled at the slur, grumbled: "If you are determined to go and meet the enemy at this great disadvantage, go on: I can go as far into an Indian fight as any other man."

"By Godly," inquired McGary—it was his pet oath—"what have we come here for?"

"To fight the Indians," said somebody.

"By Godly," cried McGary, "then why not fight them?"

With that, swearing he would prove his own courage at

least, he waved his rifle over his head and rode into the river, yelling:

"All who are not damned cowards follow me, and I'll soon show you the Indians."

With the three leaders still in council, this piece of bravado was the worst sort of insubordination, but it suited the temper of the frontiersmen. Instantly men were everywhere scrambling into their saddles and splashing through the river, while the Indian scouts watching from above must have wondered if the white men had lost their minds.

The best the crestfallen commanders could do was to follow their unduly enthusiastic troops across and try to get them into some sort of formation. This they managed to do. Trigg took the right, Todd the center, Boone the left. The men dismounted, stripped to their shirt sleeves, tied their clothes to their saddles, and left their horses standing with the reins flung over their necks, but not tied. They would need them to pursue Indians. Only a few officers were still mounted. Boone himself went ahead on foot.

An advance guard of twenty-five men—commanded by three majors!—started forward, the impetuous McGary with them. The rest followed in three long narrow columns abreast of each other. They reached the top of the ridge and then started toward the ravines where Boone expected the Indian ambush. Leaving their horses behind, they moved to within sixty yards of the Indians—point blank range.

There was a rattle of shots as the advance guard stumbled into the Indians, then the fire quickened and a volley brought down all but three of them. McGary survived the mischief he had done. Within three minutes, forty men were down. On the right the Indian line extended far beyond Trigg's little force. Trigg was soon shot through the body and fell dead, or dying, with blood gushing both from breast and back. His men, disheartened, began to yield ground. The Indians not only drove them back in an instant, but swung in behind them, so that in a few minutes the Kentuckians were caught between two fires. As soon as these woodsmen—used only to their own style of go-as-you-please fighting, and never accustomed to waiting for a steadying word of command—realized that the Indians were behind them, it was every man for himself. Some of them got in three or four shots. Then it was all over. Disciplined troops might still have won. These men, equally brave, could not.

Boone's troops were the only ones who drove the enemy back and Boone himself later suspected their retreat was merely a feint. But in the excitement of battle none of Boone's fighters noticed what was going on elsewhere. Boone was elated. He was carrying an extra-long fowling piece which he rarely used, loaded with three or four balls and sixteen or eighteen buckshot.

"You be there!" he cried as he fired at an Indian and saw him fall—an exclamation so strange under the circumstances that someone remembered it afterward. The Indians dodged backward from tree to tree for about a hundred yards while Boone and his men pursued.

At this moment McGary rode up:

"Col. Boone, why are you not retreating? Todd's and Trigg's line has given way, and the Indians are all around you." Boone looked back and saw the other Kentuckians running for their lives.

The battle itself had lasted about five minutes. The rest was a panic-stricken rush for the river, more than a mile away. Men who were still on horseback rode for the ford. The rest ran for their horses, but as the whooping warriors rushed forward, the horses stampeded.

The Indians dropped their rifles and leaped ahead with

knife and tomahawk. They were in among the horses almost as soon as the fleeing white men, slashing and cutting at them as they tried to mount. The flight was over bare, open ground. There was no chance of concealment.

Alone or in small groups, on horse or on foot, as best they might, the Kentuckians made for the river, the Indians whooping among them as they plied their tomahawks or tripped up the fleeing men to stab them as they fell, or took occasional prisoners to be tortured later to a slow death, or leaped into the saddles of the Kentucky horses and rode ahead to waylay the fugitives when they reached the ford.

Knowing the country as he did, Daniel Boone saw there was only one possible chance of escape. Gathering his men together, he led them swiftly off through the woods to the west. His son Israel paused for one more shot as his father passed him. Daniel, finding a horse, told Israel to mount and ride off, while he went for another. But the boy exclaimed, "Father, I won't leave you!"

There was a shot and Daniel turned to see his son with one quivering arm still stretched in front of him, blood gushing from his mouth. As he fell Daniel gathered him up and carried him off in his arms. Once an Indian, swinging his tomahawk, got within a few feet of the burdened father before he could lay his son down and fire. Seeing that Israel was either dying or already dead, Boone laid him on the ground. Tradition says that he hid the body in a cave. Then he mounted and rode for his life. As he did so a volley rang out behind him, cutting the branch of a tree, which fell across his horse's neck. He got his men safely across near the mouth of Indian Creek, farther down the Licking River. They paused for one last volley as they reached the southern bank.

Of all the horrors of his long life, this episode made the deepest impression upon Boone. Thirty years afterward, he could not describe it without tears. Just recovering from fever, Israel had been urged to stay at home, but he had insisted on sharing the dangers of the expedition.

Squire Boone, Jr., Daniel's nephew, rode all the way back with a broken thigh. A friend got him on a horse, and rode along pushing off the frantic fugitives who tried to climb up behind the wounded man. At Strode's Station he is said to have paused, without dismounting, for a drink—of buttermilk; then to have pushed on to Boone's Station. Eventually he "got well and went to preaching."

While Daniel Boone had been struggling to save his son, another fugitive, Anthony Sowdusky, had managed to get Israel's horse and was just riding off when he heard a cry from a white man, "for God's sake not to leave him," stopped, got the man into the saddle and rode off with seven or eight bullets in his clothing but only one grazing the skin.

Boone's son-in-law, Joseph Scholl, reached the river so weak that he turned to a companion, Andrew Morgan, with the words:

"I'm afraid I can't get over the river with my rifle; I can't part with it."

"Hold on to my shoulder as we pass the river," said Morgan.

As they reached the other bank in safety, Morgan, parched with the long run under an August sun, said:

"Now you can wade out; I'll stop and drink"—which, with rifle balls kicking the water up in spurts around him, he did. One fugitive felt his wounded brother shot in his arms after carrying him half way over the stream. Of fifteen men crossing with him, he alone survived.

The river line, more than a mile in rear, now became the center of such resistance as was still possible. It was deep enough to be an obstacle to wounded men on foot; but it was an obstacle for the pursuing Indians, too. They were a clear and helpless target as they struggled across, and by this time the Kentucky rifles were beginning to speak from the other bank.

The real hero of the retreat, however, was a certain Benjamin Netherland. In the rough banter of the frontier, cowardice was a frequent accusation, easy enough in bushwhacking forest war when escape alive was often more important than a petty local triumph. The day had not yet come when a few yards of trench were thought worth innumerable lives. This border warfare was so desperate that even men were valuable.

Netherland had been suspected of cowardice and about this very time was refused promotion because he was a "triffling" character. But it was he who partially saved the day that McGary's foolhardy bravado had lost. He had seen some fighting in the East in the first years of the Revolution, had been with Lafayette, and had fought at Guilford Courthouse. Then—as was not unusual—he had left the army and come West to Kentucky.

Well-mounted, Netherland got safely across the ford. As he looked back, he could see the slaughter all along the other bank. The way to safety was clear ahead of him. It was a matter of minutes before the woods on this bank, too, would be full of savages, crossing above and below him and racing in behind to cut him off. Netherland swung his six feet two out of the saddle and stopped the fleeing men around him:

"Let's halt, boys, and give them a fire."

From the shore his line of ten or twenty rifles opened an aimed fire at close range, blazing at every Indian that showed himself. The warriors, many without rifles, fell back to cover, and the weary and wounded fugitives began to struggle across. It was only a few minutes' delay, but it was enough. The men rushed across the ford or swam the deeper parts of the river to safety, then vanished into the forests. Netherland and his band mounted and galloped safely away, reaching Bryan's Station that evening. Nearly fifty years later, Captain Robert Patterson wrote him: "I cannot ever forget the part you acted in the Battle of Blue Licks."

Patterson himself owed his life to that very Aaron Reynolds whom he had rebuked for swearing a few weeks earlier. Although he had never fully recovered after being shot and tomahawked some years before, Patterson fought with Boone on the Kentucky left. In the retreat he had managed to get as far as the river where he stopped, too exhausted to struggle across. Meantime Reynolds had seen a horse with a dead man dragging by the stirrup, had cut the body loose, taken the horse, and ridden to the river. Seeing Patterson helpless on the bank, Reynolds jumped off, pushed him into the saddle, and himself swam safely across. But his buckskin trousers were so heavy with water he could hardly move. He sat down to pull them off. Indians had crossed safely lower down and were ranging through the woods along the river, looking for white men. They captured Reynolds unhurt, kept him for torture, and went on, leaving him with a single guard. Watching the Indian closely, Reynolds noted that his rifle was not ready to fire, and waiting till he stooped to tie his moccasin, knocked him out with his bare hands and escaped.

Ahead of Patterson, attired solely in his shirt, he reached Bryan's Station, where his story was received with incredulity until Patterson himself rode in, confirmed it, and presented his rescuer with two hundred acres. Aaron Reynolds, the mighty swearer, thereafter settled down, joined the Baptist Church, and became a model citizen—all thanks to a quart of liquor, Simon Girty, and a minor massacre. He confessed that he had begun to form a secret admiration and affection for Patterson from the very day the captain first rebuked him for swearing.

The Indians followed about two miles beyond the Licking

River and then decided, in Caldwell's words, that "as the enemy was mostly on horseback, it was in vain to follow further." They returned to have some fun with the prisoners, whose slashed bodies were later found with the hands still tied, showing that they had been taken alive and tortured to death. As Caldwell reports the results of his interrogation of prisoners, he may have saved some from torture; or he may have questioned them first and then turned them over to the savages. British officers in general discouraged the torture of prisoners as much as they could. Some torture there certainly was, for Jesse Yocum, one of the prisoners, remarked after his escape that "he did not know how many they burned, but the smell of a human was the awfullest smell he ever had in his life."

In the meanwhile Colonel Logan with the reënforcements had crossed the Kentucky River forty miles to the south about the time Boone and the others were leaving Bryan's Station. On Monday, the day of the battle, he was at Bryan's Station himself, and here learned for the first time that the pursuit had already pushed ahead without waiting for him. "Dreading the consequences that might ensue from this precipitate affair," he started after them; but a few miles beyond Bryan's he ran into the first haggard survivors with their story of the massacre. Expecting the Indians right behind them, he rushed a line of outguards forward and prepared for attack, while one by one or in small bands the men who had escaped alive from the Blue Licks straggled through the reënforcements to safety.

Logan waited in vain—the Indians had given up pursuit long before, and were now amusing themselves with the prisoners. They counted their own dead. Then they counted the scalps they had taken. They had lost sixty-four killed and had taken but sixty scalps. Four prisoners must die to even up the balance. In vain the British officers protested.

Five white men were forced to sit down on a log. A warrior drew them to their feet one by one and compelled them to stretch out their arms while another warrior stabbed them. The fifth man, waiting his turn with the bleeding bodies writhing on the ground in front of him, suddenly found he was to be spared. He never knew why. It was evidently because four men were enough to even up the score, and the British lieutenant-governor paid more money for prisoners than for scalps. Girty exulted that his Indians "had killed all their damned commanders."

Learning from their captives of Logan's approach, the Indians waited for him near the river. But Logan, too cautious to fall into such a trap, went back to Bryan's Station. There he gathered 470 men and waited, while all night long and part of the next day fugitives limped into the fort—wounded, bedraggled, exhausted, shattered men.

Daniel Boone seems to have hurried straight to his own station; but he was with Logan when, five days later, the second march to the Blue Licks began.

As the column came down into the valley, they could look across the river and see the scavenging birds circling over the battlefield where the bodies of the slain had been lying alone in the wilderness for nearly a week. Stripped, robbed, scalped, mutilated, bloated by the heat, gnawed by animals, and decayed, the bodies could rarely be identified.

Daniel Boone was one of the few able to recognize his dead. He found Israel's body, knew it only by the clothing, and took it back to Boone's Station. One of the burial party at the Blue Licks later told his daughter that "they couldn't tell one man from another—of the dead—the weather being so warm—they had swollen so much. He had thought he would be afraid in battle; but when he saw the dead bodies it made him feel like fighting."

As much earth as possible was scraped away. The men built a stone wall four feet high and forty feet long. Behind this they piled the dead, throwing over them rocks, logs, brush, more rocks—anything to keep the animals off. It was the best they could do—better than the usual burial of a man killed far from home in the woods. But they did not find them all. A few years later, a surveyor who carried a chain through the battleground said that he "never saw bones thicker in any place; never buried nor nothing."

The Kentuckians were nervous, and though parties of hostile Indians were still skulking about the country, Logan did not investigate but withdrew hurriedly.

"Logan is a dull, narrow body," wrote a contemporary, "from whom nothing clever need be expected. What a figure he exhibited at the head of near 500 men to reach the field of action six days afterwards, and hardly wait to bury the dead, and when it was plain, part of the Indians were still in the Country."

The critical gentleman was sitting safely at home in Virginia. Boone, who had seen the fury of the Wyandots and the horror of the defeat, was not so cocksure.

The Wyandots had brought a new kind of warfare to the frontier. They were willing to throw away their rifles after the first few shots and close with tomahawks. Braddock's bayonets had failed in 1755, but only cold steel could have stopped the Indian rush at the Blue Licks.

Kentucky rifles, however, were not fitted for the stabbing blade. Even if they had been, the pioneers did not understand its use. There were no bayonets on the frontier anyway. Washington and his Continentals needed all they could get. Back in Virginia, after the battle, Colonel Arthur Campbell saw what was needed and wrote to a fellow officer: "The method of arming and arraying our militia ought to be varied.

The Bayonet and Scymeter must be introduced to enable us now to face the Indians. And Evolutions suited to the woods should be learned by both Foot and Horse. All our late defeats have been occasion[ed] thro' neglect of these, and a want of a proper authority and capacity in the Commanding Officers. Never was the lives of so many valuable men lost more shamefully than in the late action of the 19th of August, and that not a little thro' the vain and seditious expressions of a Major McGeary. How much more harm than good can one Fool do."

Boone wrote the Governor of Virginia that they had "Marchd to the Battle Ground again But found the Enemy were gone off So we proceeded to Bury the Dead—which were 43 found on the ground, and Many more we Expect Lay about that we Did not See as we Could not tarry to Search very Close, being Both Hungry and weary, and Some what Dubious that the Enemy might not be gone quite off."

By that time, however, the greater part of the enemy had been gone for some days. When Logan did not immediately appear, they resumed their march toward Ohio. A hundred and forty-two miles to the north, Caldwell was just reaching Wapatomica and composing a formal report to his superiors.

The blow at the Blue Licks had fallen heavily upon all Kentucky, which had had an average of three hundred marauding savages within its borders at intervals every year for four years. The defense of Bryan's Station had been heroic—but it had been in vain. It had been a mere prelude to the Blue Licks defeat. The losses had been terrific for that struggling little outer fringe of civilization. The Indians were a perpetual terror. In six years, "Eight Hundred & sixty fell, the matchless massacread victims of their unprecedented Cruelty." The country was full of widows and of orphans. It looked as if all the settlers would be driven out—"the welthy will forthwith Emigrate to the Interior parts of the Settlement & the Poor to the Spaniards.

Sir

You are hereby required to be ready to go on the intended Expedition against the Shawnese Your Service will be required as a field Officer agreeable to your late Recommendation made by the County Court in the mean Time I expect every exertion will be made by you to forward the Business [illegible] agreeable to the Orders hereto issued relative to the Same

I am Sir your most Obed^t Servt

Daniel Boone

Fayette Octob^r 25th 1782

To Lieut Col. Robt Patterson

DANIEL BOONE ISSUES ORDERS

Colonel Patterson was apparently too badly exhausted at the Blue Licks to join the retaliatory campaign immediately. Reproduced by permission from the original in the Wisconsin State Historical Society, Draper Collection.

Dreadful alternative!! Nature recoils at the thought!" One man offered fourteen hundred acres of land for one little black horse to take his family back to Virginia, "exclaiming that after all their toil they had to loose [sic] the whole country."

Practically every settlement had lost men at the Blue Licks, or in its aftermath. In one county every magistrate had been killed and the public business nearly came to a standstill. Boone wrote the Governor of Virginia that Kentucky must be either reënforced or abandoned: "I have Encouraged the people here in this County all that I Could, but I Can no longer Encourage my Neighbours nor my Seff to risque our Lives here at Such Extraordinary hazzards. the Inhabitants of these Counties are very much alarmd at the thoughts of the Indians Bringing another Campaign into our Country this fall, which if it Should be the Case will Break these Settlements, So I hope your Excellency will take it into Consideration and Send us Some Relief as quick as possaple."

There was a good deal of recrimination in Kentucky and Virginia. General George Rogers Clark thought that the officers had been at fault—in short, "the conduct of those unfortunate Gents was extremely reprehensible." Worse, "Colonel Todd's militia was excused from all other duty but that of keeping out proper scouts and spies on the Ohio and elsewhere to discover the approach of the enemy." But instead, Clark complained, "the enemy was suffered to penetrate deliberately into the bowels of the country and make the attack before they were discovered."

The victims of the Blue Licks tragedy were just as emphatic over the shortcomings of Clark's own strategy. Logan bluntly told the governor that the higher command was to blame: "I am inclined to believe that when your Excellency and Council become acquainted with the military operations in this country that you will not think them so properly conducted as to answer the general interest of Kentuckey." Clark, he said, had first called away a hundred men needed for local defense, and had then ordered more men off to build his "row galley" and other defenses. "Thus," said Logan, "by weakening One end to strengthen another the upper part of the country was left entirely exposed."

Boone's fellow officers in Fayette County agreed with him that their defenses had been weakened to protect western Kentucky and Louisville, "a Fort situated in such a Manner that the Enemy coming with a design to Lay waste our Countrey would Scarcely come with in one Hundred miles of it, & our own Frontiers, open & unguarded."

In all the bitter letters and reports that passed back and forth, however, Boone is never named as personally at fault. But his grandson observed years later that as an old, old man Daniel Boone still felt guilty because he had not been able to get his advice followed and persuade the others to attack at a more reasonable place.

Kentucky took swift revenge, in spite of its terror. At the end of September, George Rogers Clark gathered a thousand men at the old rendezvous on the mouth of Licking, with John Floyd and Benjamin Logan as seconds in command, and Boone again leading his own detachment. They advanced secretly toward Chillicothe. But four Cherokee conjurors at Piqua had used magic to foretell the white men's coming. So, at least, the Indians said. White skeptics suspected that vigilant scouting had accompanied the incantations. The expedition again burned Chillicothe, which the Shawnees had rebuilt, and also destroyed Piqua. The destruction of the September crops was a particularly severe blow to the red men.

The force fell back into Kentucky almost unmolested. Indeed, the Indian pursuit was so weak that the land-hungry Daniel Boone found time to examine the land on the Kentucky side of the Ohio River, near Maysville, with a view to future settlement when the war was over.

17. The Thirteen Fires

THE battle of the Blue Licks practically closed the Revolution, and opened a relatively peaceful period in Daniel Boone's troubled life. It was a needless battle, for the British were slowly losing ground in the East and were gaining nothing on the frontier. In November, 1782, preliminary peace negotiations were opened and about this time Sir Guy Carleton officially notified Washington that American independence could be taken for granted. Long before the treaty of peace was signed and while battle, murder, and sudden death still reigned in the frontier forests, American fishing vessels were peacefully casting their nets in the Gulf of St. Lawrence under license from an accommodating British commander. The treaty was actually signed April 19, 1783, and Daniel Boone had his first news of it from a mounted messenger who rode into Boonesborough stockade with a paper bearing the word "Peace" stuck in his cap.

There was an immediate slackening of Indian raids but not by any means an end of them. The British ceased to arm and encourage the warriors, and the wiser chiefs began to reflect ruefully what might happen if their Great Father across the Big Lake withdrew his redcoats and the Long Knives of the Thirteen Fires came to take revenge. Even so, it was by no means easy for the British to control the Indians or to stop the attacks entirely. Savage warfare is easier to launch than to halt.

The woods were dangerous for years afterward, and the flatboats which bore immigrants down the Ohio were in nearly as much danger as ever. Sporadic Indian raids continued until Mad Anthony Wayne defeated all the northern tribes and forced a treaty on them in 1795. Even George Washington had to abandon his proposed visit to the Kanawha Valley for fear of Indians. One settler deposed that "The Indians were in continual warfare from my first comeing to Strouds Station in year 1783 or 1784 Till Waynes Treaty in 1795—& some people had ventured out & setled stations & that none of them that had so Setled out, did Escape being attacted"—with a few exceptions.

About this time Daniel Boone had one of the narrowest escapes of his life. He had raised a small patch of tobacco at some distance from his cabin. Though he is said not to have been a smoker, he could still profit by his crop. Tobacco was as good as cash. Surveyors' reports were payable in tobacco at the legal rate of a penny a pound; and the State of Virginia issued currency against it.

To cure his green stalks Boone had built a small tobacco shed with a roof of cane and grass and an enclosure of rails. It was usual to split the stalks, run slender sticks through them, and hang them up to dry, one tier above another. Boone's curing shed had three tiers. He had filled one tier some time before and, finding this tobacco nearly dry, had begun lifting the stalks to the second tier, preparatory to moving new stalks in below. He was standing on the poles above when four stalwart Shawnees stalked in grinning derisively.

"Now, Boone, we got you. You no get away any more. We carry you off to Chillicothe this time. You no cheat us any more."

The white man was practically helpless. He was unarmed, high in the air, and at some distance from his cabin. If he refused to surrender, the Indians could very easily shoot him and escape. If he did surrender, they could just as easily rush him into the forest and make for the Ohio.

Again the redoubtable Sheltowee played for time, while he did some fast thinking. Glancing down with assumed friendliness, he recognized braves of the very Shawnee band that had caught him near the salt camp in 1778.

"Ah," he exclaimed affably, "old friends! Glad to see you."

But the Indians knew Boone's tricks too well. They wanted him to come down and were emphatic about it. From the rafters above, their fellow-tribesman Sheltowee explained to his red brothers just how much he would enjoy visiting dear old Chillicothe again. Sheltowee would be glad to go with his tribal kinsmen, but he really must finish his tobacco first. They could watch him closely. There was no reason for them to be suspicious, for it must be obvious that this time they really did have him.

The Indians grunted assent and Sheltowee went on with his work, quieting their suspicions by inquiring after old Shawnee acquaintances and offering to give them the tobacco when cured—though just how this would be possible if they took him off to Chillicothe is not by any means clear. At least it was conversation; and in the meantime, while Sheltowee kept up his friendly chattering, he was quietly gathering a number of sticks laden with tobacco. Suddenly he tilted them up. The pungent leaves fell directly in the upturned copper faces below as Boone leaped down, dragging with him as much dry tobacco and tobacco dust as possible.

Pushing the blinded and half-strangled braves aside, he ran for the cabin. From a safe distance he could not resist the temptation to look back and see what had become of his would-be captors. They were still there, half-blinded, feeling about in all directions, cursing themselves for fools and Boone for a scoundrel.

Nearly forty years later, just before his death, the old pioneer told the story at a granddaughter's wedding, imitating the voices and gestures of the hapless aborigines with high glee.

Soon after the Revolution Boone left Boone's Station which he had cleared and fortified in 1779. He moved to his farm on Marble Creek, a few miles west. He probably knew already that there was another claimant to the land at Boone's Station, though the Boones were not formally ousted until 1785, and members of the family may have been living there in the meantime.

Some years earlier Boone had realized the advantages of living on the Ohio River, a main artery of future trade and travel, and had looked over the ground at Limestone. He raised a crop or two on the farm at Marble Creek, but he had always hated farming. He turned the farm over to his son-in-law William Hays, and moved to Limestone. The loss of Boone's Station, though a blow, was not really serious. He still claimed thousands of acres. Nevertheless he began to be a little anxious and wrote to a business associate: "We must submit to providence and provide for the Living and talk of our Lands."

Limestone was an ideal spot for trading—an ideal spot, too, for a man interested in locating, surveying, buying, and selling land. Immigrants were entering by the Ohio River, coming ashore at Limestone, and going cross-country into Kentucky. Between October 10, 1786, and May 12, 1787, one army post along the river counted 2,689 people, 1,333 horses, 786 cattle, and 102 wagons floating down the Ohio on 177 huge flatboats en route for Kentucky.

Soon after Daniel Boone moved to Limestone the Indians became so bold that it was evident something would have to be done. As early as 1784 Boone is making a business agreement contingent on the scalping knife: "I will Bee accountable for any money put into his hands inless kild by Indians." An-

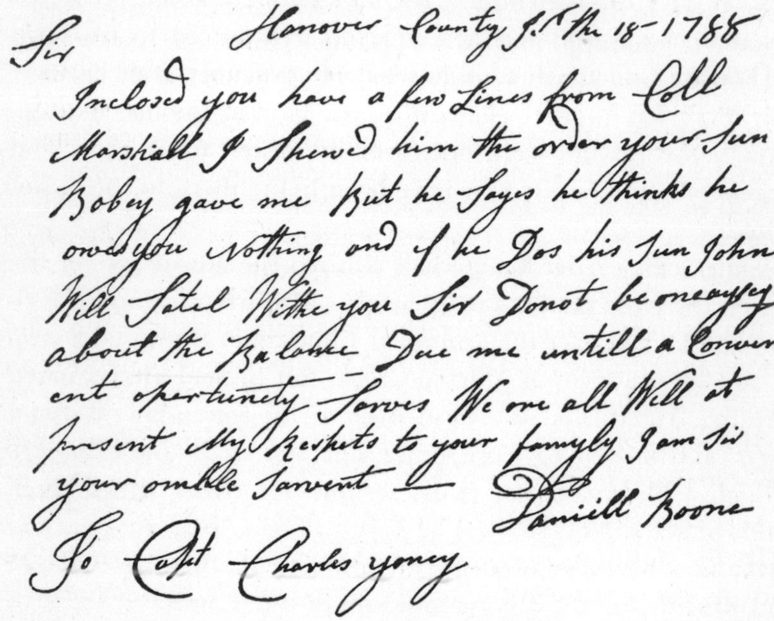

Hanover County J.t the 18-1788

Sir

Inclosed you have a few Lines from Coll Marshall I Shewed him the order your Sun Bobey gave me But he Sayes he thinks he owes you Nothing and if he Dos his Sun John Will Satel Withe you Sir Donot be oneasey about the Balance Due me untill a Conveni ent opertunety Serves We are all Well at present My Respets to your famyly I am Sir your omble Sarvent

Daniell Boone

To Capt Charles yoncy

A BOONE BUSINESS LETTER

To his friend and business associate, Captain Charles Yancey. Reproduced by permission from the original in the possession of Mrs. A. C. Pendleton, Warren, Ohio. The letter passed from Captain Yancey to his descendants, and has never been out of their hands.

other of his letters, dated August 16, 1785, reports two men killed at Squire's settlement, and adds:

> a Deal of Sine Seen in Diferent placis in purtickuler at Limston in Short an Inden Warr is Exspcted We are Cradetaly [creditably] informed that three Nations from the Waboush [Wabash] are unighted aginst us and Whatever may be the Case inLess an actul invasion it is out of the power of any ofiser of the Milititia to gave the fruntteers any asistence Know Sir I hope to Receve Such instructions from Your Honer as Will in able me to force out Scouts Spies or to Do mounthly towers at Sum of the fruntteers Stations at Least at Limston and the Blue Lick that the Salt Works may Still go on.

Agitation to make Kentucky a state had already begun, and Boone feared that the Virginia authorities might make this an excuse for refusing military aid.

"I Hope," he wrote, "our petisoning for a new State Will Bee No Baryer aganst any asistenc goverment Might gave us as it is intirely against the voce of the peepel at Large."

In the autumn, a settler near Limestone was writing: "ye indians was continually amoungst us trying to take our horses & they are so impudent. I am afraid they will take lives if opportunity suits them. there is scarcely a day but they are seen in one part of our neighborhood or another." There was a perpetual series of small raids. On May 23, 1786, a band of two hundred warriors attacked flatboats on the Ohio near the Kentucky River.

The government had been doing its best to persuade the Indians to give up prisoners taken during the Revolution, but with no great success. Some of the Shawnees defied their chiefs and insisted on keeping their captives, who were useful slaves or had been adopted into the tribe. Some of the prisoners also defied the chiefs and refused to leave. One prisoner had to be forced to part with his red friends. Others escaped from their

Kentucky rescuers and slipped back to the Indian life they had grown to love.

The Kentuckians decided that with so many captives still in Indian hands it would be advantageous to have some Indian prisoners. It was also necessary to retaliate vigorously in order to stop the perpetual raids. George Rogers Clark led one column to the Wabash, while Benjamin Logan led another to the Miami. All summer long the most careful preparations were made at Limestone. Boats, ammunition, and provisions were collected. Just before the expedition started, the women at Limestone worked all night cooking meat and "journey cake" —the modern johnnycake—and parching corn.

On the night of September 29/30, seven or eight hundred men started to cross the river. It took all night and the next day to ferry them over. Logan's advance caught the Indians at a disadvantage, since a great many warriors had hurried off to meet Clark. Those that were left fled so rapidly that it was hard to find them. At length somebody saw dogs. Boone told the men with him to follow the dogs and they would find Indians. As usual, when Indians were in question, Boone was right.

They soon encountered a small band. Boone recognized one of them with a start.

"Mind that fellow," he yelled, as the warrior ran with the whites giving chase, "I know him." It was Big Jim, who twenty-four years before had tortured young James Boone to death in Powell's Valley. As the white men closed in on him, Big Jim turned around and fired, killing one of his pursuers, then dodged into a canebrake. In its shelter he reloaded and fired again, killing or wounding another man. But not even a canebrake could conceal him long from so many enemies and he was soon run down and dispatched.

The expedition killed about twenty warriors and captured

seventy or eighty prisoners, including Daniel Boone's old friend Moluntha and his squaw. The white men were exultant when the old chief himself appeared, wearing a white robe of office and a cocked hat, and surrendered. Moluntha was not particularly disturbed by his capture. He had been working for the Americans for months, trying to get prisoners exchanged, and actually had some kind of American certificate of character in his possession. Logan had given orders about the care of Indian prisoners, and Moluntha probably knew it.

After the old man had been brought in, however, Major Hugh McGary appeared and walked up to the place where Moluntha and his squaw were standing.

"Do you remember the Blue Licks defeat?" he asked. Placidly cutting up tobacco leaf in the palm of his hand, and probably not in the least understanding the question, Moluntha replied,

"Yak, I do."

It is doubtful whether Moluntha had been present at the battle, but his words were enough to infuriate McGary.

"Damn you," he bawled, "I will show you Blue Licks play."

Seizing a small "squaw axe," he split the prisoner's head with two blows. As the chief sank to the ground McGary turned on his defenseless squaw but was stopped before he had been able to do more than slash off three of her fingers.

There was a good deal of similar brutality. One man knocked a young Indian prisoner down and scalped him alive. Clark's men are said to have shut some Indians in a cabin and killed them all. It was no worse than what the Indians had done often enough, but it horrified many Kentuckians, and Boone especially deplored it.

McGary was already regarded in Kentucky as the man really responsible for the Blue Licks defeat, and those who had lost friends and relatives in the battle still hated him. The slaughter of Moluntha was a violation of orders, which weakened Logan's position in the exchange of prisoners that was to follow. As soon as the expedition was home again McGary was court-martialed and deprived of his commission.

As a tavern- and store-keeper at Limestone, with some staunch friends in the government, Boone did a lively business provisioning the exchanged prisoners, red and white.

By October 15, 1786, Logan's redskins began to arrive under guard at Limestone, where they were treated with hospitality if one may judge by Daniel Boone's first bill to the government:

> october the 15th 1786
>
> State of Virgania Dr to Dal Boone for 19 galons of Whiskey Delivered to the Indins priseners on there first arrivel at Limeston £3–0–0

A squaw and a French Canadian were selected from among the Indian captives, given horses, equipped for the woods, and sent back to the Shawnee country with an offer to exchange. Boone "Furnished the Frenchman & Squaw" with the equipment for their journey in February—one gun, two horses with saddle and bridle, a pound of powder and two pounds of lead, twenty pounds of bread, twenty pounds of beef, and a "gard" of two men. The guards were needed to make sure no Kentuckian with a few scalped relatives to avenge should kill the returning prisoners. Apparently the pair lived briefly at Boone's tavern; his bill for them includes charges of £1.4 "To 4 Days Diett."

Backwoods diplomacy moves as slowly as the more civilized variety and occasionally Daniel Boone did what he thought the occasion required. He rescued a little girl named Chloe Flinn from the Indians. She was hardly more than a child. Her mother had died under the hardships of Indian captivity. Her brother was still a prisoner. The rest of her family had been nearly wiped out. Since no one knew quite what to do with her, Daniel and Rebecca took her into their own family and looked after the child for a year or so. Then, having located her relatives, Daniel took her up river, back to them. There is still some doubt whether Chloe was legitimately exchanged for Indian prisoners or whether Daniel made a stealthy trip to the Indian villages and stole her.

Cutting through militia red tape, Boone got a boy back in March, 1787. The Indians trusted Sheltowee, and handed the captive over when Boone offered personal pledges. Some guard-house lawyer among the militia officers protested that this was irregular. The officer may have been technically right but Daniel, who had small respect for technicalities, delivered himself of a blast to Colonel Robert Patterson: "I am hire With my hands full of Bisness and No athority and if I am Not indulged in What I Do for the best it Is Not worth my While to put my Self to all this trubel." The matter ended then and there. Daniel had saved the boy months of squalid captivity.

It was April before Naomohouoh, a Shawnee chief, arrived with a message from Captain Johnny, a young Shawnee leader who was just beginning to come into prominence. He brought four prisoners with him in token of good faith, and promised that the Indians would bring all the other prisoners to Limestone within a month. It required time to collect the captives from the scattered forest villages.

Later in April, Captain Wolf and other Shawnees came to Limestone with nine captives, for whom Boone and Patterson exchanged Indian prisoners. During the negotiation preceding these exchanges, Boone had been entertaining a Shawnee diplomat at his tavern board for nearly three weeks. One gets a general view of what was happening from his bill of April 27, 1787:

Daniel Boone Furnished the
Indians With the Following provisions

21 Gall'ns Whisky	£6. 6.0
230 Lb Flower	2. 6.8
100 Lb Bacon	4. 0.0
100 Lb Dry Beef	1.13.4
John Riggs Express Eight Days, Man & Horse and 9 men	2. 8.0
George Mifford an ascort 4 day	5. 0.0
Cash to Bare the Frenchmans Expence to Danville	1.12.0
one Beef for thir Return Home	3.10.0
Micagy Callaway Served twenty days as an Interpreter	6. 0.0
Shanee Chief 20 days diet	1.16.0

Micajah Callaway, brother of Boone's son-in-law Flanders Callaway, and nephew of Colonel Richard Callaway, had been one of Boone's men, captured at the Licks in 1778. He had spent five years and five months in Indian captivity and had naturally learned Shawnee very thoroughly.

By July Boone was feeding Indians so steadily that he opened a special account book, which he made by folding several sheets of paper, fastening them together, and labeling it:

Daniel Boones
Indan Book

It is an alluring title, but the contents are strictly business. Three pages are required to list the "Indan purvistion" which he supplied. One amusing entry is "20 lb Backer" and "2 qurts Whiskey" for the Indians and exactly the same amount of each "for the gards."

In August he was supplying Indian prisoners with "flower" in lots of one and four hundred pounds at a time and a single order of "30 galans Whiska."

The redskins, highly pleased with the treatment they had received, promised that all future prisoners from Limestone should receive the best of care. There was a certain menace in the promise, but the Indians meant it to be friendly enough.

On August 20, 1787, Captain Johnny, Blacksnake, Wolf, and other Indian diplomats appeared opposite Limestone, ready to make a formal peace. Logan, Boone, Kenton, Todd, Patterson, and others rowed over to meet them. It was almost exactly nine years since Boone had gone out alone to meet Blackfish at Boonesborough.

Captain Johnny, in ceremonial paint and feathers, made a flowery speech. It was a typical bit of Indian eloquence: "All say, let us take pity on our women and children, and agree to make peace with our brother the big knife, which our brother the big knife has always said was in our power. If we want peace we shall have peace, to which we are agreed, to come to where our old town was burnt and live brothers. These Indians who are for war, they will always be out on the Wabash, and we will make a distinction between them and ourselves, to let our brother the big knife know we are really for peace. Here will be five little towns of us that will be for peace."

Logan replied with a note of warning: "Brothers, you may see plainly, how your father over the water, who engaged you in so long and bloody a war, has treated you; that although you lost many brave warriors, yet when he gotten [sic] beaten by the great men of the United States, he made peace and gave your country away, and said nothing about you, but left you to the discretion of the Americans to treat you as they pleased. Brothers, you and all the red people may plainly see, that when your father and all his forces added to all yours, could not conquer the Americans, that it will be in vain for you (the red people) to continue a war yourselves alone."

A dance and feast, lasting most of the night, followed the exchange of prisoners. Then the Shawnee chief Blue Jacket and young Daniel Morgan Boone went hunting together to prove that at last peace really did reign beyond the Ohio.

It was not, however, a very secure peace, for the villages which had refused to sign the treaty continued to send out war parties, and even the villages which were officially friendly could not resist a slight inclination to horse-stealing. The militia continued to keep scouts out, just as they had done during the Revolution. Occasionally even these alert woodsmen were surprised or simply vanished. A report in 1790 says: "the spies put out on the fruntier of Slate Creek has not been hern of these three weeks, therefore I am much afraid they are killed."

Even in 1792, when Kentucky became the fifteenth state, Isaac Shelby, the first governor, found that "the country was then in a state of war," and that "every part of Kentucky, was a frontier infested with a savage foe." In the following year stray scalping parties were still ranging far eastward. On the Cumberland River "they ware weekly, Nay I may add daily a Murdering men weomen and childring." Along Boone's Wilderness Road, which now had been a white man's thoroughfare for nearly twenty years, it was still necessary to keep a guard of twenty militiamen moving back and forth.

Under these conditions the Indians' continued esteem for Daniel Boone was at times just a little embarrassing. Particularly so when a raider, caught red-handed, appealed to Big Turtle for aid in his predicament.

Less than a year after the treaty, in the spring of 1788, Chief Blue Jacket came down to Strode's Station, stole eight or ten horses, and fled for the Ohio. Pursued by a party of white men "who usually followed on such occasions," the raiders were caught north of the Licking River. When the whinny of the horses betrayed the approach of the white men, the Indians scattered and escaped. But Blue Jacket, happening to be on foot on a bare, open hill, had to run for it in plain sight and was quickly ridden down.

The moment the white men caught him, he exclaimed: "Boone! Boone!" and pointed emphatically in the direction of Maysville. The white pursuers were feeling good natured; they had recovered all their own horses besides some other strays that the Indians had picked up. Blue Jacket was told to pilot his captors to Maysville by the quickest way; and he knew a great deal better than to try any tricks. The captive was handed over to Boone.

It was a trifle disconcerting to a prominent member of the legislature to have his son's hunting mate brought in for horse-stealing, but Dan'l did the best he could. He saw that Blue Jacket was well tied and then put him into a new cabin for the night. It was supposed to be the securest place in the village.

Someone—was it really an accident?—had left a knife sticking in a log. Blue Jacket squirmed over to it in spite of his bonds, cut the ropes, hacked his way out of the cabin, and escaped about daybreak. His disgusted captors pursued, found his leggings where he had dropped them in the woods, but never got their horsethief back. Some days later Blue Jacket limped into his village almost naked and badly scratched by brambles. A white captive still in the village was edified to hear him adjuring his younger braves to steal their horses some other place in future.

With the treaty signed in August of 1787, Boone was free to attend the October opening of the legislature. Before he left, however, he had Logan audit his accounts and certify: "The within mentioned Artickels was nessassary for the Indiens & I think the Accounts is just." The total of Boone's charges was £101.1.6 and for once he got his money promptly. The governor laid his papers before the council October 22, and the state auditor was immediately "directed to settle the account of

Daniel Boone for supplies furnished the Indian prisoners, as certified by Colo. Logan." Boone was luckier than John Crow, another commissary, who had to feed seventy hungry redskins at his own expense for thirty days, and then petition for his money.

Boone was occupied with legislative details for the rest of the year, until the legislature closed January 8, 1788.

Daniel Boone was now one of the richest men in Kentucky. His land claims reached at least fifty thousand acres and probably a hundred thousand. Hunting and trade added to his income. His services as a surveyor were in demand on all sides.

He, who had grown up in an obscure cabin on the Yadkin, was now one of the most famous men in the nation. His reputation was beginning to reach across the sea. Strangers sought to meet and talk with him, and the Kentuckians, who knew him best, elected him to one office after another.

Now—now at last—he was reaping the reward of those years of danger, toil, privation. Again and again he had thought prosperity achieved, only to have it snatched away. His trip with Finley in 1769 had laid up a goodly stock of furs; but the Indians had robbed them. Finley had given up, but Boone had gone doggedly back and laid in a second stock. Again the Indians had robbed him of everything. Still indomitable, in 1773 he had led his little band of immigrants toward the promised land of Kentucky, only to be driven back after the murder of his son.

Grimly he tried a third venture in 1775, turned back to Kentucky with Henderson, won land for himself at last, only to lose it with the failure of Henderson's schemes. Once more he sought land, this time from the state itself. The robbery of 1780 swept all those gains away.

He had made still another struggle to rebuild his fallen fortunes. Now he had won through at last. His new land claims complied with every legal formality. Landed estates were his at last—really his own. Kentucky was a white man's country now. Immigrants were coming in. That meant the value of his lands would rise. Business was looking up. A creditable family was growing up around him. All was for the best.

With his sons, Daniel Boone engaged in general business at Limestone, ready to do anything that brought in an honest penny. He dealt in skins, furs, lands, horses, general merchandise, ginseng, and anything else that anybody wanted. He kept a tavern. He located and surveyed lands. Sometimes he was rich enough to lend amounts like £20, £4, £3.0.6, or 12s. to his friends. At other times he had difficulty raising ready cash—of which there was very little in the country anyhow. But after struggling all his life with debt, Daniel Boone belonged to the creditor class now. When he needed money himself, he could put a little pressure on those who owed him, though he was usually very mild about it.

In 1784 Boone found that he would have to "pay a Large Sum of money at Cort on tusday," and hastily wrote a man who owed him money to "Satel on monday." A year later he was writing Colonel William Christian, a prominent Virginian:

> Dear Col the Land Bissness your father Left in my Hands is Chefly Dunn and Rady to be Returned Sum I have Regestered and I have at your Requst payd by a Later payd Sum money for that bisness and Not thinking of this opertunity have Not time to Draw up your acoumpt Requst the faver of you to send me by the bearer James Briges ten pound and this Shall be your Resite for that Sum and you Will ablyge your omble sarvent
>
> Daniel Boone
>
> NB
> I have a Number of plats to Regester at the general Cort and am Scarse of Cash Plese to oblyge me if posible
>
> D B
>
> august the 23 1785
> To Cl William Cristen

Sad to relate, the bearer got only three guineas.

In another letter of this summer he finds times "a Litel Difegult" because of Indians and also because of slow collections. "I must be plan With you," he writes. "I am intirely out of Cash and the Chane men and Markers Must be paid on the Shot and I want 2 or 3 ginnes [guineas] for my own use." His "Litel Sun" was to bring back the money.

Boone was lenient with friends who owed him money, as witness the following letter:

Hanover County Ja the 18 1788

Sir

Inclosed you have a few Lines from Coll Marshall I shewed him the order your Sun Bobey gave me But he Sayes he thinks he owes you Nothing and if he Dos his Sun John Will Satel Withe you Sir Donot be oneaysey about the Balance Due me untill a Convenient opertunity Sarves We are all Well at present My Respets to your famyly I am Sir your omble Sarvent—

DANIELL BOONE

To Capt Charles Yancy

"The Land Bissness" promised well. He laid out land claims for himself and his family, for his friends, and—on shares—for others who engaged his services. People were glad to have his opinion on land titles and land values. "The Lands Mr. Mcfadden is ofering you is in Qulaty Eacqul to any you have Seen on the South Side the Cantuck," he writes a client, "and never had been Dispueted by any man as it was known to be the first Clames there by Satelment and preemtion and I believe his Wright to be good."

Everyone in the East was eager to own some of the rich land that a bounteous government was selling for a song. But not many wanted to plunge into the forests to find it. Instead, wealthy gentlemen purchased treasury warrants and entrusted them to Daniel Boone. He guaranteed to endure all the hardships, run all the risks, and find them good lands with clear titles. They guaranteed in turn to give him half of what he gained for them. His brother Squire sometimes engaged to clear forest land on much the same terms.

In 1783 Daniel was made deputy surveyor of both Fayette and Lincoln Counties. It was no very great distinction, since in about three years Fayette County had nearly a hundred deputy surveyors. But newcomers were entering Kentucky in large numbers, all eager for land. More than a decade of scouting and hunting had taught him where the best land lay, and the immigrants were well aware of that. A man who not only knew where the best land was but also how to lay it off was much in demand.

Surveying came naturally. His grandfather, George Boone, had been a surveyor. Young Daniel as a child must often have seen him at work. He himself begins to appear in the Kentucky Land Records as a surveyor by 1782, and had borrowed instruments and surveyed for himself as early as 1780. From 1783 to 1786 he made nearly 150 surveys for new settlers, and his name appears in the Fayette County records as "chopper" and chain-carrier as well as surveyor. His survey papers, still preserved, are about as good as those of the average surveyor of the time, and in one respect better. Daniel Boone is careful to include all important landmarks. Many of the others omit a few. Sad to say, Boone usually spells his assistants' names differently in all surveys. This is true even when they were made the same day.

At first assistants were any available hands; but the survey parties soon became family affairs. The eleven-year-old Jesse Boone and the fifteen-year-old Daniel Morgan Boone were chainmen. Joseph Scholl, Levina Boone's husband, was land marker, or "chopper," who marked the trees. Daniel rendered his bills in British currency. At the exchange value of the period his charges work out at about $2.75 a day for his own services, plus fees for his men and provisions for the tour (rendered by Daniel as "purvistions for the tower"), which were provided by the client.

A letter still extant describes a typical surveying trip:

July 20th, 1786

Sir:

The Land has Been Long Survayd and Not Knowing When the Money would be Radey Was the Reason of my Not Returning the works however the may be Returned When you pleas But I must first have a Nother Copy of the Entry as I have Lost that I had When I Lost my plotting Instruments and only have the Short field Notes Just the Corse Distone and Corner trees pray, Send me a Nother Copy that I may Know how to give it the proper Bounderry agreeable to the Location and I Will send the plat to the ofis a medetly if you Chuse it the Expensis is as follows viz

	£	s	d
Surveyors fees	9	3	8
Ragesters fees &c	7	14	0½
Chanmen and Marker 11 Days ea	8	0	0
purvistions for the tower	2	0	0
	26	17	8½

you will also send ma a Copy of the agreement betwixt Mr. Waler overton and my Self When I Recd the Warrants I am Sir your omble Sarvent

DANIEL BOONE

None of these activities, however, were absorbing enough to make him give up hunting. He managed to get a shot in now and then, even on survey parties. There was one stirring occasion when the surveyors knocked off work to drive a herd of buffalo into the Licking River, just for the fun of seeing them swim. Daniel Boone stood on the bank counting the number as the great beasts, snorting in terror, plunged into the water and swam across. There were, he reported, three hundred.

Though not a slave trader, he occasionally bought or sold a negro. Everyone in Kentucky kept a slave if he could afford it. The Boones usually owned a few, as tax lists show both in Kentucky and Missouri.

In this period of prosperity Daniel Boone had at least three slaves. In 1784 he secured from his relative John Grant a negro girl named "Easter," worth about seventy-five pounds. On March 4, 1786, he bought "one Negro gurle Named Loos" for ninety pounds.

A letter to a certain William Haris, dated March 3, 1791, shows pretty clearly that he once sold a negro woman and her child together. At least it is pretty hard to make sense of the letter otherwise:

> Dear Sir
>
> My Sun Dal [Morgan] Boone Wates on you for the Balance Due me for Rose and hir Child Which is 32 pounds virganea money Besides the Intrust Which I hope you will not faill to pay him and Not put me to the trubel of Coming Down my Self and he will gave you a full Resete for the Same I am Sir your omble Sarvent
>
> DANIEL BOONE

His books and correspondence show that he did a large business but most of it was in barter rather than in cash. The furtraders with whom he dealt acknowledge a single consignment of 1,790 deerskins, 729 bearskins, four otter, five black fox, and two barrels of ginseng. The account books show charges for cloth, groceries, buttons, hardware, ammunition, and a vast deal of rum and whiskey. His store gives

Cradet by Baar Skins	0.13.6
Cradet by 1 Bote	0.12.0
Cradet by 58 lb Bacon at Sixpence per pound	1. 9.0
by a Cat and Cune Skin	0. 5.0

Dear Sir March the 3d 1791

My Son Dal Boone Wates on you
for the Balance Due me for Rose and
hir Child Which is 32 pounds virganey
money Besides the Intrust Which I hope
you will not faill to pay him and
Not put me to the trubel of Coming
Down my Self and he will gave you a full
Resett for the Same I am Sir your
omble Servent

Daniel Boone

Mr
William Haris

DANIEL BOONE TO WILLIAM HARIS

(MS. HM 22393)

[By permission of The Huntington Library, San Marino, California]

Boone sometimes exchanged his pelts at a local bank, or "keep," at Louisville in return for a promise to pay cash when the skins were sold. The remarkable commercial document thus obtained could be passed from hand to hand as a kind of currency. Boone dealt with a certain John Sanders, who had set up his "keep" in a houseboat which a flood had stranded at Louisville. The "keeper," or banker, cannily took his commission first:

> Know All Men By These Pre'nts that Daniel Boone hath Deposited Six, vi, beaver Skins in My keep in good order and of the worth of VI shillings each skin and i Have took from them vi shillings for the keep of them and when they Be sold i will pay the balance of XXX shillings for the whole lot to any person who presents this certificate an delivers it up to Me at My keep Louisville, falls of ohio, May 20 1784
>
> JOHN SANDERS

The ginseng trade, to which Boone had given a little attention in his early days in North Carolina, was profitable here too. The root of this common American woods plant had long been a staple of Chinese medicine. Some of the root was probably also used by Colonial physicians and apothecaries. Ginseng has real medicinal value, though modern medicine has long abandoned it for subtler drugs. American ginseng was not quite identical with the Korean plant, but it could be exported to China all the same.

Boone may have bought from his neighbors, but he also went out into the woods and gathered "sang" himself. In the winter of 1787/88 he had nearly fifteen tons, which he took up the Ohio expecting to send it overland to Philadelphia. But on the way the boat capsized, the carefully dried ginseng got wet, and before Daniel could get to Philadelphia with it the price had fallen. He persevered in the trade and that same fall had "15 caggs of ginsang" on hand.

Horse trading was also a disappointment. The Boones tried buying "loose horses" in Kentucky and driving them overland to markets in the East. The journey was too arduous. The nags arrived in wretched condition and brought poor prices. Boone lost money on the enterprise and soon gave it up.

Another business venture was tavern-keeping. Boone's was a remarkable establishment where two months' board cost but £4.12. A traveler a year or two later pays tribute to the bountiful board Rebecca spread: "I took Breakfast with Colo. Boon and his family being the best I had Eaten for many days." Presumably Daniel and Rebecca ran a better establishment than the dreadful hovels some travelers describe. One man complains bitterly of an establishment where he was entertained. Nothing to eat but bear meat and "corn-meal dodgers." Nothing to drink but whisky at fifty cents a pint—Kentucky was already Kentucky!—and coffee "composed of an article that grew some eight hundred or one thousand miles north of where coffee tree ever did grow." This beverage was brewed from the pod of the Kentucky "coffee tree." The resulting fluid was described by a charitable geographer of the period as "not unlike coffee." Another traveler, still more charitable, described it as "a pod in which is good coffee-seed." In 1790, after the Boones had moved away, Limestone's tavern was so bad that it could provide neither "food, fire, or bed, or any other nourishment except whisky."

After statehood had been achieved the Kentucky government regulated these little frontier hotels. The keeper was required to "find & provide in his said Ordinary, good wholesome & cleanly Lodgings and Diet for travellers, and Stablage, Fodder & provender, or pasturage and provender, as the Season shall require for their Horses." Neither must he "Suffer or permit any unlawful gaming in his House nor on the Sabbath day Suffer any person to Tipple & drink more than is necessary." On weekdays, apparently, there were no limits.

More civil and military honors came to Boone in these years. In October, 1786, an act of Assembly named him trustee of the town of Washington, near Limestone in what is now Mason County, a post which he held until 1790, when he had moved away. The next year, 1787, Daniel Boone, his relative Jacob Boone, and his old friend Simon Kenton are all made trustees of Maysville; and in this year he is again a member of the legislature and complaining bitterly about the quality of the arms sent to the Kentucky militia.

Some time in 1789/90, the restless Boone moved again, this time to Kanawha County, Virginia (now West Virginia), and settled at Point Pleasant. His name appears on the county list of tithables for 1792, '93, and '94. Later he moved to Charleston, acted as pilot for immigrants, contracted to victual the militia.

He made a second trip back to the old home in Pennsylvania, too, early in 1788, and with his wife and son Nathan spent a month with the stay-at-home Boones in Berks County. Several hundred miles of the journey were on horseback, with the eight-year-old Nathan hanging on behind his father. Distance had long separated the families, but they had never wholly lost touch. Quakers do not approve of family estrangement. A letter is still extant, dated 1790, in which a friend of the Pennsylvania Boones writes back from Kentucky to send them news of Daniel. Even in 1816 old Daniel Boone is writing affectionately to an aged sister-in-law in Pennsylvania, whom he was never to see again, to give family news and to discuss religion.

In 1789 Boone is at Monongahela with a drove of "loose horses" for sale. In July of the same year he writes a client that he expects to be in Philadelphia. In October, on popular petition, he was recommended by the county court to be lieutenant-colonel of the Kanawha County militia, then just being organized. His commission did not arrive until April 1791.

Always he hunted and trapped, ranging the Kanawha and Ohio and far into the wild and dangerous country north of the Ohio after beaver. This trading and guiding and tavern-keeping and these municipal honors were all very well; but a man needed the feel of a rifle in his hands now and then, and what were town victuals to a man who had grown up on venison?

He had a few narrow escapes. In spite of the peace there were still Indians about, and north of the Ohio and even south of it, in Kentucky and what is now West Virginia, there were a good many raids. But everyone knows what Indians are like. A scalp is always a scalp, even if there is no longer a British lieutenant-governor to pay for it. An occasional brush with the redskins lent a flavor to hunting. It was interesting to hear a rifle crack, now and then, at a target that had two feet instead of four.

The Indians likewise enjoyed these innocent diversions. Raiders in Kanawha County in 1793 captured a couple of negro slaves (always welcome prisoners in the Indian villages, where ordinary labor was despised) and may have killed one or two white men. The rumor spread that "Colonel Boone and another person were killed or taken." It was officially reported that he had been captured and one son killed. In his later years someone was always spreading reports like that. All the Boones were perfectly safe. Daniel had not forgotten his old maxim: Never look for Indians in ambush—they are too well concealed. Instead, look for the rifle barrels that they can't conceal.

This is probably the alarm occasioned because Daniel stayed out on a hunting trip longer than he expected. He did, however, have a really narrow escape in 1794, on a hunt during which his son Nathan killed his first deer. One foggy night out, Daniel was wakened by the sound of distant chopping. They were near the river and he felt sure the Indians were building a raft. He roused Nathan. They loaded their canoe, and returned to the fire until the chopping ceased. Slipping down to the canoe, they hid for ten minutes until they heard the Indians paddling across the river. With the boy lying prone in the canoe, his father pushed out into the swift current of the Ohio—peering along the surface of the river between the fog and water, to see if he could detect their enemies—and slipped silently away.

He turned up one evening, a total stranger, at the home of Daniel, or "Paddy," Huddlestone, below Kanawha Falls, near the modern town of Boone, West Virginia, carrying rifle and pack and asking for shelter. No one had the least idea who he was, but of course he was taken in after the usual frontier custom. Quiet as usual and apparently tired, he went to bed soon after supper, but when morning came he was gone, though pack and rifle remained. By breakfast time he was back, with news of beaver in the river—two saplings had been gnawed down.

"Well, come, young man," he said to young Jared Huddlestone, "get your trap and go with me, and I will show you how to trap beaver." They caught five the first day, a dozen before their trapping was over. Boone presented a trap to the Huddlestones who carefully preserved it. It still exists in the West Virginia Historical Collection.

In 1791 he was a rather silent member of the Assembly, for Kanawha County. He served on the committee on religion, and another on "propositions and licenses." On December 12, 1791, just after his appointment, Lieutenant-Colonel Boone, as a member of the Assembly, advised on the defense of the county:

> For Kanaway County, 68 Privets, Lenard Cuper, Capt. at Pint plesent, 17 men; Joell Dane, Insine at Bellville, 17 men; John Young, Scout at Elke, 17 men; John Morris, Insine at the Bote yards, 17 men.
>
> Two spyes or scutes will be Nesesry at the Pint * to sarch the

* This is almost certainly Point Pleasant, at the junction of the Kanawha and Ohio Rivers. A writer in the *Register,* 28:153 Ap 1930, however, identifies it with Maysville.

Banks of the River at the Crosing plases. More would be Wanting if the could be aloude. These Spyes must be Compoused of the inhabitence who Well Know the Woods and waters from the pint to Belville, 60 mildes—No inhabitence; also, from pint to Alke [Elk River], 60 Miles, No inhabitence; from Alke to Bote yards, 20 milds, all inhabited.

This from your most Obedient

In December he offered to take ammunition back to Redstone (Brownsville, Pennsylvania), if given the contract to victual the Kanawha County militia. He wrote to the Governor:

Monday 13th Dec 1791

Sir

as Sum purson Must Carry out the armantstion [ammunition] to Red Stone if your Exelency Should have thought me a proper purson I Would undertake it on Condistions I have the apintment to vitel the Company at Kanhowway So that I Could take Down the Flower as I paste the place. I am your Excelency most obedent omble Sarvent,

DAL BOONE

He got the contract, but it would be idle to pretend that Daniel Boone was a conspicuous success as a quartermaster. On December 22 he gave his receipt to state officials for four hundred pounds of powder, sixteen hundred pounds of lead, and a barrel of flints. These were supplies for his own and other militiamen, which he "engaged to emply without change or barter, solely in the service of the Commonwealth." He was still delivering ammunition along the Ohio River and elsewhere as late as March 4, 1792, when he turned over sixty pounds of powder and "2 Piggs of Ladd Sepoused to be 3,010 pounds," for use along the Potomac.

He waged a private and enjoyable warfare with a militia captain, Hugh Caperton, whom he had himself recommended as "a fitt & proper person," but in whom he was speedily disappointed. On May 2, 1792, Caperton formally complained to the county lieutenant that he had been directed to raise a company of volunteers, but "Col. Daniel Boon, the person appointed by the Executive of Virginia, did not agreeably to orders provide provisions for the support of said Company." On May 26 a certain William Clendenin also complained. He understood Boone had received the powder but had failed to deliver it, and he had had to buy 105½ pounds at his own expense. The Indians were active, and by September 21, 1792, Kanawha County began to have grave doubts about its lieutenant-colonel's talents as a supply officer. He was in charge of supplies for the whole western militia of the state and was operating from Richmond and Point of Rocks. Three officers, including Caperton, waited till he was at the mouth of the Kanawha, and then went down to upbraid him. A little later Colonel Clendenin, representative in the Assembly, was again complaining of supply troubles, which he blamed on the "default of the Contractor, Colonel Boone."

There was a lively set-to over the conduct of Daniel Boone himself. Caperton complained to the authorities, October 30, 1792, that when he took command of the company defending Greenbrier and Kanawha Counties, "Col. Boon Contracted to furnish these men with rations, but for some cause or other failed. This put me under the necessity of employing other persons to do the business, making myself responsible for the money, & now stand bound for the amount of rations furnished my Company, no part of which has been paid. The Executive also directed Col. Boone to convey the ammunition allowed from Point of Fork to Greenbrier, in this he also failed, this compelled me to purchase and supply the men myself."

In 1793 Lieutenant-Colonel Boone's relations with Caperton again proved less than harmonious. The commissary simply walked out of camp with his rifle and was not seen for days.

Scouts operating on the Ohio bumped into him and complained that the rations (for which he was responsible) were exhausted. But the insubordinate quartermaster replied only: "Caperton did not do to my liken,"—which was apparently all they got out of him. Under any known system of military law, they would have been justified in taking him out and shooting him; but in the Virginia militia of those days these little differences were politely ignored.

Other officers shared Daniel Boone's objection to Caperton. He presently went before a court-martial and was relieved of his command. He admitted: "My conduct has in some degree been reprehensible during my command." So perhaps there was justification for Boone's attitude.

During these minor campaigns Boone, always a skillful healer, sometimes served as a kind of informal medical officer. He nursed one wounded man in his own home and cannily billed the state twenty-five dollars for medical services. The militia officers certified the bill, but the state auditor held it up and inquired of the Executive Council whether he ought to pay the "Claim of Colonel Daniel Boone for curing a wounded man." The record ends there. Dan'l very likely never got his money.

Though Boone was now approaching sixty, he was still the very model of the muscular frontiersman. People noticed him; they plied him with questions; and they pointed him out to one another. It must have grown a little tiresome—an acquaintance who spent four nights in the same house about 1792 observes that "there were a number of strangers, and he was constantly occupied in answering questions." There was at this time "nothing remarkable in his personal appearance." A tendency to grow fat afflicted him later, but now he was still lean and lithe: "He was about sixty years old, of a medium size, say five feet ten inches, not given to corpulency,—retired, unobtrusive, and a man of few words. My Acquaintance was made with him in the winter season, and I well remember his dress was of tow cloth, and not a woollen garment on his body, unless his stockings were to that material." Buffalo had vanished and their wool was now unknown on the frontier; sheep had not yet come.

There is still a more personal—indeed, a very personal—description of him a few years later. A visitor at his home says: "I recollect to see him strip off, and go to bed. He had a fair skin—a Roman nose—rather high cheek bones, rather reddish tinge. The fairest skin, for his amount of exposure, of any man you ever saw."

18. Land Trouble

DANIEL BOONE had fought the Indians and won. He was fighting white men now and losing steadily. Year after year, a series of legal troubles plagued him. Indians with knives, rifles, war clubs, and tomahawks held no terror for Daniel Boone. Lawyers with calf-bound books, writs, summonses, and suits conquered him easily enough.

He had opened the land, cleared it, defended it. His daughter had been kidnapped. Two sons and a brother had been killed. Risking his own life had been such a commonplace for years that it was hardly worth mentioning.

Daniel Boone had the odd idea that he might own some of that land, particularly as he had received certificates from the state's own officials, specially appointed to give clear and valid title. However, he was wrong again. The lawyers explained that to the judge easily enough, though it was never quite clear to Daniel.

He was in no worse plight than other pioneers. Many a man discovered that the land which he had surveyed, cleared, cultivated, and defended was not his. Somebody else had owned it all the time—often somebody who had never endured the labors and dangers of the frontier. The heroic band who had fought through the desperate days at Bryan's Station were among those who discovered they were merely trespassers. In 1784 a traveler from Virginia pulled up his horse at the stockade gate. He had

John P. Ross

DANIEL BOONE'S CABIN

Located on Brushy Fork in modern Nicholas County, Kentucky, and identified by C. Frank Dunn.

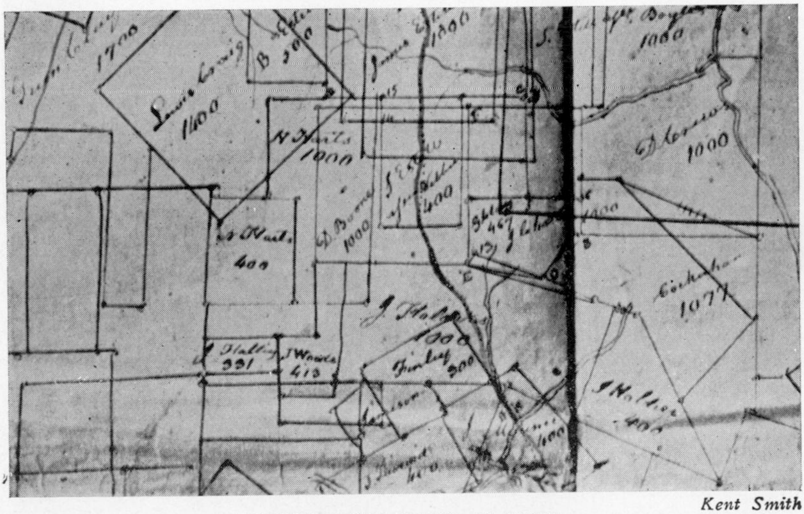

Kent Smith

"SHINGLED" LAND CLAIMS

From an original surveyor's map in the possession of Professor Jonathan Truman Dorris.

seen no fighting there. He had never been in Kentucky before. But now the war was over. He was the rightful, or at least the legal, owner of Bryan's Station, and he had plenty of paper to prove it. He took possession.

However, the law is slow, even in taking a pioneer's claims away, and it was a good ten years or more before it had wholly stripped Daniel Boone of all his first-class land. Some of these disasters were in great part due to Boone's own carelessness. Surveying hundreds of acres in thickly wooded country, where the only landmarks were blazes slashed in bark with tomahawks, it was easy for various claimants to lay out the same ground several times over without suspecting that others had been there before them.

Land legally belonged to the man who could prove that he had been first to buy his warrants, make his surveys, file his claims, and get his certificates. Most Kentucky land maps of those days are criss-crossed with "shingled" claims, so called because they overlap each other like shingles on a roof. One wonders, not that there was confusion in the land claims, but that the courts ever managed to untangle such conflicts at all. Two of Boone's land claims in Madison County conflict with those of at least four other claimants.

Another cause of Boone's difficulties was his frequent failure to take the necessary legal steps to complete his claims. New settlers were coming in. He was making money surveying for them. He postponed or neglected his own legal business until later. To make matters worse, his friend John Floyd was killed by Indians at the very time when he was handling many of Boone's land claims. Floyd's papers were lost and many of Boone's titles were left in doubt.

Nor did Boone lose all his lands in ordinary ejectment suits. Another fruitful cause of trouble was the frequency with which, in all good faith, he sold title to land that he did not really own.

A good deal of the land which he is supposed to have lost in ejectment suits he had actually sold to other people before his own title had been questioned. In 1795, for example, he sold a tract of 409 acres in Madison County for one thousand pounds, and in the same year he and his son-in-law Joseph Scholl sold twenty-five acres in Fayette County for sixty pounds. He had already sold many of his earlier Kentucky land claims to raise money with which to buy still more land warrants. Many, many years later, in his old age, he was still selling land in Missouri. But the money he acquired in these transactions was invariably swallowed up either in new land schemes or in meeting old claims against him.

Boone acquired additional enormous land holdings in Kentucky by surveying lands on shares for wealthy gentlemen in the East. In all such cases Boone guaranteed to secure good lands with clear titles. When he failed to do so he not only lost his own share but found himself in debt to the men to whom he had given the guarantee. When the original titles to lands he himself had sold proved faulty, the first purchasers naturally looked to honest Daniel to make good. Sometimes they brought suit. With all these elements combined against him, he soon found himself hopelessly loaded down with debt.

Boone never really learned to deal with civilized man. He never quite got over the scrupulously honest man's delusion that all the rest of the world is honest, too. Alert, suspicious, sensitive to the least hint of danger in the forests, he never acquired a sense of the risks in practical affairs.

Sometimes he was a victim of downright fraud. He went security on a five hundred pound bond for a certain Ebenezer Platt, quite unaware that in England the man had been condemned to Newgate Prison. Not content with this piece of folly, he loaned Platt a negro slave and a horse, saddle, and bridle for a trip to Louisville. Platt was next heard of in New Orleans. The negro, horse, saddle, and bridle were never heard of.

That smooth adventurer, Gilbert Imlay, later the lover of Mary Wollstonecraft, mother of Mary Shelley, arranged to buy land. Boone took his bond for one thousand pounds. Imlay sold

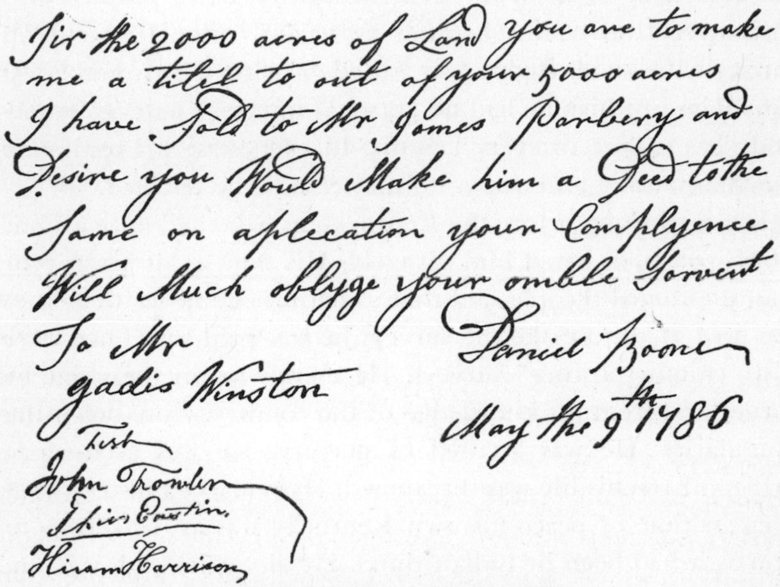
Sir the 2000 acres of Land you are to make me a titel to out of your 5000 acres I have Sold to Mr James Parbery and Desire you Would Make him a Deed to the Same on aplecation your Complyence Will Much oblyge your omble Sorvent

Daniel Boone

To Mr
Jadis Winston

May the 9th 1786

Test
John Fowler
Elias [illegible]
Hiram Harrison

DANIEL BOONE SELLS LAND
From the Original in the Haverford College Library.

the land to others. In 1786 he wrote apologetically to say that he could not meet the bond. Thereupon he sailed for England, fell in love with Mary Wollstonecraft, begot an illegitimate daughter, and died not long after. As usual, Daniel Boone was the loser, though he probably had no idea of Imlay's last adventures.

It was probably Imlay who brought Boone's adventures to the attention of the British public and, at several removes, eventually to Lord Byron's. It was slight consolation to Boone that the English poet would one day celebrate him in *Don Juan* as "happiest amongst mortals." His own difficulties in the meantime had been nearly overwhelming.

He, who had been hero and leader for twenty years, now suddenly became the most hated man in Kentucky. Nobody knew quite so much about Kentucky lands as Daniel Boone. He had made many of the first surveys. As other people's lawsuits over land claims became more and more frequent all through the state, Boone was called as witness in numberless squabbles in which he had no personal interest whatever. Somebody has to lose in every lawsuit. In every case his testimony inevitably made an enemy, no matter how he testified.

It was not long before the Kentuckians, who had once all but worshiped him, hated him savagely. His honesty as a surveyor was questioned. People said that sometimes he never went into the field at all to make the surveys he was paid for. They were just "chimney corner" surveys. He merely sat in the chimney corner and from his knowledge of the country wrote down the boundaries. He was accused of perjury. He was accused of bribery. Even his life was threatened. He remarked bitterly that even in time of peace his own Kentucky was as dangerous to him as it had been in Indian times. He alone, he said, was singled out for assassination.

"He had settled in that country to end his Days," a relative said later, "but they got up so maney squabbles over land, that it anoied him, and he Did not want to Die among them."

"I have often defended you in public against calumny and abuse," wrote his business associate, Charles Yancey, February 29, 1796. Yancey recounts his own losses at Boone's hands as follows:

> The thousand acres warrant that I first put in your hands cost me dear when the money was good, which you promised me should be laid on good land. But I have neither warrant nor land as yet.

> A number of the locations you charged me for are not surveyed or returned and may possibly be lost to us forever, and I am told Hughes' survey of two thousand acres will the most of it be lost, owing, as I am informed, to its not being surveyed according to location. Boone's settlement and pre-emption, I am told, has claims on it, and, I fear, may be lost, at least in part, as I fear it was not located in time, and Bridges' pre-emption and settlement, I am informed by Wm. Lipscomb, that he can find no deeds to him either in Fayette or Lincoln Counties, and that many settlers are on all those lands, and that it may finally be lost also, which different surveys, some of which I have sold, and cannot, I fear, make a proper right to, and it may cost much of my small fortune to make good.

Yancey's syntax is rather mixed, but obviously Boone's surveying clients were highly dissatisfied.

The sensitive Boone was at first surprised, then hurt, then bitter. He gave up official life, withdrew more and more from the world. It is no wonder he was angry. As a member of the legislature he had always been going back and forth between the frontier and the settlements. On these trips he was always being importuned to make land entries for other people. Now the good-natured help he had given his neighbors turned out to be a constant source of trouble. Whenever there was dispute over a land entry—and there always was dispute over a land entry—he was blamed.

Eventually Boone grew weary of perpetual recrimination. He determined never to defend another land suit. He decided to go away and leave everything. He turned his business interests over to a nephew, Colonel John Grant. At least one claim was still not "shingled over." He left it in Grant's hands to be used in paying off anyone with an honest claim against him. He never asked Grant what he did with it, and Grant later had a hard time getting him even to answer letters about his Kentucky business. Boone advised his children never, after his death, to contest any land claims that might remain to his estate. One or two of them later went back to Kentucky, looked over the documents, and decided that they were rightful heirs to about forty-four thousand acres. He said bitterly that he would rather be poor than own an acre or a farthing with a claim against it.

A friend noted "the soreness of the feelings he entertained, as I heard from others, and which he displayed to me, occasioned by the conduct he received from many of the citizens."

He turned to the sure comfort of the wilderness. A wanderer in the forest came upon the Boones bear-hunting along the Sandy. Daniel, Rebecca, two of their daughters with their husbands, were all living deep in the woods with no shelter but the usual "half-faced" hunters' camps. They were eating all their meals from a common rough tray, "very much like a sap trough," set on a bench. Their forks were made from stalks of cane. They had only one butcher-knife among them, and nothing to eat but bread and the game they killed.

But the bear-hunting was magnificent and Daniel was jubilant. He had just killed "the master bear of the Western country," two feet across the hips. The camp was full of drying bear skins and salted bear meat, which the hunters intended to sell at the salt works on the Kanawha River.

By 1795 Daniel and Rebecca were back near the Blue Licks, building the only one of all his cabins that has survived the years intact. With his wife and son Nathan, he landed at Limestone and went overland to Brushy Fork, a little stream near Hinkston's Creek, in what is now Nicholas County. Here they settled, apparently on land belonging to their son Daniel Morgan Boone. It had never been cleared and the family worked for a year to get ten acres opened up and ready for crops. By 1796 the new land was clear enough to grow one, and it yielded another in 1797.

The cabin which they built and lived in has only recently been identified. Most of these old log buildings moldered away or were torn down long ago. This one survives because some later owner, dissatisfied with so uncivilized an exterior as logs, covered them over with clapboards and so accidentally preserved them. Its twentieth-century owner intended to raze the cabin about 1936 in order to erect a new farm building, but its history was discovered just in time to save it.

That it was actually Daniel Boone's cabin is, in the nature of things, unprovable. But at least it stands where his cabin must have stood and it is of the proper period.

Deer were getting scarce near the new farm, and though both the colonel and his son killed one occasionally, the Boone family—probably for the first time in its life—lived on purchased provender, mostly mutton. One can see why Daniel was uneasy about the crowding that accompanied the approach of civilization. Bad as the hunting was, he could hardly enjoy it, for he was so crippled with rheumatism that Rebecca had to go along on hunts to carry his rifle. But even with this handicap he killed more deer than anybody else. When the rheumatism was so bad that he could not hunt he turned to trapping, though sometimes he had to be carried to his trapline.

From his cabin doorstep the sexagenarian could look out over the country where he once had made history. Not far from here he had rolled on the ground with laughter at Stoner's misadventure with the buffalo. That was in 1774 when they and the surveyors they had come to warn were the only white men in Kentucky. Near here he had rescued his kidnapped daughter from Hanging Maw's camp. Near here the Shawnees had caught him in '78. The fatal Blue Licks were only twelve miles away. Close to this spot where his cabin stood he had marched—already worried about the suspiciously open retreat of McKee, Girty, and their Injuns—with the Kentucky militia. Through these very woods he had fled for his life, and had come back with Logan's men to bury the dead. Such dead as they could find. Young Israel's body would be lying up there now, if Daniel had not had the luck to recognize it when the Indians were gone.

The Warriors' Path ran close at hand. Not many warriors on it, now. Just skulking redskins. But instead, and more alarming to the old pioneer, a stream of immigrants, people from the states, people from the Old World, not used to the wild back-country. It didn't seem very wild to Daniel Boone, but it was too wild for them. Well, it was lucky for them folks old Daniel Boone had opened the way. Most of them didn't look as if they could do real pioneering, and their cabins began to clutter up the landscape.

The old life was nearly gone. And no wonder, for in England extraordinary tales were being circulated by eager land agents and ardent pamphleteers of the new, rich land of Kentucky, where the earth was fabulously fertile; where a man was a citizen and not a subject; where taxes were ridiculously low. A single issue of the London *Gazetteer,* August 31, 1792, advertised two hundred thousand acres for sale, mostly in Fayette and Nelson Counties.

There was talk at the new state capital of opening the Wilderness Road so that wagons could make the journey to Kentucky. Wagons moving openly where for twenty years the pack trains had fought for their lives! Daniel Boone thought he had some rights in the Wilderness Road. He had opened it for 'em in '75, and he hadn't been paid yet. All he ever got was land claims that always turned out to be good-for-nothing when the lawyers and legislators went to work.

Daniel Boone sat down with his goosequill in the little cabin on Brushy Fork, February 11, 1796, and wrote a few of his thoughts on this matter to Kentucky's first governor, Isaac

Shelby, whom he had known when Shelby was a surveyor at Boonesborough in 1775-1776:

> Sir—After my best Respts to your Excelancy and family I wish to inform you that I have sum intention of undertaking this New Rode that is to be cut through the Wilderness and I think my Self intitled to the ofer of the Bisness as I first Marked out that Rode in March 1775 and Never rec'd anything for my trubel and Sepose I am no Statesman I am a Woodsman and think My Self as Capable of Marking and Cutting that Rode, as any other man Sir if you think with Me I would thank you to wright me a Line by the post the first oportuneaty and he will lodge it at Mr. John Milers on Hinkston fork as I wish to know Wheer and when it is to be Latt [let] So that I may attend at the time I am Deer Sir
>
> your very omble servent
>
> DANIEL BOONE

What Shelby answered no one knows. It is quite certain that others got the contract for the "New Rode." Daniel was not very much surprised. They hadn't paid him in 1775. They didn't intend to give him the contract now. But it was his road all the same. A year or two later he left his cabin on Brushy Fork, and in 1798 he was living on the Little Sandy and clearing land for the spring crop. He led a bear hunt on the Big Sandy and helped kill forty or fifty. There was plenty of bear oil and bear bacon that winter.

But Daniel Boone went back home to his cabin in disgust. Kentucky had had plenty of use for him in 1775 and 1782 and the dark and bloody years between. They didn't have much use for him now. Daniel began to wonder. This country was too full of people and a great deal too full of lawyers. He was not completely impoverished yet, but it looked as if he soon would be if he stayed in Kentucky; and he still dreamed of wealth.

All of his best land was gone, but the tax returns for 1796 or 1797 show that he still owned twenty-six thousand acres of "second rate" and fifteen hundred acres of "third rate" land. There is, however, absolutely no mention of slaves, personal property, horses, or cattle. Jesse Boone owns two slaves, two horses, six cattle, while Daniel Morgan Boone has three slaves, four horses, five cattle, and five hundred acres. Perhaps the old hunter had turned over all this property to his farmer sons, while he, who detested farming, lived by roaming the woods with "Old Tick-Licker."

Stories were trickling in from across the Mississippi. Daniel Morgan Boone, his son, had gone out there in 1795. Zenon Trudeau, the Spanish lieutenant-governor, had received him royally. His Excellency hinted that Spain had need for pioneers and would gladly welcome so distinguished a settler as the celebrated Lieutenant-Colonel Daniel Boone, of Kentucky. Missouri was a new, wild country. Fertile, full of game, his son said. The trapping was excellent. The price of beaver pelts was high. Better than the six shillings a trapper used to get.

Daniel Boone did some thinking.

19. "Elbow-Room"

KENTUCKY was a confused and puzzled part of the world in the period immediately after the Revolution. In ten breathless bloody years the country had been wrested from the Indians, while the thirteen Colonies were winning their independence from the British. Kentucky had been a wilderness in 1774, with nothing in it but game, wandering Indian hunters, and a few white surveyors. It was still backwoods in the 1790's; but each ship that docked in Philadelphia and Baltimore sent the ripple of white settlement just a little farther into the western wilderness. As the settled portion of new states grew more crowded, men pushed west toward new country that offered land and fortune and that was now safe from the Indians—well, pretty safe.

Backwoods and settlements have never loved each other. Friction between them had helped send Daniel Boone westward into the Dark and Bloody Ground. Now the settled East seemed more preoccupied with its own interests than ever. Was the American government forgetting its western settlements? Why didn't it protect their interests? The British at Detroit clung silently to the fur country which (on paper) they had ceded long ago. The King of Spain closed the Mississippi at New Orleans. What good was the United States government to Kentucky if it let Kentucky be cut off from the sea?

Just what was Kentucky, anyhow? Part of the United States?

It didn't look as if there was going to be a United States very long. The Articles of Confederation hadn't worked. No one knew whether the new Constitution was going to work any better. The states were still jealous of each other. Connecticut and Pennsylvania had fought an unofficial but very lively war for years over the Wyoming Valley around Wilkes-Barre. Hostilities had been suspended during the Revolution but would have broken out again if in 1782 a federal commission had not handed the country back to the Pennsylvanians. Most of the states had waged tariff wars with other states.

From beyond the Mississippi, the Spaniards watched all this and waited. Monarchists, they did not trust these rough-and-ready Republicans. Catholics, they had their doubts about this predominantly Protestant young power. Absolutists, they were disturbed by these turbulent devotees of freedom.

The Americans had driven the British out, most conveniently for Spain. Spanish dominion now ran (in theory) from St. Louis to Cape Horn, from the Mississippi to California. The Mississippi was a wide, wide river; but already these strange, young, new people, these Americans, were part way along one bank.

Americans had a way of spreading out. Suppose they did become a nation. Then what? Louisiana? Florida? Texas? California? Mexico? Panama, perhaps? All Spanish territory now, but all dangerously empty. A standing temptation to these lean stalwart pioneers who spread, and spread, and spread—always a little farther westward.

In Havana, his Excellency, Señor Don Esteban Miró, Governor and Intendant of the Provinces of Louisiana and West Florida for his Catholic Majesty, shook his head.

Into this situation came a man of large ideas, extravagant habits, and elastic honor, one James Wilkinson, late brigadier in George Washington's army. He had soldiered with Benedict

Arnold; but so far—at least no one knows anything to the contrary—he had been loyal. The war over, he had come to Kentucky in 1784 to make a fortune. The fortune proved harder to achieve than the brigadier had anticipated.

He looked around for easy money. Arnold had done that, too, years before.

The British were gone.

The Spaniards?

Brigadier-General Wilkinson took a boat for New Orleans. He had a long and very private conference with Spanish officials there. When he came back, the brigadier had found his easy money. He rejoined the United States Army later; but still he kept that easy money.

Eventually he went before a court-martial. His enemies were entirely correct in suspecting unutterable treason. Wilkinson had actually asked the Spaniards for arms to use against the United States. The trouble was that, though his accusers knew they were correct, they could not prove it. All the evidence was neatly tucked away in the Spanish government's archives in Havana. It was a hundred years before historians dug the incriminating documents out, and by that time even the Judge Advocate General himself could not reach this slightly mercenary brigadier.

The Spaniards paid Wilkinson for two plans. In his first scheme he undertook simply to encourage the immigration of Kentuckians to the Spanish dominions. It had a flavor of legitimacy unusual in Wilkinson's schemes; but he made up for this bit of respectability in the second part of his design, which was treason, pure and simple. The Kentucky settlers were discontented. Some merely wanted to break loose from Virginia and become a fifteenth state—as they actually did in 1792. Others wanted to leave the United States entirely—or so Wilkinson, in a highly confidential memorandum, told his Spanish friends. If the Spaniards would supply the necessary arms, the general offered to separate Kentucky from the United States by force and bring it over to Spanish rule.

Brigadier-General Wilkinson thought also that it might be possible to assist nature with a few bribes. He made a little list—a beautifully cynical little list—of some leading men with notes on their qualifications, and prices. United States judges were getting one thousand dollars a year. The brigadier suggested that two thousand dollars apiece to a few of them would help matters enormously. His list also contained Boone's old fellow Indian-fighter, Benjamin Logan, and a good many other names. It was, in short, a list which several eminent American families would find distinctly embarrassing today.

But why waste time proving that somebody's distinguished great-great-grandfather was not all he might have been? The curious may go to the Archiva Histórico-Nacional in Spain. And there, in Estado Legajo No. 3898 B, they will find the whole treasonable scheme writ large.

There is actually no real evidence that Logan or several others on Wilkinson's list had any idea of his schemes. Wilkinson may just have used their names for what they were worth to him. He may have done so without the least authority—Wilkinson was that sort of man.

Now the dons of the Supreme Council of State in Havana were wily old gentlemen. It was not hard to see that Wilkinson was something of a scoundrel. One step at a time was quite fast enough for the Supreme Council of State in any dealings with him. Even before Wilkinson had presented his list of proposed bribes they had, in 1788, decided to wait until Kentucky, on its own impulse, broke away from the United States. Then, perhaps . . .

Wilkinson had asked for arms to speed the process. That would hardly do. But in the meantime they recommended "that all be allowed to enter as settlers who might come of their own accord, or might be brought by the brigadier aforementioned, with their families, property, and cattle, exclusive of mere vagabonds, and granting to the settlers the private enjoyment of the religious faith they profess, though not the public observance of it, for the churches must be Catholic."

Wilkinson planned a "whispering campaign." He proposed to send confidential agents around to arouse Kentucky interest, praising the lands available in "Louisiana," which then extended as far north as the Missouri River and beyond. He wanted "to win over to the actual service of His Catholic Majesty the distinguished 'notables' of Kentucky." His plan needed, he said, "two or three prominent men of the most select kind in every district."

It is no wonder that from 1787 on American interest in "Louisiana" grew mightily. Wilkinson was not alone in his efforts. At least two other, and more reputable, agents were also active in promoting immigration from the United States. In addition, George Rogers Clark himself wrote to the Spaniards, despairing of security for property in the weak United States, and offering to bring settlers to Spanish territory in return for land. Gradually Kentuckians began to cross into Spanish Missouri, quite unaware of the dark and devious schemes that had helped to clear the way.

It was a long time before any of this reached Daniel Boone. He is never mentioned in any of Wilkinson's correspondence. Even Wilkinson knew better than to offer Daniel Boone a bribe. As for legitimate land offers, when the Spanish schemes first began Boone had all the land he could possibly desire. Only when these lands were wrested from him did "Louisiana" begin to interest Daniel and his sons. If the Spaniards wanted Kentucky "notables," however, here was the most notable of all.

Early in the eighteenth century old George Boone had sent a son ahead to spy out the new land of Pennsylvania before he tried to settle there. At the century's end, Daniel Boone, his grandson, sent his own son to examine this new land of Missouri. Caution—when possible. That was the Boone way.

Daniel Morgan Boone was the first to venture. Between 1795 and 1797 he was hunting and trapping along the Mississippi, sometimes accompanied by his brother-in-law Joseph Scholl and one or two others. Deciding to see the Missouri country, he took Scholl and a companion along, but when the trip was only half over they decided to return, much as the elder Boone's fellow-hunters had done during the wilderness trip of 1769-70.

Young Boone visited Don Zenon Trudeau, the lieutenant-governor, and knowing that his father was already interested in the Missouri country, discussed settlements. Quite aware of Daniel Boone's reputation, Trudeau was extremely cordial to his son. He hinted that if Daniel Morgan Boone's celebrated father wished to move farther west, the government of the Most Catholic King of Spain would treat him handsomely. He even wrote a letter to the old frontiersman waiting in Kentucky, promising him a huge grant of land for himself, and smaller tracts of either four hundred or six hundred arpents * for any families he might bring. The Spanish government would make further land grants of forty acres for each wife, child, or servant. The younger Boone hurried back to Kentucky.

In 1798 he was on his way to Missouri again, this time with three negro slaves, prepared to found a settlement. In the spring of 1799 he returned for a final consultation with his father. By this time Daniel Morgan Boone had taken up land on a bluff about a mile from the Missouri River, at Darst's Bottom in St. Charles County, some twenty-five miles beyond the village of St. Charles, and about sixty miles from St. Louis. He may have claimed the land as early as 1795. Whatever the earliest date of his arrival, he was soon sending back to Kentucky enthusiastic

* The arpent was .85 acres.

accounts of the warm welcome which the Spaniards gave to "notables," the richness of the soil, the admirable climate, the abundance of game.

It was the beginning of the last stage of Daniel Boone's career. The end turned out to be a curious recapitulation, on a smaller scale, of his earlier exploits. Just as the wild fastnesses of Kentucky had inflamed his imagination when he dwelt on their border in relatively settled country, so now from the newer settlements of Kentucky, the wild land in the Ozarks lured him westward. He was entering upon a new period of land claims, legal troubles, more hunting, more exploration, more trapping, and more Indian fighting—the old story over again. From the very beginning he had held office in Kentucky; he was immediately made an official in Missouri. The Indians had twice robbed him in Kentucky; the Osages were lesser men than the wily Shawnees: but if they succeeded in robbing the old Indian-fighter only once, there was at least one other occasion when they tried their best.

The lawyers did not yet have possession of quite all his land. Indeed, land in Daniel Boone's name was carried on the assessors' books of Kanawha County as late as 1803. But the hopes he once had cherished of that little ten acres painfully cleared on Brushy Fork had ended in disappointment. Prospects in Missouri grew more alluring.

When the last of his land was nearly gone, Daniel Boone was footloose once again. Kentucky did not seem to want him very much. The country was too full. The game was vanishing. Newcomers from the crowded East might think it plentiful but Daniel remembered the days when you could kill a deer at any lick. New Englanders were coming in; and Daniel held the entire breed in abhorrence. He declared he had never been deceived by an Indian who had once announced himself a friend, but you never could trust New Englanders, and he never wanted to live "within 100 miles of a d–d Yankee." Besides, people were clearing the land. No wonder the game was vanishing.

For a year or two, Daniel Boone still clung briefly to the Kentucky land that he still hoped to hold, then turned westward to a new life that was to be amazingly like the old life he had known and loved. In 1798 he spent a little while on the Big Sandy. About this time he is said to have wandered over into Tennessee.

He may even have wandered briefly into North Carolina. In her old age a little girl born in 1793 remembered traveling through the North Carolina mountains with her father. On the way they met a man in hunting dress, carrying a rifle. It was Daniel Boone. Her father threw his hat into the air with joy, and so did Boone, as they recognized one another. The story is almost certainly true—it is exactly the kind of thing a child remembers forever—and it is hard to find any other possible date for the incident.

In 1798 the sheriffs of Mason and Clark Counties put up more than ten thousand acres of his lands to be sold for taxes. With unconscious irony, Kentucky chose that very year to name a new county Boone in his honor. It was pleasant to be honored, but the honors somehow seemed a little empty. What Daniel wanted was land, and they had taken most of it away, though he did survey five hundred acres more in September of 1798 and patented it in 1800, after he had left for Missouri.

Daniel Boone cut down a huge tulip poplar growing on the bank of the Big Sandy, and made a dugout canoe sixty feet long, capable of carrying five tons. The poplar stump was still being pointed out in 1851—a by no means impossible survival, since an old sycamore that stood at Boonesborough during the siege lasted far into the twentieth century, and was cut out of the ground only a year or two ago. In 1857 one old man still remembered that he had seen Boone cut down the tree to make the canoe, and had later seen him start for Missouri. An old clergyman remembered seeing Daniel Boone "on pack-horses, take up his journey for Missouri, then Upper Louisiana."

The contradiction is only apparent. Actually, Daniel himself did go overland; but the household goods and most of his family traveled in the big canoe. Daniel's sons Daniel Morgan and Nathan, and his brother Squire traveled with Rebecca and her daughter Jemima down the river. Jemima's husband, Flanders Callaway, appears to have taken the overland route.

Old friends and neighbors went along to Missouri, among them the faithful Stephen Hancock, who had fought through the siege of Boonesborough. However Kentucky may have treated its erstwhile hero, his family and friends had a touching and implicit faith in the man. So many of them went along that they must have needed a small flotilla of additional dugouts. All his life long the pioneers were ready to "pull up stakes" and set off for a new settlement at a word from Daniel Boone.

Boone's departure in September, 1799, was a public event, the date and place of which were announced far in advance. Down the rivers in canoes and through the forests on foot or on horseback, old friends came to see the veteran wanderer off to his last frontier. While the dugout drifted down the Ohio, Daniel Boone, with some white companions and a negro slave or two, drove the stock to Missouri. Hence a relative's statement that "the old man walked every foot of the way, with his rifle on his shoulder, through a trackless wilderness, a large part of which was infested by bands of bloodthirsty savages." It is rather an exaggeration. The journey was certainly arduous, but many Americans had already made it. The wilderness was by no means trackless now and the savages at the moment not in a particularly bloodthirsty mood.

Nathan Boone voyaged in the dugout only as far as Limestone, where he secured a marriage license and started back alone to the Little Sandy, seventy-five miles away. Here he married Olive Van Bibber, said to be the prettiest girl north of the Ohio River, on September 26, and by October 1 the newly married couple were also on their way to Missouri.

There is a legend that Daniel Boone halted on the wharf at Cincinnati. It is an unlikely stopping place for a pack train, but a likely one for boats. Perhaps Daniel crossed the Ohio River to see how the rest of his family were faring. There was a mild sensation in Cincinnati when word spread that the famous pioneer was there. Some officious fool asked why he was leaving Kentucky and received a famous answer: "Too many people!" said the veteran. "Too crowded! too crowded! I want more elbow-room."

By October both parties had reached St. Louis. This was the kind of Kentucky "notable" that the Spaniards wanted. Lieutenant-Governor Zenon Trudeau had just been superseded by Lieutenant-Governor Carlos D. Delassus, but he was still there; and the two governors and their officials treated the immigrants as distinguished guests.

American and Spanish flags were displayed. The garrison paraded, and Lieutenant-Colonel Boone, late of the Kanawha County Militia, was received with the honors due his rank. It was probably the first time in his life that the tough old fighter had ever seen the frills and furbelows of army life. The militia in Kaintuck' simply went out, killed its Indians, and hurried home to its families, troubling its heads very little over military pomp and pageantry, thankful enough to have them still unscalped.

When the official formalities were over, the simple old man in the leather hunting shirt with a couple of knives in the belt mounted his "sad looking horse," took his rifle, whistled to the three or four hunting dogs that accompanied him, and set out for the home of his son Daniel Morgan Boone, sixty miles farther on. He camped out on the way, avoiding villages. Here Nathan and his bride had already preceded him. Daniel Morgan Boone's negroes had planted fifteen acres the previous spring, so there was plenty of food for everyone, even without hunting. Neither Daniel Boone nor his sons went out that winter on a "regular hunt," but simply shot enough venison to supply the household.

Daniel Boone had a great deal of work to do in parceling out land. Trudeau had used his influence to make sure that all his promises to the Boones should be kept by his successor. Boone had brought so many other settlers with him that the Spanish officials made no effort to assign the lands themselves, especially as the Kentuckians chose the land farthest west, on the wildest frontier, westward, toward the unknown. They left the details to Señor Boone. He had a list of the people actually with him, and allotted to them the grants which the Spanish officials had made out in blank and given him to distribute. These were about four hundred acres each, with allowance for children and dependents. The actual choice of land sites was also left to Señor Boone, and he continued for some years to assign lands to newcomers.

There was talk of ceding the country to France and the provincial lieutenant-governor in St. Louis was not quite sure that this might not have happened already. To make quite certain, therefore, that all land grants fell within the unquestioned period of Spanish jurisdiction, they were carefully antedated. Daniel Boone's first grant bears the date of January 28, 1798, a time when he was still in Kentucky. It was a futile precaution, as events turned out.

In recognition of his distinction and the official position he was soon to occupy, Señor Boone was given more land than the others—one thousand arpents to be located wherever he chose to survey it in the District of the Femme Osage. This officially included nothing less than the entire area north of the Missouri River, and extended westward indefinitely. There was a pleasing boundlessness about it, gratifying to a frontiersman's soul.

Boone chose a site in the Ozarks, sixty miles from the mouth of the Missouri and about twenty-five miles from St. Charles. It was mostly bottom land, between the river and the acreage on the bluff beyond, which had been granted to Daniel Morgan Boone. For the sake of convenience the elder Boone built his cabin on his son's land. That was a serious legal blunder, as Daniel was eventually to discover.

There was only one difficulty. Nathan Boone had waited to be married. He had not come out with the Boone party and—presumably for that reason—had received no grant. There was no way to get him one now without direct personal pressure on Spanish officials at St. Louis, sixty miles away. Moreover, there was some doubt whether he could legally receive it. Bachelors and newcomers without property had to wait three or four years before they were entitled to land. Nathan was a boy of twenty who had been married only a few weeks. He certainly owned no property. The Spaniards might not have regarded him as a settler at all.

Daniel, who fretted to the end of his life because he could not provide better for his family, was greatly disturbed because he was unable to make Nathan and his bride a wedding present of land. However, he and his sons made the best arrangement they could. Nathan traded off his last horse, including saddle and bridle, to one Robert Hall, in return for a four-hundred-arpent tract. The original Spanish grant to "Robben Hall" is dated January 23, 1798, but this is probably pre-dated. It is worth noting that Daniel Boone himself paid Hall's taxes and that Hall sold his tract to Nathan Boone January 20, 1800, probably just after Nathan's arrival in Missouri.

Squire Boone also secured a grant on which he started to build an elaborate stone house; but two of his sons came out to Missouri and persuaded him to come home with them. Squire built another stone house back home, "packing" the stone himself and adorning it with couplets more remarkable for piety than versification.

I set and sing my soul's salvation
And bless the God of my creation.

Keep close your intention
For fear of prevention.

My God my life hath much befriended,
I'll praise him till my days are ended.

Missouri never knew what it escaped!

Family and personal ties were always strong among the Boones and within a few years the Boone and Callaway families and Rebecca's nephew Jonathan Bryan were all living close together in Missouri. By 1800 the Bryans and the Boones were once more so close that they could see each other's houses through the trees.

Amity reigned even when it was discovered that Daniel Boone's old dog Cuff had formed the habit of dropping in at Jonathan Bryan's water mill to lick up the ground meal as fast as it ran down from the millstone into a pewter basin on the floor. Poor Cuff was indiscreet enough to howl when the meal came too slowly. Bryan substituted for the basin a coffee pot too small for the dog to get his head in and all was well.

In February, 1800, just after their arrival, Daniel and Rebecca went out to Nathan Boone's land, constructed one of their usual "half-faced" camps, and lived there for several weeks, tapping the maple trees and boiling down three or four hundred pounds of maple sugar.

Together the Boones proposed to lay out the town of Missouriton, sometimes called "Daniel Boone's Palatinate." They hoped to bring in wealthy settlers and slaveholders from Virginia. For a time the town prospered sufficiently to be proposed as territorial capital; but the shifting Missouri changed its course, nibbled at the banks, and eventually much of the land fell bit by bit into the flood and was swept away to make sandbars in the Mississippi and deltas at New Orleans. The modern post-office of Missouriton is some distance from the spot where the Missouri now rolls over another of Daniel Boone's land schemes.

At first Daniel Boone's Missouri hunting trips were mainly for amusement—mere "home hunts" from which he "hoppused" the deer home on his own shoulders. But from the very beginning his sons went farther afield with an eye to commercial hunting and the old man soon began to join them. Deerskins were fetching forty cents a pound in St. Louis and these western dealers did not even insist on having them "grained"; they would buy deerskins hair and all. Late in the summer of 1801 Daniel began deer-hunting again in a serious way.

On one of these trips the veteran discovered beaver sign on the Barbeuse River. That looked exciting. Taking a negro boy of twenty years or so along as "camp-keeper," Boone set off for the winter, but had rather a bad season, returning with only thirty or forty pelts. His sons, who spent the winter on the Niango River, a branch of the Grand Osage, came back with a hundred pelts. Neither party had seen any sign of Indians. Thereafter the Boones devoted themselves to regular fall and winter hunts, mainly after beaver. The best luck was Nathan Boone's, on his 1802 hunt along the Grand River, when he and a relative by marriage took nine hundred beaver skins, then worth about two dollars and fifty cents apiece. Indians found and looted a cache of one hundred pelts, but even so two thousand dollars' worth of furs remained. Most of this fur went back to Kentucky, though sometimes hatters came out from Lexington and bought from the Boones in Missouri. At other times Nathan took the furs back himself. In 1802 he used Daniel Boone's share to help pay off old claims of merchants there against him.

1802 was otherwise a bad year for Daniel. He caught his hand in one of his own beaver traps one freezing winter day. Unable to get the jaws open with his foot, the old trapper had to trudge back to camp with two of his fingers gripped in the steel.

As if that were not enough, his camp was robbed by Indians. Boone himself had just saddled up and ridden off, leaving his colored camp-keeper in charge. There was an outburst of shots and yells and eight or ten Indians came charging in. The colored youth fled, but Boone, glancing back, observed that the Indians were merely firing into the air and seemed more intent on scaring the colored boy than on actual fighting. He rode calmly back to camp, was jerked off his horse, lost his coat, and was forced to "give" the Indians most of his powder and lead, plus most of his pelts. But he called the colored boy back, parleyed with the Indians, and eventually managed to finish his winter's trapping in spite of the robbery. He came home with about two hundred skins. It was, however, his last long hunt for some time. During the next winter or two his old enemy rheumatism crippled him again.

Within a couple of years the Spanish authorities proposed that Boone should bring in a hundred American families and should have as his reward an additional ten thousand arpents, also to be located in the district of the Femme Osage. The man's prestige was enormous. He had been forced out of Kentucky; he had been defeated by his lack of business sense; but the people still knew him for a master of the wilderness. Furthermore, they trusted him completely. They had followed him when he had led the way to Kentucky. They were ready to follow when he led the way again. A word from Daniel Boone was enough. The new pioneer families that the Spanish authorities wanted came; and Daniel Boone's ten thousand arpents (8,500 acres) were duly awarded to him. But—as usual—it turned out later, when the lawyers took a hand, that there was a flaw in the title.

Boone settled easily into the life of the new country. There might have been religious difficulties with a Roman Catholic government, for the new settlers were Baptists and Methodists, some of them rather bigoted. One good old missionary Baptist refused to admit that the sermons of the Romish priests were genuine "gospel preaching" at all. But the Spanish Catholic officials—having promised the new colonists the private practice of any religion they pleased—proceeded to stretch the law until its letters cracked. They were legally compelled to examine all newcomers to determine their orthodoxy. With much tact, they were careful to ask only such questions as: "Do you believe in God Almighty? in the Holy Trinity? in the true apostolic church? in Jesus Christ our Savior? in the holy Evangelists?" Any believer of any sort could answer such questions loud and clear and with a good conscience. Delighted with the highly orthodox responses they always received, the Spanish officials blithely pronounced each Methodist or Baptist American immigrant a good Catholic.

The traveling missionary parsons who soon appeared, sent out by eastern Protestants, were dealt with just as cleverly. The governor, well aware who they were and what they were doing, invariably waited until each missionary had nearly completed his tour, and then sent him a fierce official warning that unless he left the territory within three days he would be arrested. It looked well in the records, especially as the missionary, his duty done for the time being, invariably complied. When he returned on his next tour, he always found the broad-minded governor conveniently blind until his work was done, after which the official warning duly arrived.

There were very few Catholic priests in this wild country anyhow, and most of them were in little churches in the sparse towns, whereas the Protestant Americans were outside the towns, scattered along the frontiers. There was slight chance for religious friction.

Trudeau, while lieutenant-governor, had sternly forbidden Protestant worship. That was against the law. But, as he explained to one missionary Baptist preacher, if the Americans wished to gather in each other's houses for religious discussion or addresses, or if they wished to sing hymns and pray, there could obviously be no objection to these pious exercises—which, as Trudeau very well knew, constituted the only Protestant services desired. Still, he explained in an official tone, all children must certainly be baptized by priests. That was not a matter of deep concern to these Baptists; they did not believe in infant baptism anyway. The further prohibition of a church bell on the house in which they met was equally innocuous; they hadn't any church bell.

There was a formidable-sounding Spanish regulation which declared severely: "The commandants with the greatest strictness are to watch that no Protestant preachers, or preachers of any other sect not Catholics, introduce themselves; for they shall be made severely responsible for the least neglect in this respect." But, in spite of that, the commandant of the Femme Osage sometimes made one of the congregation when the Baptist preachers were holding forth.

None of this mattered very much. The Protestant Daniel Morgan Boone lost no time falling in love, and duly went through the prescribed form of Catholic marriage in the parish of St. Charles Borromeo at St. Charles, Missouri, March 2, 1800.

His bride, thoroughly Protestant, was an American girl from the wholly American settlement of Bon Homme, a little farther down the river.

Boone had his own thoughts on religion, when he had time to ponder, and he lived most of his life under the shadow of death; but doctrinal subtleties meant little to him. A good many of his family were Baptists. He went to Baptist preaching himself sometimes. He was one of the congregation when the Reverend John M. Peck, his future biographer, preached at Flanders Callaway's house in 1819. Sometimes the missionary parsons talked with him about his soul and making a "profession of faith," but their crude theology never impressed Daniel Boone very much.

"He never made a profession of religion," said one of them, "but still was what the world calls a very moral man. I asked him if he thought he loved God? He replied, 'I hope so.' I asked again, 'Do you ever remember the time, Colonel, when you experienced a change in your feelings towards the Savior? He replied, 'No, Sir, I always loved God ever since I could recollect.' He listened to preaching with apparent interest; but the above was all I could ever learn from [him] upon the subject of experimental religion."

Toward the end of his life, when he had a little enforced leisure as his hunting and trapping grew less arduous, he read a great deal in his Bible; but he never felt any particular need to join the church.

Like his brother Squire, Dan'l had an interest in the life after death and once agreed with a friend that the one who died first should try to communicate from beyond the grave. Nothing came of it, of course. Squire Boone made his sons promise to wait at the mouth of the limestone cave he had himself selected for his tomb, on the night after they buried him. Nothing came of that, either, though the sons, having waited for some hours, made camp near the tomb and spent the night there, hoping for communications from their father's spirit.

Daniel Boone once wrote out a few of his thoughts on matters theological for the benefit of a sister-in-law:

> Relating to our family and how we Live in this World and what Chance we Shall have in the next we know Not for my part I am as ignurant as a Child all the Relegan I have to Love and feer god beleve in Jeses Christ Dow all the good to my Nighbour and my Self that I Can and Do as Little harm as I Can help and trust in gods marcy for the Rest and I Beleve god neve made a man of my prisepel to be Lost and I flater my Self Deer Sister that you are well on your way in Cristianaty.

As for his son's marriage, well, since Catholic marriage was the law of the land, a Catholic marriage let it be. The listening priest jotted down the record from the replies of the bridal couple and their parents. The marriage record, which still exists among the archives of the Parish, is worth quoting:

> On this day, the 2nd of March 1800, there appeared before me, Fr. Leander Lusson, Recolet Priest and Pastor of the parish of St. Charles of Missouri:—on the one hand Daniel Morgan Boone, of age and legitimate son of Daniel Boone and Rebecca Bryan his wife, the Father and Mother living in St. Charles, Mo.; on the other hand Sarah Griffin Lewis still a minor, and legitimate daughter of John Baptist Lewis and Elizabeth Harvé his wife, as Father and Mother living at the Post of St. Andrew. The couple assured us it was their intention to be married; and with their oath upon the Bible they promised to answer truthfully to the questions I would put to them.
>
> 1 Qu.—I asked: What Religion do you profess?—The said Daniel Morgan Boone said he professed the Presbyterian religion; and the said Sarah Griffin Lewis replied that she professed the Protestant religion.
>
> 2 Qu.—To my question whether they were willing to bring the children that might be born to them to the church nearest

their home, in order to be baptized and to be instructed, they replied "Yes."

3 Qu.—To my inquiry as to any impediments of relationship which according to their religion forbid Marriage, they answered in the negative.

4 Qu.—I next inquired into their birth-place or country. Daniel Morgan Boone replied he was a native of Virginia in the diocese of Baltimore, and that he now lived with his parents. Sarah Griffin Lewis said she also was from Virginia, and now lived with her father and mother.

5. To my query, whether respective parents, or others upon whom they might be dependent gave their consent to this marriage.—The parents who were present replied in the affirmative.

6. Again I asked, whether there wasn't any constraint on the part of anyone authorized who by threat or violence compelled them to enter into this union? Their answer was in the negative.

After the above mentioned informations were taken, the publication of the Banns having been made on three successive Sundays at the door of our church of St. Charles in Missouri, as also at the gates of Sire Mackay, Commandant of the village and Post of St. Andrew of Missouri,—the said Daniel Morgan Boone in our presence took the said Sarah Griffin Lewis for his wife and legitimate spouse, pledging to her his marriage troth. In like manner Sarah Griffin Lewis took Daniel Morgan Boone as her husband and legitimate groom and pledged unto him her troth. And thus we have received their mutual consent; according to the Ordinance of His Majesty, given on the 30th day of November 1793. Moreover, there were present Messrs. William Hays, Philip Milla [Miller], Nathan Boone, Francis Howell, and several others, all of this Parish and the Post of St. Andrew, as witnesses to this transaction, who all have signed with us on the same day and year as given above.

Two months after the marriage, July 11, 1800, Carlos D. Delassus, the new lieutenant-governor, appointed Boone "syndic" for the Femme Osage. Under Spanish law this placed Daniel Boone in more or less complete administrative charge, civil and military, of the whole area. In his official signatures, Boone refers to himself as "Commander of the District of the femme Osage."

By a curious coincidence a similar appointment in a Missouri district farther down the Mississippi was granted to Louis Lorimier, once a controlling influence among the Shawnees who had raided Kentucky. He had been one of the Frenchmen present when Boone was captured at the Salt Licks in 1778. Bird's expedition had passed through his station on its way to the capture of Ruddle's and Martin's Stations in Kentucky. Though there is no positive evidence, it is likely enough that the two old rivals met sometimes to compare experiences.

Not long after his arrival in Missouri, Boone had renewed his acquaintance with his old Shawnee enemies, an acquaintance which ever afterward was friendly. He ran into a Shawnee hunting camp on a deer-hunt in 1801. Two or three surviving Indians remembered the days when Sheltowee lived among them as a fellow tribesman. He met once more Jimmy Rogers, for whom he had stocked a rifle in 1778, the man who had told the Shawnees that Sheltowee would get safely back to Boonesborough. Joseph Jackson, who had been one of the captured salt-makers in 1778, now a Shawnee warrior named Fish, was back with his adopted brothers once more after a brief return to white civilization in 1799. Boone paid at least one visit to the permanent camp of the Shawnees northwest of St. Louis. One of his granddaughters, on a later occasion at Fort Leavenworth, Kansas, was surprised by the friendliness of an old squaw. She was one of Blackfish's daughters, adopted sister of Daniel Boone!

His new position made Daniel Boone a powerful official. He was already the leading man of the new community. He assigned vacant lands. He kept order. He punished crime. He was official witness to notes. He settled estates. At the request of the

Spanish governor he acted as guide to a visiting capitalist who thought of starting an iron mine. The people around St. Charles, observed Meriwether Lewis, as the Lewis and Clark Expedition passed up the Missouri River, "yeald passive obedience to the will of their temporal master, the Commandant."

"The settlers in these districts," wrote the geographer Jedidiah Morse in 1798, "are under the immediate orders of the military commandants, and subject to martial law, with an appeal from stage to stage, up to the viceroy of Mexico. The property of the subject at his dicease, is to be managed by the commandant, whose fees are settled by law, and amount to 25 per cent." Even in 1816, when he was himself past eighty and had long ceased to be an official, Boone was still being asked to act as estate administrator.

As a magistrate of the Spanish Crown, Daniel Boone dealt justice. He held court under the "Justice Tree" near his cabin. Here, in moccasins of buckskin and clothing of buckskin or homespun, the old man heard offenders and awarded penalties according to methods of his own devising. The rules of evidence were of his own devising, too. His knowledge of law was only such as he had picked up in numerous appearances as a witness in land suits; in that dismal series of legal troubles in which he was invariably the loser; or in the fairly frequent courts-martial of the Kentucky militia. His position as commandant suited him exactly. No regular records were required. He could issue his own decrees and more or less manufacture the law as he went along. There was no one to dispute his judgment. His decision was final and, as a practical matter, without appeal except in land cases, which had to be referred to the Crown or its representatives.

Daniel Boone had seen a lot of courts, but he didn't think much of them. He preferred his own judicial methods. So, apparently, did his neighbors. It was a somewhat rough-and-ready justice he administered, but there was no complaint. Whipping posts were common in Missouri then—even St. Louis had one—and the lash was Boone's principal penalty. He is said to have made sure that the blows were "well laid on," as the law itself later specified. What was the use of sending a man all the way to St. Charles to lock him up in the calabozo? A hickory sapling near the Justice Tree provided a convenient whipping post, and here the culprits were "whipped and cleared." Thereafter, Missouri tradition says, they were restored to reputable standing in the community as having paid the full penalty. The phrase itself, still familiar in Missouri, arose when a man sentenced to the lash by Daniel Boone was asked how he had made out. The victim replied cheerfully enough: "First rate. Whipped and cleared." At this time the lash carried no social stigma.

Severe measures were unquestionably needed. It was a rather turbulent district, as is shown by the cases with which the American syndic of the Femme Osage had to deal:

June 30th, 1804

This Day Came before me Justice of the Peace for the District of the Femmeosage, Francis Woods, Peter Smith & John Manley and made oath that on the 29th of June of said Month at the house of David Bryan a Certain James Meek and the Bearer hereof Bery Vinzant had some differance Which Came to blows and in the scuffle the said James Meek bit of a piece of Bery Vinzants Left Ear, further the Deponent sayeth not Given under my hand and seal the day and Date above written

DANIEL BOONE [Seal]

Other legal documents remain, some entirely in Boone's own handwriting. One is a note which he drew up for a relative and officially witnessed:

June the first 1802

I promis to pay or Cause to be paid unto James Callaway Eighteen Dolors in good Well Shaved Marihentable [Mer-

chantable] pelterry on or before the 25th day of Desember Next insuing for valour Recd. of him as Witness my hand
OLIVE WOOD FRANCIS WOOD X his mark
DANIEL BOONE
Commander of the District of
the femme Osage

The other document is an effort to clear up another man's land title:

I do Cartify that I gave Benjamon gardner purmistion to Satel on a pees of vacant Land Coled the Little purrarey on the Misurry Sum time in Desember 1802 given under my hand this 23d Day of Febury 1806

DANIEL BOONE

A certain murder charge which he had to investigate must have been painful for Boone. The defendant was a fellow trapper and hunting companion; the dead man was his own son-in-law William Hays. James Davis, a shoemaker, had an altercation with William Hays, which ended when Davis shot Hays down. The crime was committed December 13, 1804, after the United States had taken over the territory, but no American officials had as yet arrived on Boone's wild frontier and Boone, as a Spanish syndic, took charge. After holding a preliminary hearing, he remanded Davis to the "calabozo" at St. Charles to await action by the grand jury—which for some reason had only the twelve members of a petit jury. Of the twelve, eleven could not write their own signatures. The sole literate was chosen foreman and the others signed with their marks, but the indictment follows the traditional legal form, alleging:

That one James Davis, late of the District of St. Charles, in the Territory of Louisiana, Laborer, not having the fear of God before his eyes, but being moved and seduced by the instigation of the Devil, on the 13th day of December, in the year of our Lord one thousand eight hundred and four (1804), at a place

> called Femme Osage, in the said district of St. Charles, with force of arms, in and upon William Hays, in the peace of God and the United States, then and there Feloniously, wilfully and with malice aforethought, did make an assault, and that the said James Davis, with a certain rifle gun, four feet long, and of the value of five dollars, then and there loaded and charged with gun powder and one leaden bullet, with said rifle gun the said James Davis, then and there in his hands had and held, fired and killed William Hays.

Davis was bound over for trial under three thousand dollars' bond. Boone signed the bond alone and when Davis came to trial he was cleared. It was a plain case of self-defense.

The vagueness as to legal detail in some of these documents and the casual way in which Missouri lands were assigned are typical of Boone's methods. It is no wonder that land troubles plagued him in Missouri as they had in Kentucky, troubles which even his more cautious children did not wholly escape.

But for once Boone felt secure in his lands. The lieutenant-governor himself had made the grant. Boone was the chief official of the area. As for the lawyers and their writs, he was running the court himself now, wasn't he?

Under Spanish law it was necessary to occupy the land and to clear ten acres annually until one tenth of the whole had been "improved." This would have meant one hundred acres of improvements for Boone's first tract and one thousand for his second. But Delassus said, rather vaguely, that in view of Boone's special services to the government this could be dispensed with. It was customary to exempt officials. Old Daniel never thought to have that promise written down. It was also desirable to file papers with the government at New Orleans. But it was a long way down the river; mails did not go with any regularity; and Boone was rather busy with a good many pressing affairs. Like many another settler, he let it go. It seemed just one more of these legal formalities.

But things were happening far away.

Only a few months after Boone had become syndic of the Femme Osage, Spain agreed to cede Louisiana to France; though at the moment it was impracticable for the French to take possession.

What did a few scraps of paper at a European diplomatic conference matter in far-off Missouri? Mr. Jefferson, however, had a stupendous and faintly illegal idea. Diplomats conferred and haggled. There was a great deal of bargaining. At length some papers were signed.

It was the Louisiana Purchase. Mr. Jefferson had casually bought half a continent, and some people said he had no right to do it. On March 9, 1804, Spain formally transferred sovereignty to France. Next day France turned Louisiana over to the United States. But the Americans were a long time coming and meanwhile life in the Femme Osage went on very much as it had before.

As he laid his office down, Lieutenant-Governor Delassus had a last thought of Boone. Thomas Jefferson had given the new American officials instructions to conciliate the inhabitants of Missouri and to make as few changes as possible. Stoddard, the new American governor, asked Delassus for a list of his subordinates and notes on their personalities. Among others whom Delassus listed for his American successor was: "Mr. Boone, a respectable old man, just and impartial, he has already, since I appointed him, offered his resignation owing to his infirmities —Believing I know his probity I have induced him to remain, in view of my confidence in him for the public good."

It was all very handsome, but Delassus never thought to certify to those conversations about land titles. Nor did Daniel Boone think to ask him to. The evil fate that had dogged the pioneer's footsteps all his life was preparing still another blow.

Fortunately, the difficulties with his land titles which afflicted Daniel Boone's last years were not quite so serious as the earlier ones in Kentucky. Trudeau had in a letter formally promised him a grant of land. The grant had duly been made. The survey had been properly executed and certificate of survey issued January 9, 1800. Furthermore, this time Daniel Boone really was the first and only claimant. There were no conflicting surveys "shingled" across his Missouri lands.

Remembering what had happened in Kentucky, Boone had saved all these papers. He was able to present them when the American land commission appeared shortly after the Louisiana Purchase, and everything seemed secure. When his claim was heard, his neighbor and kinsman Jonathan Bryan appeared to swear "that he knew Daniel Boone in this country in the year 1800." But the law required occupation, improvement, or cultivation of the land; and Boone had relied upon the assurance of the new lieutenant-governor Delassus. Daniel and Rebecca had simply settled down near Daniel Morgan Boone and had done nothing whatever with their own land.

> Colonel D. Boone stated to the Board, that, on his arrival in Louisiana, he took up his residence, with his lady, at his son Daniel M. Boone's, in the said district of Femme Osage, and adjoining the lands he now claims; that they remained there until about two years ago, when he moved to a younger son's, Nathan Boone, where he now lives. It is proved that the said claimant is of the age of about seventy years, and his wife about sixty-eight. He further stated, that, having inquired of Charles D. Delassus as to the propriety of improving and settling his land within a year and a day from the date of the concession, as directed by the Spanish laws, he was informed by said Delassus, that, being commandant of the said district, he need not trouble himself about the cultivating of the same as, by the commission he held of commandant of said district, he was not considered as coming within the meaning of said laws.

Delassus was wrong. Boone's claim was quite illegal—or so the commissioners held. Congress, later, was not quite so sure. There was nothing for the Board to do but decide "that the claim ought not to be confirmed."

The predicament in which Daniel Boone now found himself was not unusual. There were scores of similar cases. His son Nathan lost 420 arpents which Delassus had granted him and even lost land which he had already cultivated. Another man, it appeared, had cultivated it a year or two earlier. The faithful Jonathan Bryan appeared to testify for Nathan, as did Daniel Boone's informally adopted son Isaac Van Bibber. But the board, after first confirming the grant, changed its mind and awarded it to the first occupant. Daniel Morgan Boone also lost four hundred arpents. In the Mississippi territory Squire Boone lost four tracts. At Cap Girardeau, Louis Lorimier, Boone's old enemy, also lost his lands, partly no doubt because of his exorbitant claims, one of which was for thirty thousand arpents.

It was not, however, so tragic as it sounds. There was still a good deal of land in the family. The Boones always stood together, and the Boones saved something. Isaac Van Bibber, the adopted son, got four hundred arpents; Daniel Morgan Boone secured six hundred; Squire seven hundred; Flanders Callaway eight hundred. The children had lost hundreds of acres, to be sure, but they had kept hundreds of other acres; and for the most part the land they lost was simply land that they had not needed enough even to cultivate. Missouri might turn out to be "a great speck" even yet.

The United States had given its board of land commissioners no discretion. Land claimants had to show that they were making use of their lands, not merely speculating. Other settlers proved "cultivation," "possession, inhabitation and cultivation," or at least possession prior to survey. Boone had done none of these things. His children had taken more land than they needed, wherever they could get a grant, however; and even though they lost some of it, there was plenty left. No great hardship had been wrought to Daniel himself. Though his land formally reverted to the Federal Government, no one else had the effrontery to claim it.

Moreover, the situation was too grotesque to be accepted. The one man who had done most to open up new lands was now without a square inch of his own, while others had plenty. The injustice of it impressed people.

Daniel Boone had powerful friends, of whom the most devoted was Judge John Coburn, formerly of Kentucky. He had at one time been a land commissioner himself. As a judge he had met Daniel Boone and esteemed him. Not only did Coburn know the law; he knew how to handle Congressmen. Coburn made up his mind Daniel Boone should have his land again.

He apparently investigated and learned ahead of time that the land board's decision would be unfavorable. He got ready for the next step at once. The decision is officially dated December 1, 1809; but on October 5 Daniel Boone is already writing to Coburn about a "survivate" for Squire and adds: "I Shall Say Nothing about our petistion but Leve it all to your Self." It sounds as if his petitions to the Kentucky Legislature and to Congress were already being prepared and copies circulated for his friends' signatures.

Boone lived quietly on in Missouri, hunting and trapping while his seventies ran toward his eighties, and Coburn struggled with the legislators back East. There seems to have been no real difficulty, except the usual delay in maneuvering a private bill through a Congress which had the War of 1812 on its hands.

The land commission had not reached Missouri for some

time after the purchase. When it did, there were thousands of cases to hear and consider. Testimony was taken in Daniel Boone's claim on February 13, 1806, but it was nearly four years before an official opinion was rendered.

The Kentucky Legislature—which had, of course, no jurisdiction, since Boone's lands were now in Federal territory—did what it could by adopting a resolution urging the two Kentucky Senators "to make use of their exertions to procure a grant of land in said territory, to said Boone, either the ten thousand acres [actually arpents] to which he appears to have an equitable claim . . . or to such quantity, in such place, as shall be deemed most advisable by way of donation."

"Taking into view the many eminent services rendered by Colonel Boone in exploring and settling the western country, from which great advantages have resulted, not only to this state, but to his country in general," the resolution deplored "that, from circumstances over which he had no control, he is now reduced to poverty, not having, so far as appears, an acre of land out of the vast territory he has been a great instrument in peopling."

The legislature thought it was "as unjust as it is impolitic, that useful enterprise and eminent service should go unrewarded by a government where merit confers the only distinction."

Boone's own petition to Congress is an extremely astute document which plainly shows the guiding hand of Coburn or some equally practical attorney. It makes neither claims nor complaints. It simply states the hard facts and then throws the petitioner upon his countrymen's sense of justice.

The Eleventh Congress received a report upon the petition from Colonel Return Jonathan Meigs. Boone was in friendly hands at last. The colonel with the queer name had commanded in St. Charles County after the Louisiana Purchase, from 1804 to 1806. He knew all about Colonel Boone, he was now in Congress, and he meant to see justice done.

The Committee on Public Lands rendered another report in Boone's favor to the Thirteenth Congress, December 24, 1813. Except for his failure to cultivate, they said, "the claim of the petitioner was good in every other respect." They were even inclined to think that his appointment as syndic really had exempted him from the necessity of cultivating. In that case, he had "a good, equitable claim against the Government." For, they argued, "it is known that the Spanish officers frequently received exemptions from this condition as a matter of favor or right; and, as the petitioner was induced to omit this settlement and cultivation, by the suggestion of the said Delassus, *that it was unnecessary,* his claim ought not, on that account, to be rendered invalid. It also appears to the committee, that the petitioner is in his old age, and has, in early life, rendered to his country arduous and useful services; and ought not, therefore, to be deprived of this remaining resource by a rigorous execution of a provision of our statute."

That report really settled the matter. Daniel would probably have received all of his ten thousand arpents, but fate had a last little irony up her sleeve. Two of his sons had been careful to send a memorandum with the petition, emphasizing his claim to the ten-thousand-acre grant. But Missouri Territory's delegate to Congress officiously remarked at the last moment that all Boone really wanted was just his original thousand arpents. Supposing that the delegate—who though he did not have a vote was the official representative of the Territory—knew what he was talking about and that they were carrying out Boone's own wishes, the sponsors of the act altered it to provide for the smaller tract only. They thus provided merely "that Daniel Boone be, and he is hereby, confirmed in his title to one thousand arpents of land, claimed by him by virtue of a concession made to him under the Spanish government."

The bill went through the house January 4, 1814, and through the Senate February 8, 1814. President Madison signed it two days later, and the recorder in far-off Missouri promptly entered the title, "by special act of Congress, February 10, 1814." The law had a final fling at Boone, however. Under "Acts of ownership," the entry reads: "nil." It didn't matter any longer, but they put it in anyway.

Out in Missouri, old Daniel furiously protested that he would rather have no land at all. He wanted his ten thousand arpents. He even threatened to reject outright the gift of only one thousand. Fortunately Congress had adjourned, and before it reassembled he had time to cool off and recover his usual equanimity.

Securing the land didn't help much at that. Two or three Kentuckians who had read in the papers about the grant to Boone hurried out to Missouri. They wanted to be first with their claims. Wearily, the old man set to work to settle these demands. He sold the whole thousand arpents in May, 1815, and most of the funds thus raised must have gone to satisfy the creditors.

Last of all came another man with a claim that was too much even for the patience of Daniel Boone. Years before, in entire good faith and simply out of kindness, he had given a tract of Kentucky land to an orphan girl. Like so many of his other claims, it turned out to be worthless. Her husband arrived just after the other claimants. He wanted Boone to replace the gift land with money, after all these years. By that time Boone probably had no money left, or at least very little. It was too much.

"You have come a great distance to suck a bull," said Daniel, inelegantly. "And I reckon you will have to go home dry."

It is usually said that Boone had nothing left after these last claims were satisfied, and, in a relative's words, that he died "not owning as Much Land as would Make him a grave." Happily this was not quite true. On January 20, 1819, Jonathan Bryan and Mary, his wife, deeded to Daniel Boone a tract of three hundred acres, for which he paid them eighteen hundred dollars. It was the last and most successful of his land deals; it made him a landed proprietor for the rest of his life.

So rapidly did the old debts and claims use up the proceeds of Daniel's trapping and land sales that he even made an effort to get money for the two old cannon that he had left on the Wilderness Road in 1779. He heard a rumor that they had been brought to Kentucky for the use of the militia, and he had his son Jesse write from St. Louis requesting payment for them. The cannon, Jesse Boone pointed out, had never belonged to the militia. "They are our own private property a present from Col. Carter of North Carolina to my father." Further, said Jesse, "It is nothing but right that I should be paid for them." There is no reason to suppose that anything ever came of this odd claim.

20. Last Frontier

UP and down, northward and westward, Daniel Boone ranged tirelessly with his traps and his rifle in those last years. The price of beaver pelts was between two and a half and eight or nine dollars apiece at times. An honest man who had left debts behind him in Kentucky could do something in a country like this, where even the taxes were payable in deerskins.

The fur traders at St. Charles gave bad prices. To get better ones meant a trip sixty miles down river to St. Louis. The scattered farmers along the Missouri's banks got used to seeing Boone's huge canoe, with housing built over the cargo in the middle, a sure sign of furs aboard, come down the Missouri every year, the white-haired old trapper in the stern, on his way to sell the proceeds of his winter hunt. Travelers passing his daughter's house could often see the veteran in the yard, playing with otter and beaver that he had caught young and brought home to tame.

He had begun trapping almost as soon as he reached Missouri. A receipt in French, dated March 14, 1801, testifies that Daniel Boone, "saindic de l'établissement de la Femme Osage" had delivered sixty-two beaver skins, two otter skins, and forty-two deerskins. He kept it up when he was past eighty, even though his family and friends opposed any more expeditions. Rebecca, he used to explain, needed little delicacies and "refreshment" like coffee now and then. Trapping was the way to get them. A good winter on the trapline would yield four hundred to eight hundred dollars in furs alone.

There were Indians of course, mostly Osages. The tribe was new to Dan'l, but Injuns were Injuns, and he felt entirely capable of coping with them. Were they really quite up to the Shawnee standard of wiliness and terror? There were times when something seemed lacking.

Once a wandering band of Osages caught the old trapper on one of his expeditions and made ready for a little quiet robbery. There was only an old man and a negro boy, the latter of no particular use in the lively few minutes that followed. Boone had been robbed three times by Indians in his early Kentucky years and at least once in Missouri. Another robbery was distinctly too much. He picked up his rifle, and this early share-the-wealth movement came to an abrupt and violent end as the Indians fled.

Somehow, one's sympathy perversely goes out to those astounded Osages who—anticipating nothing but a little harmless fun with an elderly and apparently helpless trapper—suddenly found that they had blundered on the fiercest, most experienced Indian fighter in the world, a man who had been the terror of their red brethren farther east for twenty years! Blackfish or Moluntha or many another Shawnee brave could have warned them how rash it was to trifle with Sheltowee. But Blackfish and Moluntha were only whitening bones now, somewhere along the Ohio.

This little skirmish did not end Daniel Boone's Indian adventures. He paddled his canoe up the Grand River from the Missouri one winter and made a secret camp in a little cove sheltered by high bluffs. He was not being obtrusive that year, for the northwestern Indians were troublesome and he was in or near Iowa, close enough to their country to make safety-first a wise policy. A little hunting provided food for the cold months that lay ahead, when furs would be at their best, and then Boone settled down to his trapping. But the trapline was hardly laid when a fair-sized band of Indian hunters appeared alarmingly close at hand.

The only escape was by canoe down the open river, and that meant certain discovery, even if it was still possible to get through the ice. Boone withdrew to his hidden camp and lay quiet, hoping against hope that no red hunter would stumble on the trapline and suspect a white man's presence. Such a discovery meant a thorough search of the entire country, which he could hardly hope to evade. There were no canebrakes to hide in this time.

That night there was a heavy snowfall. The traps were safe now, and so was Boone. If he strayed from camp, his tracks in the snow would reveal him as they had at the salt-camp in 1778. But that was an elementary error which Daniel Boone took good care not to commit. Why stir? The traps were safe and so was he. He lay snug in his camp, cooking only at night to conceal the smoke, as he and Squire had done in Kentucky thirty-odd years before. Why worry? Plenty of venison to eat, thanks to those hunting trips at the beginning of the season. The furs would be safe enough, frozen in the traps. Stay quiet and be safe.

It was all exhilaratingly like earlier days. Old, was he? He'd show them redskins—or rather, he would show them not a trace. A pity, too—they would never know how badly he had fooled them. But the old trapper confessed later "that he never felt so much anxiety in his life for so long a period." The Shawnees had been a good deal closer back in Kentucky, when Kentucky was really wild. He had hidden from them, all alone, for three whole months in the spring of '70. But this time he had had the misfortune to go into winter quarters close to a semi-permanent Indian hunting camp. He lived nearly next-door to the Indians for three whole weeks.

All went well. By the time the snow melted and revealed his traps, the Indians were gone. Daniel placidly went about his business. They would not be back. Indians knew enough to keep away from an area that had been thoroughly hunted.

As the Indians had been quiet during the first few months at Boonesborough, so as the War of 1812 approached there was the same lull before the storm. In Missouri it lasted longer than it had in Kentucky, but at last the British began to stir up the tribes. Tecumseh and his brother the Prophet roused the Indians and brought them down upon the settlements. Alarms were frequent from 1811 to 1815. Missouri escaped the full fury of the storm, which was directed farther east, but there were enough hairbreadth escapes near La Charette to make Daniel Boone feel completely at home. Twice he and Nathan had to race four miles in the dead of night with their families to reach the strong local fort at the home of Daniel Morgan Boone. It was the way the Boones had "forted up" again and again since those early days on the Yadkin.

Daniel Boone himself volunteered as a soldier, but to his disgust was rejected as too old for active service. Only seventy-eight and yet they wouldn't take him! What an army! His sons joined up instead.

Though not by any means up to Kentucky standards it was a savage little frontier war, with some thrilling incidents. Some were amusing as well as thrilling. The blockhouse at Côte sans Dessein, in Callaway County, was desperately defended and saved only by an indecorous expedient which caused a good deal of ribald laughter later on. Time after time the Indians set fire to the fort, until the last drop of water was exhausted. At the next critical moment one of the women brought out a gallon of milk. Again the Indians set the fort on fire—but at this instant a Frenchwoman appeared, carrying "a vessel familiar in all bed-chambers, that contained a fluid more valuable now than gold." The fire was put out, and the Indians retired—though not from modesty.

While both his sons saw action and his grandson James Callaway was killed, Daniel Boone himself was not personally engaged in any very active Indian fighting, though he was out with his rifle and ready for them. But he did come to the rescue of his neighbors after one of the most dreadful raids; and there was an exciting skirmish at the home of his kinsman Jonathan Bryan within sight of the Boone doorstep.

It began with an attack on the neighbors—rather close neighbors, since they lived only fifteen or twenty miles away. One of the very last outlying settlements toward the dangerous West was that of a certain Aleck McKinney, a frequent hunting companion. His position was so exposed that the militia officers kept one of their armed rangers living there constantly, ready to lend a hand in defense.

One May morning, while McKinney was plowing and the militia guard was placidly engaged in shooting squirrels, the dogs became greatly excited, running into the wheat field, barking, and then dashing out again with their hair bristling. McKinney stopped plowing, called the ranger, and searched the field. They found nothing, but McKinney decided that it would be well to prepare for attack and retreated to the farmhouse. Later, a more thorough search revealed the spot where six Indians had lain watching the house.

The wandering raiders coming in from the West had reconnoitered the first settlement they reached; had been disturbed by the dogs; and had gone on to the settlement of Robert Ramsey. They attacked about sunrise. Mrs. Ramsey was milking, with her husband near and several children playing about. The first warning they had was the uneasiness of the cattle, which shook their horns, snuffed, and bellowed. Before the Ramseys could get away the warriors were upon them, rushing out of the woods waving their tomahawks.

Mrs. Ramsey reached the house safely. Her husband, having a wooden leg, was slower and was badly wounded just as he reached the door. But as he fell he reached for the long tin trumpet that was kept to give the alarm, and blew a blast which frightened the Indians, who knew the signal would bring the rangers down on them. Before retreating, they tomahawked three children. A fourth child squatted like a frightened animal in the weeds near a fence and escaped. The son of Jonathan Bryan, Boone's neighbor, had been sent to the Ramsey home on an errand that morning but had just left. Another lad, hunting his father's horses near the Ramsey farm, stumbled on the tracks of the raiders just as the sound of yelling and firing burst out at the farmhouse. He ran off to give the alarm, and by eight o'clock a band of rangers were on the trail. A messenger found the veteran Daniel already out and waiting for Indians, meantime walking quietly back and forth in front of the stockade with his rifle on his shoulder, softly whistling to himself after his usual habit. It was exactly the way he had waited for Indians outside Boonesborough in '78.

The old man was not needed for the pursuit, but the Ramsey family were in dire need of his rough-and-ready medical skill. An eye-witness describes the scene at the Ramseys' that morning: two children lying on the floor, blood and brains oozing as they struggled for breath; a third child with only a fighting chance for life; Mrs. Ramsey groaning in agony in premature delivery in another room; her husband lying on a bed while Boone composedly probed for the bullet, which had passed through the groin and come up close to the surface. "The old pioneer was quiet and unexcited, as usual, but his lips were compressed and a fire gleamed in his eyes."

Exaggerated reports spread of a band of eight hundred to a thousand Indians, and Flanders Callaway decided to abandon his farm, the result being the total loss of Boone's second and only authentic biography. Urged by his friends, he had for some time been writing or dictating his own narrative in his own inimitable style. His manuscript, with various other articles, was placed in a canoe and taken down river toward Boone's fort, while Daniel himself traveled overland. The canoe struck a snag and capsized. Callaway barely escaped with his life. His cargo was lost. Boone found the labor of writing so tedious that he never tried again, though he did dictate some reminiscences to members of his family. He hoped to make a little money by publishing these, but never finished; and after his death the manuscripts were lost.

Though the fort at La Charette was not itself attacked, there was a savage though fruitless raid on the home of Jonathan Bryan. After the attack on the Ramseys, most of the settlers were drawn off in pursuit. The women and children were left almost unprotected. No one supposed that the Indians would strike twice in the same place. The next day, however, Mrs. Jonathan Bryan and her negro woman were startled by the screams of a negro boy. They looked up to see a warrior who had climbed over the fence into the yard and was running toward them, tomahawk in hand. They got to the house in safety, mainly because the Indian was afraid to use his rifle for fear of alarming the Boones not far away. He was so close behind the fleeing women, however, that before they could slam the door shut, he was halfway through. The heavy door caught the luckless redskin with his body outside and his head and right arm within the cabin. While Mrs. Bryan held the door shut with all her might, the negress pulled the tomahawk out of the warrior's hand and brained him.

At that moment the negro boy screamed again. The women

looked out to see another Indian only a few feet from the house. Mrs. Bryan snatched the still-loaded rifle of the dead warrior and shot his comrade. The bodies were buried near a sandstone boulder in the "horse lot" behind the house. The Bryan family ever afterward spoke of the dead warriors with a curious gentleness as "strangers who died while traveling that way."

No one knows just how far Daniel Boone wandered in these last years, both before the War of 1812 and after. He always liked to see the country—it was a taste he had indulged even in his Kentucky days—and now he had very little else to do. In Missouri he is said rarely to have trapped the same grounds two winters in succession. Ordinarily he did not travel far beyond the western boundary of modern Missouri, but he got into Kansas and also to the headwaters of the Arkansas River.

Officers at Fort Osage, near modern Kansas City, were astonished to see him plodding in when he was eighty-two. He wore "the dress of the roughest, poorest hunter." One of them wrote home to the papers:

> We have been honored by a visit from col. BOONE, the first settler of Kentucky; he lately spent two weeks with us. . . . The colonel cannot live without being in the woods. He goes a hunting twice a year to the remotest wilderness he can reach; and hires a man to go with him, whom he binds in written articles to take care of him, and bring him home, dead or alive. He left this for the River Platt, some distance above.

The old man had heard tales of Salt Lake, perhaps from Kit Carson, who is said to have been a kinsman of the Boones. He was busily planning an expedition these wonders to behold.

"I intend by next autumn," he announced, ". . . to take two or three whites and a party of Osage Indians, and visit the salt mountains. lakes and ponds, and see the natural curiosities of the country along the [Rocky] mountains. The salt-mountain is but 5 or 600 miles west of this place." With all his romantic wanderings, Dan'l always had an eye to business. He may have suspected that there was an honest living to be made out of a land where salt was plentiful. From his early Kentucky days he still remembered how valuable salt could be, and how perilous it had once been to make. He discovered a number of salt springs in Missouri, some of which were worked for decades afterward. His sons set up a salt works at Boone's Lick, where they did a business large enough to supply salt to far-away New Orleans.

There is a story, plausible enough, that he reached the Yellowstone—wild, grand, innocent of tourists—and for a season or two trapped there, along the Rockies. If he really did carry out his intention to explore five or six hundred miles westward, he must have followed the River Platte, which would take him almost to the Yellowstone country. He had announced his intention of going to "the mountains," and Dan'l had a way of seeing what he went out to see. Where other Missouri trappers were already going, Daniel Boone was not likely to be far behind. Men who knew Boone told their descendants they had made the journey with him.

Threatened by Indians on one of these trips, the colonel showed his companions his favorite Kentucky trick of lying outside his own camp, ready to waylay possible assailants. At least once he was in danger from Indians as the boats came down the Platte or the Missouri. He escaped by pretending to camp and then slipping away when a thunderstorm came up during the night.

Death might come any time, now. A man couldn't live forever, though a tough old pioneer could come as near it as anybody. But no redskin was going to collect the scalp that Daniel had borne triumphantly against all the wiles of Girty, McKee, Caldwell, DeQuindre, Blackfish, Moluntha, Saucy Jack, Captain Will, and Captain Johnny!

The wild young people of 1818 indulged in a few gibes, not all in the best of taste, at the legendary man's expense. As Kentucky had filled with settlers before, so now Missouri, too, was filling up. "Old Col. Boone," observed a writer in *Niles's Register,* might yet "be driven to the Rocky Mountains, and even there be disturbed in 8 or 10 years, if he lives so long."

His love of solitude had become an American proverb, almost a part of folklore. Boone, said one traveler, was "a recluse by choice, and trains up his sons in the same path." After his death the story kept up. In Europe my lord Byron, elegantly amused, wrote some verses about it:

> 'Tis true he shrank from men even of his nation,
> When they built up unto his darling trees,—
> He moved some hundred miles off, for a station
> Where there were fewer houses and more ease.

"The late celebrated Colonel Boone," said another traveler, "always wished to live remote from society." Washington Irving remarked that Boone "kept always in the advance of civilization and on the borders of the wilderness, still leading a hunter's life."

The old man was mildly annoyed by the things they said about him. He told a visitor that "nothing embitters my old age but the circulation of the absurd and ridiculous stories that I retire as civilization advances, that I shun the white man and seek the Indians." And he added: "You know all this to be false."

False or exaggerated, perhaps, but really Dan'l's own fault. He had always been fond of that little joke about elbow-room and being crowded. He had made it even on the Yadkin. "I think it time to remove," he once remarked, "when I can no longer fall a tree for fuel so that its top will lie within a few yards of my cabin." One day not long before he left Kentucky, a new settler came by with his son. Boone asked where he was living. It was, said the traveler, about seventy miles away. Dan'l turned to Rebecca:

"Old woman, we must move they are crowding us."

Later on he indulged in the same jest on the wharf at Cincinnati. Arriving in Missouri, he still retailed the good old joke with gusto, and then was much annoyed when people thought him misanthropic. Again asked why he had left Kentucky, he replied: "They crowded me too much, I would not stand it & wanted to go on where I could not be crowded so much by neighbors;—I am too much crowded now where I live in Missouri." Except for the Bryans, his nearest neighbor at the moment was fifteen or twenty miles distant.

Is it any wonder people began to believe him?

He also resented *The Mountain Muse,* a would-be epic treatment of his Kentucky adventures by one of his wife's relatives. The tale was epic, but the verse was not. Daniel, discussing the author with a visitor, emphatically regretted "that he could not sue him for slander." Such productions, he added, "ought to be left till the person was put in the ground."

But no matter how much he resented this sort of thing, the old pioneer was delighted with the alleged autobiography which appeared in 1784. John Filson, a backwoods school teacher, had secured a good deal of information from interviews with him. He wrote this out in the first person, as if it were Boone's own work. Comparison of Filson's orotund, pseudo-Johnsonian style with the blunt, simple, and vigorous language of Dan'l's illiterate but salty letters and official reports reveals the pious fraud at once.

Boone, however, had no objection to ghost-writing. He was

enchanted. Like other backwoods heroes, he took an innocent joy in being written up—in such elaborate language, too. Why, the thing was literature, real book language, nearly as good as *Gulliver's Travels,* which he had carried in the wilderness.

It was published as an appendix to Filson's book *Kentucke* and Boone joined with Levi Todd and James Harrod in an endorsement quite in the modern tone:

> WE the Subſcribers, inhabitants of Kentucke, and well acquainted with the country from its firſt ſettlement, at the requeſt of the author of this book, and map, have carefully reviſed them, and recommend them to the public, as exceeding good performances, containing as accurate a deſcription of our country as we think can poſſibly be given; much preferable to any in our knowledge extant; and think it will be of great utility to the publick. Witneſs our hands this 12th day of May, Anno Domini 1784,
>
> DANIEL BOON,
> LEVI TODD,
> JAMES HARROD

Boone even commended the biography's accuracy to a chance visitor at his Missouri retreat and talked as if he had really written it. He liked to hear it read aloud.

"All true! Every word true!" he would exclaim delightedly. "Not a lie in it!"

As a matter of fact, there are a good many lies in it. Filson mixes up dates badly, represents Boone's hasty estimates of Indian forces as if they were exact calculations, and blunders in describing incidents. His errors can be shown easily enough from contemporary documents and from the reminiscences of contemporaries. But at least, republished in England and translated on the Continent, Filson's *Kentucke* spread the fame of Daniel Boone far and wide in America and abroad.

Despite inaccuracies, Boone was more fortunate in his biographer than was his old friend Simon Kenton. The early exponent of "novelized biography" who wrote up Kenton made the fatal mistake of inventing dialogue. He caused the fiery Simon to reply to a question by his Shawnee captors with a respectful "No, sir." Simon was infuriated. He might have been a prisoner, but "I never said *'sir'* to an Ingin in my life; I scarcely ever say it to a white man." The unfortunate quotation always roused the old man's ire.

Simon had a temper. Once he tripped over a wagon tongue. Someone laughed. Simon scrambled to his feet, raised his rifle, and pulled the trigger. The lock clicked harmlessly. His fall had knocked the priming out of the pan. In an instant Simon had recovered himself and apologized, but for that one savage moment he had meant murder. These literary fellows! Just as well the inexact biographer was not about at such a moment, though apparently Kenton liked to hear his own biography read aloud as much as Daniel Boone did.

Daniel Boone had become a kind of patriarch, not merely to Missouri but to the whole United States. His name was known abroad, and traveling foreigners wanted to know all about him. Adlard Welby, a visiting Englishman, inquired after him as he journeyed: "From another party which passed, I learned that the well-known Colonel Boon is still alive in the Missourie country; though the journals laterly gave a circumstantial account of his death."

Welby had read the false and famous story which spread through the country about 1818 and was copied in one newspaper after another. The old hunter had been found dead at a deer lick. He was kneeling by a stump, his cocked rifle resting in his hands across it, in the very act of firing. Boone smiled tolerantly when they told him the story. He had been reported dead so often that the novelty of the thing had quite worn off. Besides, as he remarked, the thing was impossible. His eyes were not keen enough for hunting now. Even with white paper on the sights, he was no longer the infallible marksman of the old days. No more hunting. A man could still trap, though.

Voyagers to the Far West passed up the Missouri, bound for remote lands, the other rim of the continent, which Boone would never see. Lewis and Clark went by on their way to Oregon in May of 1804. In July of 1806 came Zebulon M. Pike and his explorers, working their way up the Missouri to explore the Far West and putting in at La Charette "at a little after the dusk of the evening," meeting there the expedition's medical officer, Indians, and interpreter.

In April of 1811, John Bradbury, member of a scientific expedition, was so excited when the old pioneer was pointed out to him that he leaped ashore, preferring to overtake his boat on foot rather than miss a chance of talking to Daniel Boone:

> On leaving Charette, Mr. Hunt pointed out to me an old man standing on the bank, who, he informed me, was Daniel Boone, the discoverer of Kentucky. As I had a letter to him, from his nephew Colonel Israel Grant, I went ashore to speak to him, and requested that the boat might go on, as I intended to walk until evening.

The conversation seems to have lacked brilliance. The colonel told him that he was eighty-four years old; that "he had spent a considerable portion of his time alone in the backwoods [which was not exactly news], and had lately returned from his spring hunt with nearly sixty beaver skins." Bradbury trudged off after his boat feeling well repaid.

After about a decade in Missouri, Boone's bitterness toward Kentucky had slowly faded, and he made at least two trips back. At first, however, he cherished his resentment and not even the offer of support for life could tempt him back. Not many years after he reached Missouri, a letter had come from the oddly named Green Clay, a prominent Kentuckian, asking him to return as witness in a land suit. Clay was prodigal in his offers:

> You & your old lady (who I hope is well) are both old & in a new country where there will of course be many hardships to encounter & could you believe that you are able to travel back to Kentucky, & will come & shew the lines, or the corners, or one or two corners & lines of Jacob's two claims, or either of them, I will provide for the support of yourself and your lady all your lives afterwards: and a handsome legacy for to leave to your children I will either let you have negroes, or stock, or cash, whichever will be your choice to accept, & which you may think will be agreeable to you two. . . . I know you were very ill treated by many persons for whom you did business, & I also know the great difficulties you labored under, & the great distress you suffered by doing business for people who gave you no thanks for your trouble—nor even paid you your just due. These people ought to suffer. I have but a small part in these two tracts of land, & I would willingly divide my interest with you, to come at my rights,

Boone replied that he preferred laying his head on the block to "stepping" his foot on Kentucky soil again. The lawsuit had to get on without him.

He seems, however, to have visited Kentucky about 1810, while on a visit to his brother Squire, then living on the Indiana shore of the Ohio River. It was probably on this trip that Boone met Audubon, a ne'er-do-well, a very unsuccessful frontier store-keeper, a shiftless creature who was always in the woods drawing pictures of birds when he should have been making a success of life. It was obvious that the fellow could come to no good end. But he and the old colonel took a fancy to each other and had a famous ramble together. Old as he was, Dan'l took his new friend out and demonstrated "barking off squirrels," which Audubon thought "delightful sport."

> We walked out together, and followed the rocky margins of the Kentucky River [he wrote] until we reached a piece of flat land thickly covered with black walnuts, oaks and hickories. As the general mast was a good one that year, squirrels were seen gambolling on every tree around us. My companion, a stout, hale, and athletic man, dressed in a homespun hunting-shirt, bare-legged and moccasined, carried a long and heavy rifle, which, as he was loading it, he said had proved efficient in all his former undertakings, and which he hoped would not fail on this occasion, as he felt proud to show me his skill. The gun was wiped, the powder measured, the ball patched with a six-hundred-thread linen, and the charge sent home with a hickory rod. We moved not a step from the place, for the squirrels were so numerous that it was unnecessary to go after them. Boon pointed to one of these animals which had observed us, and was crouched on a branch about fifty paces distant, and bade me mark well the spot where the ball should hit. He raised his piece gradually, until the *bead* (that being the name given by the Kentuckians to the *sight*) of the barrel was brought to a line with the spot which he intended to hit. The whip-like report resounded through the woods and along the hills in repeated echoes. Judge of my surprise, when I perceived that the ball had hit the piece of bark immediately beneath the squirrel, and shivered it into splinters, the concussion produced by which had killed the animal and sent it whirling through the air, as if it had been blown up by the explosion of a powder magazine. Boon kept up his firing, and before many hours had elapsed, we had procured as many squirrels as we wished; for you must know, that to load a rifle requires only a moment, and that if it is wiped once after each shot, it will do duty for hours.

Boone also told Audubon the story of a fourth Indian captivity not otherwise recorded. At least, the account which Audubon gives does not agree with the known accounts of the two times when Captain Will took Boone prisoner or the captivity in Blackfish's camp:

Daniel Boon, or, as he was usually called in the Western Country, Colonel Boon, happened to spend a night with me under the same roof, more than twenty years ago. We had returned from a shooting excursion, in the course of which his extraordinary skill in the management of the rifle had been fully displayed. On retiring to the room appropriated to that remarkable individual and myself for the night, I felt anxious to know more of his exploits and adventures than I did, and accordingly took the liberty of proposing numerous questions to him. The stature and general appearance of this wanderer of the western forests approached the gigantic. His chest was broad and prominent; his muscular powers displayed themselves in every limb; his countenance gave indication of his great courage, enterprise and perseverance; and when he spoke, the very motion of his lips brought the impression that whatever he uttered could not be otherwise than strictly true. I undressed, whilst he merely took off his hunting shirt, and arranged a few folds of blankets on the floor, choosing rather to lie there, as he observed, than on the softest bed. When we had both disposed of ourselves, each after his own fashion, he related to me the following account of his powers of memory, which I lay before you, kind reader, in his own words, hoping that the simplicity of his style may prove interesting to you.

"I was once," said he, "on a hunting expedition on the banks of the Green River, when the lower parts of this State (Kentucky) were still in the hands of nature, and none but the sons of the soil were looked upon as its lawful proprietors. We Virginians had for some time been waging a war of intrusion upon them, and I, amongst the rest, rambled through the woods in pursuit of their race, as I now would follow the tracks of any ravenous animal. The Indians outwitted me one dark night, and I was as unexpectedly as suddenly made a prisoner by them. The trick had been managed with great skill; for no sooner had I extinguished the fire of my camp, and laid me down to rest, in full security, as I thought, than I felt myself seized by an indistinguishable number of hands, and was immediately pinioned, as if about to be led to the scaffold for execution. To have attempted to be refractory, would have proved useless and dangerous to my life; and I suffered myself to be removed from my camp to theirs, a few miles distant, without uttering even a word of complaint. You are aware, I dare say, that to act in this manner was the best policy, as you understand that by so doing, I proved to the Indians at once, that I was born and bred as fearless of death as any of themselves.

"When we reached the camp, great rejoicings were exhibited. Two squaws and a few papooses appeared particularly delighted at the sight of me, and I was assured, by very unequivocal gestures and words, that, on the morrow, the mortal enemy of the Red-skins would cease to live. I never opened my lips, but was busy contriving some scheme which might enable me to give the rascals the slip before dawn. The women immediately fell a searching about my hunting-shirt for whatever they might think valuable, and, fortunately for me, soon found my flask filled with *monongahela* (that is, reader, strong whisky). A terrific grin was exhibited on their murderous countenances, while my heart throbbed with joy at the anticipation of their intoxication. The crew immediately began to beat their bellies and sing, as they passed the bottle from mouth to mouth. How often did I wish the flask ten times its size, and filled with aqua-fortis! I observed that the squaws drank more freely than the warriors, and again my spirits were about to be depressed, when the report of a gun was heard at a distance. The Indians all jumped on their feet. The singing and drinking were both brought to a stand, and I saw, with inexpressible joy, the men walk off to some distance and talk to the squaws. I knew that they were consulting about me, and I foresaw that in a few moments the warriors would go to discover the cause of the gun having been fired so near their camp. I expected that the squaws would be left to guard me. Well, Sir, it was just so. They returned; the men took up their guns, and walked away. The squaws sat down again, and in less than five minutes had my bottle up to their dirty mouths, gurgling down their throats the remains of the whisky.

"With what pleasure did I see them becoming more and more drunk, until the liquor took such hold of them that it was quite impossible for these women to be of any service. They tumbled down, rolled about, and began to snore: when I, having no other chance of freeing myself from the cords that fastened me, rolled over and over towards the fire, and, after a short time, burned them asunder. I rose to my feet, stretched my stiffened sinews, snatched up my rifle, and, for once in my life, spared that of Indians. I now recollect how desirous I once or twice felt to lay open the skulls of the wretches with my tomahawk; but when I again thought upon killing beings unprepared and unable to defend themselves, it looked like murder without need, and I gave up the idea.

"But, Sir, I felt determined to mark the spot, and walking to a thrifty ash sapling, I cut out of it three large chips, and ran off. I soon reached the river, soon crossed it, and threw myself deep into the cane-brakes, imitating the tracks of an Indian with my feet, so that no chance might be left for those from whom I had escaped to overtake me.

"It is now nearly twenty years since this happened, and more than five since I left the Whites' settlements, which I might probably never have visited again, had I not been called on as a witness in a law-suit that was pending in Kentucky, and which I really believe would never have been settled, had I not come forward, and established the beginning of a certain boundary line. This is the story, Sir.

"Mr —— moved from Old Virginia into Kentucky, and having a large tract granted to him in the new State, laid claim to a certain parcel of land adjoining Green River, and as chance would have it, took for one of his corners the very Ash tree on which I had made my mark, and finished his survey of some thousands of acres, beginning, as it is expressed in the deed, 'at an Ash marked by three distinct notches of the tomahawk of a white man.'

"The tree had grown much, and the bark had covered the marks; but somehow or other, Mr —— heard from someone all that I have already said to you, and thinking that I might remember the spot alluded to in the deed, but which was no longer discoverable, wrote for me to come and try at least to find the place or the tree. His letter mentioned that all my expenses should be paid, and not caring much about . . . going back to Kentucky, I started and met Mr ——. After some conversation, the affair with the Indians came to my recollection. I considered for a while, and began to think that after all I could find the very spot, as well as the tree, if it was yet standing.

"Mr —— and I mounted our horses, and off we went to the Green River Bottoms. After some difficulties, for you must be aware, Sir, that great changes have taken place in those woods, I found at last the spot where I had crossed the river, and waiting for the moon to rise, made for the course in which I thought the Ash tree grew. On approaching the place, I felt as if the Indians were there still, and as if I was still a prisoner among them. Mr —— and I camped near what I conceived the spot, and waited until the return of day.

"At the rising of the sun, I was on foot, and after a good deal of musing, thought that an Ash tree then in sight must be the very one on which I had made my mark. I felt as if there could be no doubt of it, and mentioned my thought to Mr ——. 'Well, Colonel Boon,' said he, 'if you think so, I hope it may prove true, but we must have some witnesses; do you stay here about, and I will go and bring some of the settlers whom I know.' I agreed. Mr —— trotted off, and I, to pass the time, rambled about to see if a deer was still living in the land. But ah! Sir, what a wonderful difference thirty years makes in the country! Why, at the time when I was caught by the Indians, you would not have walked out in any direction for more than a mile without shooting a buck or a bear. There were then thousands of buffaloes on the hills in Kentucky; the land looked as if it never would become poor; and to hunt in those days was a pleasure indeed. But when I was left to myself on the banks of Green River, I dare say for the last time in my life, a few *signs* only of deer were to be seen, and, as to a deer itself, I saw none.

"Mr —— returned, accompanied by three gentlemen. They looked upon me as if I had been WASHINGTON himself, and walked to the Ash tree, which I now called my own, as if in quest of a long lost treasure. I took an axe from one of them, and cut a few chips off the bark. Still no signs were to be seen.

So I cut again until I thought it was time to be cautious, and I scraped and worked away with my butcher knife, until I *did* come to where my tomahawk had left an impression in the wood. We now went regularly to work, and scraped at the tree with care, until three hacks as plain as any three notches ever were, could be seen. Mr —— and the other gentlemen were astonished, and, I must allow, I was as much surprised as pleased myself. I made affidavit of this remarkable occurrence in presence of these gentlemen. Mr —— gained his cause. I left Green River for ever, and came to where we now are; and, Sir, I wish you a good night."

The famous story of another whisky bottle also probably belongs to this period. Boone is said to have returned to Kentucky to settle a land dispute, a service which he had resolutely refused to perform during his earlier years in Missouri. The case turned upon the identity of a particular tree. Boone testified that he had hidden an empty whisky bottle there. A little chopping soon revealed it, now surrounded by the growth of wood.

Probably at some time between his two trips, Daniel is said to have lent a hand in the construction of the stone house, the finest in Missouri, which his son Nathan built. It is said to have taken eight years to complete, the plaster being set aside one whole winter to "ripen," while the blue limestone was taken out of a hillside on the farm and painfully cut into blocks. There were three rooms downstairs (in one of which Daniel Boone was to die) and four rooms upstairs, with wide halls between. The house still stands. The thick beams show marks of the adze, and the woodwork is fitted together with walnut pegs. The seven carved mantelpieces are said to be the work of Daniel Boone himself; and some years ago when an earlier owner tore out some of the plaster—because he thought it a useful medicine for sick cows!—fine handmade laths of pine were revealed. Boone is said to have built his own little cabin a short distance from the big house.

There were innumerable grandchildren by this time, who, as children always did, adored the old man. Never was there a grandfather with such tales to tell—always in the low, gentle voice typical of the woodsman who has spent his life moving silently in the forests. One little girl remembered afterward: "The pleased attentions of such a man irresistibly won the confidence and love of a child, and I am not conscious of feeling a greater degree of safety here in my parlor than I did sixty years ago when borne on the shoulders of Boone over the hills, or than when he was paddling me in a canoe, or on logs across the Missouri. Of the Boones neither father nor son [Daniel Morgan Boone] were ever rude or boisterous, but both were mild, gentle and pleasing." Next to the children, the old man probably got most amusement out of the otter and beaver cubs he brought home to tame.

He made another trip in 1817. Judge Montgomery of Greenupsburg, Kentucky, wrote to Missouri inviting the old man to visit him while he was selling his property and preparing to move west. Daniel arrived in July, 1817, coming so quietly that practically no one noticed him. Much had been forgotten and forgiven during the intervening years. The word went round that Daniel Boone was back. Everyone wanted to see him.

During his flatboat journey to Missouri the old lion paused at Maysville where he had once kept store. They gave a dinner for him, and afterward he went—with a rather wry face—to a reception in his honor. Gray old pioneers like himself, men who had fought by his side, gathered to do him honor; and with them came youngsters eager to see the veteran. Old Dan'l spun them a few yarns of the old days. It was all very flattering, but the guest of honor muttered to a young man near him: "I dislike to be in a crowd where I have to receive so much attention." Eventually he slipped away. Farther down river, at Cincinnati, he met Simon Kenton for the last time. That was a meeting!

Boone paid off, probably on this trip, every creditor who still had a claim against him. It was a proud moment. The old man's bookkeeping was rather shaky, though some of his government accounts are models of precision. He was not sure exactly what his obligations were. With characteristic simplicity and directness, he inquired of each man what he owed him, and paid the sum that each man said was due. He had, after all, been bred a Quaker. According to tradition, he had only half a dollar left when he reached Missouri again.

John M. Peck, the itinerant parson, who knew many of the Boone family, and who saw and talked with Daniel himself many times, records the old trapper's comment on his return:

> Now I am ready and willing to die. I am relieved from a burden that has long oppressed me. I have paid all my debts, and no one will say, when I am gone, "Boone was a dishonest man." I am perfectly willing to die.

It is a pity that all the early biographers, who had a chance to quote directly, preferred to elaborate the old man's simple utterances into their own dreadful rhetoric. The unctuous tone of the cleric is apparent enough here. Old Daniel's observations, even the pious ones, were livelier than that. But even through the edifying haze cast, with the best of intentions, by the Reverend John M. Peck, one glimpses plain, old-fashioned, uncommon honesty, grim, uncompromising, resolute, up-standing. The Quaker blood again.

Once, on a hunting trip, Boone thought that death had come for him at last. He was camping on the Osage with a pack train, his only companion the negro boy whom he often took along as camp-keeper, to get the fire going, gather wood, skin game, and cook. Daniel laid in winter supplies as usual, and then was taken ill. For days he lay there. It was desperate. Daniel Boone was really ill, this time; a new experience.

But with a stick he could still hobble. He took the scared little black boy to the top of a hill. Always in love with "high, far-seeing places" was Daniel, had been ever since he scrambled up the mountains from the Yadkin to look across into his promised land, or since he had stood on Pilot Knob and looked on a new empire. He instructed the little black camp-keeper. He must wash Boone's body carefully and lay it out decently. He must wrap it in the cleanest blanket. He would be able to drag it to the grave. Boone showed him where. It wasn't far. He must make a shovel for himself, and a hatchet would be a great help in digging. Daniel Boone always had a great head for details.

As for the grave, there must be a post at head and foot—his friends would want to find the place—and poles would have to be laid side by side across it. Wild animals would try to dig. (Did he remember James Boone's grave in 1773? They always covered bodies with logs in the Kentucky woods. Did he remember Israel and the Blue Licks graves?) Also, he remembered, the little slave must blaze the trees to help people find the grave.

When that was over, the black boy must catch the horses, pack up the pelts, and take them home to Femme Osage. Special care of the old rifle and a few messages to friends—all as calmly delivered, the boy said afterward, as any other instructions for the day's work.

It was all needless. Boone got well. The tough old woodsman took a lot of killing. But he did decide that perhaps he had had enough hunting for one winter and came home without his usual stock of peltry.

Boone wanted Christian burial for those old bones. He bought himself a fine coffin of the best black walnut. The wood was not much admired in those days, but Daniel liked it. He insisted on the best work the settlement carpenter could do. Some say he made it himself. To the dismay of his grandchildren, he kept it under his bed or in the cabin loft. A little gruesome, maybe, but Daniel Boone had seen too many men dead in battle or worse to trouble over a macabre touch or two. He used to lie down and try the coffin now and then, to make sure the size was right.

Eventually the old man decided it was a bad fit after all. He had a tendency to get fat as he grew old, though his weight fell off again in the very last years. Life was getting too easy there in the settlement. His relatives conspired to keep him from arduous hunting and trapping. He didn't have to live on parched corn and jerked venison these days, and he had a hopeless partiality for sweet potatoes—starchy food, very bad for a pioneer's figure.

Boone had always been generous anyway. A neighbor died suddenly. He gave his cherished coffin away and had another made. Cherrywood, this time. He kept it about the cabin, too. They used that one eventually, and it turned out not to be a very good coffin after all. When they dug into Daniel Boone's grave a couple of decades later, it had moldered quite away.

Rebecca died at Jemima's house March 18, 1813, while the war with the British was raging. She had just spent a month in camp making maple sugar, and was ill only a week. Most of her seventy-three years, she and Daniel had lived together—except, of course, when Daniel was off adventuring. She had been only a slip of a girl when they were married. A good rifle, a good horse, a good wife. The good wife was gone now. He hadn't much chance to use the rifle these last few years, nor much occasion to ride the good horse.

Daniel picked a place on a mound overlooking the Missouri. It looked a little as if the Indians had built it—there were lots of Indian mounds in that country. Boone told them to lay him there, too, when the time came. He had land of his own now. The United States said so—or would, as soon as they could get the bill through Congress. The United States said it was his, and he had helped to win their independence; they wouldn't take this land away from him.

The sturdy old man was growing old. He had recovered from the sudden illness in his hunting camp, but he had had a number of others. Once a skin disease forced him to rent a house in St. Charles, then a town of about a thousand inhabitants, and submit to medical treatment for about two months. Except for rheumatism, he had enjoyed nearly perfect health for more than seventy years, but he was well over eighty. After all, one cannot hope to escape all the ills that flesh is heir to. His eyesight was failing. Toward the end he even gave up trapping. According to one account, his last hunt was in 1816, when he was eighty-two. According to another, he went hunting with James Boone, a grandson, in the winter following his eighty-third birthday, highly elated to be out again. His later hunting trips had not been very strenuous and he often stayed about camp, preparing skins, while the others stalked game or followed the trapline.

On this particular trip he suffered a great deal from the cold, had to stop and build a fire, and eventually sought shelter in a settler's cabin at Loutre Lick. He was too weak to be moved and word was sent back to Nathan Boone that his father was dying. By the time he reached his father's bedside, however, the old colonel was a great deal stronger. A physician, happening to pass that way at the critical moment, had saved him. He rode home on horseback and severely criticized the coffin that Nathan in his alarm had hastily ordered. It was, he said, a great deal too rough. Probably this dissatisfaction caused him to order a coffin of his own ahead of time, but the exact chronology is far from clear. The incident may have happened just after he had given away his black-walnut coffin.

Old Dan'l's mind was clear as ever. He loved to think back over his lifetime of adventures and to talk of them to visitors. When trappers began to penetrate the Rocky Mountains, whose foothills at least Boone may have seen himself, he was intensely interested in the adventurous plans of younger men. He extolled the joys of trapping, hunting, exploring as a career, urging them on to new exploits, dilating sometimes on the wonderful climate of California. He was amazingly well informed about the Pacific coast, probably from talking with Indians who had been there.

One lad of nineteen or twenty spent the last winter of Boone's life listening to the old man's tales by the fireside. Wild with enthusiasm for such a life, he was soon off to California with Kit Carson. Toward the end, however, these tales were denied to chance arrivals. Boone kept them for his friends, and as his hearing failed, used to take his cane and slip off to avoid strangers. He had had a paralytic stroke in 1818 from which he never fully recovered.

In spite of illness, the old age that closed this stormy and adventurous career was peaceful as a twilight sky.

> That which should accompany old age,
> As honor, love, obedience, troops of friends,

he had in abundance. Eventually he left the settlement of Flanders Callaway and Jemima at La Charette, and though he sometimes visited them, made his permanent home with his son Jesse. Respectful clergymen with biographical ambitions came to listen to his stories as his grandchildren had been listening for years.

Though he could be silent enough in the perilous forests,

Daniel Boone by the fireside at home was a sociable soul, who loved cheerful talk and could spin amazing yarns. "Grandfather was not taciturn by any means, but on the contrary delighted in conversation."

He was never boastful—he didn't have to be: the facts were startling enough. But woe betide the luckless listener who expressed incredulity. A mere suggestion of doubt and the old man froze up. Not another word would he utter until the man who had questioned his tale was gone. People who wanted to hear more stories usually shooed the poor wretch away.

His hair was now completely white, but still so thick and long that a dutiful granddaughter "used to comb and plait his silver locks in his old age." Plaiting the hair had been the old frontier fashion on the Yadkin. New ways might be coming in, but Daniel Boone clung to the old ones.

He scraped powder-horns to translucent thinness, through which the powder was visible, in the style the old woodsmen admired—carved them, cut his name on them, then gave them away. He liked to talk about the hunting he was still going to do. In 1818 a visitor at a granddaughter's cabin found the colonel rather indisposed but exceedingly vivacious. He picked up a piece of glass and commenced scraping a powder-horn, remarking that he would need it for his fall hunt. Soon he laid it aside and forgot about it. The master of the household quietly whispered to the visitor that the old hunter had been working for a long time on the same powder-horn, for a fall hunt that never happened. In the winter of the same year, a visitor found him, dressed in neat homespun, "as interesting a gentleman as I ever conversed with"—still talking about hunting.

To the end of his days Boone loathed the "New Style" modern calendar, and still reckoned the date of his birth in the old way. "I was 84 years old on the 22 day of October last," he told his visitor, "and if I had not over heated myself by running after my horse, a short time Ago when he got loose from me and took A bad cold I now would of been out in the woods A hunting."

These winter hunts remained pretty strenuous almost to the end. Returning from one of them when he must have been nearly seventy-five, he fell through the ice in the Missouri River. But Boone and his sons were all carrying long poles as a precaution against that very accident. The old man scrambled out unaided, shouting to the other two to keep back lest they, too, break through. One of them got a fire going while his father was still in the icy water. They warmed him up and dried him out when he reached shore, none the worse except for a cold.

One of his last visitors—just in time, for the old colonel was getting a bit feeble these days—was Chester Harding, a wandering artist sent by St. Louis admirers to paint his portrait. Missouri was filling up with newcomers who knew little about the old days, and Harding had some trouble finding where Boone lived. The story, as he tells it in the *Egotistigraphy* that he wrote for his family's edification, is hard to improve:

> In June of this year, I made a trip of one hundred miles for the purpose of painting the portrait of old Colonel Daniel Boone. I had much trouble in finding him. He was living, some miles from the main road, in one of the cabins of an old block-house, which was built for the protection of the settlers against the incursions of the Indians. I found that the nearer I got to his dwelling, the less was known of him. When within two miles of his house, I asked a man to tell me where Colonel Boone lived. He said he did not know any such man. "Why, yes, you do," said his wife. "It is that white-headed old man who lives on the bottom, near the river." A good illustration of the proverb, that a prophet is not without honor save in his own country.
>
> I found the object of my search engaged in cooking his

dinner. He was lying in his bunk, near the fire, and had a long strip of venison wound around his ramrod, and was busy turning it before a brisk blaze, and using salt and pepper to season his meat. I at once told him the object of my visit. I found that he hardly knew what I meant. I explained the matter to him and he agreed to sit. He was ninety years old, and rather infirm; his memory of passing events was much impaired, yet he would amuse me every day by his anecdotes of his earlier life. I asked him one day, just after his description of one of his long hunts, if he never got lost, having no compass. "No," he said, "I can't say as ever I was lost, but I was *bewildered* once for three days."

He was much astonished at seeing the likeness. He had a very large progeny; one grand-daughter had eighteen children, all at home near the old man's cabin: *they* were even more astonished at the picture than was the old man himself.

Harding, however, left out the best part of the story. The colonel either could not, or would not, hold his head still. He had had a fever and was still weak. A friend had to stand behind him and hold his head steady while the artist worked.

When the end came, it was quick and merciful. He was taken ill while visiting Flanders Callaway. Attended by a physician who had married one of his granddaughters, he soon felt better, and in spite of warnings insisted on mounting his horse, Old Roan, and riding off to Nathan's house with only a negro as companion. Here he was taken ill again. It was acute indigestion, apparently brought on by too many sweet potatoes. His illness was probably helped along by his adoring grandchildren, who clustered around him bringing too many other delicacies.

In the little room just inside the front door of the new stone house he lay in bed three days. Then he "passed off gently, after a short illness, almost without pain or suffering," Sept. 26, 1820. The Missouri Legislature adjourned, and wore mourning badges for twenty days. In the Happy Hunting Grounds that night, Blackfish and Moluntha grunted, held out their hands, buried their tomahawks, and lit the peace pipe. Sheltowee had joined the tribe at last.

The coffin he had cherished so long was needed now. They laid the old fighting Quaker by his Rebecca on the little knoll looking down to the river through the trees, and left him there in peace on his last frontier.

But not for long. After twenty-five years, there were stirrings in Kentucky. The state he had made wanted its hero back. Missouri consented.

A highly official delegation came to get the bodies of Daniel and Rebecca. The indignant owner of the land where they lay, finding that excavation was in progress, hastily stopped it. Only when he had ascertained the willingness of all the surviving relatives he could interview did he let them go on.

This time the Kentuckians did not take his land away from Daniel Boone. They took his body away from his last bit of land instead, meaning to do him honor. There was more elbow-room, the elbow-room that Dan'l had always craved, out on that silent knoll in Missouri. But no one thought of that. Kentucky brought the old pioneer home—home with his Rebecca. No more separation. No more anxious, solitary years or months in the cabin with the children—and Daniel God knew where.

There was not really much left of Daniel Boone, but Kentucky did the best it could with what it found in the grave. A medical man arranged the bones in proper order in a fine new coffin. They made a cast of his skull.

Kentucky, which had driven him out, received him back with splendor. Nearly every county was represented, and there were a lot more counties in Kentucky now than Daniel Boone had ever heard of. Four white horses drew the hearse and the pall-bearers who followed it were noted pioneers from all parts of the state. There was an orator to celebrate to the crowd in wingèd words and ringing periods the virtues of the solitary silent Daniel, who hated crowds. It was the Honorable John J. Crittenden, a senator, an attorney-general, no less.

There was a "brilliant military procession." The Kentucky militia of Lieutenant-Colonel Boone's day had been more remarkable for straight, fast, and deadly shooting than for brilliant uniforms; but the militia had not been wearing homespun hunting shirts for a good many years now.

The Kentucky militia was burying its Lieutenant-Colonel in the land he found and fought for, and they did the thing in style. The soldiers stood at a rigid present arms. (If anyone ever stood at present arms with a Kentucky rifle, it is not in history.) Their arms were very bright now. Their steel was burnished, their leather was immaculate, their buttons glittered. (It wouldn't have done in the woods, you know; too easy for the Injuns to see you.) The rifles crashed their salute across the grave. (There wasn't much of that sort of thing in old Kaintuck' as Dan'l had known it; though they did fire a salute—a rather ragged one—the day Henderson's party rode into Boonesborough in '75.) The swords flashed. (Dan'l knew something about swords. Hadn't he owned the only one in the whole Kentucky militia? Colonel Todd borrowed it before the fight at the Blue Licks, and lost it in the river—but they got it back in the end.)

Once in his life, once in his death, Lieutenant-Colonel Boone received the military honors due his rank. (The Spaniards had received him formally in St. Louis.) But a Kentucky Colonel in Daniel Boone's day didn't worry much about salutes; he was lucky if he could get his orders obeyed—sometimes.

Then taps. The bugle, thin and piercing sweet. That long-drawn, plaintive call. Gently melancholy but never wholly sad, not even by a new-made grave. The only exquisite thing a soldier hears. (Bugles—yes, De Quindre brought a bugle along when he attacked Boonesborough and tried to fool them with it. It hadn't done him much good, or Blackfish either. But they were good fighting men, them two, that redskin and that Frenchman.)

It was over.

From the Happy Hunting Grounds—where the buffalo never fail, where the deer always come to the lick, where the immortal beaver are strangely incautious about traps, but where there are still a few Indians about, just enough to do a bit of sniping and lend a little zest to existence—from the Paradise where all good hunters go, there was borne on the wings of the west wind a faint, sardonic chuckle.

It is to be feared that the ghost of Dan'l winked at the ghost of Rebecca. Back to Kaintuck' at last, eh?

Well, there was plenty of elbow-room up here.

ACKNOWLEDGMENTS

Acknowledgments

IT IS, alas, impossible to acknowledge all the friendly aid that has been given me in the studies preparatory to this biography. Kentuckians have long been notable for hospitality and for an interest in their own history—an interest which appears in every walk of life. Many a useful bit of information has been provided by men whose names I still do not know, and though such data naturally have to be supported by documents before they can be used, I am none the less grateful for them. A friendly state policeman helped me find the ravine used by the Indian kidnappers who stole Daniel Boone's daughter. Residents on the scene supplied the inscription which had vanished from a tablet. In one county courthouse, the janitor admitted me to the impeccably kept eighteenth-century records with a genial drawl of "He'p yo'se'f, suh." On another occasion, the judge himself did the honors. A busy lawyer made time for me in the midst of business hours. A railroad executive let me browse for a long evening among his Boone notes, manuscripts, and bibliographies, better arranged than those of many a professional scholar. A farmer took time to show a total stranger the pioneer carving on the mantel of his eighteenth-century home and to identify the exact spots where the Indians came raging across the peaceful acres that he now cultivates.

Even an indignant little group at the country store opposite Boonesborough at length magnanimously admitted that perhaps after all it was permissible for a Yankee to write the life of Daniel Boone—at least, a Pennsylvanian Yankee, since Boone also came from Pennsylvania.

Everywhere there was a friendly willingness to help an investigator—no matter how much time he took or how many questions he asked—and an equally friendly interest in his studies, all a refreshing contrast to the attitude one sometimes encounters in the archives of less hospitable lands.

Though one cannot acknowledge so many debts, it is pleasant to be able to set down a few of the greatest. I have had every aid in a number of libraries, especially the Library of Congress, the New York Bar Association, the New York, Boston, Cincinnati, Detroit, Denver, and Lexington (Kentucky) Public Libraries; the Harvard College Library; the Henry E. Huntington Library; and the Columbia, New York, Virginia, North Carolina, Kentucky, Wisconsin, and Chicago University Libraries. The specialized libraries of various historical societies have been equally generous, notably those of the Historical Society of Pennsylvania, the Presbyterian Historical Society, the Kentucky State Historical Society, the Filson Club, the Wisconsin State Historical Society, the State Historical Society of Missouri, at Columbia, the Missouri Historical Society, at St. Louis, the Western Reserve Historical Society, at Cleveland, and the Historical Society of Berks County, Pennsylvania.

Individual librarians have been tireless in locating obscure manuscripts and the rarer printed sources. Among them, I am especially indebted to a group of New York University librarians: Mr. Robert B. Downs, Director of the Libraries; Dr. Theodore F. Jones, Director of the University Heights Library; Mr. Mulford Martin, Librarian of the Commerce Library; Mr. Nelson W. McCombs, Librarian, Mr. Alfred B. Lindsay, Assistant Librarian, and Mr. H. Gambier-Bousfield, Chief of the Readers' Department, of the Washington Square College Library; to Miss Gladys Sanders and Miss Winifred Ver Nooy, of the University of Chicago Library; and to Mr. W. B. Briggs, Mr. R. H. Haynes, and Miss Alice Reynolds, of the Harvard College Library.

A form letter asking for Boone manuscripts, sent to every college and university library in the United States, has invariably met with prompt and courteous attention and has in several cases unearthed new and unsuspected material. Several hundred librarians cheerfully aided in this search and made numerous suggestions.

The keepers of archives in the various state historical societies have submitted to endless questioning with an admirable grace and intelligence. It is a pleasure to return thanks for months of detailed correspondence with Dr. Louise Phelps Kellogg and Miss Annie A. Nunns, of the Wisconsin State Historical Society, whose intimate familiarity with the Draper MSS. and with frontier history has been invaluable. Other specialists who have been generous both of time and knowledge are Dr. Thomas C. Pears, of the Presbyterian Historical Society, Philadelphia; Mr. Julian P. Boyd, of the Historical Society of Pennsylvania; Miss Ludie J. Kinkead, of the Filson Club,

Louisville; Mr. G. Glenn Clift of the Lexington Public Library; Mrs. Jouett Taylor Cannon, of the Kentucky State Historical Society; Miss Nettie H. Beauregard, of the Missouri Historical Society; Dr. Floyd C. Shoemaker, of the State Historical Society of Missouri; and Mrs. Innis C. Davis, State Historian and Archivist of West Virginia.

In Kentucky, Judge Samuel M. Wilson, Mr. C. R. Staples, and Mr. C. Frank Dunn, of Lexington, gave me every possible assistance and free access to the special materials in their possession. Professor Jonathan Truman Dorris, of the Eastern State Teachers College, Richmond, Kentucky, not only guided me to the scene of Twitty's Fort, but also opened to me the hitherto unused MSS. in his possession. Mrs. Mary T. Moore, Librarian of the Kentucky Collection, in the Western State Teachers College at Bowling Green, provided special analytic bibliographies, called my attention to several rare items, and arranged for copying. Professor W. S. Lester, of Kentucky Wesleyan, very kindly sent his collection of photostats to New York for me to use at my leisure. Mr. Charles L. Clift, Circuit Court Clerk of Mason County, Kentucky, was particularly helpful with the records now in his care. Dr. Frank T. McFarland, Professor of Botany in the University of Kentucky, has provided material on canebrakes.

J. Henry Bartlett, Custodian of Records of the Yearly Meeting of the Religious Society of Friends, Philadelphia, S. Irene Eavenson, Secretary of Exeter Meeting, and Miss E. Virginia Walker, of the Friends Historical Library of Swarthmore College, kindly allowed me to use the Friends records in their charge. Miss Elizabeth Madox Roberts, the novelist; Mr. P. M. Hamer, Chief of the Division of Reference, National Archives; Miss Mildred Rex, of the State Historical Society of Colorado; Mr. John Van Male, Director of the Bibliographical Centre for Research, Rocky Mountain Region, of the Denver Public Library; and Dr. Willard Rouse Jillson, of Frankfort, Kentucky, have all been helpful in securing special data.

Mr. M. W. Stirling, Chief of the Bureau of American Ethnology, Smithsonian Institution, has aided me with the various problems raised by Boone's Indian friends and enemies; and Professor C. F. Voegelin, of De Pauw University, one of the few living scholars acquainted with the Shawnee language, has kindly aided with Indian linguistics. Dr. Roy B. Cook, of Charleston, West Virginia, has been of great aid in verifying local documents. Dr. Archibald Henderson has helped me with disputed points in Boone's early life in North Carolina; and his published writings have been unusually valuable. Mr. Horace F. Grimm, State Director of the Historical Records Survey in Missouri, aided by his field worker, Mr. C. A. Pigg, has had church and county records in St. Charles examined for me, and in so doing has uncovered several unknown legal transactions by Daniel Boone and his relatives. Miss Elizabeth B. Parker, State Director of the Historical Records Survey in Virginia, and her field-worker Miss Ruth Sweeney, have done me a similar service with the Daniel Boone records at Christiansburg. Senator C. Hale Sipe, of Freeport, Pennsylvania, helped me locate the Revolutionary cartoon reproduced facing page 164 and now in the possession of Mr. Earle R. Forrest, of the *Washington Reporter,* Washington, Pennsylvania. Mr. Forrest has generously given me permission to include this unique bit of Americana, first printed in his *History of Washington County, Pennsylvania.* The Reverend Father W. B. Sommerhauser, S.J., rector of St. Charles Borromeo, St. Charles, Missouri, supplied the record of Daniel Morgan Boone's wedding from the parish archives. Miss Marcia Williams, of O'Fallon, Missouri, went to considerable pains to secure local information for me. Dr. Francis B. Haas, President of the State Teachers College at Bloomsburg, Pennsylvania, and County Superintendent A. F. Kemp, of Berks County, provided source material on education in Colonial Pennsylvania. Miss Ruth Granniss, Librarian of the Grolier Club, has been of material aid in locating obscure Boone manuscripts. Mr. Jack Dalton, of the University of Virginia Library, and Mr. Virginius Dabney, of the Richmond *Times-Dispatch,* have cheerfully answered a series of questions on Tarleton's raid.

My sister, Mrs. F. A. Nason, patiently motored me about from one ancient Kentucky settlement to another, and Mr. Kent Smith, of Cleveland, devoted the better part of a week to making microfilms of newspapers, maps, documents, and historic sites. My wife has helped ceaselessly in bibliographical matters, has typed more reams of paper than I care to think about, and has added to her benefactions by assisting with the index.

BIBLIOGRAPHY AND NOTES

Bibliographical Essay

SINCE a bibliographical guide to the printed accounts of Daniel Boone's life and adventures already exists in Mr. William Harvey Miner's "Contributions toward a Bibliography of Daniel Boone" (*Publishers' Weekly,* 59:614-617, 930-940 2 Mr, 6 Ap, 1901; reprinted, New York, Dibdin Club, 1901), I have not burdened this book with repetition of its contents. Publications subsequent to that date are readily available in the card index of any large library and in the usual bibliographical sources. A good many of them are in the bibliography included in Dr. Willard Rouse Jillson's *Adventures of Col. Daniel Boone* (Louisville, Standard Printing Co., 1932) and in the mimeographed "analytics" issued by the Western State Teachers College, Bowling Green, Kentucky. Mr. E. G. Swem's *Virginia Historical Index* (Roanoke, Stone Printing and Mfg. Co., 1934) is a valuable guide to local Virginiana. My own references to all this material are indicated in the notes.

Since the extant Boone documents have never before been catalogued, I have included a check-list of them. This is based on correspondence with every college and university library in the United States, the principal public libraries, and the historical collections specializing in the period. It is, therefore, reasonably complete, but it is probable that other Boone documents will turn up after publication.

The abundance of source material is partly due to the unusual group of local historians in Kentucky, who have devoted themselves with much competence and diligence to searching out and printing early maps, surveys, letters, depositions, accounts, court records, and documents of every kind. The results of this truly heroic labor are available in the *Register* of the Kentucky State Historical Society, of Frankfort, Kentucky, and in the *History Quarterly* and the sumptuous volumes of the Filson Club, of Louisville, Kentucky. Such collections as the *Pennsylvania Archives, Pennsylvania Magazine, North Carolina Records, North Carolina Booklet, American Archives, American State Papers, Calendar of Virginia State Papers,* and the *Missouri Historical Review* provide a mass of other material.

There are important MSS. at the office of the Yearly Meeting of the Religious Society of Friends, Philadelphia; the Friends Historical Library of Swarthmore College, Swarthmore, Pennsylvania; the State Historical Society of Pennsylvania; the Wisconsin State Historical Society, Madison; and the University of Chicago. Isolated documents are indicated in the check-list.

The British side of the story is told in the papers of General Frederick Haldimand, which include many reports from Lieutenant-Governor Hamilton. These contain a few direct references to Boone and are a mine of information about the Indians he had to fight. The originals are in the British Museum. Copies, in the Canadian Archives at Ottawa, are calendared in the *Reports of the Public Archives of Canada, 1884-1889.* The portions most important in American history have been printed and indexed in the *Michigan Pioneer and Historical Collection.*

There is some Boone material in the records of Bucks and Berks Counties, Pennsylvania, and Rowan County, North Carolina. The latter have been searched by Dr. Archibald Henderson. There is a little material in the archives of Kanawha County, West Virginia, which have been examined by Dr. Roy Bird Cook, of Charleston, West Virginia, and transcribed by W.P.A. workers. The records of St. Charles County, Missouri, have a few Boone documents, several of which appear here for the first time. Kentucky courthouses contain a wealth of records.

The Boone family records kept by Daniel Boone and James Boone are represented among the Draper MSS. These, as well as another set of records, are reproduced by Mrs. Hazel Atterbury Spraker in her book, *The Boone Family.*

The great detail in which we can trace the life of Daniel Boone is mainly due, however, to the lifelong and indefatigable labors of the late Dr. Lyman C. Draper. For more than half a century this painstakingly thorough and meticulously accurate investigator devoted practically all his time, energy, and money to assembling the huge collection of manuscripts relating to Boone and other frontier figures, now known as the Draper Collection in the Wisconsin State Historical Society, Madison, Wisconsin. Draper's MS. biography of Boone, in five volumes, reaching more than seven hundred pages, is still the most authoritative work on the subject. It has never been published and the author's microfilm copy appears to be the only one ever made. Draper died without completing his book, and it therefore covers only about half of Daniel Boone's life.

Of even greater importance are the more than thirty volumes of Boone MSS. (Series C), which Draper assembled. Many of these are original holograph or autograph. Draper journeyed far and wide interviewing surviving pioneers and noting down their stories. He talked and corresponded with everyone he could find who had known Daniel Boone or had information about him. He conducted a voluminous correspondence with the descendants of pioneers. He even lived for a month with Nathan Boone, eagerly writing down all that Nathan Boone and his wife could tell him about Nathan's father. He searched corncribs and attics and gathered up family records, thus saving many a manuscript which without his care would have moldered away unregarded.

All this material he carefully cross-referenced, annotated, and classified in some five hundred volumes. It has had admirable care in the Wisconsin State Historical Society's Library and is today a historical collection absolutely unsurpassed for richness and completeness in its special field. There is a great deal of additional Boone material in Series CC, Series S, and elsewhere. All this is readily located by the use of a carefully indexed catalogue.

Draper's work had been preceded by that of John Shane, who, intending to write a history of the Presbyterian Church in the West, interviewed innumerable pioneers and luckily wrote down all they told him, whether it bore on his particular subject or not. He seems to have abandoned a regular clerical career in order to supply charges temporarily in areas where he thought he might secure material. He thus preserved a great deal of information that could not possibly have been preserved in any other way. Part of his material is in the Draper Collection, which also contains a catalogue of the sale of his books and manuscripts. The rest is in the Presbyterian Historical Society, Philadelphia. This part of the Shane Collection is especially important because it contains the family papers of Daniel Boone's friends, the Harts, and of his wife's family, the Bryans. There is an account of Shane in the fourth volume of the *History Quarterly*.

Second only to Shane and Draper was the late Colonel R. T. Durrett, of Louisville, who gathered up practically all that his predecessors had missed. After a successful career in business, this remarkable man retired in middle life to devote himself to MS.

and book collecting and to research in frontier history. After his death, his MSS. were sold to the University of Chicago. When they reached the university, they were stored in 269 boxes, plus another series of boxes lettered A-R. They have since been bound. The history of the collection has been described in a pamphlet by Edward A. Henry: *The Durrett Collection* (np., nd.).

The Tipton Papers, now in charge of Professor Jonathan Truman Dorris, of the Eastern State Teachers College, Richmond, Kentucky, contain some Boone data and much material useful as background.

The story of Boonesborough's founding is told in three contemporary documents. The MS. of the diary which William Calk kept while on the way to Boonesborough with Richard Henderson is still in the possession of his family. The present owner is Mrs. Price Calk, Mt. Sterling, Kentucky, widow of William Calk's great-grandson. The Filson Club and the University of Kentucky own photostat copies. It has been thrice printed—in Thomas Speed: *Wilderness Road* (Filson Club, No. 2), pp. 34-38; in Archer B. Hulbert: *Boone's Wilderness Road* (Historic Highways, VI); and in Lewis H. Kilpatrick: "Journal of William Calk," *Mississippi Valley Historical Review,* 7:363-377 (1921).

Richard Henderson's own diary is in the Draper Collection. It is part of an eighty-page memorandum book. The diary concludes: "The Occurences of tomorrow & so on you'l find in another stitched book cover'd with brown paper & begins with Wednesday 26th July 1775." This has disappeared entirely. The surviving portion was loaned to the historian Mann Butler by Pleasant Henderson, Richard's brother. Butler seems to have placed it in the Kentucky Historical Society about 1839. It passed into Draper's hands and went with the rest of his papers to the Wisconsin State Historical Society. It is quoted here from the partial transcript in George W. Ranck: *Boonesborough* (Filson Club, No. 16), pp. 169-180. There is another in Hulbert, *op. cit.,* 101-107.

Felix Walker's narrative, written long after the events it describes took place (perhaps about 1824), was published in *DeBow's Review,* 16:150-155, F 1854. Daniel Boone's own letter describing the attack at Twitty's Fort is now known only in copies, which, however, agree among themselves fairly well.

A diary and two genuine manuscript biographies written or dictated by Daniel Boone himself have been lost. The autobiography that fell into the Missouri River in 1814 is obviously gone forever. The other two documents may some day reappear.

There are several guides to Kentucky MSS., of which the most important are:

Willard Rouse Jillson: "Kentucky Acts and Legislative Journals, 1792-1800. A Preliminary Locating List." *Register,* 35:196-197.

Willard Rouse Jillson: "Bibliography of Lincoln County." Ibid., 35:339-359 (1937).

Willard Rouse Jillson: *The Kentucky Land Grants: a Systematic Index* (Filson Club, No. 33).

Willard Rouse Jillson: *Old Kentucky Entries and Deeds.* (Filson Club, No. 34).

Mildred Hasse: *Index to Economic Materials in Printed Documents of the State of Kentucky* (Carnegie Foundation).

Irene T. Myers: "Archives of the State of Kentucky." In *Annual Report of the American Historical Association,* 1910. Reprinted as *11th Annual Report Public Archives of Canada,* App. C, 1912.

C. R. Staples: "New Discoveries Among Old Records." *Register,* 33:307-325 (1935). This includes the first effort to list the Shane documents.

The Kentucky State Historical Society has abstracted and published Fayette County records (*Register,* 33:319), and Mr. Staples has abstracted a number of valuable depositions in *Register,* 32: *passim.*

There is much valuable data in the *Notes on Kentucky* which the early printer, John Bradford, published in his *Kentucky Gazette,* beginning on August 25, 1826, and ending January 9, 1829. In 1827, George W[ashington] Stipp, a publisher of Xenia, Ohio, reprinted in his *Western Miscellany* the first twenty-three sections, which dealt with the Indian wars. These articles with some additions have been collected and edited by Douglas S. Watson (San Francisco, Grabhorn Press, 1932. Rare Americana Series, No. 5).

Bradford's *Kentucky Gazette* is a very rare periodical. The most complete file, now in the Lexington (Kentucky) Public Library, has unfortunately been badly mutilated. Through the efforts of Mr. G. Glenn Clift, of the library staff, missing issues and other gaps are gradually being filled by photostats. Judge Samuel M. Wilson, of Lexington, has collected manuscript copies of fifty-eight out of the sixty-two installments of Bradford's history.

The best account of Boone's life in Missouri is a series of articles by a collateral descendant, William S. Bryan, which ran, with a good deal of repetition, through the third and fourth volumes of the

Missouri Historical Review. It is not documented and appears to be based mainly on family and local tradition. There is further material in *Pioneer Families of Missouri,* long out of print but now available in a modern edition. In this work Bryan collaborated with Robert Rose. The latter worked indefatigably to set down the memories of old Missouri pioneers, including many who had known the Boones both there and in Kentucky. Much of what he recorded is trivial and, having been orally transmitted over a long period, cannot be very accurate, but it has an incomparable vividness. For the circumstances of its composition, see *Missouri Historical Review,* 28:255-259 (1933-34).

The earlier printed lives are the merest fabrications. Some credit, however, must be given to three biographers who have been too much sneered at. John Filson's "autobiography" is of value when cautiously used and checked by other records. After all, it was twice endorsed by Boone himself. Timothy Flint's biography was, according to its own author, written to sell and not to use, but Albert Gallatin Boone called it "the most correct history of my grandfather's career" (*Missouri Historical Review,* 30:214 Ja 1836). Flint was a Baptist preacher who taught school at St. Charles and had Albert Gallatin Boone as one of his pupils. He often visited Daniel Boone, interrogated him, and took notes. His inaccuracies have been demonstrated but it will not do to dismiss him out of hand. John M. Peck also talked with Daniel Boone in his Missouri home, but unfortunately did not always make notes as he had originally no intention of writing a biography (*Wisconsin Historical Collection,* 3:303n. (1876); *American Pioneer,* II:316 (1843)).

Much valuable material has been lost in three disastrous fires—the burning of Spring Hill, Nathaniel Hart's home near Versailles, Kentucky; of James Robertson's home at Nashville, Tennessee, which destroyed Transylvania Company records; and of Dr. Archibald Henderson's collection at Chapel Hill, North Carolina.

DANIEL BOONE DOCUMENTS

(This list endeavors to include all extant manuscripts written or signed by Daniel Boone. The usual abbreviations are employed: A.L.S.—autograph letter, signed; A.L.—autograph letter; L.S.—letter, signed; A.D.S.—autograph document, signed; D.S.—document, signed; np.—no place indicated; nd.—no date indicated.)

Receipt and memorandum, A.D.S. Draper MS. 28 C 10.

Boone genealogy. Draper MS. 6 S 17.

One page, folio, D.S. Also signatures of William Hays and Septimus Davis. W. F. Gable Sale, February 13-14, 1924.

One page, sm. 4to. Orders to Andrew Stell [Steel?] to furnish provisions for a paroled prisoner. Probably Maysville, 1786-87. E. Hertz catalogue, October 19, 1926; Anderson Galleries, Tristram Coffin Sale, January 17, 1927.

Receipt for surveyor's fees. Draper MS. 28 C 59.

Joint claim of D. Boone and Isaac Winston (map) adjoining a claim by Lincoln. With certificate of genuineness by Lyman C. Draper. N. Y. Public Library, MS. Room.

Land entry of Daniel Boone and Isaac Winston, adjoining "Hananighah" Lincoln. Obviously referring to item above. Collection of Oliver R. Barrett, Chicago.

Order written by Boone and signed by Charles Yancey, np., nd. Haverford College.

Dated or Covering Specific Periods

1733. Family Tree of the Boone Family. Berks County Historical Society, Reading, Pa. Also originals in Draper Collection.

1734-66. Boone Family Bible records. Present location of original unknown but probably in Missouri. Photostat in Historical Society of Pennsylvania, Philadelphia. Reproduced in Hazel Atterbury Spraker: *Boone Family*. This is distinct from the similar record in the Draper Collection.

1734. Survey of land in Oley Twp., Philadelphia County, now Berks County, Pa., to George Boone. With diagram. Made and returned by Surveyor General Benj. Eastburn, 1738. Berks County Historical Society.

1740. Release of Squire Boone. Berks County Historical Society.

1749. Two indentures of George Boone and Deborah his wife. Berks County Historical Society.

1751. Agreement of George Boone with George Scull. Berks County Historical Society.

1774(?). Daniel Boone's discharge from the army, presumably at the close of Lord Dunmore's War. Said at one time to have been in the Library of the University of Tennessee, Nashville. This has disappeared.

1775, April 1. Boone to Richard Henderson. Original lost. Copies in Draper and Durrett Collections. This was copied by Draper from James Hall: *Sketches of History, Life, etc.*, and also from John Floyd's copy in the *Frankfort Commonwealth*. Draper MSS. 3 B and 17 CC 166. Ranck alludes to the original but says that he takes his text from Hall.

1775-76 (?). Memorandum and account book, A.D.S. 7 small pages. Draper MS. 4 C 75.
1776. Another survey book. Draper MS. 25 C 29-50.
1776, Sept. 7. Boone to William Preston. Draper MS. 4 C 77.
1780-87. Another survey book. Draper MS. 25 C 84.
1781-87. Another survey book. Draper MS. 25 C 102-115.
1781, Dec. 17. Memorandum of agreement, D.S. Draper MS. 25 C 78.
1781, Dec. 24. A.D.S. Henkels Sale, January 26, 1921.
1782, Aug. 30. Letter to governor of Virginia. Virginia State Library. Copy in Durrett Collection.
1782, Oct. 9 and 25. Instructions to Lt.-Col. Robert Patterson. Both on same page. Draper MS. 25 C 80.
1783-85 (?). Survey book. Most entries by Boone. Draper MS. 26 C 18.
1783, Jan. 6. Orders to Capt. Hazelrigg. A.L.S. Draper MS. 14 C 2.
1784-85. Account book with most entries by Boone. Draper MS. 26 C 113-129.
1784. Survey book, probably in Boone's hand. Draper MS. 26 C 9-11.
1784. Survey book with entries by Boone. Draper MS. 26 C 13.
1784, April 28. Letter to Jacob Cohen. Historical Society of Pennsylvania.
1784, May 20. Receipt of John Sanders to Daniel Boone. Facsimile in William Hayden English: *Conquest of the Country Northwest of the Ohio,* II, 929. Said to come from the Durrett Collection but not now included in it.
1784, June 18. Survey of land in Lincoln County, for Philip and James Moore and John Donaldson. Massachusetts Institute of Technology Library.
1784, July 23. Promissory note to Squire Boone, with various annotations and transfers on back. American Art Association, W. F. Gable Sale, February 13-14, 1924.
1784, Aug. 6. A.L.S. to Lawrence Thompson. Draper MS. 14 C 5.
1785. Order to Thompson on Holley. Draper MS. File 1785.
1785(?). Boone's survey notes with signature, nd. Draper MS. File 1785.
1785, May 21. Land survey with signatures of Daniel Boone and Simon Kenton. Collection of Oliver R. Barrett, Chicago.
1785, May 30. Letter to Charles Yancey. Virginia State Library.
1785, Aug. 16. A.L.S. on Indian raids, military preparations, Kentucky statehood. N. Y. Public Library, Emmet Collection, 6277.
1785, Aug. 23. Letter to William Cristen [Christian]. Original lost.

Two identical forgeries in N. Y. Public Library, Forgery Collection. Copy and photograph of same in Missouri Historical Society, St. Louis. There is no trace of the original, but the two forgeries were probably traced from a genuine document, perhaps by Robert Spring, a well-known forger of Americana.

1786, May 1. Boone to pay James Hone (?) £150 or else give him 300 acres. W. F. Gable Sale, February 13-14, 1924.

1786, May 9. Letter to Geddes Winston, regarding a grant of lands, A.L.S. Haverford College.

1786, July 20. A.L.S. to John Overton, Lincoln County, including bill for surveying. Presented to the Kentucky Historical Society by Grant Green, Esq., and his wife, Mrs. Catherine Overton Green. See Jillson in *Kentucky School Journal,* 13:64 S 1934.

1786, Dec. 16. Promissory note, A.D.S. Durrett Collection.

1787-97. Survey book in Boone's hand. Draper MS. 26 C 156-173.

1787-1801. Account book with entries by Daniel Boone. Draper MS. 26 C 181-189.

1787, Mar. 16. A.L.S. to Lt.-Col. Robert Patterson. Draper MS. 26 C 176.

1787, May 28. Promissory note, D.S. Perhaps a copy. Draper MS. 26 C 177.

1788-1800. Documents relating to Kentucky land entries, signed by Daniel Boone and others.

1788. Jan. 18. A.L.S. to Charles Yancey. [Original in possession of Mrs. A. C. Pendleton, Warren, O.]

1788, Aug. 20. Bond for £32.1.10 jointly with William Hall on appeal of a judgment, D.S. Huntington Library, H.M. 990.

1788, Sept. 6. Joint promissory note with Thomas Hart, D.S. Clawson and Wilson Sale, January 18, 1917.

1788, Dec. 8. Apparently two documents. Dated Maysville, Ky. Deeds relating to Boone's lands there. Sold at American Art Association, December 6, 1921. Another D.S. sold by Stan V. Henkels, November 3, 1916.

1789, May 7. Letter to Thomas Hart, A.L.S. photostat. Durrett Collection.

1789, May-1790, July. Boone's account with Thomas Hart. Not in Boone's hand. [Original in possession of Charles R. Staples, Lexington, Ky.]

1789, July 30. Letter to John Philips and John Young. Historical Society of Pennsylvania.

1789, Dec. 16. Agreement on land, A.D.S. Sold by Stan V. Henkels, December 5, 1918.

1790-95. Account book, A.D. Draper MS. 27 C 19-41.

1791, March 3. Letter to William Haris, A.L.S. Huntington Library, H.M. 22393. Sold at Jones Sale, December 2, 1918.

1791, June 14. Survey for William Allin. West Virginia Historical Society, Charleston, W. Va.

1791, Dec. 13. Letter, obviously written at Richmond, to Governor Henry Lee, of Virginia. Owned by Daniel Boone, New York City.

1791, Dec. 15. Letter to same. Historical Society of Pennsylvania.

1795, May 27. Letter to William Crow on Kentucky stream names, A.L.S. Stan V. Henkels Sale, June 2-8, 1907. Copy in Durrett Collection.

1796, Feb. 11. Letter to Isaac Shelby. Virginia State Library. Copy in Durrett Collection.

1796, June 2. Deposition, Mason County, D.S. Draper MS. 15 C 30.

1797, March 30. Warrant for 2,000 acres in Montgomery County, for Abraham Outen. University of Pittsburgh, Darlington Collection.

1797, May 31. Deposition regarding land entry made by Boone in June, 1780, for Richard Allen, D.S. Huntington Library, H.M. 991.

1797, July 3. Deposition, Mason County, D.S. Draper MS. 11 C 69.

1802, June 1. Promissory note to James Callaway, A.D.S. Missouri Historical Society, St. Louis.

1803, May 6. "To the Worshipel Cort of the District of St. Charles." Mrs. Lewis C. Winkler, Manhattan, Kan.

1804, June. Deposition, A.D.S. Durrett Collection.

1805. Petition to the Court of Quarter Sessions, St. Louis, for a Missouri River ferry. Signature only. Missouri Historical Society, St. Louis.

1806, Feb. 23. Certificate of permission to settle to "Benjamon gardner," A.D.S. Missouri Historical Society.

1806, Aug. 31. Signature of Joseph Haynes' fee bill against William Hayes. Mrs. Lewis C. Winkler, Manhattan, Kan.

1809, Oct. 5. Letter to Judge Cobrin [John Coburn], A.L.S. facsimile. The original was in the possession of "James P. Boyd, Esq., of Kentucky," about 1850. It is reproduced by John Jay Smith: *American Historical and Literary Curiosities,* I, 65.

1811. Receipt by Daniel Boone to Joseph Bryan of Jefferson County, Kentucky. Mrs. Lewis C. Winkler, Manhattan, Kan.

1816, Oct. 19. Letter on religion to "sister." Probably to sister-in-law, Mrs. Samuel Boone. Draper MS. 27 C 88.

Notes

IN THE following notes, the first figure represents the page reference and the second the paragraph. An incomplete paragraph at the head of the page is counted as the first.

"Bogart," "Bruce," "Ellis," "Filson," "Flint," "Peck," and "Thwaites" refer to the biographies of Boone by those authors. Other abbreviations are: Bradford—John Bradford: *Notes on Kentucky; Cal. Va.—Calender of Virginia State Papers;* Collins—the 1878 edition of Lewis Collins: *History of Kentucky;* Ill. Hist. Coll.—Collections of the Illinois State Historical Library; *H.Q.—History Quarterly* of the Filson Club; *Life*—Draper's unpublished MS. life of Boone; *Mich.—Michigan Pioneer Collection; Pion. Fam.*—W. S. Bryan and Robert Rose: *Pioneer Families of Missouri;* Ranck—George W. Ranck: *Boonesborough; Reg.—Register* of the Kentucky State Historical Society; *Va. Mag.—Virginia Magazine of History and Biography.* The usual abbreviations for state names are used.

References to the Draper MSS. follow the system of numbering devised by Draper himself. Each series is indicated by a letter, "C" for Boone, "CC" for Kentucky, and so forth. A preceding numeral indicates the volume, a following number the MS. itself, a numeral in parenthesis the folio number in that MS. Thus 16 C 21 (1) indicates volume 16 of the Boone series, MS. No. 21, folio 1.

3.2. It is sometimes stated that George Boone, the elder, came from Bradninch, near Exeter. This was the home of his son, George Boone, the younger. Gwynedd Meeting records show clearly that the father came from Collumpton. *Cf.* Hazel Atterbury Spraker: *Boone Family,* p. 19; Draper MSS. 1 C 1, 1 C 49.

3.3. The exact relationship of the Bohuns and the Boones has never been established. No one doubts that it exists. See William Boone Douglass: "Ancestry and Boyhood of Daniel Boone," *Kentucky School Journal,* 13:13 S 1934; "Boone Records," *Reg.* 14 (No. 40): 17-35 (1916).

4.2. Draper MS. 22 C 14.

4.3. As George Boone, the younger, married the American-born Deborah Howell on September 27, 1713, he must have arrived in America very early in 1713 or even in 1712. James Boone, in Draper MS. 1 C 1, says he came "a few years before" his father. Quaker custom discourages hasty marriages. *Cf.* Spraker, *op. cit.,* p. 27; Draper MS. 1 C 27.

5.4. *Pennsylvania Archives,* Ser. 2, XIX. 64, 644. *Cf.* Douglass, *loc. cit.;* Spraker, *op. cit.,* p. 28; Morton L. Montgomery: *History of Berks County* (1886), p. 974.

6.1. Historical Society of Pennsylvania, Misc. MSS.; Penn-Physick MSS. IV 19; Peters MSS. IX 113 and III 1751; Penna. Misc. MSS. Penn and Baltimore, fol. 64; Penn MSS. Warrants & Surveys, fol. 94.

6.2. Gwynedd Meeting, pp. 15, 40; Spraker, *op. cit.,* 590-592; Douglass, *loc. cit.; Reg.,* 5:42 (1906); Bogart, 19-20. Nathan Boone, in Draper MS. 6 S 5, says that his father's "ancestors were Quakers." On Deborah Boone, see *The Friend,* 32:403 (1858-59). See Abingdon Meeting records, now in care of Ann R. Jenkins, Jenkintown, Pa., under dates 27 Fifth Month, 1713; 26 Eighth Month, 1713; and 26 Tenth Month, 1720. Transcriptions here are from printed sources which do not in all textual details agree with the custodian's transcription.

6.3. The date is Seventh Month (Old Style) 23, 1720. *Gwynedd Meeting Book,* A. 15, 33 (see also pp. 34, 35); *Women's Meeting Book,* A. 9-10; Douglass, *op. cit.,* p. 16; Spraker, *op. cit.,* 28; John S. Ritenour: "Lincolns of Fayette County [Pa.]," *Western Penna. Hist. Mag.,* 4:19 Ja 1921; *Life,* p. 13.

7.2. *Deed Book No. 23,* Bucks County Records, Doylestown, Pa. *Cf.* Spraker, *op. cit.,* p. 33; Berks County Records, Book A, Vol. VI, pp. 1-2; Draper MSS. 1 C 38, 1 C 64 (3), 2 C 7 (2), 25 C (3-4). Draper MS. 2 C 7 (2), a deed, gives the complete history of the title.

The early biographers, ill-informed and careless, give a wide variety of dates for Daniel Boone's birth. The date here given is authenticated by the Boone family Bible recently owned by James H. Boone, of Leeton, Mo., and a page from another Bible in the Draper MSS. Several pages of the former are reproduced by Spraker. The family records kept by James Boone give the year as 1733. Daniel Boone himself commented on this discrepancy but insisted that 1734 was correct. See Draper MSS. 6 S 5, 13, 16-20.

The place of birth is fixed by Squire Boone's residence in Oley (later Exeter) Township, Berks County. Writers unfamiliar with Pennsylvania confuse Bucks and Berks Counties, and others indulge in less pardonable fantasies. Berks County was cut off from Philadelphia County in 1752, after Squire Boone's family had left the colony. Thus Daniel Boone was technically born in Philadelphia County, but in the portion now known as Berks. See Morton L. Montgomery: *Political Hand-Book of Berks County,* p. 9.

The publishing family of Littell also used the Christian name, Squire.

7.3. Israel Daniel Rupp: *History of Berks,* pp. 231, 422.

8.2. Morton L. Montgomery: "Daniel Boone," *Hist. Register* (Pa.) 191; Draper MS. 1 C 91.

8.3. *Life,* p. 12½; Rupp, *op. cit.,* pp. 95, 111, 125, 231.

8.5. *Pennsylvania Archives,* 1st Ser. I, 215, 217, 218.

8.6. *Life,* p. 20.

9.1. D. B. Brunner: *Indians of Berks County, Pa.,* p. 25.

9.3. Draper MS. 6 S 21; *Life,* pp. 21-22.

10.1. Draper MS. 22 C 14.

10.4. Rev. Henry Melchoir Muhlenberg. Quoted in report for Berks County, in *Report of the Superintendent of Public Instruction of Pennsylvania,* 1877, p. 60. The Germans established a church in Oley in 1736, when Daniel Boone was two years old. Usually they established a school at the same time, but there is no evidence they did so in this case.

10.5. Draper MS. 6 S 26; *Life,* p. 27.

11.1. Douglass, *op. cit.,* p. 15.

11.2. *Reg.,* 5:42 (1906); Douglass, *op. cit.,* pp. 15, 18; *Life,* Appendix III and p. 24; Draper MSS. 1 C 19, 6 S 5; Bruce, 9.

11.3. Draper MSS. 19 C 49, 60, 122; *Pion. Fam.,* pp. 4-5.

13.1. *Life,* p. 24.

13.2. *Life,* pp. 24-26. Daniel Boone told this story to his son Nathan. Draper MS. 6 S 44.

13.3. Draper MS. 19 C 49; *Life,* p. 27.

14.1. Draper MS. 19 C 60; *Life,* p. 30.

14.2. Draper MS. 6 S 43; *Life,* p. 19. The word "gorrel," meaning "youth, lad or boy," according to the *Oxford English Dictionary,* does not occur in England after 1650, and even then is doubtful. It is interesting to note its survival in America a full century later.

16.1. *Exeter Monthly Meeting Book,* A. 32-33; *Women's Monthly Meeting Book,* A. 22, 23, 29; Draper MSS. 1 C 24, 35, 55, 87. The *Women's Book,* A. 23, shows that the mother was also rebuked and expressed penitence. The Friends records are full of turmoil because other Boones insisted on "marrying out." In 1761, Daniel Boone's cousin, Ann Boone, was dealt with by Exeter Meeting for marrying a worldling whose name happened to be Abraham Lincoln—a common name among the Berks County Lincolns, from whose stock the Emancipator sprang. See John S. Ritenour: *op. cit.,* and typescript of Samuel H. Boone: *Boone Family,* p. 8, Durrett Coll.

17.2. *Exeter Monthly Meeting Book,* A. 74-80; Draper MS. 1 C 35; *Life,* p. 31.

17.3. Indenture of Squire and Sarah Boone, Draper MS. 25 C 3; *Exeter Monthly Meeting Book,* A. 61-62. The letters were technically called "certificates."

17.5. On the Boones and Lincolns, see Ritenour, *op. cit.,* pp. 11-27.

18.1. Draper MS. 1 C 93; Ritenour, *op. cit.,* p. 19; "Lincoln, Hanks and Boone Families," *Mo. Hist. Rev.,* 1:72-84 (1906).

18.2. Draper MS. 1 C, *passim; Reg.,* 5:45, 14:27 (1907, 1917).

18.3. Draper MSS. 6 S 6, 4 C 32; *Life,* p. 33. The dates are approximate. Nathan Boone asserted the family reached the Yadkin by 1752.

18.3. On the sojourn in Virginia, see Draper MS. 6 S 24; Spraker, *op. cit.,* p. 36; John W. Wayland: *Hist. of Rockingham County, Virginia,* pp. 428-429; also his *German Element,* p. 206.

19.1. Draper MS. 8 C 187. Rowan County, N. C. *Records,* Book III, p. 37, contain the grant. There are other deeds from Granville to Squire Boone in the same book. They have been copied in the Draper MSS. See also Books IV and V; Jacob Calvin Leonard: *Centennial Hist. of Davidson County,* p. 190; Henry Sheets: *Hist. of Liberty Baptist Assn.,* p. 122; Jethro Rumple: *Hist. of Rowan County,* p. 189.

19.3. N. C. *Records,* V, pp. 275-276; Draper MSS. 2 C 62, 8 C 82, 22 C 14 (9-10).

20.1. *Life,* p. 37, apparently quoting the *Maryland Gazette,* Dec. 6, 1753.

21.3. John Redd: "Reminiscences of West Virginia," *Va. Mag.,* 7: 242 Ja 1900. For Walker's journal of his explorations, see *Ibid.,* 19:166-172 (1911). See also *Life,* Appendix II.

21.4. Military records are not available and other accounts do not agree. *Life,* p. 40, says he was in Hugh Waddell's Company. Archibald Henderson: *Conquest of the Old Southwest,* p. 50, says he was in Dobbs's Company.

22.2. *Apology for the Life of George Anne Bellamy,* I, 194; V, 155; Winthrop Sargent: *Hist. of an Expedition against Fort Duquesne,* Appendix VI, p. 417.

22.4. *Gentleman's Mag.,* 25: 378 Ag 1755; *Penna. Arch.,* 1st Ser. II, 583, 598, 638; *Va. Hist. Rev.,* 5:126 Jy 1852; Lewis Burd Walker: *Burd Papers, II. Settlement of the Wagoners' Accounts relating to General Braddock's Expedition.*

23.1. Draper MSS. 6 S 7, 30-31; 4 C 46. Nathan Boone was merely "inclined to believe" that his father and Finley met on the Braddock expedition, but the story is plausible and generally accepted. On Daniel Boone's memories, *cf.* 6 S 308-309, 2 C 23.

25.1. Alfred Moore Waddell: "North Carolina in the French and Indian War," *North Carolina Booklet,* 7:6-7 (1907); Archibald Henderson: *Conquest of the Old Southwest,* pp. 54-55.

26.4. Draper MS. 6 S 40-41, 288; *Life,* p. 55, following family tradition.

27.2. *Life,* p. 56, from Daniel Boone's own account. The date is also given in the family Bible. See Spraker, *op. cit.,* p. 564, and Draper MS. 1 C 49.

27.3. Many of the early biographers tell this story. They have had bad reputations for accuracy. It is denied by Rebecca's relative, Daniel Bryan, in Draper MS. 22 C 16 (7).

28.2. Draper MSS. 16 C 57; 6 X 17½.

29.3. *Life,* p. 58. Flint has a similar rhapsody.

30.3. Interview with Joseph Scholl, grandson of Daniel Boone, Draper MS. 24 S 217. The couple's children and their dates of birth are listed by Douglass, *op. cit.,* p. 19: James (May 3, 1757), Israel (Jan. 25, 1759), Susannah (Mrs. William Hays, b. Nov. 2, 1760), Jemima (Mrs. Flanders Callaway, b. Oct. 4, 1762), Levina or Lavinia (Mrs. Joseph Scholl, b. Mar. 23, 1766), Rebecca (Mrs. Philip Goe, b. May 26, 1768), Daniel Morgan (Dec. 23, 1769), Jesse (May 23, 1773), William (June 20, 1775, died in infancy), Nathan (Mar. 2, 1781).

30.5. Draper MSS. 8 C 3, 39-41.

31.2. Draper MSS. 2 C 1, 19 C 57; *Life,* p. 69; Spraker, *op. cit.,* p. 38. Statements of William Grant, son-in-law of Squire Boone, the younger, and of Grant's daughter.

31.3. Draper MSS. 2 C 50 (2), 57, 74, 76, 79; 19 C 59; 6 S 309-315, 321-322; Atkinson's *Casket,* No. 11:487 N 1832.

31.4. Draper MS. 7 C (3-5) records Daniel Boone's own account of the Juniata episode, as told to a friend. *Cf.* Draper MSS. 2 C 53-57.

31.5. Rowan County *Records,* Book III; Draper MSS. 8 C 17, 22, 93, 98.

32.2. John P. Arthur: "Trail of Daniel Boone," *Skyland Magazine,* 1:652 S 1914. Burrell, the old slave, told the story to Col. James Martin Isbell, of King's Creek, N. C. Col. Isbell's grandmother, Mrs. Jordan Councill, daughter of Burrell's owner, verified the story. She had herself known Daniel Boone.

32.3. There are numerous versions of this inscription. The text here is taken from a tracing in Draper MS. 17 C 13, which also contains numerous photographs of the original tree. *Cf.* Draper MSS. 6 C 79, 9 C 45, 6 S 313. The 1773 inscription was cut out of the tree and is now in the possession of Miss Margaret Preston, Abingdon, Va. Changes in the bark make exact transcription difficult. The carving may be read: "D BOON/ KILED A BAR— / O THE TRE —/ 1775." The last figure is obscure. A third inscription in the Filson Club, Louisville, found on a tree formerly standing in Iroquois (Jacob) Park, reads: "D. BOONE KILL A BAR/1803/ZOIS." The word "Bar" might be "Der," i.e., deer. It is now nearly illegible. No one knows what "Zois" means. *Cf.* William Brent Altschuler: *Illustrated Outdoor World and Recreation,* 48:256-257, 290, Ap 1913, for photographs and evidence of the commonness of such inscriptions. A mere list of the references to tree carvings in the Draper MSS. would cover the better part of a page. *Life,* p. 91, says J. G. M. Ramsey's correspondence shows that the 1760 carving was known and accepted as genuine as early as 1843-44. Many early printed accounts accept it as genuine. See Ramsey: *Annals of Tennessee,* p. 67; John Berry M'Ferrin: *History of Methodism in*

Tennessee, I, 16; Lewis Preston Summers: *History of Southwest Virginia,* p. 76; *Mo. Hist. Rev.,* 23:216 (1928-29); St. Louis *Post-Dispatch,* Nov. 7, 1928.

33.1. The inscription is in Draper MS. 6 C 85 (3). Original has not been seen since 1809.

34.1. Draper MS. 5 C 67-71. *Cf.* 9 C 73-77. No accurate transcript.

34.4. *Life,* 113-116; Draper MS. 6 S 282-285½; *Penna. Gazette,* March 11, 1756.

35.2. Archibald Henderson: "Life and Times of Richard Henderson," Charlotte (N. C.) *Observer,* March 23, 1913, p. 20; May 11, 1913, p. 26. Dr. Henderson states in a letter to the author that he possesses further evidence of Boone's financial dealings with Henderson. See his article in *Am. Hist. Rev.,* 20:103 (1914).

35.3. Jethro Rumple: *op. cit.,* pp. 37-38; N. C. *Records,* V, 528.

36.2. See **67.2.**

37.1. Collins, II, 416; John Haywood: *Civil and Political Hist. of Tennessee,* p. 48 (ed. 1891). Nathan Boone doubted the story, Draper MS. 6 S 38. The sale of the farm is in Rowan County *Deed Book,* V, 450. See Draper MSS. 8 C 61, 99, 128; 2 C 101, 1 C 49.

37.2. Draper MS. 22 C 14 (10).

37.3. Draper MSS. 2 C 62, 22 C 14 (23), 6 S 58.

38.3. Draper MSS. 6 S 69-70; 2 C 62, 66 (3); S 49 XX, Nos. 16-24, James Madison to Executors of William Riddle; Western Reserve Hist. Soc., Cleveland, Vault MS. 2342, fol. 1, verso.

38.4. Draper MS. 2 C 66 (5).

39.5. Bill for a rifle, etc., to John Nelson, July 26, 1782, Durrett Coll. For further references see Hugh James in *Journ. Am. Military Hist.,* 3:33-34 (1939).

40.1. Redd, *op. cit., Va. Mag.,* 7:248 (1900).

41.1. On the Florida trip, see *Life,* 122, 127; Draper MSS. 4 C 75, 19 C 124-125, 22 C 33, 6 S 7, 34, 35.

42.3. Nathan Boone visited the district with his father in 1796-97 and heard the story from Daniel Boone himself. Draper MSS. 6 S 6, 7, 39-40.

44.2. Finley's name is variously spelled. Documents relating to him are included in the *Life.*

44.3. Draper MS. 19 C 1.

45.1. Draper MS. 22 C 5 (4); *Life,* p. 153.

45.3. Draper MS. 22 C 14.

45.4. Deposition of David Hall. Fayette County *Complete Record Book,* E. 361; *Reg.,* 32:246-247 (1934), abstracted by Charles R. Staples. *Cf.* Draper MSS. 4 C 46, 126, 128; 22 C 5 (4), 6 S 309.

46.1. Draper MS. 22 C 14 (10).

46.2. Rumple, *op. cit.,* pp. 37, 38.

46.3. Haywood, *op. cit.,* pp. 50-52; N. C. *Records,* VIII, 231-234, 652-654; Henderson, *loc. cit.,* April 13, 1913, p. 19; April 19, 1913, p. 7.

47.1. Draper MS. 6 S 6.

47.3. Archibald Henderson in *Am. Hist. Rev.,* 20:97-98 (1914).

47.5. Stuart, or Stewart, was the husband of Boone's sister Elizabeth. *Life,* p. 195. Marriage record in Spraker, *op. cit.,* 564.

48.1. Henderson, *op. cit.,* April 6, 1913, p. 19; May 11, 1913, p. 26.

48.2. Archibald Henderson in *Am. Hist. Rev.,* 20:103 (1914).

48.4. Filson, p. 1, gives the name as Cool, but Col. and Mrs. Nathan Boone and other members of the family heard both Daniel and Squire Boone, the younger, pronounce it "Cooley." *Life,* p. 155 n. Bradford, p. 4, gives Mooney's name as "Monay." Draper MS. 22 C 5 *ff.* gives details of route.

48.5. Draper MS. 6 S 47 *ff.; Life,* p. 156.

49.3. "Station Camp" was a common term among the hunters. See Ward *vs.* Fox's Heirs, 1 Ky. 424 (Hughes, 1801). There is disagreement as to the site of Boone's Station Camp, but two of his nephews were positive that this statement of Draper's (*Life,* p. 159 n.) was correct. See Mrs. Walter Cox in *Lexington Leader,* June 30, 1938, Sect. IV, p. 8. The stream must not be confused with Robertson's Creek, a branch of Laurel Run in Laurel County, which the Long Hunters called Station Camp Creek. See *Life,* pp. 231, 235.

49.5. *Life,* pp. 159-160.

50.1. *Life,* p. 161; Boone's petition to Kentucky Legislature; Filson, p. 51; Filson: *Kentucke,* p. 8.

50.4. *Life,* pp. 166-170, based on statements of Daniel and Squire Boone to their children, and narrative of Daniel Bryan. See Draper MSS. 4 C 60, 22 C 5.

52.1. *Life,* pp. 179-180; Randolph C. Downes: "Lord Dunmore's War," *Miss. Valley Hist. Rev.,* 21:312 D 1934.

52.2. Draper MS. 14 C 30; Thomas Speed: *Wilderness Road* (Filson Club, No. 2), p. 69. Dreaming Creek is shown near Richmond, Ky., on U. S. Geological Survey, Richmond Quadrangle (21.5—45).

52.4. *Life,* 232-233; Draper: *King's Mountain,* p. 429; Draper MS. 4 C 60; Collins, II, 417-418.

53.2. Draper MS. 6 S 49-52.

54.1. Upcott Collection of Newspaper Clippings, N. Y. Hist. Soc., dated Jan. 3, 1772; Newspaper Extracts, 1756-78; Draper MS. 2 C 26; *Life,* p. 178.

54.2. The meeting with Squire is based on Peck, p. 30. Flint tells the same story. Both men knew Boone, and Peck at least tries to be accurate. But see Draper MSS. 3 C 59, 22 C 5 (6), and *Life,* p. 176, which says that Boone caught up with Finley's party and found Squire among them.

55.1. Deposition of Daniel Boone, Clark County *Deposition Book,* I, 156, Sept. 15, 1796; Draper MSS. 2 C 80, 3 C 74.

Swift's names are, of course, inaccurately recollected. On Boone as a reader, see Draper MS. 4 C 55.

55.3. Draper MSS. 6 S 56-61, 22 C 5 (7); *Life,* p. 196. Peck, p. 31, Bradford, p. 6, and Humphrey Marshall: *Hist. of Ky.* (1824), I, p. 19, tell a different story but seem to be in error. It is certainly odd, however, that the two diaries of 1775 do not mention the skeleton.

55.6. Draper MSS. 19 C 62, 6 S 281.

56.4. Draper MS. 19 C 62.

57.3. Stewart Edward White: *Daniel Boone,* p. 59. Boone is said to have used the wild grape vine again when escaping from the Shawnees in 1778, but the whole story has been questioned. See Draper MS. 16 C 80 (3).

57.5. Filson, p. 13.

58.2. Gray's *New Manual of Botany* (7th Ed., 1908), p. 171.

59.1. Draper MS. 2 C 25; *Life,* p. 202, based on conversations with Nathan Boone.

59.2. *Life,* p. 213; Draper MSS. 6 S 65-66, 2 C 42 (3), 4 C 45, 3 C 66, 70; 16 C 31; Virginia Hays Asbury and Albert N. Doerschuk in *Mo. Hist. Rev.,* 23:539

(1928-29); Louise P. Kellogg in *Report of the Daniel Boone Bicentennial Commission,* p. 51; *cf.* p. 53.

60.4. *Life,* pp. 213-214. Draper heard this rather "tall" story as a cherished tradition of old settlers on Dick's River, and was later assured of its accuracy by Isaiah Boone and others. See Draper MSS. 1 C 20, 3 C 67, 19 C 115. But *cf.* 4 C 149. See also Draper MS. 4 C 151.

60.5. Draper MS. 4 C 33, 37, 45-46.

61.3. Filson, p. 56. Draper MS. 22 C 5 (7) says Squire brought a nephew along with him.

61.4. *Life,* p. 217 and note, on the authority of early settlers, at least two of whom knew Boone personally.

62.1. Col. Boone Hays, a grandson, had the wolf story from Daniel Boone himself. *Life,* p. 218; Draper MS. 6 S 294. On the question of headgear, see *Mo. Hist. Rev.,* 30:408 (1936); Thwaites, p. 29.

62.2. Most books ignore this second journey of Squire's. See *Life,* p. 219, and Draper MS. 6 S 67. Draper heard the story from Col. and Mrs. Nathan Boone and from Daniel Bryan. Draper MS. 16 C 75 says Squire Boone brought a servant with him. *Cf.* Note **61.3.**

63.3. *Life,* pp. 239-240 n., quoting Nathan Boone. Presumably David Hall, who mentions hunting with Boone about this time, was with the Long Hunters. *Cf.* his deposition, Sept. 1, 1801. Fayette County *Complete Record Book,* E. 361; *Reg.,* 32:246-247 (1934); Draper MSS. 2 C 24, 3 C 62, 5 C 73-74, 19 C 72. Draper bases his statement on a MS. by John B. Dysart, one of the Long Hunters.

63.4. *Life,* p. 241. It is often said that Neeley died on the way back to the settlements. See White, *op. cit.,* pp. 58-59; Redd, *op. cit., Va. Mag.,* 4:402 Ap 1900. But Draper's statements (*Life,* pp. 241-243) are based on statements by Neeley's family and of W. Hall, who had the facts from Neeley himself. Draper MSS. 19 C 72, 6 S 286.

64.3. *Life,* pp. 247-248, based on MS. notes on conversation with Squire Boone's sons, Moses and Isaiah; Nathan Boone; Boone's Memorial to Kentucky Legislature, Draper MSS. 19 C 62-65, 126-129.

65.1. The quotation is from Draper MS. 4 C 73. There is a variant in Bradford, p. 7.

66.1. *Life,* p. 268, based on statements of Nathan Boone and Henry Rutherford. The latter had heard a hunting-companion of Boone's describe these expeditions.

66.2. The account is in Draper MS. 11 DD 8. See also 4 C 73, 128. Some of Shelby's other accounts are in the Durrett Collection. See Samuel Cole Williams: *Dawn in Tennessee,* pp. 344, 353, and J. J. Audubon: *Ornithological Biography,* I, 504.

67.2. Archibald Henderson: "Occupation of Kentucky," *Miss. Valley Hist. Rev.,* 1:349 D 1914. See also article in Charlotte (N. C.) *Observer,* May 11, 1913, p. 26; Haywood, *op. cit.,* p. 53; *Life,* p. 340 n.; and the memoir of his brother, by Pleasant Henderson, who says specifically that Boone induced Richard Henderson to attempt the purchase of Kentucky. *Cf.* Draper MS. 2 C 25, 106.

68.1. *Life,* pp. 269-270; R. A. B. McAfee: "Sketches of the Settlement of Kentucky," *Frankfort* [*Ky.*] *Commonwealth,* June 1, 1841. Copy in Draper Collection. See also the McAfee Diaries in the *Woods-McAfee Memorial* (University of Chicago Library); M. J. Spalding: *Sketches of the Early Catholic Missions of Kentucky* (1844), pp. 7-8.

68.3. Draper MS. 22 C 5 (7).

68.4. Henderson, *op. cit., Miss. Valley Hist. Rev.,* 1:349 (1914).

69.3. The account by M. B. Wood in Ranck, p. 146, says that they started in March, presumably confusing Boone's preliminary reconnoissance with the real expedition. See Peck, p. 38; Draper MSS. 22 C 5 (7); 4 C 64.

71.1. *Life,* p. 272; Draper MS. 11 CC 12; Thwaites, pp. 102-103.

71.2. On this massacre, see Draper MSS. 6 C 7-20, 6 S 79-83, 11 CC 12, 13 C 133, 22 C 5, 14; *Am. Arch.,* 4th Ser., I, 278, 707, 873, 975, 1015, 1169; *Life,* 280 n.

73.1. The story of the counter-attack rests on the statement of M. B. Wood in Ranck, pp. 146-147. See John H. Wheeler: *Hist. Sketches of North Carolina,* II, 448; *National Portrait Gallery,* II (1852); Draper MS. 4 C 26 (5-7).

73.5. *Life,* pp. 278, 329; *Am. Arch.,* 4th Ser., I, 873.

74.2. Draper MSS. 11 CC 12, 15 J 4-88, 3 QQ 40; Thwaites and Kellogg: *Documentary History of Lord Dunmore's War,* pp. 38-39, 374-375; Public Record Office, London, Colonial Papers, America and West India, CCXIII, 13; Charles Campbell: *History of the Colony and Ancient Dominion of Virginia,* p. 597; *Life,* p. 298; Haywood, *op. cit.,* p. 56.

74.3. Draper MS. 19 C 5-65; *Life,* pp. 278-283, 285; *Woods-McAfee Memorial,* p. 469; Daniel E. Johnston: *Hist. of the Middle New River Settlements,* p. 40; Henry Sheets: *Hist. of the Liberty Baptist Association,* pp. 122-123 (copy in Divinity School Library, University of Chicago).

74.4. Trabue's reminiscences, Draper MS. 57 J.

75.1. Draper MS. 6 S 83; *Life,* pp. 295-297.

76.5. *American Pioneer,* 1:7-9, 13-16, 22-23, 188-189, and *passim* (1843); Samuel G. Drake: *Biog. and Hist. of the Indians* (11th Ed., 1851), p. 537; Joseph Doddridge: *Notes on the Settlement and the Indian Wars* (1876), pp. 230-232; *Dictionary of American Biography,* XI, 362.

77.3. The killings are listed in *Life,* pp. 292-293.

77.6. *Life,* pp. 300-302; Thwaites, p. 106; Draper MSS. 6 C 96, 103, 105; 3 QQ 46, 50; 33 S 35-49; Thwaites and Kellogg, *op. cit.,* pp. 49-50.

78.3. On the diary, see Draper MS. 6 C 96.

79.2. Draper MS. 6 S 85-86.

79.3. *H.Q.,* 8:187 (1934); Collins, II, p. 518; Draper MS. 12 C 28 (2); *Life,* p. 305, quoting Mercer County Court records; *Am. Arch.,* 4th Ser., I, 75; Draper MS. 12 C 22 (1-3), deposition of Mrs. James Harrod.

81.1. Draper MS. 6 C 96; Lewis Preston Summers: *Hist. Southwest Virginia,* pp. 156-157.

81.2. On Boone's share in the war, see *Life,* pp. 309-320; *Am. Arch.,* 4th Ser., I, 805; Draper MS. 6 C 10, 11, 93, 95, 96; and Preston Papers, in Draper Collection, *passim.*

82.4. Ranck, p. 147.

83.1. On this whole subject, see William S. Lester: *Transylvania Colony, passim;* Archibald Henderson: *Conquest of the Old Southwest,* pp. 201, 357, and 137 n., also his article in Charlotte (N. C.) *Observer,* May 11, 1913, p. 26; St. George L. Sioussat, review in *Miss. Valley Hist. Rev.,* 7:378-383 (1921); Draper MS. 2 CC 34; Mann Butler: *Hist. Ky.* (1836), p. lxvii n.

83.5. Archibald Neilson to Andrew Miller, Jan. 28, 1775, N. C. *Records,* IX, p. 117; Ranck, p. 5; *Miss. Valley Hist. Rev.,* 1:351 (1914). The original MS. is in the office of the Secretary of State, Raleigh, N. C.

84.2. Draper MSS. 1 CC 10, 1 CC 1.

84.3. *Life,* pp. 332, 340; Draper MSS. 6 C 99, 3 QQ 134; Ranck, p. 2;

Reg., 31:1-8 (1933); Archibald Henderson in *Am. Hist. Rev.*, 20:105 (1914).

84.4. Draper MS. 4 QQ 1; Henderson, *op. cit.*, May 11, 1913.

85.2. *Cal. Va.*, I, 158; *Life*, pp. 341, 431-432; Draper MSS. 6 S 87, 15 S 100, 2 CC 23 (1); *Am. Arch.*, 4th Ser., III, 847.

86.3. Redd, *op. cit.*; *Va. Mag.*, 7:2 Jy 1899.

86.4. *Life*, p. 342-344.

87.2. *Cal. Va.*, I, 292; Ranck, p. 157; Draper MS. 1 CC 133.

87.2. Draper MS. 12 S 110.

87.3. James Phelan: *Hist. Tenn.* (188), p. 18; Haywood, *op. cit.*, pp. 58-59.

87.4. Draper MS. 12 S 109-112.

89.1. *DeBow's Review*, 16:150-155 F 1854.

90.2. These documents were discovered in 1935, when the fire warden ordered the removal of old papers found lying in the attic of the Court House at Christiansburg, Va. Mr. Charles Crush, Commonwealth Attorney, examined them and found the Boone documents. They are now kept in the Court House vault in an unnumbered file, identified by pencil notations on the back.

90.3. Felix Walker's Narrative, *DeBow's Review*, 16:150-155 F 1854; reprinted by Ranck, p. 62. *Cf.* William Calk's MS. Diary, fol. 1.

91.1. Filson, p. 15; Bradford, p. 23; *Life*, pp. 349-351½; Draper MSS. 19 C 65-66, 22 C 14-16, 7 DD 110, 179; Boone's letter to Henderson, April 1, 1775. John Crook's survey of John Kincaid's land indicates "a place shown for Twitty's Fort." See Tipton Papers, in possession of Professor Jonathan Truman Dorris.

92.1. Nathaniel Hart, Jr., in *Frankfort Commonwealth*, 25 Jy 1838; Ranck, p. 11.

92.4. Walker's Narrative; Ranck, p. 166. On Boone's medical skill, see *Reg.*, 28: 253 (1930); Isaac Shelby to "Mrs. Hartt," Jan. 13, 1785, in Presbyt. Hist. Soc., Shane Coll. Hart Family Papers, XIX, I, 41.

93.2. On Martin's cabin, see *Woods-McAfee Memorial*, p. 475. The quotations from Henderson's diary are from Ranck's reprint.

93.3. On Abraham Hanks's relationship to Lincoln, see Caroline Hanks Hitchcock: *Nancy Hanks*, pp. 127-128. On his journey, see Lewis H. Kilpatrick in *Miss. Valley Hist. Rev.*, 7:370 (1921).

94.2. Draper MS. 17 CC 166-167 (late copies of the original).

94.3. Calk's MS. Diary, April 7, 8, 1775.

94.4. *Ibid.*, April 10, 1775.

95.3. Alexander Cocke's own account, quoted in the *Life*, p. 358 n., is in Draper's MS. 2 CC 1—Cocke's bill of complaint in U. S. Sup. Ct. of Equity, Terr. of U. S. South of the River Ohio, Washington District, Oct. 1, 1796, together with draft of reply. There is a partial copy in the Durrett Coll. See also Henderson's letter to the proprietors, June 12, 1775, reprinted in Ranck, pp. 184-193; *Life*, pp. 357-362; *cf.* Draper MS. 7 C 76.

96.4. Calk's MS. Diary, April 11, 16, 1775.

97.2. Daniel Trabue's Diary, Draper MS. 57 J 35, 39. This is reprinted in Lillie Du Puy Harper: *Colonial Men and Times* (1916), but has been much altered.

98.1. Robert B. McAfee: "Early Settlement and Settlers of Kentucky," Charles Cist's *Cincinnati Miscellany*, 2:137 S 1845.

98.2-3. Calk's MS. Diary, April 18, 19, 20, 1775.

98.4. Henderson's letter to proprietors, June 12, 1775; Ranck, p. 187.

99.3-5. Henderson's Diary, April 21, 27, 1775; Ranck, pp. 173-174.

100.4. Deposition of Daniel Boone, Draper MS. 6 C 105; *H.Q.*, 1:101 (1927).

101.4. Henderson's Diary, May 14, 1775; Ranck, p. 177.

102.2. Henderson's Diary, May 25, 1775; Ranck, p. 178. On the other settlements, see R. A. B. McAfee's article in the *Frankfort Commonwealth,* June 1, 1841.

102.6. The speeches are from an original furnished by James Alves to Mann Butler in 1835. Alves descended from James Hogg, a member of the Transylvania Company. The text is given in Ranck, pp. 196-212. *Life,* pp. 384-388.

104.2. Henderson's Diary, May 28, 1775; Ranck, p. 178; *H.Q.,* 8:189 (1934).

105.1. Redd, *op. cit., Va. Mag.,* 7:1 Jy 1899.

105.2. *Life,* p. 391; Ranck, p. 29.

106.1. J. F. D. Smyth: *Travels in the United States of America,* pp. 325-356 (copy in N. Y. Public Library).

107.4. Draper MS. 6 S 16-17; *Life,* pp. 410-419; *Louisville Literary News Letter,* May 9, 1840 (copy in Wisconsin State Hist. Soc.); Henderson and Luttrell to proprietors, July 18, 1775.

107.5. *Life,* p. 427; Ranck, pp. 212-214.

107.6. Survey by John Crooke. Original in custody of Professor Jonathan Truman Dorris, Eastern State Teachers College, Ky.

108.6. *Life,* pp. 428-430; Ranck, p. 215; Diary of John Adams, Oct. 25, 1775; Archibald Henderson: *Transylvania Company and the Founding of Henderson,* Ky., p. 11.

110.1. Date of return in *Life,* p. 422.

111.1. Filson, p. 60.

112.2. Draper MS. 5 CC 85; McAfee, *op. cit.,* June 1, 1841.

112.4. *Life,* p. 424.

112.5. *Life,* pp. 422-423; *H.Q.,* 3:226 (1929); Draper MS. 12 C 27; Redd, *op. cit., Va. Mag.,* 7:1 (1899).

115.1. Draper MS. 4 QQ 52; *Life,* p. 448.

115.2. Willard Rouse Jillson: *Old Kentucky Land Entries and Deeds,* pp. 16, 79, 176.

115.3. *Life,* pp. 421, 448½; *Louisville Literary News Letter,* May 9, 1840; Callaway to Richard Trump, Jan. 3, 1780; *H.Q.,* 9:243 (1935); Samuel M. Wilson: *First Land Court of Kentucky,* p. 17.

116.2. Filson, p. 66; *Life,* pp. 558-559.

117.2. *Life,* p. 448¼; Ranck, pp. 190-191; Henderson to proprietors, June 12, 1775.

117.4. Filson, p. 16.

118.1. John Williams to Transylvania Company, Jan. 3, 1776; N. C. *Records,* X, pp. 382-387; *Am. Arch.,* IV, 558; Ranck, pp. 237-238; Draper MS. 5 CC 85; *H.Q.,* 3:226-227 (1929); *Life,* pp. 435-437; Hall: *Sketches,* I, 259-260, 246-247.

119.1. Filson is vague as to this episode. *Life,* p. 437 n., quotes Captain Gass's distinct statement that Sanders disappeared entirely.

119.2. John Williams to proprietors, Jan. 3, 1776; Ranck, p. 238.

119.3. Thwaites, p. 126.

120.5. Ranck, pp. 244-247; John Floyd to Col. J. Martin, May 19, 1776; Draper MS. 1 XX 10. See also his letter to Col. William Preston, May 19, 1776, Draper MS. 33 S 294.

122.4. *Life,* p. 426.

123.2. *Life,* p. 454.

124.1. Draper MS. 11 CC 11. Reprinted in *Lexington Leader,* April 29, 1934. The Boone cabin was "right where the ferry is," or well outside the stockade. A modern bridge has now replaced the old ferry but its location is perfectly clear. The statement that cabins had been built on the other side must refer to "cabiners" such as the pursuit encountered. See Ranck, p. 51.

124.3. Draper MS. 9 C 68.

125.1. An important source is Draper MS. 7 C 43 (5), Daniel's Boone's own story as told in Jemima's home. See also Draper MSS. 22 C 5 *ff.*, 11 CC 11, 12 CC 200, 6 S 96-98; John Floyd to William Preston, July 21, 1776, Draper MS. 4 CC 84; *Penna. Packet,* 20 Ag and 10 S 1776.

125.2. Redd, *op. cit., Va. Mag.,* 7:1 Jy 1899. Redd does not speak from first-hand knowledge.

125.3. Draper MSS. 12 C 6 (2), 12 C 16 (1), 12 C 27 (13), 13 C 74 (2), 16 C 76, 6 S 94-100, 6 S 301-306; *Life,* p. 457. Indians were often called "yellow boys" or "yellow fellows."

126.1. Draper MS. 11 C 11 (39).

127.2. Draper MS. 6 S 78-79.

127.5. Draper MS. 16 C 76; *Life,* p. 459.

128.2. Draper MS. 6 S 301-302.

129.1. Draper MS. 11 C 11. Reprinted in *Lexington Leader,* April 29, 1934.

129.2. Collins, II, 576; *Life,* p. 470; Draper MS. 11 CC 11.

129.5. Draper MS. 6 S 96.

130.1. Draper MSS. 11 CC 11, 12 CC 75.

130.3. Draper MS. 12 C 6 (2).

130.4. John Floyd to William Preston, July 21, 1776, Draper MS. 17 CC 171-175; Ranck, p. 250; *H.Q.,* 21:171-173 (1928); Draper MSS. 11 CC 11, 12 C 10 (6-7), 12 C 13 (3).

131.3. *Life,* pp. 467-468.

132.3. Floyd, *loc. cit.*

133.4. Draper MS. 16 C 76.

134.2. Draper MS. 11 CC 5-15; *H.Q.,* 10:168 (1936).

135.2. The mutual discovery is described by John Floyd, *loc. cit.* Floyd wrote his account within a few days. See also Draper MSS. 11 CC 75, 14 C 84-85, 7 C 78, 7 C 76, 84, 95, 115.

135.3. *Life,* p. 174; Draper MSS. 6 S 99, 1 C 78, 4 C 49. According to another and probably less accurate account Jemima cried: "That's Daddy's rifle." It was, of course, easy to distinguish between the reports of different rifles. See Virginia Hays Asbury and Albert N. Doerschuk in *Mo. Hist. Rev.,* 23:537 (1928-29).

135.5. Draper MS. 9 C 68.

135.6. Draper MS. 22 C 20.

135.7. Draper MS. 22 C 5 (10). On the throwing of knives, see William Faux in Thwaites: *Early Western Travel,* XI, p. 221.

136.2. *Life,* p. 474; Collins, II, 526.

136.3. Floyd, *loc. cit.*

136.4. On Blackfish's son, see Draper MSS. 7 C 16, 12 CC 200 (80). On Hanging Maw (Scolacutta), *New York Magazine,* My 1796 (Draper MS. 4 C 21); Draper MS. 4 C 22; Com. of Claims Report, Jan. 17, 1797.

136.5. Capt. Matthew Arbuckle to Col. William Fleming, Aug. 15, 1776, Draper MS. 2 ZZ 7 S; Thwaites and Kellogg: *Revolution on the Upper Ohio,* p. 185; *Life,* p. 475 n.

137.2. Redd, *op. cit., Va. Mag.,* 7:2 Jy 1899.

138.2. Draper MSS. 7 C 16, 18, 20, 97.

138.5. *Life,* p. 481. Some accounts say that Daniel Boone performed the ceremony, but this is doubtful. See also Charles W. Bryan: "Richard Callaway, Kentucky Pioneer," *H.Q.*, 9:44 (1935); *Va. Mag.*, 7:11 Jy 1899; *Life,* pp. 481-482; William Stewart Lester: *Transylvania Colony,* p. 250.

139.4. Redd, *op. cit., Va. Mag.*, 7:1 Jy 1899; W. G. Simms: *Views and Reviews* (1845), I, p. 120; John H. Wheeler: *Hist. Sketches of N. C.* (1851), II, p. 446.

141.1. *Life,* pp. 441, 478; Ranck, p. 51; *H.Q.*, 2:171 (1928).

142.1. *Ill. Hist. Coll.*, VIII, 210-212. On "scald feet," see James McAfee's Journal, Aug. 11, 1773, in *Woods-McAfee Memorial,* p. 437.

142.2. *Life,* pp. 483, 485; Daniel Boone to Col. William Preston, Sept. 7, 1776, Draper MS. 4 C 77.

142.4. Life, p. 487; *Ill. Hist. Coll.*, VIII, 20, 214-215; Collins, II, pp. 466-467; Draper MS. 4 CC 84 (5-6).

142.5. *Life,* pp. 478-480, 489; John Floyd to Col. William Preston, July 21, 1766, Draper MS. 4 CC 84 (6); Edna Kenton: *Simon Kenton,* p. 81.

143.2. Ellis, pp. 36-37.

144.3. Floyd, *loc. cit.*, Draper MS. 4 C 77.

144.5. *Ill. Hist. Coll.*, VIII, lvi and note 4; Draper MS. 11 C 44; *Life,* p. 493.

145.3. This form of Blackfish's name is given by William Albert Galloway: *Old Chillicothe* (Xenia, O.: Buckeye Press, 1934), p. 56. *Life,* p. 529, gives it as Cot-ta-wa-ma-so.

146.1. Edna Kenton: *op. cit.*, p. 84, says he went to Boone's Station, but this did not yet exist. See also Draper MS. 11 C 4; James McBride, *Pioneer Biography,* I, p. 227.

146.2. *Life,* pp. 493-494; Draper MSS. 12 C 15 (1), 12 C 16 (1-5), 27 (4-7), 28 (2), 12 C 17, 19 C 6-7; *Ill. Hist. Coll.*, VIII, 21, 215-216. There is for once not much doubt about the number of Indians. Young Ray thought there were 47, but Coomes, who had them under painfully close observation, said seventy. See also M. J. Spalding: *Sketches of the Early Catholic Missions of Ky.*, pp. 35-37.

147.1. Draper MS. 12 C 17 (3).

147.3. Draper MS. 4 CC 30 *ff.*, 19 C 7.

147.4. Spalding, *op. cit.*, p. 36.

147.4. Spalding, *op. cit.*, p. 37.

148.1. Draper MSS. 12 C 15 (1), 12 C 28 (2), 19 C 6, 12 C 16 (14), 12 C 28 (2), 19 C 6, 4 CC 30.

148.4. *Life,* p. 496; William Littell: *Political Transactions* (Filson Club, No. 31), p. 7; Draper MSS. 12 C 15, 12 C 16.

149.1. Draper MS. 12 C 27 (14).

149.2. *Life,* p. 495 and note, quoting diaries and statements of George Rogers Clark, John Cowan, Levi Todd, Robert Hancock, Joseph Kennedy, and William Cradlebaugh. The two latter were actually in Boonesborough. For the scouts' own depositions, see Draper MS. 11 C 6-21.

149.4. Filson, p. 61, says April 15, but is obviously wrong. Clark's Diary fixes the day. *Cf.* Ranck, p. 57 n., and Draper MS. 4 CC 30.

149.5. In frontier warfare, strength reports are rarely accurate. Clark says "forty to fifty" (*Ill. Hist. Coll.*, VIII, 21). Filson says "above a hundred," but he is often inaccurate and derives most of his information from Boone, who was incapacitated during this attack. On the cows which gave the alarm, see Draper MSS. 11 CC 12 (40), 12 C 5, 13, 15, 27; *Ohio Arch. and Hist. Qy.*, 22:132 (1913).

150.2. *Life,* p. 498.

150.3. *Life,* p. 499; Draper MSS. 11 CC 12, 6 S 101-102; R. W. M'Farland: "Simon

Kenton," *Ohio Arch. and Hist. Qy.*, 13:15 Ja 1913. M'Farland talked with Kenton himself (p. 17).

151.3. M'Farland, *loc. cit.; Life*, p. 501; Edna Kenton, *op. cit.*, pp. 86-88.

151.4. Draper MS. 11 CC 12; *Life*, p. 500.

152.2. Draper MSS. 12 C 28 (5), 19 C 7, 4 CC 30; *Life*, p. 506; *Ill. Hist. Coll.*, VIII, 22, 70, 557.

152.4. Draper MSS. 12 C 15 (3), 12 C 16 (7-8), 19 C 8, 73-74; *Life*, pp. 513-514.

153.1. Draper MS. 4 CC 84 (5); James Handasyd Perkins: *Memoir and Writings*, II, p. 272; Bradford, p. 35; Speed: *Wilderness Road*, pp. 44-45.

153.2. *Hesperian*, 2:97 D 1838; *Life*, p. 501, however, says that July was quiet.

154.1. Draper MS. 22 C 5; *Life*, pp. 514-515; *Ill. Hist. Coll.*, VIII, 23, 216; Thwaites, p. 143.

154.2. *Ill. Hist. Coll.*, VIII, 23.

154.3. Filson, p. 62; Draper MS. 12 C 16 (7).

154.4. *Life*, pp. 519-520.

156.1. *Life*, pp. 523-524; Draper MSS. S 4b 146, S 4b 169-176; Filson, p. 63; William Hickman MSS. and MS. copy of Isaac Shelby's autobiography in Durrett Coll.

156.3. Thomas D. Clark: "Salt, a Factor in the Settlement of Kentucky," *H.Q.*, 12:42-52 (1938); J. F. D. Smyth, *op. cit.*, pp. 141-143.

158.2. Ranck, p. 64 n.; John W. Monette: *Hist. of the Discovery and Settlement of the Mississippi*, p. 16; Jedidiah Morse: *American Universal Geography* (1802), I, p. 631; Gilbert Imlay: *Topographical Description* (1792), p. 119; Alexander Scott Withers: *Chronicles* (Ed. Thwaites, 1895), p. 265 n.; *Life*, pp. 524, 563; Thomas Jefferson: *Notes on Virginia*, p. 31.

158.4. Bradford, p. 37. "We made a few bushels of salt," according to a survivor. See deposition of Jesse Copher, May 15, 1805, *Complete Record Book* of Fayette County, D. 259; *Reg.*, 32:5 Ja 1934.

159.1. *Life*, p. 525. The fight in which Boone is said to have shot one Indian and knifed another is supposed to have happened on one of these trips. Though recounted by Flint and represented in sculpture in the Capitol at Washington, it is now regarded as apocryphal.

159.3. Draper MSS. 6 S 95, 11 C 28-30, 11 C 62, 6 S 103-109, 6 S 287, 4 C 44; depositions in *Complete Record Book* of Fayette County, D. 223, 259; *Reg.*, 32: 8, 9, 15-16 (1932).

161.1. Bradford, p. 36, says there were 102 Indians, but in view of the vote at the council, Draper's figure of 120 (*Life*, pp. 528-529) is probably correct.

The statement of Joseph Jackson, Draper MS. 11 C 62, is a valuable source since he lived for twenty-one years among the Indians who captured him. See also Draper MS. 6 S 287 and Ranck, p. 65.

161.3. A woman chief of the Shawnees, about this time, had several negroes, "taken from Virginia in time of last war, and now esteemed as her property." David Jones: *Journal* (Ed. 1865), p. 87.

162.1. *Life*, pp. 525-526.

164.4. Draper MSS. 22 C 5 (12), 6 S 108.

164.6. The dialogue is reported in Daniel Trabue (Draper MS. 57 J) and Joseph Jackson's statement, Draper MS. 11 C 62 *f*.

166.1. Joseph Jackson dictated the speech to Draper in April, 1844. See *Life*, pp. 533-534, and Draper MS. 11 C 62 *ff*. Except for one sentence the text follows Draper's original notes. The added sentence is from the *Life*. The vote is described by Jackson. See the series of depositions in Draper MS. 11 C.

167.4. Hamilton to Carleton, April 25, 1778. Canadian Archives, B 122, p. 35; *Mich.*, IX, 435 (1886).

168.4. Draper MSS. 11 C 62 *ff.*, 19 C 76, 6 S 109-110, 6 C 46.

169.1. On the gauntlet, see Withers, *op. cit.*, Notes 31, 32, 34, and *Early Times in Middle Tennessee*, p. 220.

169.3. *Life*, p. 541. *Cf.* Draper MS. 11 C 62.

170.2. W. B. Smith to G. R. Clark, Draper MS. 48 J 19; *Ill. Hist. Coll.*, VIII, 40. *Cf. Ibid.*, 48 J 20, 3 NN 105-106, and VIII, 42; *Wis. Hist. Publ. Draper Series*, III, 252.

171.2. Draper MS. 11 C 29.

172.1. Draper MS. 7 C 14; C. Hale Sipe: *Indian Wars of Pennsylvania*, pp. 506-509.

172.3. Hamilton to Carleton, April 25, 1776, Canad. Arch., B 122, p. 35; Mich., IX, 435 (1886); Draper MS. 11 C 56.

172.4. The conversation is reported in *Life*, p. 548.

173.3. Filson, p. 64; Draper MSS. 11 C 29, 6 S 112, 11 C 83, 12 CC 74. On the powder-making, see Henry Howe: *Hist. Colls. Ohio*, I, 694; *Life*, pp. 550-551; Gilbert Imlay: *Topographical Description*, p. 122. Boone's own formula is in his 1790-95 account book, Draper MS. 6 C 35.

173.4. R. B. McAfee in Cist: *Michigan Miscellany*, 2:139 S 145; Draper MS. 11 C 56. Capt. Samuel Brady, hero of the Pennsylvania frontier, also carried his old British commission, wearing it in a bag around his neck. See C. Hale Sipe, *op. cit.*, p. 855. See also *Life*, p. 542.

174.2. Draper MS. 12 CC 74.

174.3. Draper MS. 12 CC 76.

175.2. Draper MSS. 4 B 174-176, 6 CC 26-28, 12 CC 74, 6 S 114-115; *Life*, pp. 552-554; William Stewart Lester: *Transylvania Colony*, p. 205.

175.5. Draper MS. 12 CC 76-77, derived largely from a hunting companion who had the story from Andrew Johnson himself.

176.2. Draper MSS. 4 C 79-80, 11 C 5-9, 17-18, 62 (27), 71; 12 C 28, 12 CC 200 (80), 16 S 5-8, 11 CC 94; Journal of the Virginia House of Delegates, Dec. 2, 1781; *Wis. Hist. Soc. Publ. Draper Series*, V, 185; *Wis. Hist. Coll.*, XXIII, 114, 244 (1916), note 1; *Mich.*, XIX, 258 (1891).

176.3. Boone's Indian name is also spelled "Cheltowee" and once "Shwisher-towah" (Draper MS. 22 C 12).

177.1. Mann Butler: *Hist. Ky.* (1836), p. 42.

177.2. Peck, 73-74; *Life*, p. 557; Ranck, p. 66.

178.2. Draper MS. 6 S 121; *Life*, pp. 558, 571.

178.3. Draper MS. 12 CC 200 (80).

179.2. Draper MS. 4 C 46-47 gives another version.

179.4. Draper MSS. 22 C 28; 19 C 9.

180.1. Filson, p. 65; Draper MS. 22 C 28.

180.3. Draper MS. 16 C 76; *Life*, p. 565; Peck, p. 75.

180.4. Carter *vs.* Oldham, 1 Ky. 347 (Hughes, 1800).

181.1. Draper MSS. 4 C 47, 11 C 62, 22 C 5 (12).

181.2. Draper MS. 16 C 7-8.

181.7. Henry Howe: *Hist. Coll. Ohio*, I, 693-694; Theodore Roosevelt: *Winning of the West* (National Ed., 1926), I, p. 63. *Life*, p. 563, says this incident occurred on the march from the Blue Licks to Chillicothe, but as Boone had just killed a buffalo, it is hard to see why the Indians starved. Draper says that Boone told this story to Joseph Wood, of Marietta, O., who passed it on to Howe.

182.1. *American Pioneer,* I, p. 374 (1842).

182.2. *Life,* p. 564; Ranck, p. 69.

182.4. Draper MS. 11 C 62 gives the story as told by Joseph Jackson, who was living with the Indians at the time. See also Draper MSS. 9 C 79, 19 C 77-78, 22 C 5 (13-14), 12 CC 99 (87), and *Life,* pp. 565-566. But *cf.* J. H. Perkins: *Annals of the West* (Ed. 1857), p. 297.

183.7. *Life,* p. 568; Draper MSS. 6 D 125, 11 C 62. Some accounts say Boone killed a wild turkey, probably because the Indians were hunting wild turkeys when he escaped. Joseph Jackson says a deer. On the depositions, see Draper MSS. 11 C 64, 15 C 25, 16 C 88, 11 C 69 (original with autograph signature); Collins, II, p. 555; *Life,* p. 568 n. Depositions dated Sept. 28, 1795, and July 3, 1797.

184.3. On Boone's crossing and arrival, see *Life,* p. 567; Peck, p. 76; Draper MSS. 4 C 47, 22 C 5 (12), 9 C 68.

185.3. The cat story is in Draper MS. 11 C 107, as told by John Tonner, who had it from Daniel and Rebecca Boone. It is confirmed by Boone's nephew, Daniel Bryan, in 22 C 12. See also 6 S 141.

185.6. John Todd to Patrick Lockhart, June 29, 1778, *H.Q.,* 2:160 Jy 1928; Temple Bodley: *Kentucky* (1928), p. 153.

186.3. *Life,* p. 579.

189.3. *Life,* pp. 579-580; Trabue, Draper MS. 57 J; printed version, pp. 31, 36.

189.5. *Life,* p. 579; Ranck, pp. 96-97.

190.2. Deposition of William Cradelbaugh, Fayette County *Complete Record Book,* D. 274; *Reg.,* 32:9 Ja 1934. One of these kettles, handed down in Simon Kenton's family, is now in the Blue Licks Museum.

190.6. Draper MS. 4 C 79, 12 CC 99 (87); *Life,* pp. 579-580; Withers, *op. cit.,* p. 267.

190.7. Draper MSS. 11 C 62, 11 CC 94 (44); *Life,* pp. 572-573; Hancock's deposition, *Life,* pp. 580-581; Draper MS. 4 C 79; *Wis. State Hist. Soc. Coll.,* XXIII, 114 (1916). See also Chapter XIII of the present work.

191.5. The letter is in Draper MS. 4 C 79-80.

192.2. *Life,* pp. 582-583; W. B. Smith: "Attack upon Boonesborough," copies in Durrett MS. 2; deposition of Jesse Hodges, Draper MS. 11 C 65-66; Collins, II, 59, 664.

192.3. Draper MS. 4 C 78; *Wis. State Hist. Soc. Coll.,* XXIII, 123; *Life,* p. 581 n. There is a laudatory note in John Almon's *Remembrancer,* 7:340, dated from Williamsburg, Oct. 9, 1778. *Cf. South Carolina Gazette,* Nov. 12, 1778, Draper MS. 11 C 57.

193.1. *Life,* p. 583.

193.2. Draper MS. 4 C 45. The story was told to Draper by Abner Bryan, who asserted he had it from Daniel Boone. Other accounts ignore the episode, which may belong to another period. Boone estimated that the second band of Indians numbered 30, Simon Kenton 40 (*Life,* p. 584). For some reason W. B. Smith says there were 250 Indians (Durrett MS. 2, fol. 4).

194.1. Draper MSS. 11 C 62, 22 C 5 (13); *Life,* p. 583; John A. McClung: *Sketches of Western Adventure* (1852), p. 89; Withers, *op. cit.,* pp. 267-268; James Handasyd Perkins, *op. cit.,* II, 277; R. W. M'Farland, *op. cit., Ohio Arch. and Hist. Qy.,* 13:16-17 (1904); *North American Review,* 62:99 Ja 1846.

194.4. Draper MS. 11 C 62; *Life,* pp. 584-585.

195.2. *Life,* p. 585; Withers, *op. cit.,* p. 268 n.
195.3. There are specimens of the bullet molds in the Blue Licks Museum.
196.1. Hamilton to Cramahe, Canad. Arch., B 122, pp. 122, 149; *Mich.,* IX, 464, 465. W. B. Smith insists on "not less than six hundred Indians, in three divisions of about two hundred each" (Durrett MS. fols. 5-6). Daniel Trabue (Durrett TS. copy) says 1000! Joseph Jackson thought there were five to six hundred (Draper MS. 11 C 62).
196.2. Hamilton to Haldimand, about Sept. 1, 1778. Canad. Arch., B 122, p. 149; *Mich.,* IX, 473 (1886).
196.3. The ford has now disappeared as the result of modern dam building. On the Indian approach, see Bradford, p. 40; Ranck, pp. 75-76; and Withers, *op. cit.,* p. 268 n.
198.1. Draper MS. 19 C 9, 78.
198.2. Draper MSS. 12 CC 74-75, 11 CC 12, 6 S 124; W. B. Smith, Durrett MS. fol. 6.
199.4. The solemn foolery of this diplomatic conversation is reported by *Life,* p. 588. Draper MS. 12 CC 74 has a report by J. Collins, who was in Boonesborough during the siege. On Boone's further question as to the skirmish, see Draper MS. 12 CC 65; *Reg.,* 33:149 Ap 1935. On the new commander, see Draper MS. 12 C 5 (7).
199.10. Draper MSS. 12 C 5 (7), 11 C 98.
200.1. Draper MS. 11 CC 12-13.
200.3. *Life,* p. 589; Draper MS. 6 S 121; but *cf.* 19 C 80.
200.4. Draper MS. 11 CC 13.
200.5. Draper MSS. 11 CC 94 (44), 12 CC 205.
201.2. *Life,* p. 593, estimates forty riflemen.
201.3. Hamilton to Haldimand, about Sept. 1, 1778, Canad. Arch., B 122, p. 149; *Mich.,* IX, 465 (1886).
202.1. Ranck, p. 83.
202.2. The two men, De Quindre and Chêne, or Chesne, are frequently mentioned in official correspondence and are both carried on Hamilton's strength report for Sept. 5, 1778. Canad. Arch., B 22, p. 149; *Mich.,* IX, 470 (1886).
202.3. Bradford, p. 41; *Life,* p. 591.
202.4. W. B. Smith mentions the panther-skin incident but places it earlier.
203.2. Draper MS. 19 C 79.
203.3. Bradford, p. 40; *Life,* p. 57; Draper MS. 12 CC 75.
205.1. Ranck, p. 86.
206.2. *Life,* p. 594.
206.3. John Bowman to George Rogers Clark, Oct. 14, 1778, Draper MS. 48 J 42.
207.4. *Life,* pp. 596-597; Draper MS. 11 CC 13.
208.1. Draper MS. 11 C 76; *Life,* p. 597.
208.2. Bradford, p. 44.
208.4. Draper MSS. 11 C 76, 12 CC 75; *Life,* p. 599.
209.1. Bradford, p. 44.
209.5. Draper MSS. 22 C 5 (16), 6 S 141; *Life,* p. 600.
210.1. Draper MS. 11 CC 13.
210.2. Draper MSS. 11 C 76, 12 C 5 (10); Bradford, p. 43; Withers, *op. cit.,* p. 269; *Life,* p. 602. *Cf.* Journal of Ebenezer Denny, *Mem. Penna. Hist. Soc.,* 7:276 (1860) under date Jan. 8, 1786.

210.6. Bowman to Clark, Draper MS. 48 J 42; Daniel Trabue, p. 33; Ranck, p. 252; W. B. Smith, Durrett MS. p. 13; Draper MSS. 11 C 98, 19 C 81.
212.1. Ranck, p. 90. This incident may be confused with James Ray's similar experience at Harrodsburg. *Cf.* p. 153 of the present work.
212.2. Draper MSS. 19 C 14, 82; 11 CC 12, 12 CC 200 (80).
212.3. Draper MS. 12 CC 200 (80).
212.4. Draper MSS. 12 C 5 (7), 11 CC 13; *Life,* pp. 606-607.
213.2. W. B. Smith, Durrett MS. p. 14.
213.4. Draper MSS. 11 C 98-99, 12 C 5 (8-9), 12 CC 75; *Life,* p. 612.
214.1. Boone had lived four months among the Shawnees. Even before his captivity, members of the party who rescued Jemima Boone and the Callaway girls could identify Shawnee words. Traders and trappers in modern Ontario and Minnesota often have a good working knowledge of Ojibway. The story of the pretended departure is in Ranck, p. 91.
215.4. Draper MS. 12 C 5 (9); *Life,* p. 611.
216.2. *Life,* p. 614; Smith, *op. cit.,* p. 15; Withers, *op. cit.,* p. 270; Ranck, p. 93.
217.3. Draper MSS. 11 C 76, 19 C 20, 82; 4 C 48. The quotation is from Daniel Trabue (57 J 27) with some re-punctuation.
217.5. Draper MS. 6 S 138, 142. *Cf.* 22 C 16 (26).
218.1. Draper MS. 19 C.
218.3. Elijah Bryan insisted that he had this story from Boone himself. See Draper MS. 4 C 33, 48. Peck, pp. 86-87 n., who also knew Boone and several other survivors of the siege, tells the same story. Boone's remark is from *Pion. Fam.,* p. 27, also based on the recollections of survivors. But *Life,* pp. 613, 622, says Pompey was shot by William Collins on the river bank. See also Draper MSS. 11 CC 13, 16 C 81, 6 S 143, 295.
218.4. Peck, *loc. cit. Life,* p. 613, says the body was never found, but this may mean merely that his informants did not see it. *Cf.* Draper MS. 19 C 7-8.
218.5. *Life,* pp. 613, 624. Washington's headquarters displayed a flag as early as 1776. The Continental Congress passed a flag resolution June 14, 1777. The Kentucky militia received military supplies like the other Virginia forces and these probably included colors.
219.2. Bradford, p. 44; Draper MS. 11 CC 13; Ranck, pp. 95-96.
220.3. Draper MSS. 11 CC 13, 19 C 85; Smith, *op. cit.,* p. 14; *Life,* p. 619.
221.1. Draper MS. 12 C 2 (15); Trabue, Draper MS. 57 J 27-28; *Life,* pp. 624-625.
222.3. Draper MSS. 11 CC 14, 6 S 143; Bradford, p. 45; Ranck, p. 97. Ranck decorously edits the actual language used.
222.6. Draper MSS. 12 C 5 (9), 16 C 7-8, 19 C 18. The allusions to Pompey are in Draper MS. 11 CC 13 and *Life,* pp. 614-615. A manuscript Shawnee vocabulary in the Durrett Coll. gives "nipwaah" as "dead."
223.1. Draper MSS. 4 C 24-26 (10-11), 12 C 5 (9). The Draper MSS. also allude to an article in the *Progressive Age* (Scott County, Va.), 27 S 1883.
223.5. Draper MSS. 4 C 48, 19 C 18, 22 C 37, 11 CC 13; *Life,* pp. 616-617. Ranck is obviously wrong in saying that Colonel Callaway made the cannon. He is obviously following Daniel Trabue in Draper MS. 57 J 26, but Trabue was not at the siege.
223.6. Trabue, p. 33.
224.2. Draper MSS. 19 C 18, 11 CC 14, 57 J 27; *Life,* p. 617.
224.4. Trabue, p. 34.
224.9. *Wis. State Hist. Soc. Coll.,* XXIII, 115, 126-127; Draper MS. 4 C 80.

225.1. Draper MSS. 11 C 29, 62; 24 C 159-160; Heckewelder to Brodhead, March 12, 1779, Washington Papers in *Wis. State Hist. Soc. Coll.*, XXIII, 244-245.

225.2. Statement of "Drewyer" (*i.e.*, Peter Drouillard) to Simon Kenton at Detroit, Draper MS. 11 C 77; Ranck, p. 101.

225.5. Draper MS. 11 C 76-77.

226.1 *ff*. Draper MS. 57 J 28.

227.1. *Life*, p. 629.

228.2. *Va. Mag.*, 6:403 (1899).

230.2. *H.Q.*, 2:98-100, 106, 119, 127 Ap 1928.

230.5. Hamilton to Carleton, April 25, 1778, Canad. Arch., B 122, p. 35; *Mich.*, IX 435 (1886); *Wis. State Hist. Publ.*, XXIII, 283-284 (1912).

232.3. Draper MSS. 8 C 43, 64, 85, 89; 14 CC 191, 22 C 41, 6 S 144, 288; *Pion. Fam.*, p. 132.

232.4. Thwaites and Kellogg: *Frontier Retreat*, pp. 22-23.

233.1. Bradford, p. 32; William Littell: *Political Transactions* (Filson Club, No. 31), p. 7. The British made a similar offer to a Pennsylvania officer. See C. Hale Sipe, *Indian Wars of Penna.*, p. 617. Boone's remark is in Draper MS. 11 CC 14.

233.3. See the Shane Coll. in the Presbyt. Hist. Soc., Philadelphia, especially the Madison Papers, S. 49. XX. Nos. 14-15; McDowell Papers, S. 39. IX. 1; Order Book, 2nd Virginia Regt., S. 61. XXXII.

234.1. Draper MS. 57 J 44, followed by *Life*, pp. 630-632. The printed text has been much edited at this point. Practically all our knowledge of the court-martial is based on this one document.

236.2. Samuel M. Wilson: "Daniel Boone 1734-1934," *H.Q.*, 8:192-193 (1934).

236.5. Draper MSS. 11 CC 94, 12 CC 205, and 4 C 44, statement of Abner Bryan, apparently on information from Boone himself.

237.1. *Wis. State Hist. Soc. Coll.*, XIII, 126-127 n.; *Ill. Hist. Soc. Coll.*, VIII, 71; John Almon's *Remembrancer*, 7:340 (1778-1779); Draper MSS. 4 B 252, 57 J 32, 11 C 84.

237.5. Draper MSS. 11 C 61, 22 C 14, 20-22.

238.2. Kenton, in conversation with Hon. John H. James, was commenting on McClung's reflections against Boone. Draper MS. 11 C 76; *Life*, p. 605.

239.3. Draper MS. 6 S 144.

240.1. Filson, p. 70, says 160 men. Henry Hall in Draper MS. 12 C 1 (2-7) says about 230. Bird to Lernoult, June 9, 12, 1779, Canad. Arch., B 122, pp. 351, 352; *Mich.*, X, 336-337, 352 (1886); Draper MSS. 11 C 6, 7, 10, 62; 12 C 1 (2-7), 12 C 38 (2).

241.2. Draper MSS. 12 C 16, 11 C 107, 109; 13 C 192, 22 C 16 (9), 12 CC 124; Thwaites, p. 174.

241.4. Hening's Statutes, p. 135; William Littell: *Laws of Kentucky*, III, pp. 538-540; Samuel M. Wilson in *Report of the Boone Bicentennial Commission*, p. 38.

242.1. Deposition of Peter Schull, *Complete Record Book* of Fayette County, B 62; *Reg.*, 31:115 Ap 1933. James McMillan, in a deposition for William Calk, distinguishes between Boonesborough and Boone's Station in April or May of 1780 or 81. See photostat copies of the Calk Papers, Library of the University of Kentucky.

243.2. The earliest copy of the certificate book, not itself an original, is in the custody of the clerk of Fayette County Court. It has been reprinted by the

Kentucky State Hist. Soc., XXI, January, 1923. See pp. 1-2, 82-85, 87, and *Ill. Hist. Coll.*, VIII, cxv.

244.1. On the robbery, see Draper MSS. 4 C 49, 13 C 1, 22 C 16, 6 S 145-146, 162, 309-310; Petition to Kentucky Legislature (1812); Peck, pp. 94-95; Bogart, p. 241; Thwaites, p. 176. It is mentioned in *Va. Gazette,* No. 73, p. 2, 26 Jy 1780. There is an original in the Virginia State Library and a photostat in the N. Y. Public Library. On Boone's dreams, see 6 S 282. On pioneer belief in dreams, see Joseph Doddridge: *Notes on the Settlement and Indian Wars* (1876), pp. 65-66.

245.6. The original letter, from the papers of Miss Lucretia Hart, is in the library of the Presbyt. Hist. Soc. The transcription here given is the author's, made after three careful examinations of the original. Hart's hand leaves room for doubt, however. There is a slightly different transcription in the society's *Journal,* 14:343 (1930-31).

246.2. See Clawson and Wilson Sale, Anderson Galleries, Jan. 18, 1917, No. 18; Boone's letter to Thomas Hart, May 7, 1789, Durrett Coll.; and in the library of the Presbyt. Hist. Soc.: Thomas to Sarah Hart, Aug. 12, 1783, Shane Collection, Hart Family Papers, XIX, II, No. 32; letter of Thomas Hart, Oct. 4, 1781, *Ibid.,* XIX, III, No. 27; Thomas to Nathaniel Hart, April 22, 1782, *Ibid.,* XIX, III, No. 29. Nathaniel Hart's letter is Draper MS. 13 C 1.

246.4. Draper MS. 22 C 16 (9). Professor Jonathan Truman Dorris has a MS. note by Stoddard Johnson describing a conversation of French Tipton with one of the losers, still furious against Boone, years after the loss.

246.5. Lewis Preston Summers: *Annals of Southwest Virginia,* quoting Court Records of Washington Co., Va., March 21, 1781.

247.1. Charles I. Walker: "Northwest during the Revolution," *Mich.,* III, 25-26 (1881); Canad. Arch., B 103, p. 491; *Mich.,* XX, 271 (1892). Haldimand refers to a bill for Indian goods of £64,035.8.8½. Haldimand to DePeyster, July 6, 1780, Canad. Arch., B 121, p. 50. See also Gen. John Forbes to Richard Peters, Aug. 28, 1758, in State Hist. Soc. Penna.

247.3. Western Reserve Hist. Soc., Cleveland, O., Vault MS. 2342, fol. 1, verso.

248.2. Arthur Campbell Goodwood to Col. William Preston, June 7, 1780, *John P. Branch Hist. Papers,* IV, 311; *Wis. State Hist. Coll.,* XXIV, Draper Ser., V, 192. On Chapline, see also *Ill. Hist. Coll.,* VIII, 23 n., and Swearingem *vs.* Higgins, 1 Ky 7 (Hughes, 1787).

248.3. Bowman to Brodhead, May 27, 1780, Draper MS. 16 S 5; *Wis. Hist. Publ.,* XXIV, Draper Ser., V, 185-192; *Wis. State Hist. Coll.,* XXIII, 244-245, 259; *Mich.,* XIX, 528 (1891); Draper MSS. 11 C 62 (27), 24 C 159-160, 4 NN 80; *John P. Branch Hist. Papers,* IV, 311.

248.5. Bird to DePeyster, July 24, 1780, Canad. Arch., B 100, p. 436; *Mich.,* XIX, 546 (1891); Haldimand to DePeyster, July 24, 1780, Canad. Arch., B 104, p. 146; *Mich.,* XIX, 546-547 (1891).

250.1. Draper MS. 11 CC 268.

250.2. McKee to DePeyster, Canad. Arch., B 100, p. 413; *Mich.,* XIX, 543 (1891).

250.4. *H.Q.,* 2:107 (1928).

251.1. DePeyster to Bolton, May 16, 1780, Canad. Arch., B 100, p. 370; *Mich.,* XIX, 520 (1891); Draper MS. 11 C 56; *Vt. Hist. Coll.,* II, 344.

251.2. Wilbur H. Siebert: "Kentucky's Loyalist Proprietors," *Miss. Valley Hist. Rev.,* 7:114 S 1920.

252.3. "An Act covering escheats and forfeitures," passed in May, 1779. Henning: *Statutes,* X, 293-295; Siebert, *op. cit.,* p. 123; R. T. Durrett: *Centenary* *of Louisville,* pp. 23-27, 131, 133, 154 *ff.;* Collins, II, p. 183, 360. On Connolly, see Clarence M. Burton: "John Connolly, a Tory of the Revolution," *Proc. Am. Antiq. Soc.* (NS), XX, 71 *ff.;* Percy B. Caley: "Life and Adventures of . . . ," *Western Penna. Hist. Mag.,* 11:248 O 1928.

253.1. From the original in the Durrett Coll.

253.4. Homan to Bird, Aug. 15, 1780, Canad. Arch., B 122, p. 523; *Mich.,* X, 418-419 (1886).

254.1. DePeyster to Powell, Canad. Arch., B 101, p. 42; *Mich.,* XIX, 614-615 (1891); Delawares and Shawnees to DePeyster, Aug. 22, 1780, Canad. Arch., B 122, p. 533; *Mich.,* X, 565-566 (1886); XIX, 554, 614-615 (1891); and Draper MS. 13 C 2, 5.

254.2. *Life,* App. VI, 10-11; Draper MS. 2 ZZ 75 (14); *Ill. Hist. Coll.,* VIII, 396-397, 399, 401; Bryan's Station Petition, March 13, 1780, *Cal. Va.;* Draper MSS. 50 J 18, 20; 11 C 62, 12 C 5 (12), 62 (29).

254.3. Bogart, p. 270; Draper MS. 22 C 14 (26).

255.1. Presbyt. Hist. Soc., Shane Coll., Bryan Family Papers, S. 47, XVIII, VI, a MS. account book. The document is so badly written and so faded that the text is sometimes doubtful. The fourth line from the bottom may read: "and 2 got in."

255.4. Draper MS. 13 C 104-105. Joseph Ficklin had this story from a man who was present. The date is uncertain but Draper sets it as 1780, on account of the unusually cold weather. The winter of 1779-1780 was famous as the "hard winter."

255.5. On Boone's solitary scouts, see James Handasyd Perkins: *Memoirs and Writings,* II, 265. Perkins had access to a great deal of information and a reputation for accuracy. *Cf.* I, 319.

256.2. Collins, I, p. 49.

257.1. There are many accounts of this incident. I have in the main followed that of Daniel Bryan (Draper MS. 22 C 7) who often heard Daniel Boone recount his adventures. See Bradford, pp. 115-117; statement of Daniel Boone to Col. Daniel Thompson, Draper MS. 12 C 10 (7); and Draper MSS. 7 C 83, 84, 91; 11 CC 52, 65; 12 CC 109, 12 CC 76, 22 C 2, 6 S 96, 147-148.

258.2. Draper MS. 13 C 29; *H.Q.,* 8:197 (1934).

258.3. Redd, *op. cit., Va. Mag.,* 7:118 O 1899; Draper MSS. 13 C 16-23, 6 S 149-150; St. George Tucker to his wife, *Mag. Am. Hist.,* 7:202 (1881); *H.Q.,* 8:197 (1934); Thwaites, pp. 182-183.

259.6. Draper MSS. 6 S 150, 13 C 16-23, 79 (19); Tarleton: *Hist. of the Campaign,* pp. 297-298.

259.8. *Pion. Fam.,* p. 132.

260.1. Draper MS. 13 C 21.

260.2. Draper MS. 6 S 151.

260.3. Draper MSS. 1 C 45 (299), 6 S 151, 1 C 35, 36, 38, 46.

260.4. Ellis, pp. 132-133.

261.1. Draper MSS. 19 C 29-30, 51 J 53; *Ill. Hist. Coll.,* VIII, 557.

262.1. Ranck, p. 124.

263.1. Boone to Governor, *Cal. Va.,* III, 280-281; II, 314; Reuben T. Durrett: *Bryant's Station* (Filson Club, No. 12), p. 206; Draper MS. 51 J 79; *Ill. Hist. Coll.,* VIII, 582.

263.2. Charles I. Walker, *op. cit., Mich.,* III, 25-26 (1881); DePeyster to Powell, April 4, 1781, Canad. Arch., B 101, p. 421; *Mich.,* XIX, 614-615 (1891); De-

Peyster to Powell, Aug. 17, 1782, Canad. Arch., B 102, p. 130; *Mich.*, XX, 44 (1892).

264.1. This is the accepted view of Girty. For a more favorable and perhaps juster view, see Joseph M. Hutchen: "Simon Girty," *Am. Pioneer,* II, 282-285 (1843) and Draper MS. 11 C 62. See also 11 CC 267.

264.5. Ranck, p. 126.

265.3. Clark to Harrison, *Cal. Va.*, III, 345; Durrett, *op. cit.*, p. 206.

270.3. Draper MS. 12 CC 245 (15); R. S. Cotterill: "Battle of the Upper Blue Licks," *H.Q.*, 2:29-30 (1927); Shane's interview with Clinkenbeard, Draper MS. 11 CC 1-4; *H.Q.*, 2:118-119 (1928); Durrett, *op. cit.*, p. 223.

271.4. Logan to Harrison, Aug. 31, 1782, *Cal. Va.*, III, 280; Durrett, *op. cit.*, p. 226.

273.1. McKee to DePeyster, dated "Wakitunickie," July 23, 1782, Canad. Arch., B 102, p. 112; *Mich.*, XX, 32-34 (1892).

273.4. Girty's speech is reported by Bradford, presumably from the account of some white captive who heard it. See note by Willard Rouse Jillson, *Reg.*, 36:17 (1938). The florid tone is an unhappy mingling of aboriginal eloquence and eighteenth-century translation, but the content is probably reported with fair accuracy. Among an illiterate people, speeches are long remembered and much commented upon. Among modern Indians one can sometimes pick up reminiscences of famous speeches which have been handed down for years.

274.3. Bradford, p. 123. There is, of course, no absolute certainty as to the route.

274.4. Draper MS. 13 C 79 (3-34).

275.1. Doddridge, *op. cit.*, p. 222. See p. 213 of the present work for a case where this happened repeatedly.

275.2. Thwaites, pp. 185 *ff*.

276.2. Draper MS. 13 C 74.

277.4. Draper MSS. 13 C 61, 11 C 188, 13 C 64.

280.6. Draper MS. 11 C 117 (1).

282.3. 13 C 188 (3).

283.4. The story that, when they found everything quiet, they decided there had been a false alarm, is hardly plausible. In that case, they would all have marched in together. But see Bradford, p. 127; Draper MS. 13 C 110.

284.3. Draper MSS. 13 C 116, 13 C 117 (2-3).

285.1. Bradford, p. 128; Draper MSS. 13 C 69, 13 C 79 (6).

285.3. Draper MSS. 13 C 74, 13 C 180 (1-2).

285.4. Draper MS. 11 CC 243.

286.2. Draper MSS. 13 C 74, 79, 110, 116; Bradford, pp. 127-128; Perkins, *op. cit.*, p. 391; Withers, *op. cit.*, p. 351; Cist's *Cincinnati Miscellany,* 1:138 Ap 1845. Strange to say, Thwaites condemns this well attested episode as "probably fictitious."

287.3. Bradford, p. 130; Draper MSS. 13 C 74-79, 110 (1-2), 116; 11 CC 231, 11 CC 243; Durrett, *op. cit.*, p. 119; Perkins, *op. cit.*, p. 391.

288.1. Draper MS. 12 C 16 (8).

288.2. Durrett, *op. cit.*, pp. 217-218.

289.2. Caldwell to DePeyster, dated "Wakitamiki," Aug. 26, 1782; Canad. Arch., B 123; Durrett, *op. cit.*, pp. 158, 208-209.

290.2. Collins, II, p. 654, quoting the Galena, Ill., *Mercury,* July, 1847. The sword is said to have been recovered a few years later and identified by Mrs. Todd.

291.2. McKee to DePeyster, dated "Shawanese County," Aug. 28, 1782; Canad. Arch., Colonial Office Papers, Ser. II, Vol. 20, p. 288; Durrett, *op. cit.*, pp. 211-215 n.

291.5. Perkins, *op. cit.*, p. 395; Draper MS. 12 CC 134, a statement by one of the scouts.

293.1. Samuel M. Wilson: *Battle of the Blue Licks*, pp. 55-56; but *cf.* DePeyster to Haldimand, Sept. 4, 1782, Canad. Arch., B 123, p. 310; *Mich.*, X, 634-635 (1887), which says Caldwell had 30 picked rangers and about 200 Lake Indians.

294.1. Draper MS. 12 CC 134; Perkins, *op. cit.*, pp. 295-296; Wilson, *op. cit.*, p. 46, quoting Joseph Scholl.

294.2. Conversation recorded in Draper MS. 5 C 51. *Cf.* Draper MS. 5 C 50, 52, 53; Hist. Ky. MSS. ML. 41/N42, fol. 84, in Presbyt. Hist. Soc.

296.2. Draper MS. 12 C 39 says 500. Boone's official report is in *Cal. Va.*, III, 275-276. Quoted portions here are from the original. The printed manuscript is careless. *Cf.* Draper MSS. 4 C 50, 6 S 151-163.

296.3. Draper MS. 13 C 175; Wilson, *op. cit.*, p. 14.

296.7. Draper MSS. 13 C 34, 12 CC 134, 13 C 180 (3), 6 S 153; Wilson, *op. cit.*, pp. 57-58; *H.Q.*, 9:324 (1935).

297.1. Draper MSS. 12 C 24 (4), 39; 6 S 152-153.

297.4. Draper MSS. 12 C 39, 6 S 163; Levi to Robert Todd, *Cal. Va.*, III, 333; Daniel Boone to Governor, Aug. 30, 1782, *Cal. Va.*, III, 275-276; Durrett, *op. cit.*, p. 215.

298.3. Draper MS. 6 S 153-158.

298.4. Draper MS. 6 S 153-154, 158.

299.3. Draper MSS. 4 C 50, 13 C 175, 6 S 164-165; Wilson, *op. cit.*, p. 79; Peck, 127 n.; Draper MSS. 4 C 50, 6 S 164-165, 13 C 175.

300.2. Draper MSS. 13 C 30, 19 C 99, 6 S 156-157, *H.Q.*, 2:115 Ap 1928.

300.3. *H.Q.*, 8.224 (1934).

300.4. Wilson, *op. cit.*, p. 79.

300.8. Draper MSS. 13 C 180 (4), 13 C 181 (7).

301.3. Draper MSS. 13 C 29, 79; 4 C 50.

302.1. Durrett, *op. cit.*, p. 183.

302.2. John W. Van Cleve: "Colonel Robert Patterson," *Am. Pioneer*, 2:344-347 (1843); Draper MS. 13 C 35; Hist. Ky. MSS. ML. 41/N62, fol. 88, Presbyt. Hist. Soc.

303.1. Caldwell to DePeyster, dated "Wakitamiki," Aug. 26, 1782, Canad. Arch., B 123; Durrett, *op. cit.*, pp. 208-209; Logan to Governor, Aug. 31, 1782; *Cal. Va.*, III, 280; Durrett, *op. cit.*, p. 223; Draper MS. 12 CC 135; *H.Q.*, 9:236 (1935).

303.2. Logan to Governor, Aug. 31, 1782; *Cal. Va.*, III, 280; Durrett, *op. cit.*, p. 223.

303.3. Draper MS. 12 C 39 (4).

304.1. Draper MS. 13 C 197; Collins, II, pp. 662-663. Girty's remark is in Draper MS. 12 C 33.

304.3. Boone to Governor, Aug. 30, 1782; *Cal. Va.*, III, 275-276.

304.5. Draper MS. 6 S 165. But *cf.* 19 C 99. See also *H.Q.*, 9:236 (1935); Draper MS. 12 CC 50.

305.1. Draper MS. 11 CC 54-66; *H.Q.*, 2:98 (1928).

305.3. Campbell to Davi[e?]s, Oct. 3, 1782; *Cal. Va.*, III, 337; Durrett, *op. cit.*, p. 222.

305.6. *Ibid.*

306.2. Boone to Governor, Aug. 30, 1782; *Cal. Va.*, III, 275-276. The text here follows the original letter which has not been perfectly transcribed in the *Calendar*. The diary of William Brown, who reached Kentucky in July, 1782, just before the battle, gives Logan's force as 470 and the losses as 43 dead and 22 missing. It is now in the Durrett Coll.

306.4. Steele to Governor, Sept. 12, 1782; *Cal. Va.*, III, 303-304; Durrett, *op. cit.*, p. 204. On other raids at this time, see Draper MSS. 11 C 11, 13 C 124-125; *H.Q.*, 2:133 (1928).

308.1. Draper MS. 12 CC 50 (38); *H.Q.*, 9:236 (1935). On the impression created by the battle, see Hart *vs.* Bodley, 3 Ky. 104 (1807).

308.2. Boone to Governor, Aug. 30, 1782; *Cal. Va.*, III, 275-276. Copy in Durrett Collection. The text here follows the original in the Virginia State Library.

308.3. Clark to Governor, Nov. 30, 1782; *Cal. Va.*, III, 345; Durrett, op. cit., p. 207.

308.4. Logan to Governor; *Cal. Va.*, III, 281; Durrett, *op. cit.*, p. 206. Text follows original in Virginia State Library.

309.2. Officers to Governor, Sept. 11, 1782; *Cal. Va.*, III, 301; Durrett, *op. cit.*, pp. 206-207. Text follows original.

309.4. Draper MS. 11 C 62 (65).

309.5. On Clark's expedition, see Draper MSS. 11 C 62 (65), 13 C 31, 9 J 21. This first is the statement of Joseph Jackson, who was a prisoner in the Indian camp during the attack. See also Collins, II, p. 563; Morehead (1840), p. 103; *Reg.*, 29:110 (1931); *Mem. Hist. Soc. Penna.*, 7:218 (1860); *Ill. Hist. Coll.*, VIII, 477; M. J. Spalding: *Sketches of the Early Catholic Missions of Kentucky* (1844), p. 17; DePeyster to Maclean, Jan. 8, 1783; Canad. Arch., B 103, p. 1, *Mich.*, XX, 87 (1892).

311.1. Collins, II, pp. 477, 564, 565. In May, 1791, Israel Donalson was captured near Boone's former home at Limestone. Washington's Diaries (Ed. 1925), II, 279-280. Washington was still on a list of taxables, assessed with 6,000 acres on Rough Creek, as late as 1804, long after his death. See Durrett MSS., 1804. See also the deposition of Joseph Young in W. Calk *vs.* &c. Aug. 31, Sept. 1, 1813, Calk Papers. Photostat in University of Kentucky Library.

311.2. See the Virginia Acts of 1783 and 1787; Ky. Act of 1792; Jones *vs.* Kenny, 1 Ky. 96 (Hardin, 1807); Roy Bird Cooke: *Annals of Fort Lee* (1935), p. 29.

312.1. Though it has often been questioned, this story seems to be perfectly true. Nathan Boone doubted it and it was denied by others (Draper MSS. 4 C 52, 6 S 281, 306). On the other hand, it is reported by Peck, pp. 141-144, who knew Boone. Ephraim McLain heard it at first hand from Boone himself and from William Hancock at Hancock's house in the autumn of 1810 (Draper MS. 16 C 8; Ellis, pp. 173-176).

313.2. Draper MSS. 14 C 6 S 160; *cf.* Levi Todd to Patrick Henry, June 22, 1786, *Cal. Va.*, IV, 151.

313.3. Daniel Boone to Charles Yancey, May 30, 1785. Original in Va. State Library. See also Draper MSS. 14 C 3, 14, 22; 22 C 14, 6 S 167-175, 329.

313.4. Gen. Joseph Harmar to Secretary of War, May 14, 1787. *Publ. Hist. Soc. Penna.*, 7:422 (1860).

315.1. MS. Room, N. Y. Public Library.

315.5. Journal of Ebenezer Denny, March 20, 1786, May 23, 1786, *Publ. Hist.*

Soc. Penna., 7:283, 288-289 (1860); Isaac Ruddell to "Col. Mutir," Sept. 12, 1785, copy in Durrett Coll.

316.2. Draper MSS. 11 CC 83, 14 CC 192, 16 CC 297; Canad. Arch., Q 56-3, p. 674; *Mich.*, XXIV, 37 (1894).

316.4. Draper MS. 6 S 160-161, 166.

317.2. On the killing of Moluntha, see Draper MS. 22 C 235 (5), the statement of A. Thompson, who was only twenty or thirty paces away at the moment of the crime. See also Draper MSS. 11 C 61, 12 C 1 (11-12), 12 C 7 (1), 12 C 24 (4), 12 C 17 (6), 12 C 19, 12 C 27 (16), 12 C 39 (10), 11 C 62 (65-66), 11 CC 3 (3), 22 CC 235 (5). Thompson's account is partially confirmed by Draper MS. 11 CC 3 (3). On Moluntha's rank as chief, see Journal of Ebenezer Denny, *Publ. Hist. Soc. Penna.*, 7:277, 285 (1860, under dates Jan. 26, 27, 1786). The account in Draper MS. 4 C 50 is mostly wrong. *Cf.* Canad. Arch., Q 56-3, p. 674; *Mich.*, XXIV, 37 *ff.* (1894).

317.8. Draper MSS. 11 CC 3 (3); 6 S 158.

318.1. *Cal. Va.*, IV, 259.

318.3. David J. Bushnell, Jr.: "Daniel Boone at Limestone," *Va. Mag.*, 25:1-11 (1917).

319.1. The exact date and circumstances of Chloe Flinn's rescue are very doubtful. See Draper MSS. 1 C 73, 82; 14 C 30-31, 42-44, 50, 68; 6 S 169, 14 CC 10-13; *Cist's Advertiser*, Vol. I (No. 36) 2:23 N 1847; *Virginia Enquirer*, March 8, 1847; J. P. Hale: *Trans-Allegheny Pioneers*, p. 171; Draper MSS. 2 C 73, 13 C 75-79, 14 C 10-13; *Reg.*, 11 (No. 32): 11-12 (1913); *Va. Mag.*, 25: 1-2 (1917); *Mag. Am. Hist.*, 1:310, 312 (1877).

319.2. Draper MS. 26 C.

319.3. *Mag. Am. Hist.*, 1:437 (1877); pp. 164-165; *Penna. Packet*, No. 2631, p. 3, 12 Jy 1787; *New Haven Gazette*, 2 (No. 23); 180, 20 Jy 1787; Draper MS. 14 C 73.

321.2. G. Glenn Clift: *Hist. Maysville and Mason County*, I, pp. 62-63; Draper MSS. 11 CC 8-9, 18 CC 7-8, 6 S 166; *Kentucky Gazette*, 25 Ag. 1787; *New Haven Gazette*, 2 (No. 23): 180, 20 Jy 1787.

322.1. Draper MS. 12 CC 138-44.

322.2-3. Damon to Campbell, June 17, 1787; Edward to Innes, July 12, 1790; Isaac Shelby's autobiography (MS. fol. 26); Ewing to Shelby, May 11, 1793; Shelby to Kennedy, June 18, 1793; Brown to Hardin and Calwell, July 13, 1790; Shelby to Scott, June 19, 1793; Mitchell to Shelby, May 1, 1793; Beale to Shelby, April 12, May 2, 1793; residents of Nelson County to Shelby, May 9, 1793, all in Durrett Coll. *New Haven Gazette, loc. cit.*

323.2. Draper MS. 12 CC 233.

323.5. *Life*, p. 332½.

325.2. Draper MS. 26 C 66, also under year 1784 in C series.

325.3. Draper MS. 14 C 5.

326.2. Draper MS. 14 C 7, quoting Lockport, N. Y., *Express*, 27 Jy 1889.

326.5. *Ibid.*

327.2. Willard Rouse Jillson: "Daniel Boone as Surveyor," *Kentucky School Journal*, 13:32-36 S 1934; Draper MSS. 25 C 81, 12 C 37.

327.3. Douglass, *op. cit.*, pp. 14, 18; Draper MSS. 14 C 4, 14 C 6, 27 C 12-13, 11 CC 255; certificates in Durrett Coll., Sept. 23, 1787; C. R. Staples: "New Discoveries Amongst Old Records," *Reg.*, 23:219 (1935).

328.2. Reprinted here from transcript in Jillson, *loc. cit.*

328.3. Draper MS. 11 CC 255.

329.1. On Boone as a slave-owner, see Draper MSS. 25 C 76-77, 26 C 147-148; MSS. Ac 1175 (Kentucky Tax Lists, 1792-98) in Library of Congress; *Reg.,* 11 (No. 32): 11-12 (1913); Roosevelt: *Winning of the West* (National Ed., 1926), II, p. 44.

331.1. There is a facsimile of this document, made while it was in the possession of Colonel Durrett, in William Hayden English: *Conquest of the Country Northwest of the River Ohio,* I, p. 928. The original is not now in the Durrett Coll. See John B. Gibson in *Western Penna. Hist. Mag.* 6:307-308 (1922).

331.3. On the early ginseng trade, see *Rural Mag.* (Philadelphia), 1:380-382 Tenth Month [i.e., Oct.] 1820; Torald Sollmann: *Manual of Pharmacology,* pp. 211-212; Draper MSS. 14 C 92, 13 CC 122, 6 S 166, 330, 333; Shippen to Shippen, Dec. 13, 1775, State Hist. Soc. Penna.

332.11. Draper MS. 6 S 174-175.

332.2. The traveler was Joel Watkins. See his Journal, May 16, 1789. MS. copy from original in possession of Philip Franklin, Marshall, Mo., in Durrett Coll. See *Reg.,* 34:219 Jy (1936). On taverns, see Felix Renick: "Trip to the West," *Am. Pioneer,* I, 74-75 (1842); Collins, II, p. 554; Jedidiah Morse, *op. cit.* (1802), I, p. 633; *Discovery, Purchase and Settlement of the County of Kentuckie* (1786), p. 8 (Ed. Jillson, 1931); "Captivity of Israel Donalson," *Am. Pioneer,* I, 426 (1842).

332.3. On regulation of taverns and inns, see licenses in Durrett Coll. dated July 3, 1793, Jan. 7, 1794, May 3, Apr. 6, 1797. Another, in blank, is dated simply Jan. 1799.

333.1. William Littell: *State Laws of Kentucky,* III, p. 555; Hening's *Statutes,* III, p. 361; Clift, *op. cit.,* I, pp. 56-57; *H.Q.,* 8:199 (1934); Collins, II, p. 556.

333.2. Kanawha County Records; transcript in Dept. of Archives and History, Charleston, W. Va.

333.3. Thwaites, p. 211; *Reg.,* 11 (No. 32): 9-12 (1913); *Reg.,* 14 (No. 40): 27 (1916); Roy Bird Cook: *Annals of Fort Lee,* p. 99; Draper MSS. 1 C 46, 77, 85, 87.

333.4. Thwaites, p. 212; Cook, *op. cit.,* pp. 36, 100; Kanawha County Records, Oct. 6, 1789; *Reg.,* 11 (No. 32): 11 (1913).

334.1. John P. Hale, *op. cit.,* p. 169; *Reg.,* 11 (No. 32): 10 (1913).

334.3. Peck, p. 160; *U. S. Gazette,* Apr. 27, 1793.

335.1. Draper MS. 6 S 200-201.

335.2. John P. Hale, *op. cit.,* pp. 169-170; *Reg.,* 11 (No. 32): 10 (1913). Though Hale did not publish his book until 1886, his memories of the Kanawha country went back to 1840, and he talked with many men who had known Daniel Boone personally. Hale heard this story from young Huddleston himself. On the Huddleston family, see W. S. Laidley: *Hist. of Charleston and Kanawha County* (1911), pp. 66-67.

335.4. *Reg., loc. cit.;* Laidley, *op. cit.,* p. 82; Roy Bird Cook, *op. cit.,* pp. 38-39; *Cal. Va.,* V, 410, *Cf.* IV, 391, and dates Jan. 5, 1788, and Dec. 31, 1787.

336.3. Original reproduced in catalogue of Hearst Sale, Nov. 16/17, 1938, No. 19, Parke-Bernet Galleries, New York City; *cf.* Cook, *op. cit.,* pp. 39-40.

336.4. Cook, *loc. cit.; Cal. Va.,* V, 413, 416, 456.

337.1. Cook, *op. cit.,* pp. 44-47; *Cal. Va.,* V, 536.

337.2. *Cal. Va.,* VI, 118, 119; VII, 406.

338.1. *Reg.,* 11 (No. 32): 10-11 (1913); David E. Johnston: *Hist. of the Middle New River Settlements,* p. 114.

338.2. *Cal. Va.*, VI, 718-719, 658; Cook, *op. cit.*, pp. 54-59.

338.3. *Cal. Va.*, VI, 704, 708-709, 58-59.

338.4. Henry Howe: *Hist. Colls. Ohio,* I, 694; *Cist's Advertiser,* 1 (No. 36): 2 23 N 1847.

339.2. Draper MS. 15 CC, no folio given.

341.2. Madison County surveys of John Crooke. Original MSS. in possession of Professor Jonathan Truman Dorris, Eastern State Teachers College, Richmond, Ky.

341.4. Draper MS. 44 J 3; Louise P. Kellogg: "Fame of Daniel Boone," *Report of the Daniel Boone Bicentennial Commission* (1934), p. 53.

342.1. Fayette County, October Court, 1795. Recorded in *Complete Record Book,* E. 133. Original in possession of Earl Bishop, Campellsburg, Ky. Photostat in Library of the University of Kentucky. This sale was originally "part of a tract of Land granted to the said Daniel Boone by the State of Virginia for three hundred & Seventy Nine acres by patent bearing the 2d. day of Dec. 1785." See also Tipton papers, 351 (MS. Notebook), now in Professor Dorris's possession: "D. Boone of Boonesborough to Catherine Shirley, Madison County."

342.2. Louise P. Kellogg, *op. cit.,* quoting Nathan Boone. For original documents, see Draper MSS. 25 C 27, 74, 78; 26 C 163, 27 C 62-63.

342.4. Draper MS. 6 S 217.

343.2. Draper MS. 6 S 216, 25 C 83, 26 C 152; *Reg.*, 33:1-2 (1935); Kellogg, *op. cit.*, p. 54. Imlay's signature is in Durrett Coll., dated Dec. 22, 1785.

344.1. Byron: *Don Juan,* Canto VIII, Stanza lxi.

344.3. Draper MS. 6 S 309-310.

344.4. Draper MS. 16 C 94. See also James Gilruth in Ironton (Ohio) *Register,* 22 (No. 45): I 16 My 1872. (File in the Briggs Library, Ironton.)

344.5. Draper MS. 15 C 32.

345.3. Draper MS. 6 S 309-310.

345.4. Draper MS. 6 S 218, 27 C 79, 83; 22 C 66, 16 C 94.

346.2. Draper MSS. 6 S 309-310, 6 S 317½, 16 C 94.

346.3. Draper MS. 1 C 77, 15 C 31, 16 C 44.

346.5. The alleged cabin in Missouri seems to be a pigsty, though it may contain logs from Daniel Boone's cabin.

347.1. Discovered and identified by C. Frank Dunn, of Lexington, Ky. Mason County records show that Daniel Morgan Boone owned land in this area. See articles by Mr. Dunn in Lexington *Herald-Leader,* Feb. 20, 1938, reprinted in *Carlisle Mercury,* Feb. 24. Boone's letter to Shelby, Feb. 11, 1896, gives the address. Draper MS. 6 S 205. See also an unsigned note by Mr. Dunn, "Boone Cabin Was Subject of Articles," *Herald-Leader,* June 30, 1938, Sect. IV, p. 40.

347.3. Draper MS. 2 C 73.

348.3. Henry Toulmin (?): *Thoughts on Emigration* (1792), pp. 22-23; *Description of Kentucky* (1792).

349.2. *Acts of Kentucky, Private, 1798,* Chaps. I, II, XLV; Draper MSS. 6 S 205-206, 208, 211-212. There is a copy of Shelby's letter in Draper Coll.

350.1. *Commissioner's Book,* 1797, now in Kentucky State Hist. Society. The lands lie in what is now Nicholas County, which was cut off from Bourbon in 1799. These facts were discovered by Mrs. Jouett Taylor Cannon, who has kindly placed them at my disposal. See also Draper MS. 6 S 211-212.

352.4. The attitude of the Spaniards is clearest in one official's recommendation that American settlers already in Missouri be driven out, including "a person named Boone, who is the same one who first penetrated the wildernesses of Kentuqui." James Alexander Robertson: *Louisiana,* II, pp. 342-343.

354.3. *Am. Hist. Rev.,* 9:756 (1903-04). For text of the Memorial and Wilkinson's declaration of expatriation, see Filson Club Publications, No. 31, pp. cxix-cxxix. They were copied from originals in the possession of Don Miguel de Pontalba, Senlis, France.

355.1. *Am. Hist. Rev.,* 9:763, 749-50 (1903-04), referring to Archivo Histórico-Nacional. Estado. Legajo. 3898 B and 3893 A.

355.2. *Am. Hist. Rev.,* 9:755-760 (1903-04).

355.3. See copies of Clark's letter to Don Diego de Gardoqui, March 25, 1788; Gardoqui to Count Floridablanca, No. 282; and Clark's plan for an American company on Spanish territory, Aug. 16, 1802, all in the Durrett Coll.

357.1. Draper MSS. 11 CC 53 (13), 6 S 214-215; Anon.: *History of St. Charles, Montgomery, and Warren Counties,* p. 96.

357.3. Kanawha County Records.

358.1. Filson, 31-33; *Niles Weekly Register,* 24:166 17 My 1823.

358.2. *H.Q.,* 8:201 (1934).

358.3. This story was told by Mrs. Catherine Leonard (1793-1875) and is recorded by Jacob Calvin Leonard: *Centennial History of Davidson County,* pp. 200-201.

358.4. Draper MS. 15 C 51 lists of August and September, 1798; *Acts of Ky. 7th Gen. Assembly,* Ch. IV, p. 7, approved Dec. 13, 1798; John P. Hale, *op. cit.,* p. 172; *Reg.,* 11 (No. 32): (1932).

358.5. Collins, II, p. 562, says the tree was a poplar, presumably a local name for tulip poplar. See *Reg.,* 11 (No. 32): 11 (1932) Draper MSS. 6 S 215-216; Collins, II, p. 300.

359.1. Th. S. Hinde in *Am. Pioneer,* 1:327 (1842).

359.2. Draper MSS. 6 S 216, 221, 287.

359.4. Bryan, *op. cit., Mo. Hist. Rev.,* 3:297 (1908); Hale, *op. cit.,* p. 172; Thwaites, p. 220; *Reg.,* 11 (No. 32): 11 (1913); Draper MS. 2 C 73.

360.1. Draper MSS. 6 S 252, 332¾; 4 C 36; *Hist. of the Lower Scioto Valley,* p. 102.

360.2. Edmund Flagg: *Travels in the Far West, 1836-41,* in Thwaites: *Early Western Travels,* XXVI, p. 281. *Magnolia, or Literary Tablet,* 1:250 3 My 1834 (File in N. Y. Public Library); Draper MSS. 16 C 4-5, 16 C 54 (1-5).

360.3. Draper MS. 6 S 223; Bryan, *op. cit., Mo. Hist. Rev.,* 3:296 (1908); Amos Stoddard: *Sketches, Historical and Descriptive, of La.,* pp. 225, 249; Draper MS. 6 S 214-215.

361.1. Draper MSS. 4 C 58, 16 C 54, 6 S 224.

361.2. Draper MS. 6 S 222-223; *Am. State Papers, Public Lands,* II, 472.

361.3. Draper MS. 6 S 223. *Cf. Am. State Papers, Public Lands,* II, 473, which gives the date as Jan. 24. Draper MS. 15 C 55.

362.4. Draper MSS. 6 S 242; 27 C 67-71. Hall was canny enough to retain the right to recapture his land on payment of $120 and the cost of improvements. Nathan Boone lost the land when the U. S. Commissioners decided Hall had a prior title. See Draper MSS. 6 S 224, 27 C 68-69.

363.1. Draper MSS. 19 C 43-45, 107-109; 1 S 188, 6 S 224; *St. Louis Globe-Democrat,* 1 S 1888.

363.4. Jefferson City (Mo.) *Daily Tribune,* 19 Ap 1893; *Mo. Hist. Rev.,* 23: 653-654 (29); Draper MS. 6 S 227.

364.1. Bryan, *loc. cit.*
364.2. Draper MS. 6 S 227, 249.
365.2. Draper MS. 6 S 231.
365.3. Draper MS. 6 S 232. It is possible that this incident is really identical with the one described by Peck, in which Boone drove off the Indians.
366.2. Rufus Babcock: *Forty Years of Frontier Life. Memoirs of John Mason Peck,* p. 89; Peck, p. 170; *Pion. Fam.,* p. 46.
367.1. *Pion. Fam.,* p. 45.
367.3. Bryan, *op. cit., Mo. Hist. Rev.,* 4:30-31 (1909-10).
368.3. Draper MS. 16 C 47.
368.4. Draper MS. 6 S 277-278, 281.
369.1. Draper MS. 19 C 109, 145-146.
369.2. Draper MS. 27 C 88. Spraker, *op. cit.,* p. 59, says that this letter was written to Sarah Day Boone (Mrs. Samuel Boone). See also Draper MS. 27 C 89-91.
369.3. The marriage record, in French, is still in the parish archives of St. Charles Borromeo, St. Charles, Mo. The translation here given is by the Rev. W. B. Sommerhauser, S.J., the present rector. See also *Reg.,* 14 (No. 45): 67-68 S 1917.
371.3. Draper MS. 6 S 123, 228.
371.1. Draper MSS. 15 C 63, 15 C 66, 16 C 28, 6 S 225-226. See Stoddard: *Sketches of Louisiana,* pp. 248-274. The date of Boone's appointment is sometimes given as June, 1800.
371.2. Milo M. Quaife in *Mo. Hist. Rev.,* 21:616 (1926-27). There is reference to Lorimier in land papers of the time.
371.3. Draper MSS. 6 S 123, 228; 16 C 28.
372.1. MS. Codex O, fols. 19 *ff.* Original in American Philosophical Society. Reprinted in *Lewis and Clark Journals* (1905), VI, p. 29; Draper MS. 4 C 37. On the position of a commandant, see James Alexander Robertson: *Louisiana under the Rule of Spain, France and the United States,* II, pp. 320-321, 358.
372.2. Jedidiah Morse: *Am. Univ. Geog.,* section on "Spanish Dominions." Boone qualified as administrator of the estate of Isaac White, July 29, 1816. St. Charles County *Deed Records,* Book D. 17.
372.3. There is some doubt where the Justice Tree was. The site often pointed out near the stone house of Nathan Boone may not be correct, as Boone does not seem to have lived there during his years of office.
373.1. *Mo. Hist. Rev.,* 31:185, 189 (1937); 37:347 (1933); Peter H. Burnett: *Recollections of an Old Pioneer,* p. 343.
373.2. The original of this document was in the collection of F. C. Billon. Draper MS. 15 C 65 is one of several extant tracings.
374.1. Original in Missouri Hist. Society, St. Louis.
374.3. The Benjamin Gardner document was given to the Missouri Hist. Society by Horace Fox and is still in its possession.
375.1. On the Davis case, see William S. Bryan in *Mo. Hist. Rev.,* 3:200 (1908-1909); 4:85 (1909-1910); *Pion. Fam.,* p. 90; Draper MSS. 6 S 152, 4 C 58. The original indictment has disappeared from the records.
376.5. The note on Boone is in Draper MS. 15 C 64.
377.2. *Am. State Papers, Public Lands,* II, 473.
378.1. *Am. State Papers, Public Lands,* II, 473.
378.2. *Ibid.,* I, 880; II, 472, 495-496, 552, 619, 689, 690, 699, 880.
379.3. See Coburn's facsimile letter of Oct. 15, 1805 in Durrett Coll. about "an

unfortunate and worthy man, who is in pursuit of a claim to Land in the District of Louisiana." Thwaites: *Early Western Travels,* IV, 169 n. There is a tracing of Boone's letter to Coburn of Oct. 5, 1809, in the Durrett Coll. and a copy of the petition, evidently to be circulated for signatures, in State Hist. Soc. Penna.

380.1. *Am. State Papers, Public Lands,* II, 473.

380.2. Peck, pp. 200-201.

380.6. *Eleventh Congress, No. 161, 2nd Session. Am. State Papers, Public Lands,* II, 10. On Meigs, see *Biographical Dictionary of the American Congress,* p. 1304.

381.2. *Thirteenth Congress, No. 218, 2nd Session. Am. State Papers, Public Lands,* II, 872.

381.3. Draper MS. 6 S 250; *U.S. Statutes at Large. 6. Private Laws, 1789-1845,* pp. 127-128. HR. 71, 13th Congress.

382.2. *Am. State Papers, Public Lands,* III, 332; *Annals of Congress, 1st Session, 13th Congress,* XXVI, 805, 806, 823, 845; XXVII, 568, 622, 624, 625

382.3. Draper MS. 6 S 310.

382.4. Draper MS. 6 S 251.

382.6. Draper MS. 6 S 525. The manuscript, though obviously quoting Boone's words, is in the third person. It has been changed here to the first.

383.1. The St. Charles County, Mo., Records contain the following transactions by Daniel Boone: Daniel Boone to Jonathan Bryan, May 6, 1815, 300 acres, $600, *Deed Record* D. 179; Jonathan and Mary Bryan to Daniel Boone, Jan. 20, 1819, 300 acres, $1800, *Deed Record,* F. 18; Daniel Boone to William Cashio, 161 acres, May 6, 1815, *Deed Record,* D. 178; Daniel Boone to Abraham Shobe, Jan. 23, 1819, 500 acres, $5,000, *Deed Record,* F. 19; Daniel Boone administrator of Isaac White estate, July 29, 1816, *Deed Record,* D. 17. There are also numerous transactions by Daniel Morgan Boone.

384.1. Court of Quarter Sessions, St. Louis, Apr. 15, 1805; *Mo. Hist. Rev.,* 31:435 (1937); *Hist. of Howard and Cooper Counties, Mo.,* p. 807; Draper MS. 16 C 10.

384.3. Draper MSS. 27 C 70, 16 C 75.

385.1. Draper MS. 22 C 14.

385.3. Peck, p. 175; Ellis, pp. 196-197.

385.5. Peck, pp. 175-176, based on Boone's own statement. See also Ellis, pp. 196-197 and *Mo. Hist. Rev.,* 5:240-241 (1910-11).

386.4. Peck, Ellis, *loc. cit.*

387.5. *Pion. Fam.,* pp. 108-109.

388.2. *Wis. Hist. Coll.,* II, 199-212. There is an interesting letter, showing what the American settlers knew about the enemy's moves, in the Presbyt. Hist. Soc., Shane Coll. S. 35, v. II, John Steele to a brother in Lexington, Ky., May 23, 1813.

388.3. *Pion. Fam.,* pp. 101-104; Draper MS. 4 C 52; Gottfried Duden: *Berichte über eine Reise nach den westlichen Staaten Nordamerikas* (1829). Translated in *Mo. Hist. Rev.,* 12:270 (1917-18), 19th letter, May, 1826. Duden was one of the early immigrants from Germany to Missouri. His book was responsible for much subsequent immigration.

390.1. *Pion. Fam.,* p. 107; Draper MSS. 6 S 269, 272-273, 307-308.

390.2. W. S. Bryan, *op. cit., Mo. Hist. Rev.,* 3:204-205 (1909).

391.2. Allen's *Biog. Dict.; Biog. Americana* (1825), p. 40; Draper MSS. 4 C 61, 6 S 271.

391.3. *Niles Weekly Register,* 10:261 [361] 15 Je 1816; *Western Spy,* 2 (No. 102): 2, cols. 3, 4, 5 Jy 1816; *Mo. Hist. Rev.,* 16:27 (1921-22).

392.1. Duden, *op. cit., Mo. Hist. Rev.,* 12:261-262 (1917-18), 16th letter, Dec. 10, 1825; Draper MS. 4 C 60, 27 C 80, 6 S 246.

392.3. Draper MSS. 15 C 70-71, 16 C 13.

393.2. *Niles Weekly Register,* 14:208 16 My 1818; *Mo. Hist. Rev.,* 21:33-34 (1926-27).

393.3. *Don Juan,* Canto VIII, Stanza lxiv; *Faux's Journal,* reprinted in Thwaites: *Early Western Travels,* XI, 221.

393.5. John Woods: *Two Years on the Settlements on the English Prairies,* reprinted in Thwaites: *Early Western Travels,* X, 339; Washington Irving: *Astoria;* Olin D. Wheeler: *Trail of Lewis and Clark,* I, 146.

394.1. S. H. Long: *Account of an Expedition from Pittsburgh to the Rocky Mountains,* reprinted in Thwaites: *Early Western Travels,* XIV, 169.

394.2. Draper MS. 15 C 26. A comma has been added.

394.3. Draper MS. 8 C 126, 156, 181; 15 C 54; *Niles Weekly Register,* 24:166 17 My 1823.

394.5. Draper MS. 7 C 43 (3).

394.6. 12 C 39 (10).

395.5. Draper MS. 7 C 43; McClung: *Western Adventure,* p. 79; Charles Campbell: *History of the Colony and Ancient Dominion of Virginia* (Ed. 1860), p. 598, obviously quoting McClung; Bogart, p. 51.

396.1. F. W. Thomas: *John Randolph of Roanoke,* p. 76.

396.2. R. W. M'Farland: "Simon Kenton," *Ohio Hist. and Arch. Quarterly,* 13:36 Ja 1904.

396.3. Adlard Welby: *Visit to North America,* reprinted in Thwaites: *Early Western Travels,* XII, 212 n. The false obituary probably first appeared in the *Western Citizen,* Sept. 6, 1809. See A. G. Boone in *Mo. Hist. Rev.,* 30:214 (1936).

397.2. *Journal* (Ed. Elliott Coues), II, 363-364. On Lewis and Clark, see MS. Codex O, p. 19 *ff.*, now in the American Philosophical Society; *Lewis and Clark Journals* (1905), VI, 29, 30; VII, 4, 31.

397.3. John Bradbury: *Travels in the Interior of America,* reprinted in Thwaites: *Early Western Travels,* V, 43; Louis Houck: *Hist. Mo.,* III, p. 142.

398.2. Draper MSS. 6 S 220-221, 27 C 79.

398.3. Draper MS. 6 S 221; *Navigator* (1814), p. 24.

399.1. "Kentucky Sports," in *Delineations of American Scenery and Character* (Ed. Francis Hobart Herrick, 1926), pp. 60-61.

400.1. *Ornithological Biography,* I, pp. 503-506. Audubon's accuracy is impugned in *New England Galaxy,* 18 (No. 6): 2 7 F 1835. There is abundant evidence that Boone's stature did not "approach the gigantic."

404.2. Draper MSS. 16 C 44, 13 C 12.

404.3. *Kansas City Star,* Nov. 2, 1924; Draper MS. 16 C 28; J. W. Cunningham: "Daniel Boone and His Sons in Missouri," *Capital Gazette,* July 29, 1880.

405.1. Draper MS. 16 C 97. *Cf.* 9 C 43.

405.2. There has been much dispute whether Boone ever returned to Kentucky at all. Audubon, however, says specifically that he was with him on the Kentucky River at a time which must have been long after Boone settled in Missouri. Audubon was not always accurate but he certainly knew one state from another. The 1817 visit is minutely described in Draper MS. 16 C 24-25, by Buckner Payne. As Payne was then living in Maysville and slept in the same room with Boone, he, too, must know what he is talking about. If the Louisville tree-carving (see Note 32.3.) is genuine, Boone was there in 1803.

405.3. Draper MS. 16 C 25 (5).
406.3. Peck, p. 174; Draper MS. 4 C 51, 55.
407.3. Peck, pp. 176-177; Draper MS. 57 J 350.
408.1. Draper MS. 16 C 94.
408.2. Draper MS. 22 C 14 (23).
409.2. Draper MS. 16 C 18, 75.
409.3. "Truth" in *Missouri Intelligencer,* 27 Ag 1819.
410.1. Draper MS. 6 S 276-277.
410.2. Draper MS. 22 C 28.
410.3. Draper MSS. 15 C 70, 16 C 62, 78; 22 C 28, 6 S 277-278.
411.1. Albert Gallatin Boone, a grandson, in a letter to the *Clark County Democrat,* dated Mar. 26, 1877; *Mo. Hist. Rev.,* 30:214 (1936); Draper MS. 16 C 62.
411.3. *Mo. Hist. Rev.,* 6:86 (1911-1912).
411.4. Draper MS. 16 C 36-37.
411.5. Draper MSS. 7 C 43 (2); 16 C 43-44.
412.2. Draper MSS. 4 C 36-37, 43, 51-52.
412.4. *Egotistigraphy,* pp. 35-36.
413.3. Draper MS. 6 S 277-278; Spraker, *op. cit.,* p. 579.
413.4. Draper MS. 4 C 56.
413.5. Albert Gallatin Boone, who was in the house (and probably in the room) in which Boone died, told John P. Hale of his peaceful death. See *Trans-Allegheny Pioneers,* p. 173, and *Mo. Hist. Rev.,* 30:214 (1936). See also the accounts of the death in the *Rural Magazine* (Philadelphia), 1:473, 12th Month, 1820; *Detroit Gazette,* Sept. 26, 1820; Niles *Weekly Register,* 10:361, Ap 1816; *Cist's Advertiser,* 1 (No. 36): 2 23 N 1847; Cist's *Cincinnati Miscellany,* 2:133-134, 141-142 S 1845; J. M. Peck in *Am. Pioneer,* 1:243 (1842); Draper MS. 16 C 33.
414.4. The grave was on the farm of H. Griswold, Warren County, Mo., on a site now marked by a monument. It has been suspected that the wrong grave was opened and that Daniel Boone still lies in his original grave; but there is no good evidence for this. See Draper MSS. 16 C 82, 99; *Mo. Hist. Rev.,* 4:44 (1909-1910); 30:66 (1935); *Reg.,* 29:99 (1931); *Ibid.,* 34:105 (1936).

INDEX

Index

About the Author

JOHN BAKELESS, editor, scholar, and biographer, was born at Carlisle, Pennsylvania, in 1894. His father, Oscar H. Bakeless, was principal of the Carlisle Indian School. The Bakeless family physician was a full-blooded Apache M.D.; and John Bakeless, reared by two Indian nurses, was the first white student ever to attend Carlisle. He later studied at the State Normal School in Bloomsburg, was graduated from Williams College in 1918 (Phi Beta Kappa), and obtained his Ph.D. degree at Harvard under George Lyman Kittredge. Mr. Bakeless has been managing editor of *The Living Age* and of *The Forum,* literary adviser to *The Independent,* New York correspondent of the *Manchester Guardian,* and literary editor of *The Literary Digest.* During 1936-37 he held a Guggenheim Fellowship for the pursuit of Elizabethan studies; and he is at present in the department of journalism at New York University. Among John Bakeless's other publications are: *The Economic Causes of Modern War; The Origin of the Next War; Magazine Making;* and *Christopher Marlowe: The Man in His Time.*